THE SIGNS

of

THE NEW COVENANT

THE SIGNS

of

THE NEW COVENANT

by

Aimé Georges Martimort

Professor of Liturgy in the Faculty of Theology of Toulouse
Director of the *Centre de Pastorale Liturgique*

THE LITURGICAL PRESS

Collegeville, Minnesota

The Signs of the New Covenant is the authorized English translation of *Les Signes de la Nouvelle Alliance* by Canon Aimé Georges Martimort, published by Editions Ligel, Paris, France. To realize the author's purposes, revisions have been made in this translation in accordance with the needs of English-speaking readers, particularly in the bibliographies which have drawn on the wealth of material originally written in English or translated from other languages to substitute for the French works not available in translation.

Nihil obstat: John Eidenschink, O.S.B., J.C.D., *Censor deputatus.* *Imprimatur:* ✠Peter W. Bartholome, D.D., Bishop of St. Cloud. August 22, 1963.

AUTHOR'S NOTE

This work was first drafted at the request of the Christian Brothers to provide a theology course on the sacraments for junior religious. In their training program, the tract on the sacraments must receive very special attention. These students, destined by their vocation to the work of religious instruction and general education, needed a tool which would help them gain the right basic outlook together with clear and solid ideas. This text was, then, to answer the increasingly felt need for solid doctrinal formation, while at the same time avoiding any excessively technical presentation that might prove an obstacle, for some readers at least, to its fruitful use.

The initiators of this project felt that in asking the Director of the *Centre de Pastorale Liturgique* to compose such a text, they would benefit from the work accomplished by the Center during the last fifteen years and also aid in its dissemination, through future educators whose understanding of the sacraments, spiritual life and methods of teaching religion would be greatly enriched by the biblical, patristic and liturgical contributions characterizing the work of the Center.

To the extent to which this expectation has been satisfied, the credit should be given not so much to the author of these pages as to the whole team of professors and pastors who met together periodically for the research sessions the essence of which has been published in the review *La Maison Dieu* and in the *Lex Orandi* series.

This text, which has already been in use for some time in mimeographed form, is now offered to the public in the hope of serving other religious communities, students of sacred doctrine and lay people who wish to clarify and deepen their religious knowledge.

In presenting this course, we have tried to avoid all the dryness and excessive subdivisions which are opposed to the global character of initiation into the mystery of the liturgy, while meeting the normal requirements of systematic explanation.

The bibliography for each chapter indicates how the reader may develop and deepen his understanding of the material presented. We have tried to limit the titles to reasonably accessible works and periodicals; for this reason, technical treatises, publications in foreign languages, and collections of unpublished patristic texts have generally been omitted.

We should, finally, remind the reader that any instruction on the sacraments offered to Christians by means of the printed word can never replace the instruction which the Church herself requires pastors to give by means of the living voice. Above all, it cannot take the place of that experimental knowledge which is acquired only through participation in the sacraments, in the context of the whole liturgical life, within the Christian assembly: "Taste and see how good is the Lord" (Ps. 33).

NOTE ON SOURCE MATERIALS AND BIBLIOGRAPHY

The reader should have at hand a complete Bible, a complete Roman missal, and the texts of the sacramental rites. He should also have available for reference the following:

SCT *Sources of Christian Theology* (Westminster, Md.: The Newman Press)

Vol. I: *The Sacraments and Worship* in connection with chapters 1–4;

Vol. II: *The Sacraments and Forgiveness* in connection with chapters 5–6;

TCT *The Church Teaches: Documents of the Church in Translation,* translated and edited by the Jesuit Fathers of St. Mary's College (St. Louis: B. Herder Co., 1955);

Summa *Summa Theologica* of St. Thomas Aquinas, translated by the English Dominicans (New York: Benziger Bros., 1947), Vol. III;

Mystici Corporis, Mediator Dei, Casti Connubii, translations available from The National Catholic Welfare Conference, Washington, D.C.; The America Press, New York, N.Y.; The Paulist Press, New York, N.Y.;

NTRG *New Testament Reading Guide* (Collegeville, Minn.: The Liturgical Press);

PNLW *Proceedings of the North American Liturgical Weeks* (Washington, D.C.: The Liturgical Conference);

The Roman Ritual, 3 vols. (Milwaukee, Wis.: The Bruce Publishing Co.).

The bibliography (pp. 308-314) contains a list of titles for general background, including those referred to in more than one chapter, and also separate listings for each chapter giving full bibliographical information on the works in English referred to in that chapter, as well as additional titles developing various aspects.

INTRODUCTION

A basic reorientation is required if we are to study the sacraments according to the method proper to them. This reorientation is desirable for every Christian and absolutely necessary for catechists and educators. As St. John says no forcefully, "No man has ever seen God" (John 1:18). It is no longer granted to us today, as it was to the Apostle, to see with our eyes and touch with our hands the Word of Life (1 John 1:1-2). But the sacraments consist of things, actions, and words that do come within the reach of our senses. By the will of Christ who instituted them, they are signs, signs that are efficacious for us today; they are mysterious bonds between us today and the historical reality of Christ.

1. From what is seen to what is unseen. When we read the catechetical instructions addressed by the Fathers of the first centuries to the newly-baptized, we are struck by the concrete, visual quality of their teaching.

> Now see. The priest comes in; he says a prayer at the font; he invokes the name of the Father, the presence of the Son and the Holy Spirit. . . . You came to the font and went down into it, you saw the bishop, you saw the deacons and the priest at the font. What is baptism? (St. Ambrose, *On the Sacraments,* II).

The question is not asked until after the neophytes have been reminded of what they have seen and heard, for the answer is to be drawn out of the concrete event. Actions, words, persons, things all make up the sign, and the sign must be allowed to express its own meaning. From the very idea of what a sign is, the theologian concludes that to understand a sacrament we must handle and touch, look at water gushing from a spring or bathers enjoying themselves, we must see perfume compounded by an expert in due proportions of oil and some aromatic substance. We must see, and we must also hear; for the word pronounced by the Church transforms the ordinary human action into a mystery of faith, a divine act. St. Ambrose continues:

> You were asked: Do you believe in God the Father almighty? You answered: I do believe. . . . And a second time: Do you believe in our Lord Jesus Christ and in His Cross? You answered: I do believe; and you were washed and thereby buried with Christ, for he who is buried with Christ, rises with Christ. You were asked a third time: Do you believe in the Holy Spirit?

We must also look at the person who speaks, acts, effects the sign. For who is he? In him, it is Christ who speaks, acts, effects the sign: "When Peter baptizes, it is Christ who baptizes; when Judas baptizes, it is Christ who baptizes" (St. Augustine, *Treatise on John*, 6:7). This is an inductive, intuitive way of teaching, not based on the catechetical method of the fourth century or any other, but on the theological reality of the sacrament, and so on the order willed by Christ Himself.

But to say this is not enough; this pedagogy is also active.

2. Understanding through participation. Reading in a missal, ritual or pontifical what is done and said in administering a sacrament is wholly meaningful only to the person who has already taken part in the rite. This is so true of the sacraments of Christian initiation (baptism, confirmation, the Eucharist) that the Fathers explained the rites to the neophytes only after they had been initiated, basing the explanation on the actual experience. On the day of his baptism the candidate needed simply to open his eyes and ears to the mystery, now opened out to him with all the freshness and force of a new discovery. This could not be done today, certainly, now that Christianity no longer seems so new. Nevertheless, it is the reception of a sacrament that gives authenticity, living reality, and depth to our understanding of it.

It is true, for instance, that from one aspect only a priest understands the priesthood because he has received it, and he understands it more and more fully as he exercises it. And the layman only attains that appreciation of the sacrament of Orders which is proper to every Christian by taking part in an ordination ceremony, discovering the divine mystery hidden in the signs, praying when the bishop asks him to pray for the man whom the Lord is marking with His seal. Similarly, the faithful renew their baptismal promises most effectively when they do so during the Easter Vigil, after taking part in the consecration of the baptismal water and assisting at baptisms administered with it.

We must never be content, therefore, with textbooks, classes and teachers alone. We must also seek in the liturgical assembly itself the understanding of the sacraments it alone can give us. Textbooks, classes, and teachers serve to make this understanding clear and orderly, but they can never take its place.

3. What the Church does. The study of the sacraments can provide some surprises for the logical reasoning of the theologian. Christ entrusted the sacraments to His Church as a living treasure. And, while the Lord laid down once for all the essential elements of each sacrament, we find great flexibility in other aspects, allowing variations in usage in different times and places. Up to the twelfth century, for example, Communion was given to little children immediately after baptism; since then the Western Church has reserved it, except in danger of death, to those who have reached the age of reason and received some elementary preparation.

Again, the Acts of the Apostles show us the apostles confirming by the imposition of hands, but the Eastern Churches confer this sacrament validly by anointing with holy chrism.

It is not logic, therefore, that decides what must be done, what action is essential, what age is the right one for the reception of confirmation or the Eucharist—it is the practice of the Church. St. Thomas Aquinas often says: "It is done this way because this is the way the Church does it." We might think, for example, that since confirmation is the sacrament of Christian maturity, it should not be given to children. But we would be wrong, because the Church does confirm children, showing us that supernatural age does not coincide with physical age.

There is only one way, then, to determine the necessary action, the minister, and the conditions for administering the sacraments: to see what the Church does and has done, though this may differ in the East and West, today and in times past. She alone is entrusted with the distribution of this treasure of the sacraments.

4. A synthesis of the whole Christian mystery. When we study the sacraments, we discover in living unity the whole wealth of the Christian economy. To understand this economy we must take as our starting-point the figures that sketched out its characteristics in the Old Testament. But this is only a starting-point, for the sacraments flow from the mysteries of Christ, bringing their graces to men here and now. They also manifest the Church, since they constitute her mark of identification and her treasury. So they unite a person both with the Church, making him a member of the people of God, and with the Lord, introducing him into a unique intimacy with God.

The sacraments oblige the Christian to know and to express his faith in what God has said (the Apostles' Creed is precisely the baptismal profession of faith). They also form a whole spiritual life, organized around them and drawing its vitality from them. Baptism is the turning-point in our existence, the death of the "old man" and the birth of the new man in Christ. Confirmation inaugurates a prophetic mission. The Eucharist is the pledge of charity. And, though what we call today the "religious life" is not consecrated by a special sacrament, it has always been understood in the Church as founded on baptism and sealed in the Eucharist.

In spite of the fact that they are an entirely free gift of God, the sacraments generally require some effort on the part of man before he receives them. From this aspect, the sacrament of penance realizes in a special way the encounter between God coming to meet man and man responding to the divine advances. For here the work of the penitent, in accusing himself, repenting and making reparation, is part of the sacrament itself.

Finally, each sacrament is bound up with the past history of salvation, proclaiming it and communicating its grace. At the same time, each sacrament orients us toward the blessed resurrection to come, and gives us a pledge of it. There will be no sacraments in heaven; the Reality will be contemplated in a manner unveiled, not through signs. But that Reality is truly given to us here on earth by these signs.

CONTENTS

Chapter 1

A COMPREHENSIVE VIEW OF THE SACRAMENTS

Chapter 2

HOLY ORDERS

Chapter 3

CHRISTIAN EDUCATION

Chapter 4

THE EUCHARIST

Chapter 5

PENANCE

Chapter 6

THE ANOINTING OF THE SICK

Chapter 7

MARRIAGE

THE SIGNS

of

THE NEW COVENANT

A COMPREHENSIVE VIEW OF
THE SACRAMENTS

"After the study of the mysteries of the Incarnate Word should come that of the sacraments of the Church, for it is to the Word Incarnate that their efficacy is due" (*Summa* III, 60).

Each sacrament has its own special characteristics—so much so that it took centuries to establish precisely what the sacraments all have in common and to enumerate them exactly. The question then arises whether to study the sacraments one by one and then establish the definition and laws that apply to them all, or to use the reverse procedure. The former method was necessary for the development of a theology of the sacraments and is still the best procedure in elementary instruction. But at a later stage it is best to begin with a general presentation. This avoids repeating in connection with each sacrament what is common to all, and, what is even more important, brings out the nature of the sacramental organism as a whole and the fact that sacramentality is an essential characteristic of Christianity.[1] However, the reader would do well, after he has finished his study of the whole book, to reread this general chapter, which he will then understand more thoroughly.

"A sacrament is a sensible sign, instituted by Christ, to signify and produce grace." This definition, commonly used in catechisms and theology texts, makes clear the three elements which constitute the sacraments: (1) The sacraments are signs; (2) the sacraments are acts of Christ; (3) the sacraments effectively bestow the divine gifts which they signify.

These three elements must be analyzed separately for orderly consideration. Nonetheless, they are inseparably bound up with one another; the sacraments confer divine gifts because they are acts of Christ, but these divine gifts cannot be understood except by listening to the language of the signs that transmit them.

Article One
THE SACRAMENTS AS SIGNS

In the sacraments, the supernatural gift of Christ is transmitted to us by the physical actions of a man who stands in the place of Christ—actions often involving the use of material things such as water, oil, bread. These actions and these material things are signs which are meant, when their meaning is opened out, to reveal to us the supernatural gift which they convey in a hidden manner. To the actions and the use of things is added the spoken word to determine the supernatural significance of

[1] A. M. Roguet, *Christ in His Sacraments*, p. 11.

the sacrament and to awaken faith. The sacraments, then, include two elements: the first consisting of actions and things, the second being the "word of faith."

Theology texts call these two elements "matter" and "form", a terminology traditional in technical works since St. Thomas and the Council of Florence. But, however convenient these terms may be, they should be avoided in elementary instruction. And in any case they can lead to misunderstandings, for these terms are used here in a sense very different from the one given them in the Aristotelian philosophy from which they were borrowed.

Then, too, while these two elements by themselves constitute the sacrament and produce its divine effect of grace, it would be a pedagogical error to isolate them from the twofold context in which they should normally be located: the Bible and the liturgy. For only in this context can we appreciate their full meaning as signs.

The sacramental signs are biblical. They come to us charged with a long history of the deeds and images by which God patiently prepared His people for the revelation of Christ's mysteries. For example, the Fourth Gospel, which is a sacramental catechesis, often recalls Genesis and Exodus.

Moreover, except in cases of exceptional urgency, the sacraments are administered within a whole complex of rites and prayers which display, explain and extend their meaning. The sacraments are an essential part of the liturgy, and the liturgy is wholly sacramental, starting from the sacraments and leading toward them without any break in continuity.

Our study of the sacraments as signs will therefore include: the role of things and actions in these signs; the role of the spoken word; the role of Holy Scripture in the sacramental signs; the role of the liturgical extension of the sacramental signs.

I. THE ROLE OF THINGS AND ACTIONS

1. *Things used.* The sacraments often require the use of things, of an element of the material universe, such as water. This may be used where it is found and as God gives it, after the example of the deacon Philip when he baptized the eunuch of the queen of Ethiopia:

> As they went on their way, they came to a body of water, and the eunuch said: "See, here is water. Is there any reason to hinder my being baptized?" . . . And he had the chariot stopped; they both went down into the water—Philip and the eunuch—and he baptized him (Acts 8:36-38).

But often man's hard work is needed to find fresh water—witness the deep well dug and built by Joseph at Sichar, where the Samaritan woman went each day (John 4:6-12).

Man's work is absolutely necessary to provide the oil, perfume, bread and wine—material realities of daily life in Mediterranean countries— used for the anointing of the sick, for confirmation and for the Eucharist. Here the cooperation, as it were, of the earth and of men is needed before the grace of God can be given in these signs.

Nor should we be surprised that the matter of three sacraments is subject to geographical limitations, to countries where vines and olive trees can grow. Grace does not come to us directly from God; it comes through the Word who became incarnate, who lived in a particular land on our earth, preached when Tiberius was emperor, died under Pontius Pilate.

2. Actions performed. Yet the sacraments of penance, of Orders and of marriage do not involve things. Here the material element consists of actions alone: in penance, the judgment of guilt; in Orders, the imposition of hands; in marriage, the willingness of bride and groom to marry each other. And in those sacraments which do require material things, it is an action that indicates the use of these things. To be baptized, the Ethiopian was not asked simply to look at the water, but to go into it and be washed by the deacon Philip. In the sacrament of the sick, the oil is used as a salve, applied by way of anointings. In confirmation, the bishop perfumes the candidate's forehead.[2]

These actions may have a religious character, as does the imposition of hands or signing with the Cross. But in most cases these actions in themselves are prosaic and earthly, even "common." They are part of the daily routine, often crude and rough, of human life. But in the sacraments these everyday actions, involving such commonplace things, become signs. The Lord makes them efficacious signs of His salvation, of His grace. And this means that, in the sacraments, these do not become magic actions, unintelligible mumbo-jumbo; they are signs meant to be understood, designed to enlighten our minds as they communicate God's grace. Two questions, then, need to be asked: Why did Christ choose these signs and what is the law governing their symbolism?

3. Reasons for this use of things and actions. We should feel a healthy astonishment when we see a sacrament administered, the astonishment expressed by the early Christians at the unexpectedness of the Christian economy. Why did the Lord will to use material signs for His spiritual grace, to use actions carried out on the body in order to act on the soul, to make actions performed by men carry out the action of God? Though they are a scandal to an idealistic philosopher, whether

---

[2] The reader will note that the Eucharist has not been mentioned here. This is because this sacrament is constituted independently of its use. The bread and wine are meant to be eaten, and Christ actually says: "Take and eat . . . take and drink." Communion is the completion of the sacrament; it is required on the part of the celebrant as an integral part of the sacrifice; yet the sacrament and the sacrifice are constituted by the consecration which changes the bread and wine into the Body and Blood of Christ.

Platonic or Cartesian, the sacraments are a manifestation of the wisdom of Him who knows "of what dust we are fashioned."

Man comes to the knowledge of spiritual things by starting from what he sees, what he touches, what he does. Such a statement is not a conclusion drawn from any recent change in the conditions of human life, the materialistic atmosphere of our times, or the present decadence of culture. It is traditional among theologians, St. Thomas Aquinas in particular (*Summa* III, 60, 4-5), and expresses a fact about human nature which underlies the pedagogy of the Bible and of Christ Himself. For example, when Jesus wished to reveal His grace to the Samaritan woman, He took as His starting-point her own daily action of going at mealtime to draw water from Jacob's well (John 4:7-26). When He wished to define Himself as the Bread of Life, He started with the miraculous meal that had fed the great crowd in the desert: "You seek me, not because you have seen signs, but because you ate your fill of bread" (John 6:26). He led Peter and Andrew to their vocation as apostles by having them discover it from their trade as fishermen: "Come, follow me, and I will make you fishers of men" (Mark 1:17).

Not to understand this great law of divine pedagogy is to forget that earth is not yet heaven. In the state of glory, when the divine realities will be shown to us openly, there will be no more sacraments. But now, so long as we know "as in a mirror, in an obscure way" (1 Cor. 13:12), we must go by way of earthly signs to arrive at spiritual things.

The whole equilibrium of religious psychology, therefore, is involved in the sacraments. They allow us to find God in our human condition as it is while they inaugurate a new harmony of creation; once again we learn to find God, beginning from the things around us here below.

Man must be saved both in body and soul. It is true that "man does not live by bread alone" (Matthew 4:4), and "It is better for you to enter into life maimed than to go with both your hands to gehenna" (Mark 9:42). The faithful servant of Christ will often be torn apart in a painful conflict and have to "sacrifice his body to his country so as to keep his soul for God." Yet the normal order of things is that man is made holy with his body, and by means of his body put at the service of the spirit. The glorious resurrection will, finally, bring about the perfect harmony of this body-spirit relationship. The sacraments, then, are given to the body, and act on the soul. As Tertullian vigorously put it, some eighteen hundred years ago:

> The flesh is washed so that the soul may be purified. The flesh is anointed so that the soul may be consecrated. The sign of the Cross marks the flesh so that the soul may be strengthened. The imposition of hands overshadows the flesh so that the soul may be enlightened by the Holy Spirit. The flesh is nourished with the Body and Blood of

> Christ, so that the soul may grow strong, fed on God (*On the Resurrection of the Dead*, 8:3).

And St. Augustine explains:

> You should not be astonished when we say that water, a physical substance, reaches and purifies the soul. Yes, it reaches it, and it penetrates all the secret places of the conscience (*Sermon for Epiphany*).

The sacraments also have a social aspect. They bind the faithful Christian to his God with a bond of love and constitute him a member of a people, the Church. This social aspect, this "belongingness" requires signs, actions; men cannot communicate in any other way. The sacraments are both distinguishing signs and the bond of communion among Christians. Many recent studies have shown to what extent modern societies inevitably go back to symbols to express their social being, even when, unfortunately, this symbol is put at the service of a design to enslave mankind.

4. The nature of sacramental symbolism. The right attitude towards these signs is sometimes difficult to attain because of a poor initial pedagogy; witness the many erroneous "examples" presented in certain catechisms compiled in the nineteenth century, or even the treatises dating from the end of the Middle Ages. We must, therefore, keep in mind the true nature of the symbolism of the sacraments.

The sacramental signs are not merely conventional and arbitrary. Traffic lights on streets or railroad tracks, flags, insignia, our national colors—all these are mere arbitrary, conventionally agreed-upon signs which could be changed at will. They have no meaning other than that which men have freely attached to them. They are quite clear as soon as one knows the code for interpreting them, since they follow some logical system. But sacramental signs are not like this. Christ's choice of sensible realities as sacramental signs, far from being arbitrary, takes account of a certain natural aptness in these realities to signify the supernatural effects of the sacraments.

Neither are the sacramental signs allegorical, as they were made out to be by medieval commentators on the liturgy. For example, these authors were astonished that the Eucharist, Christ's sacrifice, is celebrated as a meal. So they tried to forget the obvious meaning of things and actions and to substitute another meaning: the altar-cloths symbolized a shroud, the box for reserving the consecrated hosts, a sepulchre; the knife with which the bread is cut in the Eastern rites took on the name of the "holy lance." By an opposite path, we reach the same error when the water added to the wine in the chalice is explained as signifying our sacrifices. Such interpretations have nothing to do with the real nature of things, they do not impose themselves; they are connected with their objects only by a forced attempt at explanation.

The sacramental signs are natural symbols elevated by divine choice. We must learn how to read the language of God, written into things at their creation and even engraved in the recesses of human souls. If there is, as it were, a divide to be crossed from the visible material thing to the hidden reality, the crossing is made easy by a truly profound view of things and actions. We have to take an intuitive attitude toward them —an attitude having nothing in common with that of either romantics or idolators, since it is in search of the language of God and submits us to Him. But to gain this attitude, to learn this language, we need to listen to God's word: the word spoken by the minister of the sacrament, the word spoken by God in the Bible.

It should be noted that God chose as sacramental signs sensible realities which are primordial, natural: water to be bathed in, perfume to give a pleasant scent, oil to soothe the sick, bread and wine for a meal. Can an industrial civilization, a scientific mentality adapt itself to such signs? The very simplicity of the sign serves to remind us, as forcibly as men of any other civilization, that here it is part of a rite; it is not a tool. It is a sign of the divine action, not the exercise of human power. It is efficacious, not because it has been taken up by man, but because it is a symbol in the hands of Christ. Its symbolic quality is, then, bound up with its native condition, its elemental character. And to the ancients, just as much as to ourselves, the sign seemed surprisingly inadequate. "How can water cause anyone to be reborn?" Tertullian, St. Ambrose and St. Augustine answer by saying: it is not water that causes us to be reborn, but the Holy Spirit by means of the water.

II. THE ROLE OF THE SPOKEN WORD

The action, by itself, is already a sign. Yet the sacraments also require spoken words, as St. Augustine explains in two passages from his commentary on St. John, passages often quoted by theologians:

> Hear the Apostle (Eph. 5:25-27): "Christ loved the Church. He delivered himself for her, so as to sanctify her through cleansing her by the bath of water that is accompanied by a word . . ." How does He cleanse her? By the bath of water that the word accompanies. Take away the water, and there is no baptism; take away the word, and there is no baptism (15:4).

> "You have already been made clean by reason of the word I have proclaimed to you" (John 15:3). Why does He not say: You have already been made clean by reason of the baptism with which you have been washed, but rather: thanks to the word that I have proclaimed to you, unless it be that in the water it is still the word which cleanses? The word is added to the matter, and then it becomes the sacrament (80:3).

These quotations refer to baptism; it is to be noted that the Epistle to the Ephesians already mentions the two constituents: the bath of water and the word accompanying it. The same law rules the other sacraments. The accounts of the Last Supper show us how the Eucharist, as instituted by Jesus, included the words pronounced over the bread and wine. St. James' Epistle says, concerning what priests should do for the sick: ". . . let them pray over him after anointing him with oil in the name of the Lord" (5:14). In the same way, in the Acts of the Apostles, the action of the imposition of hands is always accompanied by a prayer.

Action and word are united so closely as to constitute a dynamic whole. It is the same minister who carries out the action and who pronounces the word (when there are concelebrants, only the principal celebrant need perform the action while all pronounce the word).[3] But the simultaneity required is not rigid. In the ordination of a priest or the consecration of a bishop, the action of the imposition of hands is carried out first and the consecratory preface is chanted afterwards.

1. **As consecrating the action.** The sacramental action, as we saw above, in most cases consists of an ordinary, mundane, prosaic reality. And the more we understand the pedagogy of the sacraments, the more we should emphasize this basic mundane reality. Certainly the Church tries to show, by her whole worship, by the way she orders places and things, that we are to leave the profane level and rise to that of salvation: Mass is celebrated on an altar, not a simple dinner-table; the baptistry is distinguished from a pool by the fact that it adjoins a church and by its decoration; the baptismal water receives a preliminary consecration during the Easter Vigil; the bread and wine of the Eucharist are set apart from common use by the offertory rites.

But all these precautions, however important they may be, always remain accessory. They can even be left out in case of necessity (they were completely lacking at the baptism of the Ethiopian by Philip). The sacramental word alone is necessary to consecrate the action and the matter. When a penitent accuses himself of his sins, it is not a mere matter of self-criticism; he asks the priest to pronounce over him a word of pardon which only God can say. When the priest has repeated the words of Christ at the Last Supper, it is Christ who is present, under the signs of bread and wine, in His sacrifice.

2. **As opening out the meaning of the sacramental sign.** It is the spoken word, then, which makes a physical action into a divine sacrament. But this change is not effected in some magical way by the formulation of more or less intelligible articulated sounds, unrelated to the action of

---

[3] For the consecration of a bishop, the Church now requires that all the concelebrants pronounce the words after each has carried out the action of the imposition of hands. At a concelebrated Mass, one celebrant carries out the actions, but all pronounce the words of consecration.

the sacrament. On the contrary, the word is meant to complete, to fix clearly the meaning of the sign, to make it understandable. The word is not foreign to the sign—it perfects it. Furthermore, it is by means of the spoken word that the symbolism latent in the thing or the human action is revealed. The word causes us to discover the divine where we would not have expected it, and so gives our minds a new orientation. The sacramental word is, therefore, the good news, the proclamation, the *kerygma* of salvation; it expresses the mystery, the presence, of God acting through the sign.

When we study the words required for each sacrament, we realize that, with the exception of baptism and the Eucharist, the Church has been allowed great latitude as to their formulation, according to varied places and times. Adapting herself to the genius of various languages and civilizations, she can modify the sacramental formulas precisely because they are words, the bearers of a message. And when she does so, it is in full awareness of the power entrusted to her by Christ for this purpose.

The sacramental word, we repeat, brings out the meaning of the action. But it does more than this, as we can see from the fact that generally it does not do so in the way we should expect. Instead of saying: "By this washing you receive sanctifying grace," the person baptizing must name the Father, the Son and the Holy Spirit to whom the Christian is consecrated: "I baptize you in the name of the Father and of the Son and of the Holy Spirit." Again, the words of the Eucharistic consecration form part of a narrative: "On the night before He suffered . . . ." In other cases the words are prayers, causing the Christian to look not so much at the gift he is receiving as to the living God who is acting through the signs. The sacraments are the chief acts of the Church's worship, and this prayer-form is one way in which she expresses her adoration of God.

We must realize, then, that the sacramental word provides the first step in the pedagogy of the sacraments as willed by Christ. Any further effort must be founded on this, must develop it.

3. As effecting what is signified. When rightly pronounced by the "minister," the one who holds the place of Christ, the word is efficacious. It produces the actual presence, in the sign, of the divine mystery of grace. Its purpose is not merely to make us remember that Christ died on the Cross and saved us centuries ago; the sacrament constituted by this word together with the action is an act of Christ's here and now, today. As we shall soon see more clearly, it is the effect, produced here and now, of the death and resurrection of Christ. This is why the truly realistic way of celebrating the Christian Easter is to baptize catechumens, to absolve sinners, and to consecrate the Eucharist.

Human words, it is true, only have the power to signify, to translate our thoughts, our desires, our feelings, to cause our ideas and commands to pass into the minds and hearts of others. But God's word is quite different. The Bible shows us from its very first page that the word of God is creative (Gen. 1:3 ff.). The psalms delight in returning again and again to this divine power: "By his word the heavens were made . . . He speaks, and things come to be; He commands, and they exist (Ps. 32:6-9).

God can communicate this power to men. For example, the patriarchal blessing was a reality given once and for all as soon as it was pronounced, and so Isaac said sadly to Esau: "Your brother came by a trick and took your blessing . . . I have blessed him and he will remain blessed" (Gen. 27:33-35).

Christ Jesus, the Word-made-flesh, used actions and words to heal and save. His actions and words were efficacious, for it was by Him that all things were made. And so He said to the Canaanite woman: "O woman, great is your faith! Be it done to you as you desire," and from that moment her daughter was healed (Matthew 15:28). Or again: "Which is easier to say: 'Your sins are forgiven you' or 'Rise and walk'? But that you may know that the Son of man has power on earth to forgive sins, I command you, he said to the paralytic, rise up, take up your pallet and go back to your house. At once, under their eyes, he got up, took up what he had been lying on, and went home glorifying God" (Luke 5:23-25).

4. As a "word of faith". The sacramental word is therefore not simply an expression of the faith of the Church and her members. Because it acts, it makes the sign an effective cause of the grace signified. Because it is spoken, a change is accomplished here and now; here we have a fundamental difference between Catholic teaching and Protestant thought. But in stating the objective efficacy of the sacramental word, Catholic teaching also brings out the fact that it is truly a "word of faith."

On the one hand, it expresses the faith of the Church, since it translates her profound attitude to the whole sacramental sign. To find the Church's teaching on each sacrament, the theologian turns first of all to the study of the sacramental words. This is why the Creed does not need to state this teaching explicitly except by an occasional reference: "*Confiteor unum baptisma.* I profess that there is one baptism."

Secondly, the sacramental word calls for the response of faith on the part of each Christian. It is by means of the sacramental word that he learns and recognizes the mystery it effects. Since it is part of the sacramental sign, it is addressed at once to his understanding and to his faith. The sacraments call for a dialogue between God who speaks and the Christian who receives God's word, the response of the Christian being faith. In the Eastern liturgies, for example, this response is expressed externally in a very striking way when the faithful answer *Amen* after each of the two formulas of Eucharistic consecration chanted by the celebrant. (The Coptic liturgy in Egypt has even extended this dialogue to run through the whole account of the Supper).

But this response of faith is made, whether expressed in words or not, by the very fact of receiving a sacrament. As the French Episcopal Directive of 1951 states: "The sacraments are signs of faith; on the part of the person receiving a sacrament, this reception presupposes and affirms his faith in Christ and the Church" (No. 5).

In any case, this response is called for and needs to be aroused. This is why the Church requires that the faithful be given an understanding of the sacramental texts, even though, for the urgent reasons explained in her documents, she may maintain the use of an ancient language (as Latin in the West) for the sacramental formulas. This is also why catechisms traditionally require a Christian to know the formula for baptism and also for the Eucharist. But a much wider catechetical effort is needed as well. If the sacramental word is to be truly understood, it cannot be isolated from its biblical and liturgical context.

III. THE ROLE OF HOLY SCRIPTURE

When we read the catecheses delivered by the Fathers in explaining the sacraments to their people, we find the sacramental signs orchestrated, as it were, in such a way that God's deeds in the Old Testament, biblical images, miracles, the acts and words of Jesus, all concur to develop, extend, and enrich the sacramental symbolism.

We might think at first that all this was merely a play of the writer's fancy in accordance with the taste of that particular era, the taste that inspired the paintings on the walls of the Roman catacombs. But we find that this same method is always followed by the Church in the prayers and ceremonies with which she has surrounded the essential sacramental rites. Even more, it is in strict continuity with the method used by St. Peter in his first Epistle, by St. Paul in the first Epistle to the Corinthians, and in St. John's Gospel. We come to realize, therefore, that this biblical context is essential for a true understanding of the sacramental signs.[4]

1. The sacramental signs in the light of the actions and words of Jesus. The fourth Gospel, in particular, directly relates the actions and words of Jesus to the sacraments. This fact is obvious in the case of the multiplication of loaves, used by Jesus as His starting-point in announcing the Eucharist (John 6:26). This relationship is also indicated in the account of the healing of the man born blind, a miracle which shows us that baptism is illumination ("I washed and I see"—John 9:11); in the healing of the paralytic of Bethsaida as indicating the forgiveness of sins through the bath of baptism (John 5:14); in the wedding at Cana as pre-

---

[4] Here we are only giving a general idea and summary; we shall explain this method more precisely as we study each of the sacraments separately.

figuring the whole economy of redemption, especially the Eucharist (John 2:1-12).

The latest works of exegesis have served precisely to bring out the fact that the fourth Gospel is a sacramental catechesis. Among the innumerable things that Jesus said and did, St. John chose above all the words and deeds which illustrate the sign of the baptismal water and that of the Eucharistic meal: the conversations with Nicodemus and with the Samaritan woman by Jacob's well, the prophecy of the streams of living water (John 7:37), the pierced side of the dead Christ from whence streamed forth blood and water.[5]

The synoptic Gospels follow different plans, since they are presenting the primary catechesis, the *kerygma*. But they too provide important elements for an understanding of the sacraments. For example, they give us accounts of the institution of the Eucharist with the whole context that clarifies it. The true nature of confirmation is indicated by the way in which St. Luke relates the preaching of Jesus at the synagogue of Nazareth with the account of the baptism in the Jordan (Luke 3:21-22; 4:16-22; see chapter 3).

2. The lack of continuity between the "sacraments" of the Old Law and the Christian sacraments. Following St. Augustine, theologians have unanimously taught that the Old Law offered means of salvation to the faithful, sacraments of a kind (circumcision, for example). While this statement must always be maintained and while theological manuals rightly devote a chapter to the study of these signs, it would be a mistake to try to find in these means of salvation the true continuity between the two Testaments or the illumination given by the Old Testament to the sacraments of the New Law.

For one thing, the "sacraments" of the Old Law were signs that had no proper and direct efficacy. Certainly they oriented the spirit of the faithful Jew toward the Christ to come, but they could not cause grace, since this flows only from the Cross of Christ. They simply invited faith; and it was only in virtue of this faith in the Christ to come that salvation was given (cf. *Denz.* 845).

More important still, there is a break in symbolism between the sacraments of the Old Covenant and those of the New, with one exception—the paschal meal. Circumcision, sacrifices of expiation, the Aaronic priesthood, are not precisely in continuity with the signs of the New Testament. But the notable exception of the paschal meal directs us toward the true pedagogical use of the Old Testament. It is in the events of the history of God's people and in the images and themes of the Bible that we find continuity between the two Testaments and illumination of the

---

[5] See R. Brown, *The Gospel of Saint John and the Johannine Epistles*, NTRG, 13; B. Vawter, "The Johannine Sacramentary," *Theological Studies* 17 (1956), pp. 151-166; and articles on the Gospel of St. John by D. M. Stanley, in *Worship*, Vols. 32-34, 1957-1960.

Christian sacraments. These events, images and themes are what we are
now to study.

**3. The Christian sacraments in the light of the wonderful works of
God in the Old Testament.** God's intervention in history and, in a very
special way, the deliverance of the Hebrews from their slavery in Egypt,
their crossing of the Red Sea, the journey through the desert, the
covenant on Sinai, the entrance into the promised Land—these are the
chief "wonderful works" of God praised in the psalms and celebrated in
the Jewish feasts.[6]

These "wonderful works" are contained chiefly in the Book of Exodus.
And it is to these that St. Paul relates the Christian sacraments:

> I would not have you ignorant of this, brethren: our fathers were all
> under the cloud, all passed through the sea, all were baptized in Moses
> in the cloud and in the sea, all ate of the same spiritual food, and all
> drank the same spiritual drink—for they drank from a spiritual rock
> that accompanied them, and this rock was Christ—yet with most of
> them, God was not pleased, for their bodies were scattered in the desert
> (1 Cor. 10:1-5).

We shall return often to this capital text. Its apparent obscurity disap-
pears when we know the whole development of the theme of the exodus
in the books of the Old Testament and in those of the New, particularly
in St. John's Gospel and Apocalypse. In this text the water of baptism is
set in the frame of reference of the crossing of the Red Sea, the Eucharist
in that of the manna and the water from the rock. Baptism is deliverance
through water, initiation into membership in a people, the starting-point
for the journey toward the Promised Land. The Eucharist is the food of
a pilgrim people. The sacraments are the pledges of this Promised Land,
from which our hardness of heart may nonetheless exclude us.

But the continuity between the great deeds of the Old Testament and
our sacraments is assured by Christ. It is Christ for whom these deeds prepared; it is His "passage" that was inaugurated in the exodus; it is His
work that is carried out today in the sacraments. It was not by chance, but
exactly according to the divine plan, that Jesus chose the date of the
celebration of the pasch to institute the Eucharist and to offer Himself
on the Cross.

We shall also see that to appreciate the Mass fully it is important to
have an understanding of the covenant on Sinai and the ritual concluding
it; and for an understanding of the priesthood we need to know the
place accorded to Moses in the New Testament and in the liturgy.

[6]This section was written before Fr. Daniélou presented his paper on "The Sacraments
and the History of Salvation" (*The Liturgy and the Word of God*, pp. 21-32). See also
J. Guillet, *Thèmes of the Bible*, pp. 1-19; B. M. Ahern, "The Exodus, Then and Now";
The Bridge, John M. Oesterreicher, ed., Vol. I, pp. 53-74; A Martimort, *In Remembrance
of Me*, pp. 6-13; L. Bouyer, *The Meaning of Sacred Scripture*, pp. 224-241.

The book of Genesis also tells of the intervention of God in human history, His revelation to Abraham, Isaac and Jacob. Melchisedech and Isaac are essential references for the true idea of the priesthood of Christ and the Eucharistic sacrifice. The family life of these patriarchs furnishes some models of Christian marriage; the blessing of the Church calls down upon the bride the virtues of Sara, Rebecca, Rachel.

Finally, the later historical books, particularly those of Josue, Judges, Samuel and Kings, describe the preparation for the Messiah. The crossing of the Jordan, the entrance into the Promised Land, the person of Josue, the prophetic ministry, the institution of the kingship of David, all indicate the vast dimensions of the work of Christ's mediation. The anointing of kings, priests and prophets is found united in Jesus; and the sacramental character is a participation in the anointing of Christ.

4. The sacramental signs as biblical images. The Old Testament is a history, in the concrete and realistic sense of the word—so much so that Christ and His Church are included within it in strict continuity, and our God is truly the God of Abraham, Isaac and Jacob. But it is also a pedagogy of the realities of the faith, it is a message. God's mercy, redemption, forgiveness, grace—in a word, everything that is given us in the sacraments—was proclaimed, first in a remote fashion and then more clearly, throughout the history of Israel. Each stage of the road is marked by the faults, the trials of the people, and also by the new lights given by God. Sages, prophets, and the praying community discover step by step the new covenant which is to come and also the great day of the Lord which is to dawn.

This revelation is presented, not by means of ideas or abstract formulas, but by means of images which we can follow from one book of the Bible to another, while we see their content being ceaselessly enriched and purified. Some of these images are taken from material things: rock, water, fire, light, vines, bread, oil, perfume. Others come from the daily life of man: meals, marriage. And, finally, there are religious gestures, with a symbolic meaning extended beyond their ritual use: anointing, the imposition of hands.

Particular mention should be made here of the first eleven chapters of Genesis. While they are related to real facts and in this sense have a historic character like that of the rest of the book, they do not follow a historical method properly speaking, but obey the laws of a particular literary style. Here, again, the basic truths presupposed by the economy of salvation are also presented in images, so vital that the art of all ages has admired and tried to reproduce them, so charged with revelation that they are the starting-point of all later catechesis. The fruitful waters with the breath of God hovering over them, producing life; the rivers of Paradise; the destroying water of the Flood; the creation of the first human couple, "two in one flesh"—the New Testament invites us to go back to all these to understand the redemption, the Church, the sacraments, and particularly baptism and marriage (Matthew 19:4; John 3:5; Apoc. 2:7; 22:1-2; 1 Peter 3:18-21).

Thus, when Christ chose the sacramental signs, these signs had a very rich meaning for Him and for the apostles, the meaning already provided by the tradition of the whole Old Testament. It was because of this richness that He chose them.

> We generally interpret the rite of baptism by seeing in it a reference to water as cleansing and purifying. But this does not seem actually to be the most important meaning of the rite . . . On the other hand, the water of baptism is the water that destroys, the water of judgment; the waters in Jewish symbolism are actually a symbol of the power of death. But the water of baptism is also the water that brings forth a new creature, and this sends us back to the Jewish symbol of the waters as not only destructive but also creative.[7]

Yet the biblical meaning of the sacramental signs is not unrelated to their natural meaning: the biblical develops and extends the natural. Modern science is continually discovering its coherence; depth psychology in particular demonstrates this in its analysis of the symbolism of the unconscious. This reference to psychology should not surprise us, for the Creator knows what is in man, His creature. Still less should it lead us on the wrong path; biblical symbolism is bound up with a history, the history of salvation, and bound to a Person, Christ. These images, in accord as they are with our human mentality, are the vehicle of a revelation, that is, of the free and unexpected intervention of God in the life of mankind.

IV. THE LITURGICAL EXTENSIONS OF THE SACRAMENTAL SIGNS

We do not need to become specialists in the science of exegesis to acquire the biblical ideas needed to understand the sacramental signs. The Church herself offers them to her children. For, as said above, except in cases of extreme urgency, the sacraments are part of a great liturgical whole which surrounds them, prepares for them, extends them, and clarifies their meaning without any break in continuity.

It is true, for example, that the baptism of the Ethiopian recounted in the Acts was decided on in a few minutes, and celebrated without ceremony, with water found by the wayside and a brief ritual. Here the newness of the Gospel message, the intense generosity of the candidate (germinating through a long period of time through his connection with

[7] J. Daniélou, *The Bible and the Liturgy,* pp. 6-7.

Judaism), the charismatic breath of the Holy Spirit necessarily present at these origins—all this amply justified the absence of preparation and of a religious setting.

But this is not the normal way of administering the sacraments. From ancient times the celebration of baptism has been surrounded with most of the rites carried out today, e.g., ceremonies of entering the catechumenate, scrutinies together with exorcisms, clothing with a white garment.

Nor does this liturgical context include only the actions and words grouped together in the Ritual under the title "On Baptism." Normally the celebration of baptism is inserted in the Easter Virgil, and as such is prepared for by the biblical readings and the consecration of the water, and followed by the Mass. The oil and the chrism used in the anointings were consecrated by the bishop on Holy Thursday in the course of a Mass with a whole formulary setting out their significance. Even more, the whole liturgy of Lent is, as we know, organized around preparation for baptism, while Easter week is a great meditation on the graces of Christian initiation. And all this is carried out through a marvellous synthesis of biblical readings, psalm texts, prayer-formulas.

1. Differences between these ceremonies and the sacramental signs properly so called. We are meant, then, to receive and to understand the sacraments in their whole liturgical context. Nonetheless, theologians strive to work out an exact distinction between the sacramental signs properly so called and the prayers or rites with which the Church has surrounded them.

This distinction is important from the doctrinal point of view because the efficacy of the sacramental signs differs from that of the rites which the Church has added. The efficacy of the sacramental sign is inherent in the action performed, because it is the act of Christ. It produces the grace that it signifies by the fact of the act being carried out (*ex opere operato*[8]). The other rites do not have this privilege. But this does not mean that they are negligible—far from it. They are carried out in the name of the Church, whose prayers are pleasing to God because she is the Bride of Christ (theologians say that they have value *ex opere operantis Ecclesiae,* as acts of the Church and within the limits of her proper mediation).

---

[8] *Ex opere operato:* a theological formula consecrated by the Council of Trent (*Denz.* 851) meaning that the sacrament produces its effect by the fact that it is the act of Christ, as soon as the sign is carried out, and does not receive its value from the fervor, the merits, or the activity either of the minister or of the subject.
Ex opere operantis Ecclesiae: this formula applies only to the rites which, not being of divine institution, are not sacraments in the strict and rigorous sense of the term, but draw their value from being acts of the Church; she participates in the mediatory priesthood of Christ and she is His Bride to whom He always listens. See *Mediator Dei,* 27, C. Vagaggini, *Theological Dimensions of the Liturgy,* pp. 55-58; P. F. Fransen, *Faith and the Sacraments,* Aquinas Paper 31, pp. 17-22.

From the practical point of view also, it is necessary to know which rites are essential to the sacrament and which are accessory. Defects and omissions may occur in a celebration—to what extent is the validity of the sacrament impaired by these defects? This is the reason why the introduction to the Roman Missal tries to foresee all the accidents that might occur in the Eucharistic celebration and the means of remedying them. Again, the sacrament might have to be administered in exceptional conditions of poverty, of urgency or of secrecy—what is the absolutely indispensable minimum for a true sacrament? The Church has frequent experience of such cases as the necessity of baptizing or anointing the victim of a fatal accident, of celebrating the Eucharist or of ordaining in times of persecution. Such situations cannot be overlooked, and solutions have been provided.

Nevertheless, we must not exaggerate this distinction between the essential sacramental sign and what the Church has added by way of actions and prayers. The continuity between them is equally important. Moreover, it is not always easy to say what is essential to the sacrament and what is accessory.

2. Difficulties encountered in distinguishing between the essential sign and the accessory rites. In the first place, the sacramental signs were not all fixed in an invariable way by Christ, so the intervention of the Church in this domain may be determining. A remarkable example is furnished by the history of the sacrament of holy Orders. While the authors in the Middle Ages and the practical decisions of the Church at that period considered the essentials of the sacrament to be the act of anointing and the fact of presenting the candidate with the instruments symbolizing his function, the constitution *Sacramentum Ordinis* of November 30, 1947, decided that, in future, the imposition of hands and the solemn preface following it alone suffice for validity (*Denz.* 2301).

Certain rites, furthermore, although not necessary for validity, may nonetheless be required by the very logic of the sacrament, such as the Communion of the Mass which is required on the part of the priest at least as an integral part of the sacrifice, or the breaking of the bread, which repeats a gesture of Christ's.

Finally, the discipline here often differs in accordance with the tradition of different churches within the unity and catholicity of the one Church. In the case of marriage, for example, in the Latin Church the exchange of consent in the presence of the priest is all that is required, but it seems that in the East the priestly blessing is equally indispensable.

3. The ceremonies as extending and continuing the sacramental sign. The rites instituted by the Church are not a mere guard-of-honor around the sacrament. (Let us note in passing that even from this point of view they play an important role. The sacrament, reduced to the essential

signs, is a fleeting act, rapidly carried out, whereas it should be surrounded with respect and solemnity and be received in a well-prepared
soul.)

Their purpose is to clarify and to extend the sacramental sign, to develop its meaning. With baptism, for example, if we stop at the single
sign of water poured out, we are apt to see only the effect of purification
and the remission of sins. (Perhaps this is the reason why the state of
grace is so often defined as "not having any mortal sin on one's conscience.") But we need much more in order to correspond with the
graces of our baptism. So, to the sacramental sign the Church adds the
anointing with holy chrism to signify our identification with Christ and
our "divinization". And the symbolism of the water is further explained
by the consecrating preface that prepares it for baptism; marvellous poem
that it is, this prayer, orchestrating a vast biblical symphony, is essential
to a true catechesis of baptism.

Similarly, what does it mean to baptize "in the name of the Father and
of the Son and of the Holy Spirit"? It is simultaneously to give and to
require faith in the three Persons with whom original relationships of
intimacy are established. This is the reason for the baptismal questioning
about the faith, and for the presentation of the *Credo* to the candidate.
And, although the biblical theme of water suggests combat, struggle and
death, the baptismal liturgy needs to make explicit this symbolism contained in the sign—it does so by the renunciation of the devil, by the
pre-baptismal anointing, by the exorcisms.

In so serving the sacramental sign by explaining it and opening out its
wealth of meaning, these rites imitate the divine economy. They are at
once prayer and act, act making use of things: oil, light, clothing, breath,
sign of the Cross. They are biblical both in inspiration and in meaning,
so that they, in turn, are clarified by the Bible. Thus the sacrament sets
in motion, as it were, an innumerable series of waves extending further
and further, continually widening the scope of the power that gives them
their impulse.

Article Two
THE SACRAMENTS AS ACTS OF CHRIST

When we see the sacramental action and hear the words spoken, we
can easily perceive the effect that is signified. But how is this effect not
only signified, but produced, since, as we have seen, the sacramental
word is efficacious? Because it is Christ who acts; the sacrament is an act
of Christ. We must now explain this statement.

It is not enough to pay attention to the things, to the actions and to the words. We must also consider the person who makes use of these things, who carries out these actions, who pronounces these words—the minister of the sacrament. He also is a sign, for he holds the place of Christ, he plays the part of Christ, Christ acts through him. And the minister of a sacrament is not an isolated man, lost in the universe, arrogating to himself the right to carry out this mission; rather, he is the minister of the Church, of the Bride of Christ, to whom Christ entrusted the treasure of the sacraments. When Peter baptizes, it is the Church that baptizes, it is Christ who baptizes. This is why it is well to follow this order in elementary religious instruction: (1) the minister; (2) the Church, who distributes the sacraments; (3) Christ, who acts through the Church and her ministers.

At a more technical level, however, the reverse order has the advantage of encountering problems and difficulties in the very order in which the understanding of the faith is to solve them. Thus the *French Directory for Pastoral Care* begins by stating: "The sacraments are acts of Christ through the ministry of the Church exercising His priesthood, which has as its purpose at once to glorify God and to save men."

I. ACTS OF CHRIST

All grace comes from God alone, because He alone can forgive sins ("Who can forgive sins but God alone?" as the Pharisees rightly objected—Luke 5:21), and He alone can freely make a human being His adopted son. More precisely, grace is the work of the Holy Spirit. It is He who causes us to be born again of water (John 3:5); He is given to us and pours out in our hearts the love of God (Rom. 5:5).

Since, however, the Son of God has taken on our flesh, His holy humanity is the instrument of this divine work. There is no grace except through Jesus, and through Jesus as man. "There is one mediator between God and men, Christ Jesus, Himself a man, who delivered Himself as a ransom for us" (1 Tim. 2:5). In the sacraments it is Christ who gives the Holy Spirit, who forgives sins.

1. The sacraments instituted by Christ. The Church did not set up the sacraments on her own initiative as is the case with the rites surrounding and extending their celebration. They were instituted by Jesus Himself during His earthly life. The faith of the Church is quite clear on this point: "If anyone says that the sacraments of the New Law were not instituted by Jesus Christ our Lord, let him be anathema." This canon of the Council of Trent (*Denz.* 844) expresses the constant tradition of the Church. This does not mean, however, that we find the institution of each sacrament set out explicitly in the Gospels with circumstances of time and place. We do find this in the case of the Eucharist, which the New Testament shows us as instituted by Christ on the eve of His death. He Himself carried out this rite, explained its meaning, and made it clear that it was not a passing action, but a lasting institution: "Do this in memory of Me." Because the Eucharist is the supreme gift and the chief sacrament, and at the same time the sacrament of the Church's daily life, its institution must be recalled continually. The Supper is reproduced; the narrative of it is the efficacious word. The Eucharist is thus the act of Christ who offers Himself sacramentally, His sacrifice made present.

The other sacraments are found presented in the Gospels, the Acts, and the Epistles in various ways as the faithful fulfillment of a command of Jesus. Sometimes this command is expressed: "Go, therefore, make disciples of all nations, baptizing them in the name of the Father and of the Son and of the Holy Spirit" (Matthew 28:29); "Receive the Holy Spirit; whose sins you shall forgive, they are forgiven; whose sins you shall retain, they are retained" (John 20:22-23). In other cases, it is one of the apostles who hands on the message to us, as in St. James' record of the anointing of the sick (James 5:14-15). Or else we see the administration of the sacrament itself as having taken place since the first days of the Church, as in the case of confirmation (Acts 8:15-17; 19:6).

The great diversity of ways in which the sacred writers indicate Christ's institution of the sacraments is no literary caprice on their part. It expresses the difference in the bond that connects these efficacious signs of grace with the life of Jesus. The Eucharist is connected with a precise moment, a definite date, "the night on which He was betrayed." Holy orders is also connected in some way with the Supper by the Eucharist itself. But in the case of the other sacraments, it is the symbol, the sign, which is decisive, and this is determined as much by Jesus' word as by His acts and His life.

Nor should we imagine that everything about the sacraments was determined in an invariable and definitive way by Christ. The choice of each of the sacraments and their special efficacy is His work. The sign itself was designated by Him, more or less precisely. The water of baptism, the bread and wine of the Eucharist, doubtless also the oil for the sick and the imposition of hands in ordination, have been determined once for all. But other actions as well as words have in great part been left to the Church to determine. What she does in this regard is not arbitrary, since the sign must always express the hidden reality which is contained in the sacrament and which is the work of God.

2. "From the pierced side of Christ came out blood and water." Furthermore, to look for the concrete circumstances, the precise details, the exact moment when the Lord instituted one or another sacrament (with the exception of the Eucharist, as we have just said) would be to falsify, by restricting unduly, the meaning which we ought to attach to Christ's institution of the sacraments. For

> Christ is not the founder of a religion—after the manner of Buddha, Muhamed or Wesley—a man who has created a certain religious organization which goes on functioning without him, after his death, according to the rules he gave at the beginning. Christ is not only present at the historical origin, the foundation of the Church—He is its Head, living and working, here and now.[9]

Through the Church and through the sacraments of the Church, Christ continues in a mysterious way, thanks to the signs, the redemptive act accomplished once for all by His death on the Cross. It is not enough, therefore, to say that the grace given by the sacraments comes only from Christ. We must explain more precisely: it can come only from the passion of Christ. By the sacraments the passion of Christ is, as it were, made available to men, according to the formulation of the Epistle to the Romans: "Do you not know that when we have been baptized in Christ Jesus, it is in His death that we have been baptized?" (6:3). Thus we must connect the sacraments with this supreme moment in the life of Jesus as their source.

Christian tradition has emphasized the insistence with which St. John describes this supreme moment in his Gospel (19:33-35).

> When they came to Jesus, they found him dead; they did not break his legs, but one of the soldiers with his lance pierced his side, and at once there came out blood and water. He who saw it gives witness of it—and he knows that he speaks truly so that you too may believe.

According to the commentaries of the Fathers and St. Thomas, this stream flowing from the side of Christ is the symbol of the sacraments, in particular of baptism and the Eucharist; through these it is the sign of the Church, the new Eve created from the side of the new Adam as He slept (*Summa* III, 62, 5). Receiving the sacraments thus puts us in communication with the passion of Christ, the effects of which we receive; the sacramental sign is always commemorative of Christ's death and the sacraments cause us to enter into the pasch of Christ, His passing from this world to the Father.

What, precisely, is this relationship between the sacraments and the unique event of Calvary? Here again, the Eucharist has a privileged place. It makes really present, thanks to the symbol, the event which was carried out once for all. This is why it is the chief act of worship and why, as we shall see, it makes the Church. The other sacraments do not attain this unique realism; they do not contain the mysterious presence of

[9]A. M. Roguet, *Christ Acts through Sacraments*, pp. 11-23.

Christ's immolation, but only its effects.[10] And so, whenever possible the liturgy administers them in conjunction with the celebration of the Eucharist: Christian initiation (baptism and confirmation) is completed with Communion. Major Orders cannot be conferred except during a Mass. The nuptial blessing is also, in principle, connected with the Mass, and it is in the course of a Mass that the bishop consecrates the holy oils.

3. "Peter baptizes, it is Christ who baptizes" (St. Augustine).

Let us take one further step: the sacraments are acts of Christ, not only because Christ instituted them and because the grace which they signify and cause comes from Calvary, but also because Christ Himself acts through the Church and through her minister. The Church is His Body and the extension of His sacred humanity; the minister, through his intention to do what the Church does, becomes the instrument with which Christ acts. "It is He who through the Church baptizes, teaches, governs, binds, absolves, offers, sacrifices" (Mystici Corporis, 54). This is why, as we shall see later, the sin or the heresy of the minister does not impede the value of the sacrament. St. Augustine remarks:

> Those who were baptized by John (the Baptist) were given baptism again. Now Jesus did not baptize Himself, but His disciples did, and Judas was still among them. How can it be that those who were baptized by John had to be baptized again, and not those baptized by Judas? Certainly . . . because those whom John baptized were baptized by John; those whom Judas baptized were baptized by Christ.[11]

Thus the Lord Himself remains the author of the sacraments given by His ministers. The ministers are many, but there is only one Christ acting through them:

> I hear that each of you says: I am for Paul, and I am for Apollo, and I am for Cephas, and I am for Christ. Is Christ divided? Was it Paul who was crucified for you? Or was it in the name of Paul that you were baptized? (1 Cor. 1:12-13).

4. The priesthood of Jesus exercised through the sacraments.

Christ is a priest forever according to the order of Melchisedech: "From the fact that He remains forever, He has an unchangeable priesthood. Whence it follows that He can save forever those who go to God through

[10] This point has been the object of lively discussion among theologians during the last thirty years, as a result of the works of Dom Odo Casel. To attribute to all the sacraments the very presence of the mystery is to ignore what is specific to the Eucharist: it alone is the efficacious *memorial* of Christ's passion and sacrifice. In the other sacraments Christ is present only "by the power He infuses into them so that they will be effective instruments of holiness" (*Mediator Dei*, 20). Cf. C. Davis, *Liturgy and Doctrine*, pp. 75-92; "Dom Odo Casel and the Theology of Mysteries," *Worship*, 34 (1960), pp. 428-438.

[11] *Treatise on St. John's Gospel*, 5:18. We are quoting the text only as a witness and for its general sense; the true sacrament of baptism was not administered until after the resurrection, and so after the death of Jesus.

Him, since He is always living to make intercession for them" (Heb. 7:24-25).

Certainly, the priesthood of Christ is manifested above all in His passion and in His death; this was the moment when Christ through His own Blood entered into the sanctuary (Heb. 9:12). But He continues to exercise it on earth through the Eucharist and the other sacraments (*Med. Dei*, 1-3).

Being priestly acts of Christ, the sacraments are thus at the center of the liturgy. They not only carry out the work of our salvation but also the praise and adoration of God. They consecrate man to God, causing him to participate more or less closely in the priesthood of Christ "for the praise of God's glory." Here again, the Eucharist is the sacrament above all others, since it is the sacrifice of praise as well as the Blood poured out for the remission of sins and the food of eternal life. In saying that "the sacraments are for men," a most important theological adage which regulates both pedagogy and pastoral practice, we must not forget that the sacraments are part of divine worship and cause us to enter into the very prayer of Christ.[12]

II. GIVEN THROUGH THE CHURCH

It is to the Church, and to her alone, that Christ has entrusted His treasures as the deposit which she is faithfully to preserve: the faith, her mission or "sending" by Christ, and the sacraments. She who is the sole guardian is also the sole distributor of this treasure; the sacraments cannot be given except through her. She is Bride and Mother, it is she who brings forth the children of God. "No one can have God for Father who does not have the Church for mother" (St. Cyprian).

1. The Church, guardian of the sacraments.   It was not to a chance member of the crowd, but to the apostles gathered in the upper room on Holy Thursday that Jesus said: "Do this in memory of me." It was to the Eleven that Christ said after His resurrection: "All power is given to Me in heaven and on earth: go, therefore, make disciples of all nations, baptizing them . . ." (Matthew 28:18-19).

As guardian of this marvellous treasure, the Church must first of all ensure its conservation. She makes authoritative decisions concerning the conditions that are essential and sufficient for the sacraments to be effectively carried out (conditions for validity). Her magisterium, with sovereign authority, puts an end to controversies arising on this subject. For example, Popes Benedict XIII, Pius VII and Pius X rejected the opinion of the East holding that the Eucharistic consecration requires, besides the account of the institution, an invocation to the Holy Spirit

[12]See Cyprian Vagaggini, *Theological Dimensions of the Liturgy*, ch. 4.

(the epiclesis). The Council of Trent decided that the Communion of the faithful was not essential to the celebration of the Mass, and also that Communion under one species is legitimate. Pius XII determined in 1947 what was essential and sufficient for ordination, thus ending a theological dispute many centuries long.

Even more than such interventions by a single act, it is the daily life of the Church that provides the norm of the validity of the sacraments. It is from the Church's current prescriptions for the various rites, and from the customary usages established over the centuries in the East and in the West,[13] that theologians determine the laws of sacramental organization. Those laws, therefore, are founded upon concrete realities rather than upon discursive arguments.

But in virtue of the freedom of action granted by Christ to His Church with regard to the sacramental rites and within its limits, the Church's part is still more active. The formulas or prayers which constitute the word of the sacrament (i.e., its "form") are composed by her, and she may change them in accordance with the needs and modes of expression of each civilization. For example, in the various rites and in different periods these formulas are presented sometimes in the form of a prayer ("Send down, O Lord, Your Holy Spirit . . ."), sometimes as a statement ("I baptize you . . ."). The Church, then, has extensive power over the sacramental formulas.

The same thing is true—even more surprisingly for the historian—of the actions and the things concerned in the sacraments. It is possible, for instance, that the presentation of the instruments of office formed an essential part of the sign of ordination during the Middle Ages, although this did not exist in antiquity, the East has always ignored it, and the constitution *Sacramentum Ordinis* of 1947 definitely rejected the necessity of this action for validity.

Again, while the apostles confirmed by the one action of the imposition of hands, the Roman Church has made use of a threefold sign: the imposition of hands, the sign of the Cross, and anointing with chrism. The anointing has become such an essential part of the sacrament that the East uses no other action. Here again, the Church exercises an active power; though she is the guardian of a deposit that she can but transmit, she possesses a certain liberty with regard to the choice of the sign which is to express the grace attached by Christ to one or another sacrament.

2. The Church, the only distributor of the sacraments. The Church has the very presence of Christ living and acting in her. (This is why it is so regrettable that the faithful all too frequently see her simply as a kind of legislative authority, regulating and codifying religious activity.) And

---

[13] This precise formulation is needed because the ordinary (though not the solemn) magisterium of the Church is infallible only as a whole. Isolated examples, too limited as to time or space, may be merely errors or abuses, whatever the authority responsible for them.

so her role in the sacrament goes beyond what we have already mentioned: deciding on conditions of validity and determining the sign when this has been left to her discretion by the Lord. It is precisely because the sacraments are administered by the Church that they are acts of Christ. It is she who acts when a baptism or an absolution or any other sacrament is given. This is always true, even when a sacrament seems to be the affair simply of the minister and the subject, because the minister of a sacrament is necessarily the minister of the Church.

To administer any sacrament validly, the minister must be connected with the Church by his intention to carry out an act of the Church and to do so as she wishes. This intention may exist in the schismatic who has broken with the unity of the Church and in the heretic whose faith is falsified. It may even exist in the apostate or unbeliever: emergency baptism may be validly administered by anyone who has the intention of doing what the Church does and manifests this intention externally by carrying out the bare essentials of the sign. In this case, the Lord's infinite mercy, of which the sacraments are the pledge, acts through a very rudimentary connection of the minister with the Church.

All the sacraments except baptism require that the minister be baptized. And all the sacraments except baptism and marriage require that the minister also have the power of orders. This makes the connection between the minister and the Church a much closer one. The character given by ordination to bishops and priests gives them the privilege of representing the Church in the role of Christ as Head and Mediator. This bond and privilege endure even when the minister acts outside the unity of the Church.

The connection of the minister with the Church must also normally be expressed by his observing all the conditions she lays down for the administration of the sacraments. In her Code of Canon Law, in her liturgical books, in her various legislative acts, the Church regulates many questions concerning the use of the sacraments which do not pertain to the essential structure of the signs; these she decides in virtue of the power proper to her. Such questions include: to whom should a sacrament be given, to whom refused? At what age and with what dispositions is it to be received? At what times and what places should it be administered? Moreover, the Church places the sacraments within the whole economy of her worship (we have already seen the importance of this context for the sacramental sign itself, which it develops and extends).

Fidelity to these various requirements is imposed by the general duty of obedience binding clerics and faithful to the Church. But here this fidelity is imposed for the very special reason that it is the Church, and she alone, who is the distributor of the sacraments.

The Church is the sole administrator of the sacraments because it was she who, in the person of the apostles, received the command, the commission of Christ to administer them. The Pope and the college of bishops, the successors of the apostles, are the only beneficiaries of this commission. It is they who are to administer the sacraments; other ministers are only their assistants, their delegates, their substitutes, acting in their name and in union with them. No one has set out this great principle more clearly than St. Ignatius of Antioch in the letters he wrote, toward the end of the first century, to various churches: no baptism, he says, no Eucharist, without the bishop.

In virtue of this principle, ecclesiastical legislation determines the way in which this mission is verified in each case. It is given either in a permanent way, in virtue of the function to which a man is appointed by the bishop (ordinary power), or temporarily for a particular case or a series of acts (delegated power). It is supplied in cases of urgency and, besides, may often be presumed.[14]

The Church, therefore, is present in each sacrament. And this presence is realized basically through the intention and action of the minister, and, with the exception of baptism and marriage, through the character received in ordination. It is expressed still more strongly through the commission the minister has received from the bishop and through the faithful observance of all the prescriptions of the Church. As a normal consequence, therefore, it calls for the assembling of the faithful.

The community of Christians is already invisibly present around the minister as he carries out Christ's act. But when this presence becomes visible, when the faithful have been called together and actually take part, then the ecclesial dimension of the sacrament is fully manifested. This is why (except for the present discipline in the West concerning the sacrament of penance), the liturgical books always take it for granted that the Christian people will be present at the ceremony and pray at the celebrant's invitation. It is not merely a little group of parents or friends but the local Church as a whole, or at least its representatives, whom the celebrant addresses in the course of the celebration ("Let us pray, be-

---

[14] When the non-observance of certain conditions results in the nullity of the sacrament (for example, if confirmation were given with chrism that had not been duly consecrated by a bishop), we speak of conditions of *validity*. When the violation of various rules, while weighing on the conscience of those responsible and constituting a more or less serious disorder, does not nullify the sacrament, we speak of conditions of *liceity*.

Validity—An act is valid that has been truly carried out, that does not have to be repeated, and that is of itself capable of producing its proper effects. We speak of the validity of a sacrament (or even of a ceremony of the Church) when it has been administered in such a way that the sign is effectively constituted and so must produce, if not the grace *(res)*, at least the *res et sacramentum*. Validity requires: (1) that the matter or action and the word be ensured in their essentials, (2) by a minister having the necessary power and intention, (3) on a subject capable and (if he has the use of reason) willing.

Liceity—A sacrament is given licitly when all the prescriptions not bound up with validity are faithfully observed. Violating these does not, consequently, involve the nullity of the act that has been carried out, but constitutes a grave fault on the part of the person responsible and a more or less serious disturbance of the order that the Lord wills should reign in His Church.

loved brethren . . .; The Lord be with you . . .") and who respond to his invitation or greeting.

III. ACTS OF THE MINISTER OF CHRIST AND THE CHURCH

The person who carries out the action of the sacrament and pronounces the essential words is called the minister of the sacrament. The choice of this term is suggested by a phrase in the first Epistle to the Corinthians (4:1): "That we may be regarded as the servants of Christ (*ministros Christi*) and as those entrusted with disturbing the mysteries of God." The term invites us to go beyond the person of the minister and to see only Him whose representative, whose executant, whose instrument, this minister is. As the Apostle says:

> Christ has entrusted us with the ministry of reconciliation. For it was God who, in Christ, reconciled the world to himself, no longer taking account of the faults of men, and putting on our lips the word of reconciliation. We are therefore ambassadors of Christ; it is as if God were speaking through us (2 Cor. 5:18-20).[15]

All the doctrinal statements of the Church concerning the minister of the sacraments serve to illustrate and explain this idea. If the definitions of the magisterium on this subject are exceptionally numerous, it is because the Church has had, in the course of her history, to face many grave crises in which the truth of the sacraments was in danger of distortion.

1. *The sacraments as necessarily administered by men on earth.* Various poetic legends represent holy persons as receiving the sacraments through the miraculous ministry of angels or of the blessed in heaven. Theologians do not accept this pious imagery (and it should not be included in children's religious instruction). The power of the sacraments flows from the passion, which is the work of Christ's humanity, and it is through the Church on earth that He continues to sanctify men. The fact that the minister is a human being, in the earthly condition of living by faith and in danger of sin, is in harmony with the whole economy of salvation. The sacraments are instruments in the hands of Christ, an extension of His humanity.

2. *The sacraments which require the apostolic succession of ordination.* "If anyone says that all Christians have the power to preach and to administer all the sacraments, let him be anathema." This canon of the Council of Trent (*Denz.* 853) refers to the error of the Protestants who rejected the hierarchy of orders in the Church and by so doing abol-

---

[15] This text refers directly to the ministry of the word, not of the sacraments, yet the realism of this second ministry is still greater and realizes still more fully the instrumental role of him who exercises it.

ished practically the whole sacramental organism. The fact is that, with two exceptions, the sacraments cannot be efficacious as acts of Christ if the minister does not possess by ordination the basic power to carry them out. The character imprinted in an ineffaceable way by the sacrament of orders is, above all, a sacramental power.

Therefore, bishops alone possess in fullness the power to confirm, to celebrate the Eucharist, to pardon sins. And they alone can hand on their priesthood. Priests have received the power to celebrate the Eucharist and to give the anointing of the sick. But they may do so licitly only in dependence on the bishop (even though they possess this power in such a way that they can give these sacraments validly even outside of obedience to the bishop and the Church).

With regard to the sacrament of penance, it is only when express jurisdiction has been given by the bishop or by the general laws of the Church that priests can validly exercise the power to absolve. As for confirmation, it is only by special privilege or the express concession of the Roman Pontiff that certain priests receive the power to confirm within precise limits, and in a way so exceptional that: (1) the sacrament is null if a priest goes beyond these limits (such as those of function, of territory, etc.); (2) no case of urgency allows him to go beyond them; (3) that in the exercise of this faculty, the priest presents himself as being deputed to do so by the Holy See. (The case of confirmation administered by a priest illustrates the notion of the *extraordinary minister,* an idea which is fully applicable only to this sacrament, although Canon Law applies it by analogy to others).

Orders, confirmation, the Eucharist, penance, and the anointing of the sick thus require in him who administers them a priestly succession going back to the apostles, the only depositories of the power of orders instituted by Christ. This succession is ensured by the bishops. Where it exists, the sacraments are valid. This is true in the case of the separated Eastern Churches, even though their schism is very ancient. But where the succession has been interrupted, there are no sacraments except baptism and marriage; this is the case with the Anglican Church (except for individual instances) and the majority of Protestant Churches.

Baptism and marriage, however, constitute two remarkable exceptions. In marriage, the act is performed by the bride and groom themselves: they marry one another. Their action becomes a sacrament because they have been baptized, and, while the intervention of the priest is required for validity, the Church does not insist on the necessity of this condition in the same way in different times and different rites. She dispenses with it in cases where it is impossible; she does not impose it on schismatics in good faith. This is why it is commonly said that the bride and groom are the ministers of the sacrament of marriage.

As for baptism, while it is normally administered under the authority of the bishop by priests and deacons, we have already seen that it can be validly given by anyone, even an unbaptized or unbelieving person.

3. The necessity of intending to do what the Church does.

> If anyone says that, in the celebration of the sacraments, the minister does not need to have at least the intention of doing what the Church does, let him be anathema (*Denz.* 854).

This formula dates from the twelfth century. But the tradition of the Church is unanimous both in affirming the necessity for this intention and in emphasizing the minimum to which it can be reduced in the case of baptism. For the minister of the sacrament is not a robot, but a man, submitting himself in a lucid and intelligent way to Christ, the principal cause of the sacraments, putting himself at His disposal, consciously carrying out an act of the Church.

However, since we cannot see into souls, this intention is manifested by external signs: the fact that the actions are carried out with seriousness, that the words are pronounced, that the whole sign is carried out in a religious context. (Thus there is serious question as to the validity of the intention in the various rather fantastic cases imagined by canonists or by novelists in which a sacrilegious context manifestly violates the order of the Church.)

A pagan may have this intention, since he may be eager to give baptism even though he does not have the faith, does not know, or rejects the Church for himself. This intention may be valid in schismatics, in heretics and even in apostates; the Church has stated, after bitter controversies, that the faults of the minister do not nullify the sacraments.

4. The sacraments not nullified by the unworthiness of the minister.

"How can a sinner hand on grace?" This objection disturbed the African Church in the time of St. Optatus and St. Augustine, and it has periodically found a new audience, especially in times when Christian morals needed to be reformed (in the fifteenth century particularly, with Wycliff and John Huss). Nobody can give what he does not possess; the person who does not possess the Holy Spirit must be incapable of communicating Him. "Can a dead man give life, a wounded man heal, a blind man give light, a naked man clothe or an unclean man purify?" (St. Cyprian). The answer is easy: he does not act by his own power but by that of Christ, whose instrument he is, "It matters little whether the pipe through which the water flows is of gold or of lead" (St. Augustine, *Treatise on John,* 5:15).

> It is not Damasus who makes pure, it is not Peter, nor Ambrose, nor Gregory; we are the ministers, but the sacraments are Yours. Conferring the divine gifts does not come from human resources, but is Your gift, Lord (St. Ambrose, *On the Holy Spirit,* I).

The Council of Trent condemned the error of those who rejected the validity of the sacraments conferred by a minister in the state of sin (*Denz.* 855).

How can the sacraments administered outside the true Church be valid? St. Cyprian's acute sense of the unity of the Church and of the necessity for going through her to receive the gifts of God led him to consider invalid the baptism and the Eucharist celebrated by a schismatic, and still more by a heretical bishop or priest. He obliged those who had been baptized under such conditions to receive the sacrament again. The intervention of Pope St. Stephen I aroused strong reactions on the part of the African bishop, who was supported by many of his colleagues. A long time after the death of St. Cyprian, the Councils of Arles (314) and of Nicea (325) ended the controversy by stating that such baptisms are valid, providing that they have been truly given in the name of the Father, the Son and the Holy Spirit.

But the dispute was reawakened at the end of the fourth century by the Donatists, against whom St. Augustine had to defend both the true teaching of the Church and the memory of the holy martyr St. Cyprian. This time the question was concerned especially with the value of ordinations. See how he solves the objections:

> The baptism conferred by schismatics or heretics is not their baptism; it belongs to God and the Church wherever it may be found, wherever it may be given. The only thing that is really your own is your error, your sacrilege, your separation. It is the Church who begets all men by baptism, whether in her own womb or outside it . . . all those who are reborn are born as children of the Church by right of baptism (*On Baptism,* 1:14f.)

The Council of Trent took up the same principles in its canons on baptism (*Denz.* 860). Their interest is not merely historical; these principles are applied every day to the reception of Christians baptized in heresy or schism. The intention linking the minister with the Church is, consequently, not suppressed by the fact that this minister is separated from the true Church. A person cannot seek Christ without at the same time finding His Bride.

5. Conclusion: the minister as a sign of Christ and the Church. From these difficulties met and dealt with in the life of the Church, there has resulted a vivid awareness of the nature of the minister. He is a man, he carries out a human act with all the freedom, the initiative, the intention that this implies. But he does not act in virtue of his own holiness, his personal worth. He can communicate a grace that he does not possess himself. He is the minister of Christ, an instrument in His hands. With the exception of the minister of baptism, it is the sacramental character which is the basis of this identification: the baptismal character for marriage, and the character of orders for the other sacraments.

As a minister of Christ, he is necessarily a minister of the Church, her representative, and this even when he is separated from her. He carries out a work of the Church; whether he wishes it or not, he makes the Church present. Thus he is himself a sign, and an efficacious sign. This is why, in analyzing the sacramental signs, St. Thomas and the Council of Florence do not speak only of things and words, of matter and form, but also include the minister (*Denz.* 695).

Because he is a sign and because he does not act in his own name, he can occasionally be one of a "college." For example, episcopal consecration is given by at least three bishops; Mass may be celebrated by several bishops or priests as is done in ordinations in the West and much more frequently in the East; the anointing of the sick, in various Eastern rites, is administered by several priests together. All priests, in fact, are together only a single sign of the one Priest who is Christ.[16]

Article Three
THE SACRAMENTS AS CONFERRING THE DIVINE GIFTS THEY SIGNIFY

The efficacy of the sacraments can be studied fully only in relation to each sacrament separately, for, as the signs are different in each case, so are the effects signified. But particularly in connection with baptism and the practical problems that its administration has raised for the Church, the Fathers and theologians have deduced principles concerning this efficacy that are valid for other sacraments, and in some cases for all. The first three topics we are now to study, then—the connection between the sign and its effect; the indelible imprint of Christ marked on the soul by baptism and confirmation and orders; the cooperation of man with the free gift of God—have been clarified by controversies raised in the life of the Church. And we also need to consider here the ecclesial and the eschatological dimensions of the efficacy of the sacraments.

I. SIGNS AND CAUSES OF GRACE

"The sacraments contain the grace that they signify." By this traditional formulation, the Council of Trent (*Denz.* 849) brings together two ideas

---

[16] Concelebration is not possible in the case of those sacraments in which the minister does not act in virtue of the power of orders—baptism and marriage.

in themselves incompatible, since it is not in the nature of a sign to be at the same time a cause. We have just seen that it is Christ who acts through the Church and the minister. The sacrament is efficacious because the humanity of Christ is the source of grace as it was the source of healing: "The whole crowd tried to touch Him, because from Him there came a power that healed them all" (Luke 6:19). But it is quite natural that theologians should try to perceive more clearly the exact mode of this causality.

1. The sacraments as divine mysteries. From the fact that the sacraments are signs it would be possible to infer that they are merely commemorative actions. Christ died for us on the Cross, He saved us once for all. Does it not diminish the value of the unique sacrifice of Jesus on Calvary to attribute any efficacy to the sacraments themselves? Is it not enough to say that they are pledges and witnesses of the salvation already gained?

We do indeed state that the sacraments are memorials, that they recall not only Jesus' passion but also His resurrection. Moreover, we insist that grace comes only from this same paschal mystery. This is why the sacraments are the true paschal celebration of Christians. But they are not merely commemorations of past events. They constitute an effective bond between men here and now and the sacrifice carried out in the past at Calvary. The grace gained in the Blood of Christ is contained in the sacrament.

It is not even enough to say that the sacramental sign "accompanies" the invisible act of Christ. For then the sign would be a mere manifestation, a kind of notification, as giving a person certain insignia visibly expresses his nomination to some dignity or office. Christ does not give His grace on the "occasion" of the sign; He gives it *through* the sign. The formulations of the Gospels and of the apostles require this realistic view.

> Unless a man be born of water and the Spirit, he cannot enter into the kingdom of God (John 3:5).

> When the goodness of God our Savior and his love for men appeared, he was not concerned with the works of justice that we might have accomplished; but, urged only by his mercy, he has saved us by the bath of regeneration and of renewal in the Holy Spirit (Tit. 3:4-5).

> Peter and John began to lay their hands upon them, and they received the Holy Spirit. But when Simon (the magician) saw that the Holy Spirit was given by the laying-on of the apostles's hands, he offered them money, saying: Give me also this power, so that those on whom I lay my hands may receive the Holy Spirit (Acts 8:17-19).

> I urge you to reawaken the gift that God placed within you by the laying-on of my hands (2 Tim. 1:6).

The sacraments, then, are signs and also mysteries, which means that they both manifest and convey an invisible divine reality. This results in a startling disproportion between the sign and the reality signified, between the sacramental cause and the effect of grace.

> Nothing so shocks the minds of men as the contrast between the apparent simplicity of the divine works and the greatness of the promised effects. This is true here: everything takes place with the greatest simplicity, without any scenery, without any extraordinary equipment. Briefly, without other display, a man goes down into the water and is immersed in it, while a few words are said. When he comes out, he is perhaps a little cleaner or not at all so. This is why it seems so incredible that he could thereby gain eternity (Tertullian, *On Baptism*, 2:11).

But this disproportion is only apparent. We must take into consideration the nature of what is called "instrumental causality." In the hands of an artist, for instance, a pencil or brush produces effects that it could in no way effect by itself. So, in the hands of Christ, the sacraments, earthly acts, become the cause of eternal life. And the sacred humanity of Christ is itself an instrument, a living instrument united to the Divinity, the instrument which the Word uses to redeem mankind.

2. The sacraments as producing grace. The gifts bestowed by the sacraments are as various as the signs that signify them. Some are designed for the personal life of the Christian, others for a social mission. Holy orders is characterized above all by its hierarchical powers, while penance is spiritual healing and strength to amend one's life. The anointing of the sick is a medicine designed to give health of body as well as of soul. But all the sacraments have in common the power to confer the gift of God's grace, to effect the work of the Holy Spirit in the soul, the bond of life with God and configuration to Christ Jesus.

The proper effect of baptism is new birth; of penance, restoration to the baptismal state. These two sacraments are designed to give the life of God to those who do not possess it, this grace being called *gratia prima*. They are called sacraments of the dead because they carry out a work of resurrection.

The other sacraments normally presuppose that the person who receives them is in the state of grace. And yet they also bring a gift of grace. The Eucharist, the wedding feast that requires a wedding-garment (Matthew 22:11), the food one cannot eat if one is unworthy (1 Cor. 11:27), is the Bread of Life: "He who eats my flesh and drinks my blood has everlasting life and I will raise him up on the last day . . . He who eats this bread will live for ever" (John 6:54, 58).

Even when the sacraments confer a mission (confirmation, orders, marriage) there is a corresponding grace for one's personal life. It is true that the Lord who in the Old Law made use of Balaam's donkey to prophesy can make use of sinners as His witnesses and ministers. The person who has been confirmed, married people, and priests retain their divine mission even though they may be unworthy of it. But this is a state of violence, and one which also brings out very clearly the mystery of mercy which is the New Law. In receiving a mission through a sacrament, the subject receives and should conserve a grace for his interior life. For example, since it is the Holy Spirit who is given in confirmation and in orders, the prayer explaining the sacramental effects always asks the Lord that the recipient of the sacraments may receive grace to conform his life to his mission.

This *gratia secunda* received in the sacraments called the "sacraments of the living," since they require the state of grace for their reception, comes to develop and complete the spiritual organism.[17] Grace is divine life, wholly one, wholly spiritual, which we should speak about preferably in the words of the New Testament itself. We should think of its "growth", then, as meaning a greater and greater resemblance to Christ, as configuring us more particularly to Himself in His various states, as leading us to Himself by His light and strength in the various ways of life to which the sacraments commit us.[18]

Moreover, the Eucharist, which always occupies a special place among the sacraments, not only confers a gift of grace; it contains the very Author of grace.

3. The sacraments as signs of several spiritual realities. Two developments of the idea of the sacraments as signs still need to be considered. The first is in reference to the whole economy of salvation, the second to the way in which the various sacraments signify and confer grace.

St. Thomas asks himself whether a sacrament can be the sign of several realities at the same time, and concludes that it can:

> A sacrament properly speaking is that which is ordained to signify our sanctification, in which three things may be considered: viz., the very cause of our sanctification, which is Christ's passion; the form of our sanctification, which is grace and the virtues; and the ultimate end of our sanctification, which is eternal life. And all these are signified by the sacraments. Consequently a sacrament is a sign that is both a reminder of the past, i.e. the passion of Christ; and an indication of that which is effected in us by Christ's passion,

[17] The image that comes too easily to mind is that of growing in wealth, a kind of quantitative increase in grace. We should beware of such analogies in religious instruction, even though they are justified in theological exposition; the Council of Trent uses the expression, "All true justification either begins through the sacraments, or, once begun, increases through them, or when lost is regained through them" (*Denz.* 843a).

[18] Theologians generally distinguish between *sanctifying* grace and *sacramental* grace. For St. Thomas, the latter adds to the former a certain divine assistance to attain the end of the sacrament (*Summa* III, 62, 2).

i.e., grace, and a[3] prognostic, that is, a foretelling of fortune glory *(Summa III, 60, 3)*.

This is why the grace of the sacraments always means insertion into the paschal mystery and places us within the whole historic movement of the economy of salvation.

We owe the second further development of the idea of sign to St. Augustine, who was led to work it out in the course of his controversies with the Donatists. Between the sign itself, *sacramentum*, (baptism, for example) and the final reality, *res*, which it signifies (in baptism, the grace of new birth), there intervenes an intermediary reality which is at once signified and a sign, *res et sacramentum*, the baptismal character. This intermediary reality is signified and caused by the sacramental sign. Although it is not visible, it is a kind of sign because it is the permanent and direct effect of the sign. It is what expresses and causes the grace which is the final reality. We must, therefore, go from the sign to the ultimate reality,[19] by way of this intermediary reality in accounting for the signification of the sacrament and in explaining how the sacrament is the cause of grace.

This is the true way of explaining how it is that three sacraments—baptism, confirmation and orders—cannot be received more than once. When they have been received validly but without the desired dispositions, they are nonetheless irrevocably acquired. In spite of its efficacy, the sacrament is then deprived of its fruits of sanctification. In this case, the person will not be forever deprived of the grace of the sacrament despite the fact that it cannot be received again, because the sacrament has produced its inamissable, its inalienable effect: the character *(res et sacramentum)*. When the Christian regains the requisite dispositions, the character procures the grace of the sacrament previously received.

The same notion clarifies the doctrine of the Eucharist. The consecration of the bread and of the wine *(sacramentum)* brings about the real presence of Christ and of His sacrifice *(res et sacramentum)* and does so independently of Communion, since Communion is not necessary to the essence of the sacrifice and since the Real Presence lasts as long as the species endures. The grace of nourishment and the pledge of eternal life *(res)* are given to the faithful who communicate through the Body of Christ which they receive under the sign.

---

[19] *Sacramentum* (or *sacramentum tantum*) designates the outward sign: the word and the action or matter. *Res* (or *res sacramenti*, or *res tantum*) designates the effect of grace that the sacrament is to produce in a well-disposed subject. This effect is a free gift coming from God alone, but it is not automatic since the absence of the requisite dispositions may impede it. It is not final and inalienable, since grace may be lost by the fault of the subject. *Res et sacramentum* expresses an infallible effect produced by the sacrament validly performed, a stable and supernatural reality independent of the dispositions of the subject. By its intermediary, grace is given or given again. See the chart on page 55 showing how these categories apply to each of the seven sacraments.

We can thus understand how it is that a transitory act, baptism or the Eucharistic consecration, for example, can continue to be a sign when the act has already taken place, and can produce its effect of grace in a delayed way, as it were. This is precisely because the effect of the sacrament is twofold, the one caused by the other: the grace (*res*) and, in the case of baptism, the indelible imprint of Christ, the character (*res et sacramentum*).

II. THE IMPRINT OF CHRIST

With reference to baptism, confirmation and orders, the Council of Trent states: "If anyone says that in these three sacraments a character is not imprinted on the soul, that is, a certain indelible spiritual sign which makes their repetition impossible, let him be anathema" (*Denz.* 852). Starting, then, from the fact that it is impossible to receive these sacraments a second time, we come to understand more clearly the reality of the sacramental "character" as a participation in the priesthood of Christ.

1. The three sacraments which cannot be repeated. The difficulties aroused by the schisms and heresies of the first centuries served to bring out clearly the principle that baptism, confirmation and orders can in no way be received a second time. Actually, the disputes to which we referred earlier involving St. Cyprian and St. Augustine were concerned exclusively with the value of the sacraments received from a schismatic, a heretic or a sinner. When Cyprian maintained that baptism received in heresy had to be repeated, it was because he thought it to be null, invalid. The same attitude was held by those who tried to oblige bishops and priests who had been ordained by Arians or other heretics to be ordained again; they thought such ordinations invalid.

But at no moment in these disputes did either Catholics or schismatics suppose that a baptism, a confirmation or an ordination which had been validly received could be received a second time. A baptized person fallen from his baptismal state and excluded from the communion of the Church was reconciled by penance; he was never rebaptized and reconfirmed. A bishop or a priest deposed by the sentence of a Council continued validly to exercise the powers of his ordination—to the great scandal of St. Cyprian. If such bishops or priests were re-established in their charges, they took up their functions without any renewal of the rites of initiation or ordination. The instances of reordination to be found particularly in the very disturbed period of the tenth century are explained by the suspicion that the first ordination had been null and void, never by a fear that a validly conferred ordination could be nullified later on.[20]

These three sacraments, therefore, have an inalienable, indelible effect, remaining even when the man who has received them falls into sin, leaves the Church, loses his faith. This ineffaceable effect must, consequently, be distinct from the grace of holiness, since it can endure without it. This effect is called the "character."

2. The imprint of Christ. The term "character" is to be understood, not in the sense it has in modern English, but as it was used in ancient Greek: an image or inscription engraved in a permanent way on a medal, a coin, or stone. The Epistle to the Hebrews makes use of this image to describe the Son of God: "the radiance of the Father's glory, the image of His substance" (Heb. 1:3). Here the meaning is that of an indelible portrait, but also an essential likeness. On the other hand, in the Apocalypse the word recalls the practice in certain cities of marking slaves with an indelible brand; those are cursed who let themselves be marked on the forehead with the sign of the beast (Apoc. 14:9-11). The faithful, on the contrary, are marked with the sign of Christ's slaves, but here another term is used, with a much wider range of echoes in the New Testament, the "seal" (Apoc. 7).

The seal is an imprint marked on a stamp or ring and pressed on hot wax so as to give this wax its own form. Used to witness to a final contract, it is the signature of its owner. So the gift received at baptism and confirmation is the seal of the Holy Spirit:

> It is God who has strengthened us together with you in Christ and who has anointed us, who has also marked us with his seal and has placed in our hearts the pledge of the Spirit (2 Cor. 1:21-22).

> It is in him that, having heard the word of truth, the good news of your salvation, and having believed in it, you have been marked with a seal by the Holy Spirit of the promise . . . (Eph. 1:13).

> Do not sadden the Holy Spirit of God, who has marked you with his seal for the day of the redemption (Eph. 4:30).

In the quotation from the Epistle to the Corinthians, the theme of anointing recalls also the idea of an irrevocable and inamissable consecration. Saul remained the Lord's anointed even when, because of his sins, he had fallen from his royal state and had been replaced by David; consequently, it was forbidden to lay hands on him, and the man who killed him was instantly punished (2 Sam. 1:1-17). And while it recalls the

---

[20] See the conclusion of the study of L. Saltet, *Les réordinations* (Paris, 1907), p. 392: "It has always been admitted that an ordination validly conferred cannot be repeated. Reordinations do not presume the denial of the inamissable character of order; they always presume that a previous ordination was null. That a mistake might be made about the nullity of a previous ordination is undeniable; but this mistake as to the facts leaves intact the doctrine that ordination can never be repeated."

fact of being irrevocable, anointing also means resemblance to the supreme Anointed One, Christ. The engraved imprint, the seal, is an image, a portrait of Christ.

This is why theologians, following St. Thomas, define the sacramental character at once by its property of indelibility and by a likeness to Christ, a participation in the priesthood of Christ, which deputes a person to divine worship and distinguishes men as to rights, duties or powers related to worship. While it attains the greatest possible fullness only in the sacrament of orders, this likeness is realized in a certain way in baptism and confirmation: "You who have been baptized, you have put on Christ" (Gal. 3:27).

3. The special case of marriage and of the anointing of the sick. Marriage and the anointing of the sick do not belong to the category of sacraments that can be received only once. Yet they are designed to have a lasting efficacy and cannot be repeated unless the situation created by their first reception has ceased to exist. A person who has received the sacrament of marriage cannot remarry unless the other partner to the marriage has died. A sick person cannot validly receive anointing a second time in the same illness; but if, after recovering, he finds himself once more in a condition of serious illness, he is then capable of receiving the anointing again.

Tradition does not admit that these two sacraments produce a character, since this is absolutely inamissable. However, we must recognize that they have a lasting effect, distinct from grace, the fruitfulness of which will be perceived afresh in the person who, having lost grace, regains it in penance. These two sacraments bring about the consecration of a state: the state of marriage and the state of illness. They also bring about a certain special configuration to Christ: the bond of marriage is the sign of the love of Christ for the Church; the anointing of the sick offers the Christian an image of Christ who has suffered. This lasting effect is, therefore, at once a sign and the reality signified (*res et sacramentum*). (See the chart on the following page.)

III. COOPERATION WITH THE DIVINE GIFT

Because the sacraments are the source of divine grace for us, they exhibit the paradox inherent in the economy of salvation: the gift of God is gratuitous, free, and yet it requires our cooperation. The difficulty that we experience in holding to these "two ends of the chain" explains the errors that continually threaten the theology, the teaching, and the pastoral administration of the sacraments.

The *sacramentum, res et sacramentum,* and *res* of the various sacraments.

	sacramentum	*res et sacramentum*	*res*
BAPTISM	Bath of water and proclamation of the Trinity	Character (member of the Church, power to take part in worship)	Grace of a child of God
CONFIRMATION	Imposition of the hand, signing and anointing with holy chrism	Character (witness to Christ)	Gift of the Holy Spirit, grace of strength to give witness
ORDERS	Imposition of hands and consecrating preface	Character (ministerial powers in reference to the kingdom of God)	Gift of the Holy Spirit to exercise these powers worthily
THE EUCHARIST	Consecration of the bread and wine	Presence of Christ in His paschal sacrifice	Nourishment for the soul, charity, bond of unity of the Church
MARRIAGE	Expression of mutual consent	Indissoluble bond (until the death of one partner)	Grace of married life (*res contenta*) to the model of the love of Christ and the Church (*res non contenta*)
ANOINTING OF THE SICK	Prayer of the priest over the sick person and anointings with oil	Configuration (in this illness) to Christ suffering	Healing of body and soul
PENANCE	Acts of the penitent, and the priest's absolution		Return to grace with the Church and with God

To exaggerate the gratuity of the gift of God and the efficacy of the sacraments is to neglect the conditions required for their fruitful reception and the obligations that they involve. But to insist too exclusively on the work of men involves the temptation to become too severe in admitting people to the sacraments, to make their reception the mere crowning of personal achievements or the reward of a work of self-sanctification valid of itself.

1. The gratuity of God's gift. In the Old and New Testaments, the word "grace" expresses the gratuity of the love that God bears to us, of the mercy with which He comes to meet us. The intervention of God in human history in the days of Abraham, in the times of the Exodus and the desert, was an unexpected invasion. If He chose Jacob rather than Esau, it was because He is sovereignly free in His giving. Whatever be the road by which anyone goes to find God, the first advance is always on God's part, and even when such a person has had to struggle, to search out the way, it is God who has been his guide.

The incarnation of the Son of God, His redeeming death, all this is a free gift. In spite of the divine promises fulfilled by the coming of Christ, His work of salvation was still unexpected, so far did it go beyond what had been hoped for. Now this work of salvation is at once universal and individual. Those who enter into the mystery of Christ are those whom God has chosen in advance, has predestined to be conformed to the image of the Son of God (the first two chapters of the Epistle to the Ephesians should be read in this connection). But what indicates this choice, this gratuitous call of God? The sacraments that a person receives. The divine vocation of the Christian is revealed in baptism; ordination expresses the priestly vocation.

The unexpectedness of God's initiative reaches its highest point in the case of the initiation of children. They are baptized without any initiative of their own, the Church supplying their complete lack. In the East, and in the West when in danger of death, a baby also receives confirmation. And, while in the West today the Eucharist is refused before the age of discretion, this is to ensure respect for the sacrament; it is not because a small child could not receive it validly and with fruit.

Now the same absolute gratuity exists in the case of the adult also, in spite of appearances. While it is absolutely necessary, under pain of nullity, that he have the intention of receiving a sacrament; while he must have faith and repent of his sins if this sacrament is to produce in him its effect of justification; while to receive certain sacraments fruitfully he must already be in the state of grace, nothing that he does himself can earn for him the grace of the sacrament. This is given to him without any merit on his part. If he does not receive its grace (in the event that he places an obstacle in its way), the effect of the sacrament is nonetheless begun, since the intermediary reality (*res et sacramentum*) is produced, designed to cause grace to revive at the opportune time.[21]

This is why the Christian is to live in continual thanksgiving and to apply to himself the psalms that sing of God's mercy shown in the wonders of the Exodus and the desert (Pss. 77, 104, 105, 135, etc.).

2. The necessity of intention. A child who does not yet have the use of reason receives baptism, can receive confirmation and even the Eucharist without any activity on his part; these sacraments will be valid and fruitful for him.[22] He has not asked for anything, he has no awareness of the divine work that is being carried out.

But the situation of an adult is quite different. It is he who asks to receive the sacraments; in fact, God does not now act in him without his action, does not justify him without the consent of his own freedom. A sacramental action carried out on an adult who refuses it, who has not asked for it, is null and void—no sacrament, no effect is produced. We should add that his intention need not always be explicit at the very moment when the sacrament is being celebrated; it may be anterior to it and still remain valid. Thus the dying person who has asked for baptism and the anointing of the sick receives them validly, even though he has lost consciousness before receiving them.

3. Preliminary dispositions. The intention to receive a sacrament is enough to make its reception valid and to attain the first effect of the sacrament: that intermediary reality which is independent of the dispositions of the subject. In consenting to receive the sacrament, the subject effectively receives the character of a baptized person, of a confirmed Christian, of a deacon, a priest or a bishop; he contracts a valid marriage; he is consecrated in the state of illness.

Does he receive at the same time the grace that justifies? Will this valid sacrament (producing the *res et sacramentum*) also be fruitful (will it produce the *res*)? Yes, on condition that the subject does not put any obstacle in the way by his bad dispositions (*Denz.* 849). To assure the right dispositions, the person who receives baptism, for example, should

---

[21] There are two important exceptions: since the *res et sacramentum* of the Eucharist are produced on the altar, not in the soul of the faithful, he "who eats and drinks unworthily" eats to his own condemnation, without receiving in any way this seed of grace given by the *res et sacramentum* of the other sacraments. In the case of penance, the fact that the acts of the penitent form part of the sign and their absence makes the sacrament null and void might seem to detract from the total gratuity of the gift of God, but actually these acts of the penitent and the absolution that confers forgiveness do not belong to the same order of efficacy.

[22] The person who receives a sacrament is called in theology the "subject" of the sacrament. But this word designates more precisely the person who is capable of receiving a sacrament validly and licitly. This subject can only be a human being in his earthly state; angels and the dead are incapable of receiving any sacraments. And, further, baptism is necessary before the other sacraments can be received validly; it constitutes as it were the "door" to them.

have been preparing himself for it for a long time. He must have received and accepted the message of faith. He should then regret his faults and alter his way of life, learn the Creed and be initiated into Christian prayer. Again, to receive the sacrament of penance, the penitent must humble himself before God and before the Church, admit his sins, make reparation for them. Both these cases require the conditions laid out by the Council of Trent as necessary for justification: faith, hope, the beginning of love of God, repenting of one's faults and amending one's way of life (*Denz.* 797-798).

This is why, in spite of the gratuity of the divine gift and the fact that the sacraments act *ex opere operato,* men must prepare themselves to receive them. This preparation is ensured by pastors through religious instruction and by the Church through her liturgy. Moreover, progress in the Christian life and its taking root in human society require special institutions for the formation of those who are to receive the sacraments of initiation: the catechumenate is needed for adults who are to be baptized, just as the seminary is necessary for those who are to receive the sacrament of orders.

When a sacrament has been received without the minimum dispositions necessary, we say that it is unfruitful although valid. Moreover, the action of the subject in receiving it in this way is a sacrilege if he is conscious of his unworthiness. But can he gain the grace of the sacrament when he has the required dispositions and has obtained forgiveness of his sins through the sacrament of penance? Yes, with the exception of the grace of the Eucharist and of penance. The other five sacraments have left in his soul, even though it be unworthy, the *res et sacramentum* which allows grace to revive; this is what is called the "reviviscence" of the sacrament.[23]

4. Commitments involved in receiving the sacraments. Cooperation with the divine gift is even more necessary after the reception of the sacrament than as a prerequisite for receiving it. The sacraments create a resemblance to Christ which is to be manifested in daily life, and they confer a special grace for this purpose. So, for example, after the initiation of the new Christians during the Easter Vigil, the Church asks in their behalf "that in living their lives they may hold to the sacrament which they have received by faith" (Collect, Easter Tuesday). And in her Postcommunion prayer the Church prays for our faithfulness to the gift that God has given us: "Pour out in us, O Lord, the Spirit of Your love; in Your fatherly kindness, make one in heart those whom You have fed with Your paschal sacraments" (Postcommunion, Easter Vigil).

---

[23] "Reviviscence" is not a very exact term. The fact is that a sacrament which has not produced its effect of grace at the moment when it was given, due to its not having been received with the required dispositions, gives this grace later on at the moment when these dispositions are regained.

Not only for baptism and marriage, but for every sacrament, the existence of a real commitment is indicated by the liturgy and the traditional catecheses. Thus the sacraments authentically understood and lived are the foundation and the norm of all spiritual life, as can be seen in the epistles of St. Paul.

But the commitment involved in the sacraments is not the lonely adventure of a man going off by himself on a long road. It is the response to a divine advance, the entrance into a mystery of mercy. "He who has begun his work in you will complete it" (Phil. 1:6). That is why this obligation is happy and peaceful since it is founded on God alone, and also demanding, since it has no limits other than identification with Christ.

IV. THE BUILDING UP AND MANIFESTATION OF THE CHURCH

Besides having a personal effect as efficacious signs of grace for the person who receives them, the sacraments "express and bring about incorporation into the Church. Since they are signs of the Church, the sacraments are given in the community and for the sake of the community which they are meant to build up and to bind together."[24] St. Thomas expresses himself in a still more forceful way: "The Church is said to be built up with the sacraments which flowed from the side of Christ while hanging on the Cross" (*Summa* III, 64, 2 ad 32).

1. As building up the Church. This social aspect is ensured by the *res et sacramentum,* as we shall see briefly, bringing together ideas already discussed.

> The sacraments which confer a character and bring about participation in the priesthood of Christ delineate, in a way, the hierarchy of the Church. Baptism and confirmation provide the Church with consecrated members, subjects fit to lead the liturgical life, to exercise worthily the rite of the Christian religion inaugurated by the Cross and maintained through the life of the Church. The hierarchy properly so called is constituted by the character of orders and its successive stages. And the power of jurisdiction, while it is distinguished from the power of orders, is nevertheless normally dependent upon it, so that the Church, not only in the recruiting and the unity of her members, but also in their mutual relationships, is truly "fashioned by the sacraments of faith."[25]

To such an extent is the Eucharist "the sacrament that makes the Church" that it makes present the very redemptive act whence the Church proceeds: the Blood of the New Covenant poured out. The term

[24] French *Episcopal Directory for Pastoral Care,* No. 4.

[25] A. M. Roguet, *Les Sacraments,* a translation and commentary upon the *Summa* III, 60-65 (*Editions de la Revue des Jeunes*).

"Mystical Body" of Christ which up to the ninth century designated the Real Presence in the Eucharist, has come to designate the Church herself; this shift in the meaning of the word reveals the bond that exists between the Eucharistic Body of Christ and the Church.[26]

2. As manifesting the Church. It is especially by the sacraments, again, that the Church is manifested. It is around the Eucharist that Christians gather every Sunday as around the family table, an essential action of communal life. Baptism shows the Church as truly a mother, bringing forth children of God, and as the community of salvation. Orders and the Eucharist further reveal the Church as a hierarchic body in which the wealth common to all is given by some members to the others. Marriage is more particularly designed to proclaim the mystery of the Church, since it is precisely this of which it is a sign. Penance is the exercise of the power of the keys of the Church, in its aspect of mercy.

Not only are the sacraments the term of the Church's mission of evangelization, but the ministry of the Word is itself organized around them. Pastoral functions are exercised primarily in connection with the sacraments. To exclude a person from the sacraments means to exclude him from the Church, to "excommunicate" him.

Finally, the sacraments constitute the essential element of the Church's prayer, the liturgy. The other acts of this prayer simply imitate their symbolism (the sacramentals), extend their signs, or complete their work of praise and sanctification.

V. PLEDGES OF GLORY

After God had worked His wonders for the Hebrews in the desert, they did not enter into the Promised Land, as St. Paul recalls in the text already quoted from the First Epistle to the Corinthians. Yet it was in view of the Promised Land that God had brought them out of Egypt, had multiplied miracles for them, had sealed the covenant on Sinai. Their infidelity emphasizes the dialectic of God's work. Everything is already gained, and yet everything still may be endangered: "Those whom God has justified . . . he has glorified" (Rom. 8:30), and yet, "Conduct yourselves with fear during the time of your exile" (1 Peter 1:17).

In spite of this possibility of loss, the sacraments of the New Law are the beginning, the seed, of the glory of heaven through the grace they bring us. The sign with which some of them mark the Christian is a pledge of heaven, constituting an earnest of it. This is why the Church reads to the newly baptized, in the first Easter Mass, a passage from the Epistle to the Colossians containing a summary of the whole baptismal economy: "When Christ appears, who is your life, then you also will

[26] See Louis Bouyer, *Introduction to Spirituality,* pp. 108 ff.

appear with him in glory" (3:4). Even more than baptism, the Eucharist is the pledge of resurrection and glory, the earnest of eternity. It contains the risen Body of Christ; the Lord has given it to us as our food in view of eternity:

> Your fathers ate the manna in the desert, and they are dead. . . .
> he who eats this bread will live eternally. . . . and I will raise him up
> on the last day (John 6:49, 52, 55).

This perspective, so familiar to the first Christians, was expressed in a moving way in the Roman catacombs of the third century. To give the faithful who visited these graves the true reasons for hope, they depicted on the walls of their cemeteries the biblical themes of the baptismal cate-chesis.[27]

We find the same spirit in the funeral liturgy. The Church has only one reason for recommending to the Lord the Christian who has left this earthly dwelling-place—that he had been marked with the seal of the Trinity at his baptism.

But it is above all in the Apocalypse and in the Eastern liturgies that this eschatological meaning of the sacraments is developed to the full. Here the liturgy of earth and that of heaven intermingle, are united in the same signs, the same prayers, the same chants. The sacraments are the anticipation of glory as Jesus' transfiguration was the proclamation of His resurrection. Thereby the sacraments of the New Law retain a resemblance to those of the Old. Although they turn first of all toward the past, being the memorial of Christ whose passion is the sole source of grace, they orient us toward the future: "Whenever you eat this bread and drink the cup, you proclaim the death of the Lord until he comes" (1 Cor. 11:26). In the state of glory there will be no more sacraments.

Article Four
THE SACRAMENTAL ORGANISM

The study we have just made of the elements common to all the sacraments of the New Law indicates both their unity and their diversity. If these contrasts at first seem surprising to the logically-minded, they happily remind us that the sacraments are not abstract concepts, but a living organism.

---

[27] See Frederik Van der Meer and Christine Mohrmann, *Atlas of the Early Christian World*, pp. 53-55; Alfred Rush, *Death and Burial in Christian Antiquity*.

In this connection we might first ask: why seven sacraments, and not simply one, since they draw their efficacy from the divine power which is one, and from the power of the passion which is also one: "By a single oblation, he has made perfect forever those whom he sanctifies" (Heb. 10:14)? One reason is precisely because this work of Christ's, accomplished once for all on the Cross, brings about the salvation of all men through uniting them together in one body in which each member has a distinct function and in which the gifts of God are given by some to the others. Again, even though salvation can be achieved at the outset in one unique stage, as is the case with a baptized child who dies before reaching the age of reason,[28] it normally consists of a journey, a pilgrimage, re-producing the journey of the Hebrews through the desert between the crossing of the Red Sea and the crossing of the Jordan. The stages, the vicissitudes of this road are marked by the intervention of Christ in the sacraments. The personal history of each Christian is thus made part of the history of salvation itself.

1. *The number of the sacraments.*

> If anyone says that the sacraments of the New Law were not all in-stituted by our Lord Jesus Christ, or that there are more or fewer than seven . . . ; or, again, that any one of these seven is not truly and properly a sacrament, let him be anathema" (*Denz.* 844).

In peaceful possession of this number and of this numbering, a Chris-tian can enjoy finding all sorts of reasons why the number seven is suit-able, as the theologians and sometimes the catechists of the Middle Ages were not slow to do. St. Albert the Great tried to show how each of the sacraments remedied one of the capital sins, while St. Bonaventure con-nected them with the seven virtues, three theological and four moral. Having no feeling for this devotional mathematics, men of today find it more useful to study the difficulties and the slow efforts at systematiza-tion which resulted, in the twelfth century, in finally fixing the list and the number of the sacraments.

To St. Augustine, the whole work of Christ and the Church seemed to be a "unique sacrament." Even when this term came to be reserved for sacred signs only, the most varied kinds of rites were still listed under it. Christian initiation includes actions that are sacramental in the precise and modern sense of the word, and others that are not. And certain liturgical acts, such as the consecration of virgins or the dedication of churches, are also sacred signs.

We should hold to the grand continuity of this perspective of antiquity, continuity not only between the essential actions of the sacraments and those accompanying them, but also between the sacramental acts properly so called and the other rites (the sacramentals) which the Church treats

---

[28] Even here there are two stages: spiritual birth and passage to eternity.

as related to the sacraments, even though they do not fulfill the definition of sacrament. Having distinguished the "great rites" that have a major role in the economy of salvation from the "lesser rites," the theology of the sacraments has been able to state that the "great rites" are traditionally seven in number, a fact admitted in the schismatic churches and contested only by Protestantism. Here again, it is by reflecting on the practice of the Church that theological formulations have been developed.

2. The order of listing the sacraments. The traditional order of listing the sacraments has the advantage of drawing attention to the various situations for which they were instituted.

First come the three sacraments of Christian initiation: baptism, confirmation and the Eucharist, presented in the order in which they ought to follow one another when an adult is initiated in the regular way. They constitute the Christian state, even though they are not equally necessary to the salvation of each person.

Then are named the two sacraments that sooner or later come to aid the Christian who has sinned after his baptism: penance and the anointing of the sick (this second sacrament being at once a complement to penance and a grace proper to the state of illness).

Lastly are named the two sacraments designed, not for the salvation of the individual, but for a social function in the Church: orders and marriage. It is thus the economy of salvation which serves as the principle according to which this classification is made.

We can, however, examine the sacraments from other points of view, to show from various aspects how they are at the same time different and yet organically united.

3. The inequality of the sacraments: the primacy of the Eucharist. On this point the Council of Trent states:

> If anyone say that the sacraments are equal among themselves, in such a way that from no aspect would one have greater dignity than another, let him be anathema (*Denz.* 846).

In the thought of the Council this formulation was meant to enhance the value of the sacraments, not to diminish any of them. For it ends by explaining that the Eucharist is the most important of the sacraments (*Denz.* 876), as we have already noted frequently in the course of this study.

The various characteristics of the sacraments are all true of the Eucharist and with the greatest degree of intensity, because it contains the very cause of all of them. In the same way, it is the Eucharist which forms the internal unity of the whole sacramental organism, the other sacraments being ordered to it as to their end. Baptism could not even be conceived of without the Eucharist, the goal of initiation. The Eucharist is made possible by the sacrament of orders and reveals the hierarchical structure of the Church. Marriage is united with the Eucharist through its symbolism, since it represents the union of Christ and the Church. This is why the administration of the sacraments is consummated in the Eucharist and proceeds from the Eucharistic celebration, as we have already said.

4. The necessity of the sacraments. The sacraments are also unequal from the point of view of their necessity, although they are necessary as forming a whole, since the entire sacramental organism is the only normal source for the salvation of men.

> If anyone say that the sacraments of the New Law are not necessary to salvation, but are superfluous, and that without receiving or desiring them, but through faith alone, men may obtain from God the grace of justification (even though not all are necessary for each individual), let him be anathema (*Denz.* 847).

First, desire for the sacraments is always necessary, at least in an implicit way, if a person is to enter effectively into the economy of salvation through Christ.

Secondly, certain sacraments are indispensable to the Church, though not to the faithful; they are not designed for everyone since they form the structure of the body in its diversity of functions. This is true of orders, of marriage, and in some respects of confirmation to the extent that its purpose is a Christian mission to other men.

Thirdly, baptism is absolutely indispensable. Furthermore, it constitutes the "door of the sacraments"; without it no other sacramental grace can be obtained. Penance is necessary also, but only for those who, after baptism, have lost the grace of their initiation. The Eucharist is necessary, but in a less strict way, since the Western Church does not give it to children who have not reached the age of reason nor to adults who have lost consciousness. Baptism calls for the Eucharist and is connected with it by a bond so close that, in exceptional cases, this bond by itself is sufficient for salvation. And, finally, confirmation and the anointing of the sick are not in themselves indispensable to salvation. But confirmation is called for by baptism, which is incomplete without it; and the anointing of the sick is a special grace for the state of illness, and should not be neglected.

Chapter 2

HOLY ORDERS

Preliminary Remarks

Although in the traditional list of the sacraments the sacrament of orders is put sixth, we are discussing it first for two reasons. When we speak of orders, we are concerned with two things at once: ordination, a transitory action; and the lasting result of this sacrament, the sacred hierarchy of the Church. Since five of the seven sacraments require that the man who administers them be linked to the apostolic succession through ordination, orders is the immediate source of most of the sacraments. Again, the sacraments form part of the liturgy of the Church, indeed the essential part, and holy orders is the sacrament that builds up and makes clear the hierarchical structure of the liturgical assembly as being, within its unity, made up of different ranks and calling for a distribution of roles.

The term "orders" was taken over, not from the Bible[1] but from the language of the civil institutions of ancient Rome. It expressed the existence of classes, social categories with strictly and precisely defined boundaries, hierarchically related to one another in a way that could not be changed. People of that time spoke of the senatorial or of the equestrian "order." Under the Empire this strict hierarchy, these different categories and divisions were thought of as expressing the order, the peace, the beauty of the City. It is in this sense that Tertullian, whose influence was predominant in translating the realities of the faith into the Latin language, spoke of the "sacerdotal order," of the "ecclesiastical order," or even of "orders" pure and simple—a phrase that was quickly adopted since it suggested the collegial character of the hierarchy and the differentiation of members which constitutes the beauty of the Body of Christ.

We must, furthermore, avoid the error of trying to explain the realities of the Church simply in terms of human societies, or of natural religion, or even of Mosaic legislation. At periods of violent doctrinal disputes and in the legitimate desire to justify the faith on rational grounds, this method could be used. The Council of Trent does not hesitate to say that "sacrifice and priesthood are so related in the divine plan that they have both existed in every law" (*Denz.* 957). However, the priesthood instituted by Christ so far surpasses both the natural and the Mosaic that the break with them is more noticeable than the continuity. The priesthood of Christ is according to the order of Melchisedech, not according to the order of Aaron (Heb. 7:11). However, we shall see later what must be retained of the priesthood of Aaron.

---

[1] The expression, "according to the order of Melchisedech," which passed from Psalm 109 into the Epistle to the Hebrews to characterize the priesthood of Christ, is not the source of this use.

A comparison with regimes flourishing in human societies is unsatisfactory from every aspect.[2]

Only one method is satisfactory: to observe the Church in her living reality, to take note of the tradition expressed in her laws, to assist at ordinations.

Our explanation will be a kind of commentary on the definition of orders given in the Code of Canon Law, the official legal code of the Latin Church.

> Orders, through its institution by Christ, sets the clergy apart from the laity in the Church for the government of the faithful and for the celebration of divine worship (*Can.* 948).

This definition states first of all the clear distinction between clergy and laity manifested in the Church as the result of Christ's institution. Next, it distinguishes two functions of orders; "the government of the faithful" and "the celebration of divine worship."

The "government of the faithful" is the exercise of the power of jurisdiction; it includes the mission and the pastorate. The "celebration of divine worship" is the exercise of the power of orders received through ordination. It includes the priesthood of the bishop and of priests and the "ministry" of deacons and of the lesser orders. Both sets of functions and powers have their source in the apostolic succession and have several degrees, as is stated in Canon 108 of the Code of Canon Law:

> Not all clerics are of the same rank; there exists among them a sacred hierarchy in accordance with which some are subordinated to others. By divine institution the sacred hierarchy as regards order consists of bishops, priests and ministers; as regards jurisdiction, it consists of the supreme pontificate and the subordinate episcopate. By ecclesiastical institution, other orders are added.

Theologians generally separate the study of ordination and the power of orders, which they deal with in the treatise on the sacraments, from the study of the power of jurisdiction (orders as constituting the hierarchical structure of the Church), which they reserve for the treatise on the Church. But this separation entails two inconveniences: the sacrament of orders is no longer described in relation to its proper dynamism, which is that of the economy of salvation; and, because of this overly precise division, the government of the Church no longer appears as sacramental. The two poles of the activity of the hierarchy—their mission and pastorate on the one hand, and the exercise of their power in relation to the sacraments and worship on the other—are no longer seen in their proper relationship. For, while these powers are distinct, they are normally united in the person of the bishop, who dispenses them in

[2] In this connection, see the important warning given by Cardinal Suhard in his *Priests among Men*, p. 222.

various degrees to priests and ministers. Therefore, if we divide the study of orders into fragments rather than take it in its full perspective, we fail to see the significance of the bishop, the keystone of all orders.

St. Thomas Aquinas did not always know how to guard against these difficulties; unfortunately he died before writing out the questions in the third part of the *Summa* which would have set out his definitive thought on this matter. But at least he brought out clearly the principles which the Council of Trent, later theology, and the Code of Canon Law have simply developed.

We must take note of certain terms which will recur frequently in the course of this chapter. *Clerics* are those whom the Church has destined, through ordination or at least through the ceremony of tonsure, to receive, in a lasting way, a divine ministry; clerics are thereby separated from the laity (cf. Can. 108, 1).

The word *layman* is generally used to distinguish those who are not clerics from those who are. But this negative aspect of the term should not cause us to forget that the laity constitute the people of God (the word comes from *laos,* people). The clerics are at their service (Can. 682) and in many fields the laity have an important and indispensable share in responsibility for the Kingdom of God.

The *hierarchy* is made up of all the degrees, unequal and subordinated one to another, among which ecclesiastical power is distributed. It includes both the degrees of the power of orders and those of the power of jurisdiction, whose principal forms are of divine institution.

The *power of orders* has for its object the administering of the sacraments and the sacramentals and, in general, the celebration of liturgical functions, insofar as these functions have been assigned by Christ or by the Church to certain degrees of orders. This power is given by ordination; it cannot be taken away or substituted for.

The *power of jurisdiction* gives the mission and the authority to lead men to salvation; to this end, it is concerned with acts of teaching, direction, judgment, necessary decision. The full power of jurisdiction comprises, in the external forum, the power to make laws, to command, to hold courts of justice, to punish, to administrate. It is given in fullness directly by the Lord to the Pope for the universal Church as soon as he accepts his election (Can. 219). It belongs to a legitimately convoked general council (Can. 228). Bishops receive it for definite territories or persons by divine right (Can. 329). The laws of the Church determine the exact ways by which bishops are to be appointed and their flocks delimited. The other clerics receive only that portion of ordinary or delegated jurisdiction which ecclesiastical law or the will of their superior confers on them.

Ordinary power of jurisdiction is given by law, divine or ecclesiastical, for a clearly determined and fixed function (Can. 197, 1).

Delegated power (or *delegated jurisdiction*) is communicated to a person by an act of will of a qualified superior. The delegated power is, of itself, contingent and limited (Can. 197).

The *magisterium* is the charge given by Christ to the Church to conserve intact the deposit of revelation and to preach it throughout the whole world to all men. It is, then, the whole task of safeguarding and propagating the faith, a task in which the Church has the unceasing assistance of the Holy Spirit (cf. Can. 1322).

Article One
THE DISTINCTINON BETWEEN CLERGY AND LAITY

In a cursory view of the mystery of the Church, the hierarchical structure is summarized in the distinction between priests and faithful. In daily life this distinction seems satisfactory enough. The Sunday gathering of the members of the parish, the day-to-day administration of the sacraments, the communal activities of Christians are characterized by the fact that a priest presides over them. His role and powers cannot be shared; he gives and directs while the host of the baptized receive and are directed.

Actually, this is a very sketchy description of the Church. The priest has been sent by his bishop; he does not preach or command in his own name. He forms part of a priestly body and is assisted in his tasks by certain of the faithful—readers, servers, catechists—who thus momentarily exercise certain functions of "ministry," functions which are also assigned by the bishop to seminarians in a permanent and definitive way.

It is ordination which consecrates a man as irrevocably designated for hierarchical functions, since it confers on him the powers of orders. Even before ordination, however, the Church expresses this designation by the act of tonsure. The bishop cuts off a few hairs from the candidate's head, while he, in turn, proclaims his willingness to consecrate himself to the service of the Church, using a verse of Psalm 15: "The Lord is the portion of my inheritance and my cup; it is You who will restore my inheritance to me.[3] The powers of jurisdiction can, moreover, be acquired before ordination.

This is why it is well for us to speak rather generally of clerics, a term which covers the variety of hierarchical situations in the Church; those who are not clerics are laymen, that is, they constitute the Christian

---

[3] Tonsure may be celebrated in the course of the ceremonies of ordination; but it is not an ordination. It is a sacramental by which a man is designated to receive clerical rank and function.

people. "Through divine institution, in the Church, clerics are distinct from laymen, although not every clerical order is of divine institution" (Can. 107). This distinction is not meant to lessen the role or the dignity of the laymen in the Church, but merely to mark out differences in vocations and tasks, and to indicate how they are complementary.

I. A PEOPLE OF PRIESTS AND KINGS

The New Testament emphasizes the eminent dignity of the baptized in startling terms:

> Yield yourselves, as living stones, to the building of a spiritual edifice, for a holy priesthood, so as to offer spiritual sacrifices acceptable to God through Jesus Christ. . . . You are a chosen race, a royal priesthood, a holy nation, a ransomed people, meant to proclaim the praises of Him who has called you out of darkness into His wonderful light (1 Peter 2:5-9).

> He loves us and has cleansed us of our sins by his blood; he has made us a kingdom of priests for his God and Father (Apoc. 1:5-6).

> They were singing (to the Lamb) a new song: you are worthy to take up the book and break its seals, for you were slain and with your blood you have ransomed for God men of every tribe, language, people and nation; you have made them for our God a kingdom of priests reigning over the earth (Apoc. 5:9-10).

The phrase which recurs again and again, "royal priesthood" or "kingdom of priests," shows us that the new people of God enjoy the complete fulfillment of the promise made to Israel in the desert:

> Now therefore, if you will obey me and keep my covenant, you shall be my own possession among all the peoples; for all the earth is mine. You shall be to me a kingdom of priests and a consecrated nation (Exod. 19:5-6).

Taking his inspiration from these texts, St. Thomas Aquinas rightly defines the baptismal character as a participation in the priesthood of Christ deputing one to the worship of God (*Summa* III, 63, 5), a doctrine taken up again by Pope Pius XII in the encyclical *Mediator Dei*:

> By the waters of baptism, as by common right, Christians are made members of the Mystical Body of Christ the Priest, and by the character which is imprinted on their souls, they are appointed to give worship to God. Thus they participate, according to their condition, in the priesthood of Christ (88).

To the baptismal character is added, for most of the faithful, that of confirmation, the sacrament which fulfills in the Church the prophecy of Joel: in messianic times, all the sons of Israel are to become prophets. This is why the Church in our days is fostering a really positive idea of the laity. She insists on the active participation of the faithful in the liturgy and also urges laymen to realize and undertake the task which is peculiarly their own. It is they, and they alone, who are to dedicate themselves to the building-up of the earthly city, a work willed by God but not the mission of the clergy. This city can set itself up against God like the tower of Babel, or it can respect the ideal of the Gospel; but the transforming of human life on all levels is possible only if Christians are present and active therein. They are in the front lines of the combat. As Pius XII said:

> The faithful, and, more precisely the laity, are in the front lines of the life of the Church; through them the Church is the vital principle in human society. As a consequence they should always have a keen awareness, not only of belonging to the Church but of being the Church—that is to say, of being the city of the faithful on earth under the leadership of their common head, the Pope, and of the bishops in communion with him. (Feb. 20, 1946).[4]

They are also called to share in the hierarchical apostolate by taking part in activities which go beyond the simple witness given by presence and participation in temporal affairs. Pope Pius XI, in instituting Catholic Action, pointed out how basic is the role of the laity; even in the time of the apostles, laymen labored in the work of evangelization (see Phil. 4:3, a text which was often on the lips of Pius XI). The laity, therefore, are the Church, and it is for their sake and in their service that there is a hierarchy.

II. THE CHURCH, A SOCIETY OF DIFFERENT RANKS

This people of priests and kings has its priests and leaders above it. Given to the people and not chosen by them, these priests and leaders provide supernatural food for all the people; they are the shepherds of Christ's flock. The laity are the "faithful," but the faith they have has been handed to them, has been taught them. They share in the Eucharist, but they are incapable of consecrating it; they can only join the action of the priest who is presiding over their assembly. If they dedicate themselves to the apostolate, it is only through sharing in the hierarchical apostolate.

> Scripture teaches, and tradition confirms us in the belief, that the Church is the Mystical Body of Christ, a body ruled by pastors and teachers—a society of men, at the heart of which are leaders with full and perfect powers of governing, teaching and judging. As a result, this Church is essentially a society in which not all are equal, that is to say, a society comprising two kinds of persons, the shepherds and the flock: those who occupy one or other rank in the hierarchy,

[4] See Y. Congar, *Laity, Church and World.*

and the multitudes of the faithful. And these categories are so distinct that in the pastoral body alone reside the right and the authority necessary for moving and directing all the members towards their goal; as for the multitude, its duty is simply that of letting itself be led and, as a docile flock, of following its shepherds (Piux X, encyclical *Vehementer*, Feb. 11, 1906).

Is such a submissiveness compatible with "the liberty to which Christ has called us" (Gal. 5:13) and with the eminent dignity of the laity just described? Yes, because this subjection does not extinguish a single charism, because he who commands is at the service of those whom he guides towards salvation, and because supernatural goods are the free gift of God. It is the Lord who has willed that certain men collaborate in a special way with Him, that the faith, the sacraments, grace should be given to some by others, just as in a living body certain organs communicate life to others. This is why in the Church there are pastors, priests, leaders—in a word, clerics.

A man does not belong to the hierarchy of the Church as a result of heredity, in the way the tribe of Levi was destined in the Old Law for service in the temple and for the priesthood. Nor does this condition arise from the will of the Christian people, as organizations elect their officers. It is true that at one time (and even in certain cases today) the people intervened in the choice of bishops and priests. The election of St. Ambrose to the episcopacy or that of St. Augustine to the priesthood took place at the unforeseen instigation of the people; these interventions, however, do not create of themselves any right, any mission.

The power of orders is conferred solely by ordination; the power of jurisdiction is given by a commission from legitimate authority. Both must proceed from the apostles through an uninterrupted succession, for the hierarchy is not an organ which the body creates for itself, but one which precedes and builds up the Church as a community of believers. While the redemptive act of Calvary has been carried out once and for all, it is still necessary for each man to make a real and immediate connection, across time and space, with the unique work of the incarnation and the pasch of Christ (cf. Can. 109; *Med. Dei* 38-44). This is made possible precisely by the sacrament of orders.

It is in a general sense, then, that we speak of the priesthood of the faithful. "The people, since they in no sense represent the divine Redeemer and are not mediator between themselves and God, can in no way possess the sacerdotal power" (*Med. Dei* 84). The hierarchy alone is identified with Christ in His redemptive mediation as pastor and priest.

III. CLERICS AS "SET APART," "CONSECRATED"

Even the non-Christian can see that the clergy do not lead the life of the laity, that they are set apart. In the majority of countries, custom assigns to clerics a distinctive form of dress sanctioned by the law of the Church. But the clergy are even more recognizable by the fact that they cut themselves off from a number of secular activities and, in the West, by their celibacy.

Canon Law lists certain of these activities which are incompatible with the clerical state: participation in war, international as well as civil; the military profession even when there is no war; the assuming of political office, whether executive or legislative; the prosecution of civil justice; the conducting of law-suits, whether personal or financial; and business (Can. 138-142).

This banning of marriage and of certain roles in the human community is not because the Church considers these human realities suspect or tainted with sin; on the contrary, they constitute the main temporal preoccupations of the laity. It is because the clergy are exclusively at the service of the Church, whose mission must be carefully distinguished from that of human societies. The cleric is charged with bringing about unity among men—a unity deeper than anything that may divide them. Therefore he cannot take sides; he must be at the service of everyone, not of a party. He guides men toward their eternal destiny, and therefore cannot have any earthly attachments. His God-given tasks in the Church prevent him from engaging in the affairs of the human city.

There is something more. Ordination gives him a certain resemblance to Christ and, at certain moments, a presence of Christ, which require a consecration. This consecration cannot be purely exterior, as was that of the priests of the Mosaic Law. It must reach to the very depths of life, be an exclusive love of Christ, become an uninterrupted prayer. This is why the increasingly vivid awareness of the real nature of orders has brought about, in the course of the centuries, the requirement of the celibacy of the clergy,[5] and the recitation of the Divine Office for all those finally committed.

Article Two

THE HIERARCHY OF JURISDICTION: MISSION AND PASTORATE

While theologians generally subordinate the jurisdictional powers to the sacramental, the definition of orders given above from the Code of

---

[5] Only the clerics who have received the order of deacon in the East or of subdeacon in the West are from then on and forever deprived of the right to marry. The clerics in lower orders are bound by no irrevocable promise, but in the West they are required to maintain celibacy so long as they do not renounce the clerical state.

Canon Law mentions first the government of the faithful and then the celebration of divine worship.

This second method is pedagogically preferable as emphasizing an important aspect of the New Testament and of apostolic history: the kingdom of God is a work of breaking ground, of construction; it is also a journey together toward the Promised Land. Even the names chosen by the primitive Church to designate the different hierarchical ranks are significant: first are the apostles, or envoys, men sent out; then, after them, the bishops, the supervisors, guardians or shepherds; and, finally, the elders or presbyters. It was a long time before Christians were willing to adopt the vocabulary of the levitical priesthood, limited to ritual tasks as it was. It is, moreover, the nature of the priesthood of Jesus which forces us to enlarge our viewpoint. Christ is a priest according to the order of Melchisedech, not according to the order of Aaron (Heb. 7:11).[6]

I. THE MISSION AND PASTORATE OF CHRIST

We shall discuss later the sacrifice through which Christ carries out and consummates His priesthood. The priests in whom He continues His work share in His priestly act by making it sacramentally present through the Mass and by transmitting to men, through the sacraments, the grace which flows from it. But the oblation of Calvary had been preceded by three years of ministry on the roads of Galilee and Judea, during which Christ spoke, acted, gave commands. So He realized in Himself a type of priesthood different from that of Aaron, uniting all the forms of mediation between God and men marked out in the Old Testament.

1. Christ, prophet of the New Law. It is with His prophetic mission that the Epistle to the Hebrews begins its description of the role of Jesus:

> After having spoken, in times gone by, in many ways and various forms, to our fathers through the prophets, in these last days God has spoken to us through the Son whom he has appointed heir of all things, through whom also he made the world (Heb. 1:1-2).

The prophets were sent by God to some one person or to a people, to speak, to transmit a divine message. Jesus is the "One sent by the Father." He insists on this mission entrusted to Him; St. John's Gospel repeats this phrase again and again (3:17; 3:34; 4:34; 5:24,36-37; 6:29; 7:28-29; 8:42; 10:36; 11:42; 17:3,25; etc.). The Gospel of St. Luke shows the consecration of Jesus as prophet carried out in a visible way by the Holy Spirit on the day of His baptism, and His fulfillment of the prophecy of Isaias 61: "He has sent me to bring the good news to the poor" (Luke 3:21-22; 4:17-21).

[6] For the history of our present terminology, see Josef Jungmann, *The Early Liturgy*, pp. 17-18.

The message which Christ brings is a word to which we must respond with faith, a word which gives eternal life, causing us to know the true God and His Son. Only those who believe have the power to become children of God. The most precious gift that Jesus can give, one far greater than the healing of a blind man, is to speak the word which gives faith: "Do you believe in the Son of God? I am he, I who speak to you" (John 9:35-38).

2. Christ, guide and shepherd of His people. As the people of God journeyed toward the Promised Land, they were often compared in Scripture to a flock of sheep which the shepherd guides to pasture. The hand of the shepherd and the shepherd's crook are good to feel, since they are reminders of his loving care; they give comfort and security (Ps. 22). It is Yahweh Himself who is the guide and shepherd.

Appearing frequently throughout the psalms, this theme is developed at length in chapter 34 of Ezechiel. Abandoned by bad shepherds, the flock is decimated by wild beasts, the sheep are scattered and straying. But the Lord will gather them together again, going in search of those lost, healing those wounded. He will raise up a shepherd who will feed them, while He will still be the shepherd Himself.

This shepherd announced by Ezechiel is none other than Christ Jesus. He sets out to find the lost sheep (Luke 15:3-7); He knows His sheep; He wishes to bring back to the fold all those who do not yet belong to it; He gives his life for His sheep (John 10:11-18). In receiving baptism, we, who had wandered astray like sheep, now return to the shepherd and the guardian of our souls, Christ (1 Peter 2:25).

3. Christ, king and priest: Melchisedech. The theme of the shepherd is linked to the statement of the kingship of Christ. When the prophet Samuel first set Saul and then David as kings over the people, it was to have them carry out as God's lieutenants the mission of leading Israel. It is in relation to kings that Jeremias speaks of shepherds (Jer. 2:8; 10:21; 23:1-3). The Messiah whom Ezechiel announces as a shepherd, is also a prince, a new David: "I will set up over them a shepherd, my servant David, who will lead them to pasture" (Ez. 34:23).

At the annunciation the angel presents the coming of Jesus as the fulfillment of this prophecy: "The Lord God will give him the throne of David, his father; he will reign over the house of Jacob forever, and his kingdom shall have no end" (Luke 1:32-33). So far as Jesus Himself is concerned, the claiming of His kingship is the climax of His testimony before Pilate, coming as it does when this claim could no longer be misunderstood: "My kingdom is not of this world . . . I am a king, and I was born and came into this world only to give testimony to the truth" (John 18:36-37).

The kingship of Jesus, therefore, is linked with His prophetic office. It

is also closely linked with His priesthood because it is the work of re-
uniting men with God and with one another. We distinguish His kingship from His priesthood because, though He acquired His kingdom once
and for all on the Cross, it must still be continually won by conquest until
the parousia. His kingship is exercised in the history of the Church.

But these two aspects are founded on one and the same biblical figure—
Melchisedech. Jesus Christ is a priest according to the order of Melchisedech, who was himself king and priest, king of Salem, i.e., "king of justice"
(Heb. 7:1-2). Although the sacrifice of bread and wine offered by this
king did not foretell that Christ was to shed His Blood in His self-obla-
tion on the Cross, nevertheless it was an image of the effect of the sacrifice of Christ, "for the bread and wine signify the unity of the Church,"
according to the comment of St. Thomas (*Summa* III, 22, 6) who is here
following St. Augustine (*Treatise on John*, 26).

4. Christ, the new Moses. Finally, it is Moses who, above all, ideally
prefigures Christ and His mission (cf. the whole of Heb. 3). For Moses
was not only a prophet, but the prophet *par excellence* (Num. 12:7; Deut.
18:15 ff.), mediator between God and men (notice in particular the
wonderful account in Exod. 32:11-14), law-giver, shepherd and guide
(cf. Num. 27:17). After his death all his functions were divided up into
different offices, but Christ reunites these again in Himself. He is the new
Moses; He plays the role of Moses, repeating his words and actions. It is
these different prerogatives which Christ continues to exercise on earth
through the apostles and their successors.

II. THE MISSION AND THE PASTORATE OF THE APOSTLES

From among His disciples Christ chose a small group of men, exactly
twelve, whom He called apostles. This small company maintained its
unity up until the passion; it was reduced to eleven after the betrayal of
Judas and remained "the Eleven" until after the ascension.

The name apostles, "those sent," indicates a mission. This mission, for
which they were prepared in a veritable traveling seminary, they received when the risen Christ returned to His Father.

> The eleven disciples went back to Galilee, to the mountain that
> Jesus had appointed as a meeting-place. . . . Jesus came and said to
> them: All power has been given me in heaven and on earth. Go
> therefore and make disciples of all nations, baptizing them in the
> name of the Father, and of the Son and of the Holy Spirit, and
> teaching them to observe all things I have commanded you. And I
> shall be with you always, even to the end of the world (Matthew
> 28:16-20).

> Go into the whole world; proclaim the good news to all creation. He who believes and is baptized will be saved; he who does not believe will be condemned (Mark 16:15-16).

We may note how in these two texts the sacramental work (here, baptizing) is fitted into one great inclusive activity: go out, preach the faith, then, after baptism, teach observance of Christ's law.

This mission of the apostles is identified with that of Christ: "As the Father has sent me, I also send you" (John 20:21). It is first of all prophetic: "You will bear witness to me even to the ends of the earth" (Acts 1:8), in the same way in which Jesus witnesses to the Father. Their voice will be the very voice of Jesus: "Whoever listens to you, listens to me; whoever rejects you, rejects me; and whoever rejects me, rejects him who sent me" (Luke 10:16; cf. John 13:20). Their preaching will initiate the work of salvation.

> Whoever will call upon the name of the Lord will be saved. But how can one call upon him without first believing in him? And how can one believe in him without first hearing him? And how can one hear him without a preacher? And how can one preach without having first been sent? . . . So it is that faith is born of preaching (Rom. 10:13-17).

The mission of the apostles is also the building-up of a house made of living stones, in which Christ is the cornerstone, with the Apostles as foundation stones.

> You are fellow-citizens with the saints, you are of the house of God, for the building that you are has for its foundations the apostles and the prophets, and for cornerstone Christ himself (Eph. 2:19-20).

Although we do not find it stated expressly in the New Testament that every apostle has the prerogative and the responsibility of a shepherd, they obviously must have received this function since they handed it on, as Peter testifies in addressing the elders:

> Feed the flock of God which has been entrusted to you, watching over it, not grudgingly, but with good will as God wishes. . . . becoming the model for the flock. And when the chief shepherd appears you will receive the crown of glory that never tarnishes (1 Peter 5:2-4).

And St. Paul, addressing the elders of Ephesus, says:

> Guard yourselves and the whole flock whom the Holy Spirit has given to your charge, that you may feed the Church of God, acquired by him at the cost of his blood (Acts 20:28).

The task of the shepherd is that of driving off the "ravening wolves," of guarding the holy people in the midst of the temptations of the desert (see particularly the Second Epistle to Timothy), to keep Christians from falling back into the vices from which they have been rescued by baptism. This is indeed the charge of souls, as Christ Himself exercised it: "Of those whom you have entrusted to me, Father, I have not let one perish" (John 18:9).

To one of the apostles, Peter, the mission of Christ was entrusted in a very special way, with unique prerogatives. He is the rock, the stone on which the Church is built (Matthew 16:18), identified closely with Christ, the cornerstone. It is he who receives in an explicit way the charge of being shepherd for the whole of the flock: "Feed my lambs, feed my sheep" (John 21:15-17)—another way in which he is identified with Christ. He, and he alone, has the mission that contains in itself all missions, the charge of the whole Church; he even has charge of his brother apostles, whose faith he is to strengthen, since his own, through the prayer of Jesus, will never fail (Luke 22:32).

In many respects the apostles form part of that unique and irreversible historical event which can never happen again: the economy of salvation wrought by Christ. They alone were chosen by Jesus during His mortal life, and were with Him from His baptism by John until the resurrection. Matthias and Paul were added to their company and share in their dignity, but by a special intervention not to be repeated. Inspired by the Holy Spirit, the apostles continued the revelation of the New Testament; they were infallible, even taken individually. They are the pillars of the Church as no one else ever can be.

But their mission, their charge to preach, their function of shepherding must be handed on, since the flock must be led until Christ's return and the Good News must be spread to the ends of the earth and to every creature.

III. THE MISSION AND THE PASTORATE OF THE APOSTLES' SUCCESSORS

The mission and the pastoral charge which the Apostles received from Christ and handed on constitute what the Law of the Church calls "jurisdiction." But, just as the apostolic college had, in Peter, a head endowed with a special prerogative of primacy, so the hierarchy of jurisdiction which succeeds the apostles also has two degrees: the supreme pontificate of the pope and the episcopacy subordinated to the pope.

1. The two degrees of the hierarchy of jurisdiction: the pope and the bishops.   After his missionary work in different places, St. Peter settled in Rome as head of the local Church. It was at Rome that he died a martyr during the persecution of Nero; it is here that his tomb has been preserved. His successor as bishop of Rome is at the same time the inheritor of his primacy over the whole Church. Responsible for the whole flock, guardian and interpreter of the faith throughout the whole earth, he has the benefit of the guarantee given by Christ to Peter—he is infallible in his solemn pronouncements. He alone succeeds to an apostle personally.

> The Roman pontiff, the successor of Peter in the right of primacy, possesses not only a primacy of honor, but the supreme and full power of jurisdiction over the universal Church, in the domain of faith and morals as well as in that of the discipline and government of the Church spread throughout the whole world. This power is a truly episcopal ordinary power (attached by law to the office itself), and without any intermediary, over all churches, all pastors and faithful, whether taken together or separately; and it is independent of every human authority (Can. 218; cf. 197).

In contrast to the pope, the bishops do not succeed the other apostles individually but collectively. The college of bishops succeeds the college of the apostles; they are infallible collectively but not individually. However, their power of orders and of jurisdiction is that of the apostles.

> The bishops are the successors of the apostles; by divine institution they have been placed at the head of the local churches which they govern in virtue of their office, under the authority of the Roman pontiff (Can. 329).[6]

2. The importance of the apostolic succession. The early Church and the Fathers thought it of great importance to emphasize that the mission of the pope and the bishops is inherited from the apostles, that it continues their work, that they guard the deposit entrusted to them by the apostles, that their whole authority comes from the apostles. It will be enough to cite two very characteristic texts, the first by St. Clement, third successor of St. Peter as head of the Church of Rome.

> The apostles have sent us forth as messengers of the Good News received from the Lord Jesus Christ. Jesus Christ was sent by God. Christ comes, then, from God and the apostles come from Christ: these two things flow in marvellous order from the will of God. Armed with the teachings of our Lord Jesus Christ and fully convinced by His resurrection, the apostles, strengthened by the word of God, went out with the assurance of the Holy Spirit to proclaim the Good News, the coming of the kingdom of God. Preaching throughout towns and countrysides, they gained their first fruits (i.e., their first converts) in the Holy Spirit, and set these up as the bishops and deacons of the future believers. This was in no way an innovation. Scripture had long since spoken of bishops and

---

[6] This text sums up a paragraph of the Constitution of the First Vatican Council on the Church; see *Denz.* 1828; the encyclical of Leo XIII, *Satis Cognitum,* June 29, 1896.

deacons, since in one place it says: I will establish their "bishops" in justice and their "deacons" in faith *(Letter to the Corinthians,* 40).[7]

And Tertullian, toward the year 200, says in his polemic against the heretics:

> Show us the origin of your churches; list the series of your bishops as they succeed one another from the beginning in such a way that the first bishop has as a warrantor and predecessor one of the apostles or one of those apostolic men who remained until the end in communion with the apostles. . . . The churches show the names of those who, having been established by the apostles as bishops, are shoots from the apostolic stock" *(On the Treatment of Heretics,* 32).

In this connection also should be mentioned the long and celebrated passage by St. Irenaeus, bishop of Lyons, who died around 202, in the third book of his work *Against Heresies,* and the epistles of St. Ignatius of Antioch, the most beautiful works ever written on devotion to the bishop.

This same continuity between the apostles and their collaborators and successors is indicated in the New Testament itself. We see that, while the number of the apostles could not be increased after the addition of St. Paul, missionary expeditions and the founding of local churches continually demanded more and more workers. And so Silas, Barnabas, Timothy, Titus, and a great many others named in the Acts and in St. Paul's epistles received the "deposit" which they were in turn to transmit —namely, the pastoral care of a church or missionary work.

This transmission is not affected by the fact that the different functions of "bishops" and "elders" ("presbyters") in the very early days of the Church are hard for historians to delimit and were, perhaps, even interchangeable. For, in any case, the epistles are inclined to speak of the bishop in the singular and of presbyters in the plural. And, imperceptibly but very quickly (as early as the letters of St. Ignatius and perhaps even in the Apocalypse), these terms acquired the significance, which they were never to lose, of bishops and priests as we use the words today (see particularly 1 Thess. 3:2; 1 Cor. 4:17; 1 Tim. 3:1-12; 5:19-20; Tit. 1:5-10).

The pope becomes the successor of St. Peter and receives divinely sanctioned jurisdiction on the condition that he has been legitimately elected and has accepted his election (Can. 109); he can give up his office, as did Celestine V, but the Code does not take any account of the exceptional cases which occurred during the Great Schism (1378-1417) in which it was thought possible to depose a pope. According to the present law, bishops

---

[7] Isaias 60:17. We leave this translation unchanged to allow St. Clement the expression of his personal thought, though the sense of Isaias, according to the Hebrew, is quite different.

are named, or at least established in their sees,[8] by the pope who, moreover, defines their territory, may limit their competence in certain matters, can accept their removal so as to make this effective, and finally, in
exceptional cases, even has the faculty of deposing them. Thus in 1801
Pius VII required all the French Bishops to relinquish their sees in order
to bring about religious peace after the disorder of the Revolution.

3. The ministry of mission work and teaching. The first work of ecclesiastical jurisdiction is that of going out to those who are not baptized—
missionary work in the strictest sense of the term. At present the Church
is divided into regions in accordance with degrees of progress in evangelization.

Regions in which Christianity has flourished for a sufficiently long time
are entrusted to bishops who administer them with full personal right;
this does not mean that everyone in such a region is baptized or that there
is no missionary work to be accomplished there, but simply that the local
bishop is personally responsible. While he is first of all the shepherd of
the faithful, he must consider as peculiarly recommended to his care
in the Lord the non-Catholics who reside in his territory (Can. 1350, 1).

In mission countries properly so called, at present less and less numerous, the pope reserves to himself the responsibility of evangelizing (Can.
1350, 2) and provides this through more or less permanently established
delegates: vicars or prefects apostolic. However, this is not done in such a
way as to rule out collaboration by bishops: "It is not to Peter only, whose
chair we occupy, but to all the apostles of whom you are the successors
that Jesus Christ gave the command: Go out into the whole world and
preach the Gospel to every creature . . ." (Pius XI, *Rerum ecclesiae*,
Feb. 28, 1926).

The pope and the bishops are to present the faith to non-Christians as
well as to Christians, to teach it with authority, to deal with the difficulties that present themselves to men's minds, to controvert the errors
and heresies that are always arising. They have a deposit to preserve and
defend, a seed to sow, a plant to be cultivated so that it may grow and develop. Instructing those to be baptized, organizing the religious teaching
of children, preaching, providing schools of theology, are all basic
forms of this ministry, in which, as we shall soon see, the bishop calls
others to assist him.

Still more important manifestations of this ministry are the pastoral
letters of bishops and papal documents. The work of teaching as a whole
is called the "magisterium." In the name of Christ and with the continuous assistance of the Holy Spirit, the Church exercises this function in

---

[8] There are some bishops, even in our times, who are not named by the pope: the
bishops of Strasbourg and of Metz in France and all the bishops in Spain are named by
the head of the state; certain German bishops are elected by the chapter of a cathedral,
et al. In such cases the pope gives the bishop who has been named or elected "canonical
institution." In the East the intervention of the pope is less direct.

such a way that the solemn and extraordinary acts of the magisterium emanating from the assembly of the whole episcopate (a general or ecumenical council) or of the pope are infallible. But there also is a global infallibility of the ordinary magisterium.

4. The ministry of the care of souls.   The pope and the bishops bear the responsibility of caring for the souls entrusted to them. This charge is the pastorate. They have received it from the Holy Spirit Himself; they will render an account of it to God, who will judge them accordingly.

The shepherd of souls carries out his charge first of all by praying for his flock, particularly through the Sunday and other Masses which pastors are obliged to celebrate for their people. He has the right and duty to administer the sacraments to them, either himself or through his priests, to heal, guide, give counsel. To do so he must know his flock; this is why the bishop visits his diocese and informs himself about all its needs.

His is, in fact, an over-all responsibility as weighty as that of the father of a family, and also at times as distressing; it made St. Paul groan and appalled St. Augustine and St. Gregory the Great whenever they reflected on it. But the care of souls is also a source of sanctification for the person entrusted with it; it calls for many renunciations—the good shepherd may have to give even his life for his sheep.

With a bishop this responsibility is by its nature fixed and final. As the pastoral ring on his finger testifies, he is bound to his church in such a way that he is called its bridegroom by the Fathers and theologians, and a diocese is said to be "widowed" when its bishop dies. As St. Thomas says:

> Every minister of the Church under certain aspects is an image of Christ . . . and yet he is the greater who represents Christ according to a greater perfection. Now, the priest represents Christ in that Christ carries out certain ministries through him. But the bishop represents Him in that he makes ministers of others and supports the Church. . . . It is for this very reason that the bishop is called in a special way the bridegroom of the Church, like Christ (*Commentary on the Sentences*, 24, 3, 2 ad 3).

For this reason marriage is forbidden him. Actually, the care of souls has as its counterpart a more demanding love, the love of Christ.

> The fact that bishops apply themselves to tasks meant to assure the salvation of their neighbor arises from the abundance of their love for God. This is why the Lord first asked Peter whether he loved Him and then entrusted him with the care of His flock (*Summa* II-II, 184, 7 ad 2).

Bound up with their pastorate is the power possessed by the pope and by bishops to govern: to make laws, command, judge, punish, administrate. The organizations required to carry out this function and the formalities it entails make it all too easy for us to regard the Church as a society like other societies, and to equate its hierarchy, courts, offices and committees with those of civil governments. The differences, however, are far greater than the resemblances. The government of the Church is concerned with spiritual goods, with those of revelation, and with other matters closely connected with these spiritual goods and the faith. The purpose of this government is the unity of the Church and her advance towards the Promised Land. The various juridical structures of the Church are, then, a sign; in the decisions of the hierarchy the Holy Spirit is at work. "It has seemed good to the Holy Spirit and to us," the apostles said when they made important decisions in their assembly at Jerusalem (Acts 15:28).

IV. PARTICIPATION IN THE MISSION AND PASTORATE OF THE BISHOP

The bishop cannot carry out his pastorate adequately all by himself. Consequently, he shares it with his priests, his assistants and, in a more limited but no less real way, with laymen.

The proper function of priests, in fact, is to be the bishop's collaborators. When the bishop entrusts a share of his pastoral responsibilities to his priests, they do not stand in the same relation to him as do bishops to the pope. The bishops are the shepherds of local churches by divine sanction and they govern them in their own name. The power of the pope is episcopal like theirs; it is of the same nature, though superior. But it is from the bishop and from him alone that the power and the whole mission of the priest is derived. In fulfilling his functions he never acts in his own name but in place of his bishop, and the bishop can delegate to him a greater or less number of his powers.

There are two particular ways in which the bishop, within the perspective of the work of the whole Church, causes his priests to participate in his mission and his pastorate. First, he gives the power to preach, to hear confessions, to celebrate the Eucharist throughout the whole extent of his diocese, and entrusts to a priest some area of evangelization, or specialized task of dispensing charity, or the work of teaching theology, etc. (delegated jurisdiction). Secondly, he divides his territory into parishes, assigning to each a pastor who has full pastoral responsibility (ordinary jurisdiction of the internal forum). This division into parishes is obligatory (Can. 216, 1). But the non-territorial functions mentioned above are also important in carrying out the general pastorate of the bishop.

When the laity take part in the hierarchical apostolate, they receive their mission from the bishop, whether or not it comes in the form of a "mandate":

Union with and submission to the hierarchy are here essential and in the nature of things, because this is the cooperation of the laity in apostolic work, in the work of the apostolate properly so called, since the bishops are the successors of the apostles (Pius XI, *Discourse to the F.N.C.*, June, 1929).

V. THE CONNECTION BETWEEN JURISDICTION AND ORDERS

To limit the functions of the hierarchy of the Church to matters of jurisdiction would be to give a completely distorted view of it and to fall into the error of the Protestants. For there is a continuity between the exercise of this power and the exercise of the power of orders conferred by ordination—a continuity indicated by Christ Himself, as we noted above. Before the sacraments are administered, the faith must be proclaimed and therefore messengers sent out. But in celebrating the sacraments, the Church builds herself up; and it is the task of the pastor to bring the life of Christians into conformity with the sacraments they have received. The faith is not authentic as long as it has not received the seal of the sacraments; the Church is not fully expressed except through the Eucharistic assembly. Evangelization without the sacraments would remain at the stage of development reached with John the Baptist; it would not give the first fruits of the good things to come;[9] it would not assure that real and living bond of each person with the redemptive action of Christ. Evangelization is the first and necessary stage in justification, but this is fully accomplished in the sacraments.

Certainly, jurisdiction is not given to all who have received ordination; a Carthusian, for example, is excluded by his vocation from pastoral responsibility. Again, jurisdiction is sometimes given without ordination. And, finally, heads of churches who do not have the episcopal character are equated with bishops.[10]

These examples indicate a certain flexibility in the organization of the Church that allows for exceptions. But these are exceptions. Of itself, jurisdiction requires and calls for ordination; for example, a bishop who has taken possession of his see, and who is not then consecrated within six months, is deprived of his charge (Can. 2398).

In the same way, ordination of itself is ordered to the Church which is building herself up, and to the people who must be baptized, nourished with the Eucharist, governed and guided. Although every bishop does not have such a charge, and although the participation of the priest in ecclesiastical jurisdiction is not by divine right, theologians hold that

[9] As P. M. Gy says in *Christ in His Sacraments, Theology Library*, 6, (A. M. Henry, ed.), p. 317.

[10] The question here is one of temporary situations, like that of a diocesan administrator, who administers a diocese on the death of the bishop, or of delegations by the Holy See when it reserves a territory to itself, as in the case of prelatures *nullius* and the missions.

orders, taken as a whole, and particularly the episcopate, has for its final purpose the work of evangelization and the pastorate.[11]

Now we can see how the rites of ordination present us with an image of the hierarchy of the Church, in which both powers are united. This unity was realized first of all in the apostles; they received from Christ the order to consecrate the Eucharist and to go forth and preach throughout the world. The apostolic succession is not transmitted unless there is an inheritance of this mission, and also ordination.

Article Three
THE CONFERRING OF HOLY ORDERS

Ordination is the rite by which a man is established in the hierarchy of orders. The actions and prayers of this rite will be the source from which we shall derive the doctrine of the structure of the whole sacrament and each of its degrees.

I. THE RITES OF ORDINATION

It would be a most rare occasion to have, at the present time, a single ceremony conferring all the degrees of the hierarchy of orders. An episcopal consecration requires the presence of several bishops and is assigned preferably to one of the feasts of the apostles, while the other ordinations are normally celebrated on Ember Saturdays. But the popes of antiquity had them brought together on the same day of December or March or September. For example, the *Liber Pontificalis,* a collection of records made at the death of each pope, says about St. Gregory (590-604): "He performed two ordinations, one in Lent, the other in September, in which he created thirty-nine priests, five deacons, and sixty-two bishops for different places."

1. The consecration of a bishop. The ordination of a bishop is called in modern speech a "consecration". It can only take place during the celebration of Mass. The future bishop is conducted and presented by his senior colleagues to the one who is to be his principal consecrator and

---

[11] In his early writings St. Thomas insisted on the connection between the Eucharist and orders; and we shall point out in a moment that this aspect must be unconditionally maintained. He added further that the task of the priest is not only to consecrate the Eucharistic Body of Christ, but also to prepare the Mystical Body for the Eucharist— this second aspect being dependent on the first (*Summa,* Suppl. 36, 2, ad 1). Later on he emphasized more the pastoral function of orders, as, for example, in *Summa* III, 65, 1 or 3 ad 2: "Orders depute one to functions allied to those of a head of state."

who is also the principal celebrant of the Mass. Before this the candidate undergoes a public examination during which he accepts the duties of his episcopal office and the articles of the faith. For example, he is asked: "Will you teach, by word and example, what you understand of the Sacred Scriptures to the people for whom you are to be ordained?" "I will." "Will you, with the help of God, preserve chastity and temperance, and teach them?" "I will."

It is between the two readings of the Mass, that is, after the Epistle and the Gradual, that the consecration properly so called takes place. After having enumerated the functions of a bishop—"a bishop is to judge (what is of faith), to interpret (Holy Scripture), to consecrate, to ordain, to offer (the Eucharist), to baptize, to confirm"—the principal consecrator invites the faithful to pray. We should note in passing that these ceremonies are meant to take place in the presence of the people, who, far from being mere passive spectators, have a very important role to play, although it has no effect on the validity of the ordination.

Then the great litany of the saints is chanted, the indispensable accompaniment of every great constitutive liturgical action; the Church triumphant is thus associated with the Church on earth. During the litany the candidate prostrates himself in a gesture of intense supplication.

After this the consecrating bishops place the book of the Gospels upon the head and shoulders of the candidate. This is a practice of great antiquity, explained as follows by an Eastern Christian of the fifth century, Severinus Gabalus:

> Since the descent of the Holy Spirit is invisible, the Gospel book is placed on the head of him who is to be ordained high priest; and when this is done, we should see it as nothing other than a tongue of fire resting on his head: a tongue, because of the preaching of the Gospel, a tongue of fire, because of the words: "I have come to cast fire on the earth."

This is a figurative and somewhat stylized way of inviting us to see in the ordination of a bishop the reality of the mystery of Pentecost. This action of putting the Gospel on the candidate's head signifies above all that it is Christ who is acting here; it amplifies the more primitive gesture of the imposition of hands.

For immediately after this the principal consecrator and at least two of the other bishops present place their hands on the head of the candidate; the celebrant chants a long thanksgiving along the lines of the Eucharistic preface:

> Lord, we beg of You, bestow Your grace on Your servant here present whom You have chosen for the ministry of the supreme priesthood, so that there may shine forth in his life and all his actions what was symbolized in the vestments of the high priest of the Old Law by

the brilliance of gold, the sparkle of jewels, and the sheen of precious stuffs. Fill your bishop with all the graces he needs to serve You. Adorn him with a brilliant holiness, and sanctify him with the heavenly dew of Your anointing. . . .

Let the strength of Your Spirit suffuse him within and surround him from without. . . .

May his words and preaching not seek to persuade by human wisdom, but may they manifest the Spirit and power of God. Grant to him, Lord, the keys of the kingdom of Heaven. . . . May all that he binds on earth be bound also in heaven, and all that he looses on earth be loosed in heaven. . . .

Grant, Lord, that he may occupy the episcopal throne to govern Your Church and the people entrusted to his care.[12]

The singing of the hymn to the Holy Spirit, the *Veni Creator,* is inserted into the preface, during which the principal consecrator anoints the head of the new bishop with the holy chrism. At the end of the preface, the anointing of the hands recalls Samuel's anointing of David, the royal prophet. Finally the bishop is given the shepherd's crook or crozier, the bridegroom's ring ("Receive the ring, seal of fidelity, so that you may keep spotless the Bride of God, holy Church"), and the Gospel book ("Go, and preach to the people who have been entrusted to you").

The new bishop concelebrates the Mass with the principal consecrator, standing beside him at the altar, pronouncing all the words and making all the gestures with him. At Communion he receives part of the celebrant's Host and drinks of the Precious Blood from the chalice.

At the end of the Mass the bishop is enthroned. Wearing his mitre and gloves, and still vested as he was for the Mass, he is conducted to his throne by the other bishops, whereupon he gives his blessing to the people.

2. Ordination to the other orders. The ordination of deacons and of priests must be performed by the bishop in the course of a Mass which he celebrates. It takes place at the same point as the consecration of a bishop, between the Epistle and the Gospel.

The ordination of subdeacons is likewise permitted only in the course of a Mass celebrated by a bishop. This must precede the Epistle, and take place preferably at the end of the fifth lesson on an Ember Saturday (that is, during the course of the vigil celebration connected with the Mass of these special days).

The tonsure of clerics, and ordinations to the orders of porter, lector, exorcist and acolyte, can be performed by the bishop outside of Mass. But if he should wish to connect them with a Mass, they are arranged in accordance with the rite of the Mass of the day in such a way that the

---

[12] We should note here the reference to the prophecy of Isaias (52:7) concerning the heralds of the Good News, referred to in Rom. 10:15.

various grades follow one another in the order of their reception on the way to the priesthood.

The ordinations of porters, lectors, exorcists and acolytes all follow the same plan. The bishop explains to the candidates the functions of their order and the virtues these demand. Then he has them touch the objects which symbolize these functions: the porters touch the keys of the church; the lectors, the Bible (or a missal containing extracts from it); the exorcists, the ritual; the acolytes, a candlestick with a taper and an empty cruet for holding the wine at Mass. Finally, the Christian people are invited to join in the prayer which the bishop offers for the new ministers.

In many respects the ordination of subdeacons resembles the preceding ordinations. The bishop explains to them that they are to be the assistants of the deacons, that their duty will be to prepare the chalice, take care of the cleanliness of the altar, wash the linens that have been used in the Eucharistic meal. He presents them with a chalice and a paten, while one of his assistants has them touch the filled cruets to be used at Mass. Finally, he prays for them, after requesting the faithful to join him in this prayer. The subdeacons have much the same functions as lectors and acolytes.

Up until the twelfth century the subdiaconate remained a fifth minor order, as it still is in the East.[13] But in the Middle Ages the subdiaconate was raised to the rank of a major order because the obligation of celibacy was extended to subdeacons, an obligation which up until that time had extended only to bishops, priests, and deacons. This is why, today, the bishop commences their ordination by recalling the promises that will bind them:

> Up until now you are free, and you may, if you so will, still heed the call of the world. If you receive this order, you can no longer go back on your decision; it will be necessary always to be at the service of God—but to serve Him is to reign with Him—, to preserve your chastity with His aid, to be always attached to the service of the Church.

Then the litany of the saints is chanted as in the ordination of a bishop and of priests and deacons, with the same attitude of prostration on the part of the bishop and those to be ordained. The subdeacons are also given the vestments proper to their order (in modern usage): the maniple and the tunic, as well as the book of Epistles.

The future deacons and priests are presented to the bishop by one of the dignitaries of the diocese. A kind of inquiry is instituted concerning the qualities of the candidates, the people themselves being invited to give their opinion, at least tacitly (this recalls the beginning of the epis-

---

[13] In the East there are only two minor orders, that of lector and subdeacon.

copal consecration). We shall notice still other resemblances between the rites of ordination to the three higher degrees of the hierarchy.

The bishop explains to them the nature of the order they are to receive, the functions proper to it, the virtues these call for. The litany is chanted, if this has not already been done. Over the future deacons the bishop pronounces a consecratory prayer.

> Lord, look with kindness on Your servants here present whom we are consecrating as ministers of Your altar in the office of deacons. . . . We beseech you, send down upon them Your Holy Spirit that He may grant them the strength, through the seven gifts of Your grace, faithfully to fulfill the ministry of Your service.

The bishop pauses during this prayer to place his right hand on the head of each ordinand. Finally, he vests each of the new deacons in the vestments of their order: the stole, which they wear over one shoulder, and the dalmatic. And he presents them with the book of the Gospels, which they are to read and explain to the Christian people.

For priests, the imposition of hands precedes the consecratory prayer. In silence the bishop places both his hands on the head of each. All the priests present at the ceremony come up and repeat this gesture and group themselves in a circle about the bishop, keeping their right hands stretched out towards the ordinands. Now the bishop pronounces the eucharist. This begins by recalling figures of the Old Testament: Aaron assisted by his sons, Moses assisted by the elders.

> In the desert You communicated the spirit of Moses to seventy prudent men, that, aided by them, he might easily govern the countless multitudes of his people. . . . With this same forethought, Lord, You gave to the apostles of Your Son teachers of the faith to be their colleagues; aided by them, the apostles filled the world with their preaching. . . .
>
> Grant, O Almighty Father, we beseech You, the dignity of the priesthood to these Your servants. Renew in their hearts the spirit of sanctity, that they may receive from You, O God, the office of the second rank, and that by their example they may inspire amendment of conduct; that they may be heedful co-workers with our ministry. . . .

Then the bishop vests the new priests with their distinctive vestments: he takes the stole, which up to this point they have been wearing across one shoulder, and crosses it on their breast; then he gives them the chasuble. In a second prayer he asks for his priests the grace to be assiduous in reading the Bible, to preach from the abundance of their faith, to keep pure the gift of their service. "In the service of Your people, may they transform by a holy blessing the bread and the wine into the Body and Blood of Your Son."

While the *Veni Creator* is chanted, the bishop anoints with the holy oil the hands of the priests he is ordaining.

> O Lord, consecrate and sanctify these hands by this anointing and our blessing. May all that they bless be blessed, may all that they consecrate be consecrated and sanctified in the name of our Lord Jesus Christ.

Finally, he presents them with a chalice containing wine and water and a paten with some bread, the sign of the power to offer the Eucharistic sacrifice.

Immediately after their ordination, the new priests concelebrate with the bishop, pronouncing the words simultaneously with him. They truly consecrate, and this is their first Mass. The Communion of the new priests has a special solemnity, since it is the seal of their consecration. Several verses are sung from the discourse at the Last Supper: "Henceforth, I will call you no longer my servants, but my friends; you now know all that I have accomplished among you" (John 15:15, etc.). The new priests make their profession of faith and promise obedience to their bishop. He then lays his hands on them once again, and accompanies this gesture with the words spoken to the apostles by Jesus after the resurrection: "Receive the Holy Spirit. Whose sins you shall forgive shall be forgiven them; whose sins you shall retain shall be retained." Lastly, he gives them the kiss of peace and blesses them.

II. THE THREE DEGREES OF THE SACRAMENT OF ORDERS

The true import of the rites just described is explained by the Council of Trent:

> The witness of Scripture, the apostolic tradition and the unanimous consensus of the Fathers show clearly that ordination, which is effected by words and external signs, confers grace; no one should doubt that orders is truly and properly one of the seven sacraments of the Church. For the apostle Paul says: I admonish you to stir up the grace which God gave you through the laying on of my hands. For it is not a spirit of fear that God has given us, but a spirit of power and of love and self-mastery (2 Tim. 1:6-7).

> If anyone says that orders or holy ordination is not truly and properly a sacrament instituted by Christ or that it is some kind of human invention devised by men ignorant of ecclesiastical matters, or that it is only a rite of choosing the ministers of the word of God and the sacraments, let him be anathema (*Denz.* 959, 963).

This last statement refers to the Protestants who eliminated orders from the list of the sacraments, refusing to see in ordination a divine mystery efficaciously giving grace, the source of sacerdotal powers not common to all the baptized. Luther and Calvin considered ordination only a gesture signifying the choice of a man, the handing on of a mission. After ordination as before it, they said, he is only one of the baptized, nothing more.

This definition of the Council of Trent, however, refers to orders and ordination as a whole, not to each of its degrees or to each of its rites. Certain of the degrees of the hierarchy are of ecclesiastical institution (Can. 107). And certain rites are not essential, but simply extend the sacramental sign.

Which degrees of orders are sacramental? Theologians have discussed this question for a long time, their differences being explained by lack of knowledge, up to the seventeenth century, both of liturgical history and of the Oriental rites. Today it seems to be unanimously agreed that there are three sacramental degrees: bishop, priest, deacon. Minor orders and the subdiaconate are sacramentals instituted by the Church. This is suggested by the Council of Trent:

> If anyone denies to the Catholic Church a divinely instituted hierarchy consisting of bishops, priests and ministers, let him be anathema (*Denz.* 966; cf. Can. 108, 3).

Above all, the apostolic constitution *Sacramentum Ordinis* of November 30, 1947, stressed what the liturgical study of orders makes evident: the diaconal, priestly and episcopal degrees of orders have the same pattern of rites; they are conferred by the same essential gestures, the imposition of hands, accompanied by a solemn eucharistic prayer invoking the coming of the Holy Spirit. Sacramental value cannot be attributed to one of these ordinations without affirming it of all three; to refuse it to one is to refuse it to all of them. The other ordinations, on the contrary, lack these characteristic elements.

But while three degrees of orders are sacramental, all the orders taken together are but one sacrament, of which the episcopate is the fullness and the others a participation, again in accordance with the image of Moses, to whom God said: "I will take some of the spirit that is upon you and place it upon them, that they may bear the burden of the people with you" (Num. 11:17).[14]

III. THE SIGN OF THE IMPOSITION OF HANDS

For the Middle Ages, influenced by feudal usages, the sign of the sacrament of orders consisted in the presentation of the objects characteristic of the powers conferred: to the deacon, the book of Gospels; to the priest, the chalice with the wine, and the paten; to the bishop, the crozier and

[14] Here we are basing ourselves on St. Thomas (*Summa,* Suppl. 37, 1, ad 2), though he does not deduce from this principle all the consequences it implies.

ring—in the same way as a sovereign invested his vassal by handing him a symbol of his rights or fiefs. Although accepted by St. Thomas (*Summa*, Suppl. 34, 5; *On the Articles of the Faith and the Sacraments of the Church*) and by the Council of Florence in the instruction on union with the Armenians (*Denz.* 701), this opinion is now obsolete. Since the constitution *Sacramentum Ordinis*, it is the imposition of hands and this alone which must be considered as the sacramental sign.

This is the gesture described by St. Paul and the Acts of the Apostles. Timothy, who received the imposition of hands from Paul (2 Tim. 1:6-7; 1 Tim. 4:14), is in turn to carry out this action over those whom he is to choose carefully (1 Tim. 5:22). It is by the laying-on of hands that the apostles, after having prayed, established as deacons the seven whom the assembly presented to them (Acts 6:6).

This is the gesture with which Moses transmitted to Josue his spirit of wisdom and his authority, thereby making him his successor.

> And the Lord said to Moses: Take Josue, son of Nun, a man in whom dwells the spirit. Lay your hands upon him. Then have him come before Eleazar the priest and the whole community; in their presence commission him and invest him with some share in your authority, so that the whole community of the people of Israel may obey him (Num. 27:18-20).

> Josue, son of Nun, was filled with the spirit of wisdom, for Moses had laid his hands upon him. He it was whom the children of Israel were to obey, carrying out the charge that Yahweh had given to Moses (Deut. 34:9).

Even though the gesture is not mentioned, it is nevertheless suggested in Numbers 11:25, when God gave Moses the aid of the seventy elders: "He took the spirit that rested upon him and bestowed it upon them."

IV. THE EFFECTS OF ORDINATION

1. An invisible mission of the Holy Spirit.

> If anyone says that by holy ordination the Holy Spirit is not given and thus it is in vain for bishops to say: Receive the Holy Spirit. . . . let him be anathema (*Denz.* 964).

In this canon the Council of Trent expresses the unanimous tradition of the liturgy; the citations made above of the three consecratory prefaces are explicit on this point. The Holy Spirit is the author of all consecrations. To each of the three ordinations there corresponds a new sending of the Holy Spirit, distinct from that of baptism and of confirmation.

2. Permanent powers and ineradicable mark.

> If anyone says that by holy orders a character is not imprinted or that he who was once a priest can become a layman again, let him be anathema (*Denz.* 964).

Ordination cannot be repeated. The powers granted are final, unlike that of jurisdiction, which may be withdrawn. The Church recognizes as valid an ordination carried out in accordance with the essential rite by an heretical bishop. These powers constitute the character of ordination, which is ineradicable (*res et sacramentum*).[15] It is above all in the transmission of these powers that the sacrament of orders consists. He who receives this sacrament receives it for the good of others, not for himself (cf. *Summa*, Suppl., 34, 2 and 4; 37, 1 ad 1).

The sending of the Holy Spirit and the character are signified not only by the consecrating prayer, but also by the action of anointing. This, though not essential, has nevertheless been traditional in ordaining a bishop or priest since the eighth century. In biblical usage, anointing inaugurated a definitive designation to some special mission. It rendered the person who received it so sacred that, for example, David punished with death the Amalecite who had dared to strike Saul; rejected by God, deprived of his kingship, Saul was still the anointed of Yahweh (2 Sam. 1:14).

The character conferred by the sacrament is always a configuration to Christ. "Every minister," says St. Thomas, "is in a certain respect an image of Christ."[16] In fact, the sacramental powers given by ordination are exercised in the person of Christ.

3. A grace of inner sanctification.

While the principal effect of ordination consists in the powers received, nevertheless this sacrament brings with it also a grace of inner sanctification (*res sacramenti*). The exercise of the ministry calls for exceptional virtue. Those who receive ordination are placed at the head of the faithful and are to be their models—a fact which, once again, is clearly brought out in the prayers of consecration. However great may be the care which the Church exercises in choosing her candidates, she can never fathom their hearts. But God knows the depths of souls and He acts mercifully, making them worthy

[15] See St. Gregory of Nyssa, *On the Baptism of Christ* (PG, 46, 581): "The same power of the word (which makes baptism and the Eucharist) also makes the priest venerable and holy, setting him apart from the rest of men by a new blessing. Yesterday and the day before he was one of the crowd, one of the people. Then, suddenly he is elevated to be a guide, leader, teacher of piety, instructor of hidden mysteries. And he becomes so without any change of body or form. While he remains in appearance what he was before, an invisible power and grace have transformed for the better his invisible soul."

[16] *Commentary on the Sentences* cited above. We may note that St. Thomas did not grant to the bishop a special character distinct from that of the priest, because he believed that episcopal ordination could be conferred validly only on someone who had already received the priesthood; he did not know that the practice of the early Roman Church forces us to adopt another view. But he affirms, along with all tradition, that episcopal ordination confers powers not possessed by a priest and bestows a resemblance to Christ superior to that which the priest possesses (*Summa*, Supp. 40, 4 and 5).

of the powers He grants (preface of the ordination of deacons). However, this effect of grace is not received by anyone whose bad dispositions act as an obstacle to it, and it can be lost. It is produced by the intermediary of the character.

V. THE RECIPIENT OF ORDINATION:
THE PRIESTLY VOCATION

Only a baptized person of the male sex may receive ordination validly. Other conditions are also required that do not involve validity—particularly the previous reception of confirmation, the sacrament which first designates a man to give witness to Christ among his fellows.

The Church bars from orders those who have committed crimes, those who have certain infirmities, those who have carried out activities the very memory of which she deems incompatible with the hierarchical mission and ministry. These impediments are called "irregularities."

Nowadays, the Church confers orders only on those who take the initiative in presenting themselves to her to receive them. This procedure is a free and clear choice, a gift of oneself to the Lord based on faith. It calls for generosity and love. We can estimate the depth of the Christian life in a family or a society by how well it fosters the development of this desire to serve the Church.

Yet, it is the Church alone that calls men to ordination for the needs of her ministry. She makes a choice among those who present themselves, determining the aptitudes of each person and the quality of his self-giving.

Here again we must rise above the level of the visible. Through the voice of the Church and through the circumstances which have led a man to ordination, it is God who is calling: "Let no one claim this honor for himself; one is called to it by God, just as was Aaron" (Heb. 5:4). Ordination, a free gift of the Lord, is the authentication of this call, which is termed "vocation." Although God knows better than we the needs of His kingdom, Jesus has asked us to pray that workers may be sent out into His harvest (Matthew 9:38).

Article Four

THE PRIESTHOOD OF THE BISHOP AND OF PRIESTS

One of the three sacramental degrees of orders, the diaconate, establishes a man in a role with powers for service, while the two others, the episcopate and the priesthood, confer the role of the priesthood with its powers. But this priesthood is not all on the same level, and still less is it made up of isolated and independent individuals. Priests receive all their priestly power from the bishop, whose helpers and collaborators they are. Moreover, they are formed into a body, a "collegium," a unit centering on the bishop. And, finally, the bishops themselves are united around the Roman pontiff.

I. ORDINATION AS CONFERRING A TRUE PRIESTHOOD ON BISHOPS AND PRIESTS

Through Moses the Lord gave to the people of the Old Testament a liturgical organization including a temple and sacrifices of adoration and expiation, some to be performed daily (Lev. 6:1-6; Exod. 30:6-8), others once a year (Lev. 16), as well as a priesthood to offer these sacrifices to God in the name of the people. This precise organization found in the book of Leviticus is visible and external.

The New Testament also includes a visible priesthood and a ritual sacrifice instituted by Christ. This new worship abolishes the levitical cult (Heb. 7:12). And the new institution has a richness which the old does not suspect.

1. Christ as the sole Priest of the New Law. The temple of the Old Law has given way to the one temple of the New: the sacred humanity of Jesus.

> Jesus replied to the Jews: Destroy this temple, and in three days I will raise it again. The Jews gave answer: Forty-six years were needed to build this temple, and you will raise it up again in three days? But he was speaking of the temple of his body (John 2:19-21).[17]

In like manner, the sacrifices prescribed by Leviticus disappear before the single sacrifice of the New Testament, the death of Christ on the Cross. The sacrifices of the Old Law were too exclusively external; this is why the Lord, though He had instituted them Himself, declared time and again through the mouth of His prophets that He rejected them (Is. 1:10-16; Jer. 6:20; 7:21-23; Os. 6:6; Amos 5:22-25; Pss. 39,49,50, etc.).

> Coming into the world, Christ said: You did not wish either sacrifice or oblation, but you have fashioned me a body. You took no delight in holocausts or sacrifices for sins. Then I said: See, I come—for it is of me that it is written in the head of the book—to do your will, O God (Heb. 10:5-7).

---

[17] The Body of the risen Christ is the center of the worship in spirit and in truth (4:21 ff.); the place of the divine presence (1:14); the spiritual temple whence flows the spring of living water (7:37-39). This is one of St. John's great symbols; cf. Apoc. 21-22; Matthew 26:61 and 12:6. (*Bible de Jerusalem,* note on John 2:21). See comment in the *New Testament Reading Guide,* #8, p. 25; also L. Bouyer, *The Meaning of Sacred Scripture,* pp. 98-116.

The Blood of Christ, and not the blood of goats and bulls—this is the sacrifice of the New Law. The Cross is its altar. It is at once a holocaust, an act of obedience and adoration, the first fruits of creation offered to God in pure praise, and the sacrifice for the remission of sins, of which the yearly rite of expiation performed by the Mosaic high priest was only a remote image. Finally, it is the sacrifice of the covenant, setting a definitive seal on the constitution of the new people of God (Heb. 8:10) and bringing together all those who had been dispersed (John 11:53).

The mission of Jesus culminates in this sacrifice. Witness of the Father, He dies like all the prophets to give testimony to the Truth (1 Tim. 6:12-13; John 18:36-37; Matthew 26:63-66; Heb. 3:1). The Good Shepherd, He gives His life for his sheep (John 10:11-18). This sacrifice is unique; there can never be another because its efficacy is complete and it extends to men of all time. The Body of Christ is offered once and for all (Heb. 10:1-18). The one victim in the New Law, Christ is also the one priest, the one pontiff, it is He who offers the sacrifice.

> For every high priest taken from among men is appointed to intervene for men in their relations with God, to offer gifts and sacrifices for sins. . . . Let no one claim this honor for himself; one is called to it by God, just as was Aaron. Likewise, it was not Christ who attributed to himself the glory of becoming High Priest, but he received it from him who said to him: You are my son; today have I begotten you, as, again, he also said: You are a priest forever, according to the order of Melchisedech . . . (Heb. 5:1, 4-6).

> Those (the priests of the Old Law) became priests in great number, because death prevented them from remaining, but he, by the fact that he endures forever, has a priesthood that cannot change (Heb. 7:23-24).

Through the sacraments, redemption in Christ, accomplished once and for all, is actualized daily in the Church until the parousia. The remission of sins for which Jesus shed His Blood is received in baptism and penance. The redemptive mystery is itself made present in the celebration of the Eucharist. Christ communicated His priesthood to the apostles, and through them communicates it to bishops and priests, so that they may exercise it sacramentally.

2. The power to consecrate the Eucharist. Before immolating Himself on the Cross, Jesus anticipated His sacrifice on Holy Thursday evening by celebrating it under the signs of bread and wine: "This is My Body given up for you . . . This is the chalice of My Blood, the Blood of the new and eternal Covenant, which will be shed for the remission of sin."

Because the immolation on the Cross cannot be repeated—since Christ dies only once—it will be rendered present in a sacramental way throughout all time. This is why Christ added at the Last Supper: "Do this in memory of me" (Luke 22:19; 1 Cor. 11:24). He thus gave to the apostles the commission and the power to perform again the actions of the Last Supper with the same efficacy. This is the power to consecrate the Eucharist, to render the sacrifice of Christ present under the signs and to offer it (cf. *Denz.* 938, 949).

Since this memorial of the passion of Christ is to be celebrated "until He returns" (1 Cor. 11:26), the power received by the apostles to consecrate the Eucharist is transmitted through ordination to bishops and priests. One of the functions of the future bishop, the consecrator tells him, is to offer sacrifice. The most ancient consecratory prayer still preserved, that of the *Apostolic Tradition* of Hippolytus (c. 200), asks that "he offer to the Father the gifts of His holy Church."

To the priest whom he is ordaining the bishop hands a chalice prepared for Mass. "Receive," he says, "the power to offer sacrifice to God and to celebrate Mass for the living and the dead in the name of the Lord." And previously he asked God, the author of every consecration, to "bless this servant . . . in order that, in the service of Your people, he may transform bread and wine into the Body and Blood of Your Son through a holy blessing."

In contrast to the ritual sacrifices of the Old Law and those of pagan religions, the celebration of the Eucharist is not an isolated religious action. Since it is the presence of the passion of Christ, it is the renewal of the sacrifice of our redemption. On it converges all the work of establishing the Church and of sanctifying souls; from it issues the whole pastorate. Accordingly, in the theology of St. Thomas, all the other hierarchical powers are organized around the Eucharistic power: to the power over the Eucharistic Body of Christ there corresponds a power over His Mystical Body (cf. *Summa,* Suppl., 37, 2, and *Summa contra Gentiles,* 4, 74-75).

3. The power to forgive sins. While Moses was able only to implore pardon for his guilty people (Exod. 17:8-16; 32:11-14; Deut. 9:18-19), Christ forgives sins because He sheds His Blood for their remission. This divine power, exercised during His earthly life to the great scandal of the Pharisees, He transmitted to the apostles after the resurrection: "Receive the Holy Spirit. Whose sins you shall forgive, shall be forgiven them; whose sins you shall retain, shall be retained" (John 20:22-23).

After the apostles, the exercise of this ministry of mercy requires ordination and a "sending." Only a bishop who is the legitimate head of his flock can forgive sins himself or through the priests to whom he gives jurisdiction. The sentence of pardon cannot be validly uttered except by one who has received ordination as bishop or priest (*Denz.* 902, 920).

The rites of ordination give an important place to this power of absolving sins. In the preface of the consecration of a bishop it is said expressly:

> Grant him, O Lord, the keys to the kingdom of heaven. May all that
> he binds on earth be bound in heaven; and all that he looses on
> earth be loosed in heaven; may the sins he retains be retained, and
> the sins he forgives, O Lord, may You forgive.

According to the *Apostolic Tradition,* a similar prayer was in use at the beginning of the third century. In the Latin rite it was only much later that a similar prayer was added for the ordination of priests. But priests have always been called upon by the bishop to aid him in the ministry of the reconciliation of penitents.

4. A true priesthood received by bishops and priests in ordination.

It is on these powers, the two most characteristic of the priesthood, that the Council of Trent bases its doctrinal teaching concerning the sacrament of orders.

> Sacrifice and priesthood are so related through the will of God that
> both have existed in every law. Since, then, in the New Covenant
> the Catholic Church has received through the institution of the
> Lord the holy and visible sacrifice of the Eucharist, it is necessary
> to recognize also in the Church a new, visible, and external priesthood into which the old one was changed. It was instituted by our
> Savior, who gave to the apostles and to their successors in the priesthood the power to consecrate, offer, and distribute His Body and
> Blood, as well as to forgive and retain sins, as the Holy Scriptures
> show and as the tradition of the Catholic Church has always taught
> (*Denz.* 957).

> If anyone says that the New Covenant does not include a visible and
> external priesthood, or that the power to consecrate and offer the
> true Body and Blood of Jesus Christ and to forgive and retain sins
> does not exist, but only the office and the simple ministry of preaching
> the Gospel, or that those who do not preach are not priests at all,
> let him be anathema (*Denz.* 961).

When the Council insists on "a priesthood that is visible and external," it does so in order not to confuse this with the spiritual and interior priesthood attributed by Scripture to all the members of the people of God.

The priesthood of the bishop and of priests is exercised also in the anointing of the sick and in baptism. The anointing of the sick cannot be given without the intervention of a priest, and of the bishop as well since he blesses the oil. As for baptism, although it can be administered in case of necessity by a layman and even by an unbeliever, normally it is one of the functions proper to the bishop, and, in dependence on him, to priests and deacons.

5. The unique priesthood of Christ exercised through bishops and priests.

While bishops and priests have a true priesthood, they do not have it in their own name; it is the exercise of the one priesthood of Christ. Their priesthood is sacramental.

As we saw in the first chapter, it is Christ who acts when the priest baptizes, grants pardon, anoints the sick. It is in the Eucharist above all that the priest is identified with Christ. With the same efficacy he carries out again the actions of the Last Supper, says again the words of Jesus. It is Christ who offers Himself, but He does so sacramentally, that is, under the sign of the priest who consecrates the bread and wine. The priesthood of bishops and of priests is "in the role of Christ"; they "represent the person of Christ," to use the phrases classic in theology and referred to again by the encyclical *Mediator Dei*.

In the Mass, as on the Cross,

> "the priest is the same, Jesus Christ, whose sacred Person His minister represents. Now the minister, by reason of the sacerdotal consecration which he has received, is made like to the High Priest and possesses the power of performing actions in virtue of Christ's very person, wherefore in his priestly activity, he in a certain manner "lends his tongue, and gives his hand" to Christ (*Mediator Dei*, 69; see 92ff).

For this reason there is a presence of Christ in the priest who conse-crates the Eucharist—a presence no less authentic, though of a different kind, than that which exists under the sacred species after the consecration (*ibid.*, 20).

Because they exercise sacramentally the priesthood of Christ, the bishop and, in his place, priests, can preside over the assembly of the faithful, pray in His name, and appear there as mediators between God and men. This power of acting as head of the assembly, which is mentioned in the rites of ordination, is not something delegated by the faithful, but the re-sult of the priestly character and of the power to consecrate the Eucharist (*Summa,* Suppl., 37, 4 ad 2; *Mediator Dei* 84).

Finally, although Christ's communication of His priesthood is for the sake of the Church and the faithful, it must be emphasized that it is final and constitutes a mark that cannot be lost. It can even be given legiti-mately without reference to any ministry.

II. THE BISHOPS AS POSSESSING THE FULLNESS OF THE PRIESTHOOD

Priests and bishops are not equal in their priesthood. The bishop is su-perior to the priest, not by reason of mere historical chance, but through divine institution (Can. 108, 3). This superiority does not reside in jurisdiction alone, but also in the power of orders. Here is how the Council of Trent explains it.

> Besides the other ecclesiastical grades, the bishops, who have succeeded the apostles, belong in a special way to the hierarchial order. Placed, as the Apostle says, by the Holy Spirit to direct the Church of God, they are superior to priests, and can give the sacrament of confirmation, can ordain the ministers of the Church and have the power to perform many other functions that those of an inferior grade cannot (*Denz.* 960).

> If anyone says that bishops are not superior to priests, or that they do not have the power to confirm and ordain, or that this power is theirs in common with the priests, let him be anathema (*Denz.* 967).

It is the bishop alone who is the ordinary minister of confirmation. If a priest receives the power to confirm, he is only the extraordinary minister under special conditions with delegation from the Holy See. A priest exceeding these limitations makes the sacrament invalid. Even in the exceptional cases in which the priest is allowed to confirm, he must make use of chrism consecrated by the bishop; this consecration cannot be delegated (Can. 781, 1).

For some ordinations Canon Law does not require the episcopal character for validity. But here it is a question of orders instituted by the Church, not of sacramental orders (Can. 951, 957, 964). The bishop alone can administer the latter. He alone can provide successors for himself in the episcopate. He alone can ordain priests and deacons.

The historical facts sometimes advanced in discussions between theologians, facts which would seem to lessen the force of this principle, do not apply widely enough to constitute an argument of dogmatic value. Moreover, they do not weaken the definitition of the Council of Trent. An extraordinary power that may have been given in some special way to priests is not the same as the power possessed by the bishop, which is so thoroughly his own that he exercises it validly even outside the communion of the Church. Tradition is unanimous in holding that the exercise of the power of ordination shows the difference between bishops and priests.

The bishop possesses the fullness of the priestly power because he represents most perfectly the mediation of Christ as king, priest, and prophet. He has the role of Christ, not only in the exercise of some of His ministries as does the priest, but in their totality, and especially in the establishment of the Church and in the very institution of its ministers.[18]

While Christian tradition has come to speak of priesthood in reference to the hierarchy, the term was originally reserved to bishops alone. When the terminology of Leviticus was finally applied allegorically to the sacra-

---

[18] St. Thomas, *Commentary on the Sentences,* 4, 24, 3, 2; cf. *Summa,* Suppl. 40, 4 ad 3.

ment of orders, the title of pontiff and the figure of Aaron were attributed to the bishop to mark the excellence of his priesthood and his superiority over priests.

III. PRIESTS AS THE BISHOP'S COLLABORATORS

Conversely, the very definition of a priest and the particular nature of his priesthood show that he is to be an auxiliary to the bishop, a co-worker, as the preface of the Mass of ordination says. He receives his powers from the bishop and exercises them only as taking his place, in his name and in union with him. The Fathers and the liturgy proclaim the great dignity of priests by speaking of them as assistants, as priests of the second rank. They aid the bishop, but it is from the fullness of his priesthood that they receive the share in the priesthood with which they are invested, as the seventy elders appointed to help Moses received a share of the spirit that rested on him. This is why there is no baptism without the bishop, whether he gives it himself or through his priests. "Baptizing belongs to the high priest, the bishop. By him this power is communicated to priests . . . but they cannot exercise it without his authority" (Tertullian, *On Baptism*, 17:1).

There is no Eucharist without the bishop. This is a principle to which St. Ignatius returns in his letters time and again. The ancient liturgy indicated it by two eloquent signs. The first was concelebration: all the priests present about the altar consecrating a single Eucharist with the bishop and under his leadership (the Roman Church now limits this usage to Masses of ordination, while the Eastern Churches maintain it as a frequent practice). The second sign was peculiar to Rome: when the priests were dispersed in their respective parishes as heads of that part of the flock entrusted to them, they received a fragment of the Bread consecrated at the Mass of the pope, the *fermentum*, which they mingled with the Eucharist they themselves celebrated.

Since there is no Eucharist without the bishop, there can also be no mission, preaching or pastorate without him.

Two formulas of St. Ignatius of Antioch summarize the ideal of priests: they are to be "united to the bishop as the strings to a lyre" (*Epistle to the Ephesians*, 4:1). "There is only one flesh of Jesus Christ, only one chalice to unite us in His Blood, only one altar, just as there is only one bishop, who is but one with the collegium of his priests (*Epistle to the Philadelphians*, 4).

IV. THE PRIESTHOOD AS "COLLEGIAL"

Because they are all, taken together, the sacrament of the one Priest—Christ—priests and also bishops have a "collegial" priesthood. This term signifies a solidarity of responsibility, a profound community, the common exercise of certain functions, and, finally, the precedence of the "college" over the individuals who compose it.

This "collegial" quality is indicated in the collective name by which priests were designated in the early Church: St. Ignatius and many other writers call them the "college of priests," the *presbyterium*. It is also brought out in liturgical life, for example in the concelebration of the Eucharist and the "concelebration" of the consecration of the holy oils. But it is perhaps most strongly expressed at priestly ordinations when first the bishops and then all the priests present lay their hands on the heads of the *ordinandi*. For this last action, the *Apostolic Tradition* of Hippolytus gives the reason: "For they all have a common, similar spirit." Finally, the diocesan synod expresses in a solemn way the everyday reality of the common effort of the "college" of priests.

While the bishop, symbol of Christ as founder and bridegroom of the Church, is unique as the head of his own local church, still the bishops also form a "college." On the level of jurisdiction, as we said, it is collectively and not individually that they are infallible. A General Council is an extraordinary expression of this privilege. But also in daily life a most profound "solidarity" is at work. Its liturgical manifestation is the consecration of a bishop, carried out not by one bishop only (though this would be sufficient for validity) but by at least three. At the side of the principal consecrator, the others are not "assistants," as they are often called, but "co-consecrators" concelebrating the essential action of ordination (Apostolic Constitution, *Episcopalis consecrationis*, Nov. 30, 1944).

> There is among the bishops only one Church, one soul and one heart. . . . There is, through the institution of Christ, only one Church spread in many members throughout the whole world, a single episcopate represented by a multiplicity of bishops united among themselves . . . (St. Cyprian, *Letter* 66).

Article Five
THE DIACONATE AND THE MINOR ORDERS

There is a considerable spread between the diaconate and the lesser orders, since the first is a sacrament and the others are sacramentals instituted by the Church. It is interesting, however, to study them together, since the lower orders are, as it were, extensions of the diaconate, exercising some of its ministerial functions.

I. THE ORDER OF DEACON

1. Christ as "Deacon." The deacon in the New Testament is someone who serves at table (Luke 17:8; John 12:2; Mark 1:31; Matthew 4:11), but more broadly he is, by virtue of his occupation or his love, someone who is at the service of others (Luke 8:3; Matthew 27:55; Mark 15:41; Matthew 25:34-35).

Jesus wished to show Himself as a "deacon," as one who serves. At the Last Supper, before the meal, He put on an apron, washed the feet of His apostles and explained: "Who is the greater: he who is at the table or he who is serving? And yet, I am in the midst of you as one who serves" (Luke 22:27). And again, in the Gospel of St. Mark, Jesus says:

> Whoever would be great among you must be your servant, and whoever wishes to be first among you must be the slave of all. So, the Son of Man did not come to be served but to serve and to give his life as a ransom for the multitude (Mark 10:43-45).

2. The institution of deacons by the apostles. Burdened by the extension of their tasks, the apostles asked for seven men to be designated, filled with the Holy Spirit and wisdom. They imposed their hands upon them, appointing them for serving at table, so they themselves could remain "devoted to prayer and the service of the Word" (Acts 6:1-6). Far from being purely material, this service combined a liturgical function with a mission of charity. A sacramental sign inaugurated it; it also took the form of bearing witness and of evangelizing, as we see from the example of Stephen (Acts 6:8—7:60) and of Philip (8:5-40). The establishment of deacons became a regular part of the organization of every fixed community (cf. Phil. 1:1; 1 Tim. 3:8-12). On the testimony of St. Clement of Rome and of St. Ignatius of Antioch, the deacons constituted the third rank of the hierarchy, and later tradition unanimously affirms this fact.

3. The diaconate, a sacramental order. The same action of the imposition of hands, accompanied by the invocation of the Holy Spirit, has always been employed in the ordination of deacons. This establishes them in the divinely instituted hierarchy of orders (*Denz.* 962; Can. 108, 3). It is, then, a sacramental act, truly conferring the Holy Spirit and giving a character which causes the deacon to be configured to Christ the Servant.

4. Functions of deacons. In ancient times, and even today in the East, deacons perform very important functions. If their importance seems less obvious in the West today, it is because this order is given almost exclusively to future priests as a step toward the priesthood. But the functions still remain, though carried out by priests. They consist in:

1) serving the Eucharistic table. Traditionally, deacons were specially

concerned with administering the species of wine, so that their role here disappeared along with Communion under the two species. But even today (Can. 845), as in the time of St. Justin (*First Apology*, 65 and 67), they administer Holy Communion.

2) Serving the bishop (and priests). In the celebration of the liturgy the deacons serve the bishop at the altar. Their service has been extended from the bishop to priests, although this did not always happen without certain objections, as the Councils of the fourth century testify.

3) Directing the prayer of the congregation by "monitions." It is the deacon who, liturgically, has the charge of making the connection between the celebrant and the people, alerting them at different moments in the ceremony, telling them what posture to take, suggesting prayer intentions.

4) Solemnly proclaiming the Gospel in the assembly, as well as preaching as a deputy of the bishop.

5) Administering solemn baptism (Can. 741), according to the example of the deacon Philip and in conformity with ancient tradition.

6) Social-welfare functions and certain important administrative functions were carried out by deacons under the authority of the bishop throughout antiquity and the Middle Ages.

II. THE ORDER OF SUBDEACON

This order, which is not a sacrament and which in the West is classed among the sacred orders only since the thirteenth century, was treated in detail above (Article Three).

III. MINOR ORDERS

Minor orders have been, and still are, quite variable in number, according to different local churches. The East has in practice recognized only two: subdeacons and lectors. In the West outside Rome, all the orders are to be found simultaneously only since the Middle Ages.

In the Latin Church today these orders are conferred only on clerics destined for the priesthood. They constitute different stages, as it were, toward this office. By contrast, they had considerable importance in the ancient Church. They were conferred in view of carefully defined services to the community, without any intention of ascending to a higher order. Moreover, they were concerned not only with matters of worship, but also with pastoral responsibilities.

Acolytes are the deacon's assistants, charged with acting as escorts of honor for the celebrant and the Gospel book, and with serving at the altar. Their functions today are carried out by altar boys and adult clerics.

Exorcists played an important role as long as there were adults to be prepared for baptism. They assisted the bishop and the priests in caring for the catechumens. Their liturgical activity in the pre-baptismal exorcisms undoubtedly corresponded to their permanent role; we might, then, consider catechists as their exact substitutes today, especially in mission countries.

The function of lectors is regaining its importance today when many laymen are acting as lectors. The Word of God must be proclaimed in an intelligible way to the assembly of the faithful, and so the role of the lector is strictly liturgical. When the celebrant takes on this role, the pattern of the celebration is disturbed.

As for porters, they give the ceremony its true character of a gathering-together, an assembly. It is they who are to call the faithful together by ringing bells, greet them (and, if necessary, turn away those who are not to be admitted to the holy mysteries), as well as to regulate the movements of the crowd, especially at Communion time. Finally, they have the care and custody of the building in which the Christian community assembles for worship.

The Council of Trent wished to restore these different functions to their full status. It even allowed bishops to ordain married men for these functions, if they would actually exercise them (Sess. 23, Decree on Disciplinary Reform, ch. 11). The decision has remained a dead letter, no doubt because the pastoral impulse given by the Council was not followed up in this field any more effectively than it was in many others.

Appendix: Priests and Religious

In elementary pedagogy and general opinion, as well as in connection with the life of prayer, parallel is often drawn between priests and religious, the priestly vocation and the religious vocation.

This parallel is explained by the fact that the reception of orders calls for a final consecration of a man's life, for the renouncing of marriage, of financial concerns and temporal interests. In this way, the step a man takes in presenting himself to a bishop for ordination resembles that of the man or woman who chooses the life of a religious. Both require the same joyful abandoning of earthly things, good and sound as these are, the same generous self-giving, the same depth of faith, the same dynamic hope in the return of Christ.

The comparison, however, is not without great drawbacks. First of all, it overlooks actual facts: there are religious who are not priests and who have no priestly vocation; there are priests who are religious and priests who are not, for even within the one priesthood there are different ways of life (cf. Can. 107).

Above all, the parallel is liable to create confusion of mind with regard to doctrine. The religious life seeks after personal perfection. In itself it is primarily for lay people. It is a life of work and prayer in community or solitude, a life bearing witness to the heavenly Jerusalem by the silent evidence of mutual love, of sharing everything in common, like the first community described in the Acts of the Apostles (4:32-35).

By contrast, the cleric does not seek perfection and separation for their own sakes; he is led to them by the inner logic of the hierarchical responsibility with which he is entrusted. This helps to explain why such spiritual commitments have not always and everywhere appeared indispensable for clerics. While the religious life is one of free choice ("If you wish to be perfect"), the cleric is chosen and designated by the Church, separated from the laity by the free gift of ordination or of mission, even though it was he who first presented himself to his bishop.[19]

---

[19] For a discussion of the similarities and differences between the priestly vocation, the "religious" vocation, and the monastic vocation strictly so-called, see L. Bouyer, *Introduction to Spirituality*, pp. 185-242.

Chapter 3

CHRISTIAN INITIATION

Preliminary Remarks

To become a Christian and form part of the Church, we must receive faith and baptism. Baptism and faith are, in fact, so closely united that baptism is called "the sacrament of faith." But baptism cannot be understood without the other two sacraments closely connected with it—confirmation and the Eucharist. Confirmation completes and perfects baptism. The Eucharist is the family table to which baptism gives access; only after a baptized person has taken part in Mass and received Communion does he "know all the secrets of the kingdom of heaven" (Matthew 13:11). Then he is initiated.[1]

Baptism, confirmation and the Eucharist, then, together constitute Christian initiation. When an adult is received into the Church by the bishop, the three sacraments are given in immediate succession, as was the universal custom in the early Church. In the Eastern rites this is still the rule, even for infants. And even though, in the West, infants are baptized without immediately receiving confirmation and the Eucharist, initiation is incomplete without these other two sacraments. Therefore the Church in the West decrees that confirmation and Communion should be given to children at an early age, as soon as she judges them ready. We will, then, study these three sacraments as a unit, while distinguishing carefully the rites, nature and effects proper to each.

Section One

BAPTISM

Christian baptism has a very special place in the New Testament, in the writings of the Fathers, and in early Christian art, as it has in the liturgy and in the whole Christian life.

Among the Christian texts preserved with particular care are the cate-cheses, the instructions given to the baptized, by the great bishops of early times: St. Ambrose, St. Augustine, St. Gregory of Nyssa, St. Cyril of Jerusalem, Theodore of Mopsuestia, St. John Chrysostom. The biblical themes which these great teachers brought out in their oral and written teaching are also used in inscriptions on graves (for example, those of Abercius and Pectorius), depicted on the walls of Roman catacombs and primitive baptistries and sculptured on ancient sarcophagi.

[1] The Latin Fathers used the terms "initiates" and "initiation" by analogy with the vocabulary of the pagan "mystery religions."

In these early centuries, also, the baptismal liturgy was worked out with special splendor. By the fourth century its form had been fixed substantially as we have it today and substantially the same in the various Churches in spite of differences of language and culture.

Again, the paschal celebration, the focus of the Christian year, is also a celebration of baptism. Lent prepares for it, Easter week and the Easter season continue it. Moreover, the Church provides not only stages of preparation for baptism, but also occasions for recalling it and renewing its graces.

There is nothing surprising about this, for baptism inaugurates and establishes the whole Christian life. On the one hand it ends the journey, sometimes a very lengthy one, that has brought a man to Christ. On the other, it contains in embryo all the further stages of the Christian's "pasch," his journey with Christ to the Father through life and death. It is from baptism that Christian spirituality flows. In every era of the history of the Church the impulse to the religious life, to the perfection of the Gospel, to the apostolate, has sprung from a renewed realization of the implications of baptism.

Article One
BAPTISM IN THE NEW TESTAMENT

I. THE ACTS OF THE APOSTLES

One of the facts most strongly emphasized in the Acts of the Apostles is that from the time of Pentecost and the very first manifestation of Christ's Church those who believed in the word of the apostles were baptized.

> Hearing this, their hearts were pierced through and they said to Peter and the apostles: Brothers, what ought we to do? Peter answered them: Repent, and let each one of you be baptized in the name of Jesus Christ, for the remission of his sins, and then you will receive the gift of the Holy Spirit. . . . And, welcoming his word, they were baptized, and there were added on that day about three thousand souls (Acts 2:37-41).

It was the same after each proclamation of the message—for example, when the lame man had been healed in the temple (4:4) and when Philip preached in Samaria (8:12-17). Sometimes mass conversions are described (18:8), sometimes individual initiations of special importance for the direction they gave to the future of the Church, e.g., that of the

Ethiopian eunuch (8:26); of Paul (9:18); of Cornelius (10:47-48); of Lydia and her household (16:14-15); of the jailer and his family (16:29-33).

II. THE COMMAND GIVEN BY CHRIST

In administering baptism, the apostles and their co-workers were carrying out the mission entrusted to them by the risen Jesus:

> Go, then, make disciples of all nations, baptizing them in the name of the Father and of the Son and of the Holy Spirit, and teaching them to observe everything that I have commanded you (Matthew 28:19-20).

> Go out into the whole world, proclaim the good news to all creation. He who believes and is baptized will be saved; he who does not believe will be condemned (Mark 16:15-16).

III. JOHN'S BAPTISM AND CHRISTIAN BAPTISM

The term "to baptize" is never explained in the Gospels or the Acts, for it was a common one for many kinds of purifying ablutions. In Scripture, for example, Naaman, at the command of Elias, went to bathe (*baptizesthai* in Greek) seven times in the Jordan and was thereby healed of his leprosy. More particularly, John the Precursor and his disciples had baptized on the banks of the same Jordan, at the edge of the desert.

The resemblances and the continuity between John's baptism and that instituted by Christ are striking. In both cases, those who received baptism did not simply go into the water as Naaman had done, and as was the practice among the Jewish communities whose customs have been brought to light recently in the Qumran documents. In John's baptism and in Christian baptism there is the active intervention of a man acting as God's agent. John baptized, the apostles baptized. Again, both John's baptism and that of Jesus were conferred after the proclamation of a divine message announcing the messianic times and the judgment (Luke 3:3-9; Matthew 3:1-12; Mark 1:1-3). Both were given in view of the remission of sins and to inaugurate a definite amendment of life. And, finally, both gave entrance into a community of converts and disciples, thus making baptism not an isolated incident, but the beginning of a new way of life.

This continuity was emphasized by the fact that Jesus received John's baptism, the first disciples of Jesus were John's disciples, and Jesus or His disciples also baptized at the beginning of the Gospel preaching, first appearing as co-workers with John (John 3:22-26; 4:1-3).

But the baptism given at Jesus' command on Pentecost and thereafter was not John's baptism. The difference between the two was so great that the apostles rebaptized those who had received John's baptism (Acts 19:1-7). Although the action was the same and John's work had prepared men for that of Christ, John's own statement indicates the profound difference: "I baptize you in water, but he will baptize you in the Holy Spirit" (Mark 1:8). Christian baptism not only inaugurates conversion, it produces it; and it does so because Jesus has died and risen. The gift of the Spirit works a radical transformation in a man, a new birth. Finally, Christian baptism presupposes the revelation of the mystery of the Trinity and the response of faith in that mystery.

Through John the Baptist, Christ indicated both His close connection with the Old Testament which He had come to fulfill and the unexpected newness of His work, for which the Old Testament and John himself were only figures and preparations.[2]

IV. ST. PAUL'S EPISTLES

St. Paul addressed his letters to communities of Christians still in the first fervor of their initiation. Baptism, therefore, occupied such a primary place in the Apostle's thought that it is frequently implied even when not explicitly mentioned. Basic texts are Gal. 2–5; Rom. 6–8; 1 Cor. 6:11; 10–12; Col. 2–3; Eph. 1–5; Tit. 3:3-7.

We shall return to these in Article Three, but we should note here that St. Paul always places baptism in the context of the whole economy of salvation. Baptism is the entrance into the mystery of Christ, prefigured in the Old Testament, realized through the Cross and resurrection. It is the inauguration of a life which is hidden today but will appear when Christ returns, a life which should manifest itself in a constant spiritual effort. Baptism is also the entrance into a new people with no distinction between Greeks and Jews, slaves and free men, a people made up of sons of God, fellow-citizens of the saints. St. Paul does not describe the baptismal liturgy except by allusions and reminders, but the teaching and the biblical images he presents greatly influenced the later development of its rites.

V. THE FIRST EPISTLE OF ST. PETER

St. Peter's first Epistle, which has been the object of many important studies during recent years,[3] begins with a true baptismal homily, filled with allusions to the theme of the Exodus and the covenant of Sinai (1–4). And, far from being unique in this regard, the perspectives pre-

[2] See Bouyer, *History of Christian Spirituality*, Vol. I, ch. 2.

[3] See, for example, F.L. Cross, *1 Peter, A Paschal Liturgy; New Testament Reading Guide*, # 12, pp. 34ff.; Louis Bouyer, *op. cit.*, ch. 6.

sented in this Epistle correspond so closely to those found in the writings of Paul and John that it has been suggested that they must all have been based on the liturgy of the first Christian generation. Certainly they all agree on the same biblical concept of baptism.

VI. THE WRITINGS OF ST. JOHN

In St. John's Gospel the sacraments of baptism and the Eucharist underlie the choice and the explanation of many of the deeds and words of Christ. The conversation with Nicodemus (John 3) bears the same relation to baptism as does the discourse after the multiplication of the loaves to the Eucharist. And Jesus' words, "Unless a man be born of water and the Spirit, he cannot enter into the kingdom of God," are further explained by the theme of the "living water" which recurs in the conversation with the Samaritan woman (4:7-15) and the discourse at the Feast of Tabernacles (7:37-39), and in Christ's actions of being baptized by John (1:29-34) and of healing the paralytic at Bethsaida (5:1-9) and the man born blind (9:1-38). From the side of Christ pierced on Calvary flowed out the blood and water (19:34-35) which tradition has always seen as signs of the Eucharist and baptism.

St. John's first Epistle and the Apocalypse present less obvious allusions, but baptism is to be found here too under various symbols (1 John 3:1-11; 5:6-8; Apoc. 7:17; 21:6; 22:1, 17, etc.).

Article Two
THE RITES OF BAPTISM IN THE LIGHT OF HISTORY

The Roman Ritual provides two formularies for baptism, one for children and the other for adults, the first being simply an abridgment of the second. In studying the sacrament and its liturgy, therefore, we will concern ourselves primarily with the rite for the baptism of adults rather than that of children.

The Church was built up in the early centuries mainly by the conversion of adults; children were received only with their parents or after them. The adaptation of the rites to the initiation of children raised questions which served to bring out the gratuity of God's gift and also the need for the Church to supply for the child's inability to respond personally to this gift. For a vital sense of the meaning of baptism, then, a Christian community must assist both at baptisms of adults who are becoming members of that community and at baptisms of the children of its members.

The Ritual also brings out the fact that the various rites making up the liturgy of baptism are distinguished by changes of place. This sacrament is administered, as it were, "on the march": in front of the church door, inside the church, on the way to the baptistry, within the baptistry. This journey indicates the various stages of progress toward baptism which actually existed in the past and which disappeared only at the period when Christianity had no more adults to initiate. In our times the re-establishment of these stages is certainly to be desired, especially in communities where converts are numerous.[4]

I. THE CATECHUMENATE

In the very early days of the Church, Christian initiation was carried out immediately upon conversion, as on the day of Pentecost (Acts 2:37-41) or in the case of the Ethiopian eunuch (Acts 8:36-38). When those entering the Church became very numerous, and particularly after the lapses occasioned by persecution toward the end of the second century, a lengthy period of preparation and probation called the catechumenate was organized. This is still observed in its main lines today. For example, the synodal statutes of the dioceses of France and the *Directoire pour la pastorale des sacraments* (n. 27) require a minimum of three months' preparation for an adult who wishes to be baptized. In missionary territories this period may sometimes be as long as four years.

This time of special preparation should include not only instruction but should also provide for opening out the life of the Church to the candidate, initiating him into Christian prayer, aiding him to amend his life and do penance, and giving him some real awareness of the obligations of baptism. It should also be a period of probation to assure the sincerity of his intentions and their seriousness.

A person thus preparing for baptism is called a "catechumen." Although he does not yet have the power to participate in the sacraments, the Church admits him to certain of her assemblies and recognizes him as having certain rights (Can. 1239, 1149, 1152).

In the first centuries, the entrance into the catechumenate was accompanied by the actions and prayers which are now, in the continuous rite of baptism, carried out at the door of the church. First there is the proclamation of the Good News and the response of faith. To ask for baptism is first of all to ask for faith, the response to the Good News proclaimed by the messengers God has sent. (This primary message,

---

[4]See Johannes Hofinger, *Worship, the Life of the Missions,* p. 76, and pp. 211-288. Also Rev. Reinold Dijker, "The Liturgy of Baptism and the Catechumenate" in *Liturgy and the Missions* (J. Hofinger, ed.).

kerygma, the essence of the apostles' preaching in the Acts, is analyzed in all its profundity by St. Augustine in his *First Christian Instruction.* In the present ritual, this proclamation and response is summed up in a few phrases and a dialogue.)

Recalling the first creation of man, the priest breathes on the candidate: "Receive the Holy Spirit . . ." The breath of God puts the impure spirit to flight: "Be gone, unclean spirit, and give place to the Holy Spirit, the Paraclete."

The sign of the Cross is first made on the candidate's forehead, and repeated on his eyes, ears, nostrils, lips, breast, and shoulders, accompanied by wonderful prayer-formulas. It marks Christ's first taking possession of the person who wishes to enter His army and fight under His orders.

Not being able as yet to give the candidate the "heavenly nourishment" of the Eucharist reserved to the baptized, the priest gives him salt to taste in sign of hospitality. As a condiment meant both to ensure the flavor of foods and to preserve them, it recalls the wisdom which God gives together with faith.

II. THE LENTEN PREPARATION FOR BAPTISM

In the early centuries, after months or years as catechumens, those who were ready and willing would finally, before the beginning of Lent, ask to be enrolled for baptism on the coming Easter night. The catechumens who were accepted then entered on an intensive period of preparation including special meetings for instruction and prayer.

1. The "scrutinies" and exorcisms. During three of the Sundays in Lent, the liturgical assembly was particularly concerned with the scrutinies, a phase of the communal preparation of the catechumens consisting of a careful inquiry into the uprightness of their conduct, and prayer for them and their sponsors. These exercises also included biblical readings and exorcisms.

The biblical readings chosen were the following: The Gospel of the Samaritan woman (John 4:6-42), preceded by the episode of the miraculous water of Meriba (Num. 20:1-13), both now read on the Friday of the third week in Lent; the Gospel "of Abraham" (John 8:12-59), now read on the first Sunday in Passiontime, preceded by Isaias 49:8-15, now read on the preceding Saturday; the Gospel of the man born blind (John 9:1-39), preceded by Isaias 1:16-19, both now read on the Wednesday of the fourth week in Lent.

Today, as in ages past, these readings serve not only to prepare new candidates for baptism, but to reawaken in Christians an awareness of the profound meaning of their own baptism. The baptismal water, the living water offered by the Savior, is at once a grace of healing and enlightenment. Faith and baptism are thus shown as being indissolubly connected.

The exorcisms which now form part of the rite for baptism of adults are prayers for the catechumens, different for men and for women, accompanied by the imposition of hands and ending in an imperative adjuration to the demon:

> Accursed demon, now acknowledge your condemnation, and give honor to the living and true God. Give honor to Jesus Christ, His Son, and to the Holy Spirit, and depart from these servants of God. For our God and Lord Jesus Christ has been pleased to call them to His holy grace, to blessing and to the water of baptism.[5]

These exorcisms are not precisely for the purpose of driving out the demon as did Jesus from the bodies of possessed persons. They look to the future rather than the past, and are to be understood in the context of the whole Christian warfare against sin, begun during the catechumenate and to be continued throughout life. This combat is not simply a psychological struggle; here God and Satan confront one another. The demon who once tempted Jesus in the desert (see the present Gospels for the first Sunday in Lent, Matthew 4:1-11, and the third Sunday, Luke 11:14-28) now seeks to dispute with Him for the possession of our souls.[6] So St. Augustine says to the catechumens:

> What we begin in you by the adjurations made in the name of your Redeemer, you are to complete by a profound examination of your soul and by the contrition of your heart. We fight by our prayers and exorcisms against the treacherous wiles of this ancient enemy, and you for your part ought to persevere in prayer and contrition of heart (*Sermon* 216).

2. Presenting the Symbol, the Pater, the Gospels. The readings now given on the Friday of the fourth week in Lent were, in the practice of ancient Rome, the readings for the last Sunday of Lent: the Gospel of the raising of Lazarus (John 11:1-45) preceded by the account of Elias bringing the widow's son back to life (3 Kings 17:17-24). For they show baptism as being a miracle of resurrection, and this was the day on which the catechumens were entrusted with the whole deposit of faith: the Symbol or Creed called that of the Apostles, which has always been associated with baptism, the Our Father, and the Gospels.

On this Sunday the bishop commented on the Creed article by article, and on the *Pater,* petition by petition. He then gave a homily on each of the Gospels. The catechumens had to learn by heart the text of the

---

[5] With one exception, the prayer *Deus immortalium praesidium,* which is recent, these formularies are always found in the Ritual for adult baptism, n. 17-27.

[6] See Louis Bouyer, *Introduction to Spirituality,* pp. 246-249.

Creed and the Our Father from hearing them said aloud and be able to repeat them, "give them back," before their baptism. It was strictly forbidden to "betray" these prayers to non-Christians; and so they were entrusted to the catechumens only orally and shortly before their baptism.[7] In the Eastern churches, especially at Jerusalem, the commentary on the Creed was more fully developed, extending over fifteen days or more and taking up only one article a day.

The "giving back" of the Symbol and the Our Father still remains in the present baptismal liturgy. But only a vestige remains of the presentation of the Gospels, the prayer that once ended the ceremony (n. 28 in the rite for adults; n. 9 in that for children), although this was one of the most striking rites of initiation, rich in spiritual and pedogogical import.[8]

III. THE CONSECRATION OF THE CHRISM

The liturgical renewal of Holy Week in 1955 restored to this important rite its due splendor. During a special morning Mass on Holy Thursday, the bishop, surrounded by his clergy, consecrates the chrism and blesses the oil "of catechumens" used in Christian initiation. The Preface of the Mass itself and the consecratory Preface for the chrism are almost exclusively devoted to setting out the meaning of the "characters" given in Christian initiation, of which the anointings at baptism and confirmation are the signs. Consequently, these texts should be studied, commented on, and meditated. Moreover, every Christian should, at least once in his life, make a pilgrimage to his cathedral on Holy Thursday to take part in the Chrism Mass.

IV. FINAL PREPARATIONS

The rites which at present take place in front of the door of the baptistry (baptism of adults, 33-37; of children, 12-16) constitute the final preparations for baptism. In Jerusalem these were carried out in the vestibule of the sanctuary immediately before the immersion. In Rome they took place on Holy Saturday morning (a day on which the Eucharist is not celebrated). They include: *a final exorcism,* showing baptism as the carrying out of God's judgment against Satan.

The Ephpheta. With his thumb, the priest touches the ears and nostrils of the catechumens with saliva, saying "*Ephpheta,* that is, be opened!" Action and words repeat the Gospel scene of the healing of the deaf-mute

[7] A trace of this prohibition may still be found in the liturgy in the custom of sometimes saying these prayers silently.

[8] See the fine description given in L. Duchesne, *Christian Worship, Its Origin and Evolution.*

(Mark 7:31-37). By faith Christ opens our ears to the words of God and gives our mouth the power to sing His praises.[9]

The threefold renunciation of Satan and the anointing with the oil of catechumens. The candidate must publicly renounce Satan three times, corresponding to the threefold profession of faith. In the East the two series are more closely associated than in the present Roman rite. The candidates turn toward the west to express their renunciation of the demon. Then they turn toward the east, toward the rising sun, to proclaim their faith, thereby expressing clearly the re-orientation, the conversion, of the whole man required by baptism.

The formula of renunciation has not changed since the beginning of the third century: "Do you renounce Satan? I do renounce him. And all his works? I do renounce them. And all his allurements? I do renounce them." This formula echoes both the Old Testament ("the works," the labors imposed by Pharaoh—Exod. 5:3-4) and the New ("Let us put off the works of darkness"—Rom. 13:12; "The Son of God has appeared to destroy the works of the devil; he who commits sin is of the devil"—1 John 3:8). It signifies the candidate's determination to free himself from slavery to Satan and to sin.[10]

As the threefold profession of faith, the positive commitment to Christ, is connected with the baptismal washing, so this preliminary renunciation of Satan is connected with the anointing with the oil of catechumens. Taking the oil with his thumb, the priest traces a cross on the candidate's breast and between his shoulders. Formerly, the candidates took off all their clothing at this point and presented themselves completely naked to have their whole bodies rubbed with oil, the customary preparation of athletes for a contest. Even though its present form is so reduced, this anointing indicates that baptism is the entrance into an arena, the beginning of a severe struggle (cf. 1 Cor. 9:24-27; Phil. 3:12-14; 2 Tim. 4:7-8; James 1:12). To quote St. Ambrose:

> You have been anointed as an athlete of Christ, as if you were about to engage in some profane struggle. You have professed your willingness to undertake a contest. He who strives knows that he may hope. Where there is a contest, there is also a crown. You struggle in this world, but you will be crowned by Christ *(On the Sacraments, 2, 2-4)*.

---

[9] Even by the time of St. Ambrose this action had undergone a deformation, for he notes that Christ touched the lips, not the nostrils, of the deafmute *(On the Sacraments, 1; On the Mysteries, 1,2)*. It seems probable that this was the result of some confusion with an exorcism concerned with the five senses.

[10] The Latin word *pompa*, translated in the present American ritual as "allurements," meant the various kinds of showy displays accompanying the processions in honor of idols. See J. H. Waszink, "Pompa Diaboli" in *Vigiliae Christianae*, 1, 1947.

V. THE PASCHAL VIGIL

In the primitive Church, baptism was administered during the Easter Vigil, and this practice is still called fitting (*decet*) for adults, except in danger of death (Can. 772). The whole rite of the holy night is, in fact, designed to praise both the pasch of Christ and baptism, or, rather, to celebrate both the mystery of Christ and Christian initiation as two aspects of the same reality.

The catechumens kept watch with the whole community, making ready for baptism by meditating on the biblical readings, singing canticles from the Old Testament, and praying. The number of these readings has varied in different Churches and different ages. However, the account of creation (Gen. 1–2:2), of the sacrifice of Abraham (Gen. 22) and of the going out from Egypt, with the Canticle of Moses (Exod. 14–15) have always been included. The following also have frequently been used: the renewal of the Covenant, with the canticle from Deuteronomy (Deut. 31:22-32); the prophecy of the "remnant," with the canticle of the vine (Is. 4–5); the vision of the bones that became living men (Ez. 37:1-14). The present Roman liturgy has only four readings with three canticles. Their meaning is clearly baptismal, as is indicated by the prayers.

VI. THE CONSECRATION OF THE WATER

The water to be used in baptism receives a solemn consecration which, like all great liturgical acts, begins with a eucharistic formula. This consecration is not essential to the validity of baptism; in case of necessity, ordinary water may be used. But its importance is very great since it is the preparation the Church normally requires to fit the baptismal water for its sacred function. Moreover, it develops the biblical symbolism of water and so enables us to appreciate the treasures of Christian baptism. The themes it introduces are based on the apostolic catechesis; their synthesis has not changed since Tertullian wrote his treatise *On Baptism*. We should, therefore, value this prayer as a precious heritage from the first Christian generations and meditate on it so that it will become as meaningful to us as it was to them.

After this consecratory prayer a few drops of holy chrism and of the oil of catechumens are poured into the water. This was done originally simply to make the water sweet-smelling, as people today use bath-oils. But it has also become the sign of the link between the bishop and all the baptisms conferred in his diocese. It indicates that priests and deacons baptize only with the commission of the bishop and in his stead.

VII. THE PROFESSION OF FAITH AND THE
BAPTISMAL WASHING

In the majority of churches of the Latin rite today, baptism is given by pouring water three times on the head of the candidate while saying: "I baptize you in the name of the Father and of the Son and of the Holy Spirit." Immediately before these baptismal ablutions the candidate professes his faith by answering the questions of the celebrant:

> Do you believe in God, the Father almighty, Creator of heaven and earth? I do believe.
> Do you believe in Jesus Christ, His only Son, our Lord, who was born into this world and who suffered? I do believe.
> Do you believe also in the Holy Spirit, the holy Catholic Church, the communion of saints, the forgiveness of sins, the resurrection of the body and life everlasting? I do believe.

This method of baptizing differs from the ancient way in two important respects. The first is the loss of the traditional practice of immersion almost everywhere in the West since the Middle Ages. The ancient baptistries were real pools, flowing with warm and perfumed water. The candidates went down into these pools, having taken off all their clothes and adornments. This complete nakedness, descent into the water, immersion in the pool and emergence on the other side were charged with meanings illuminating the implications of Christian baptism as St. Paul explains it. The Fathers' commentaries on baptism must therefore be understood in the light of the fact that baptism was then always given by immersion.

The second difference is that in the ancient practice the profession of faith was combined with the immersion. The questions asked by the minister and the answers of the candidate were the only words accompanying the action. The dialogue took place when the candidate was in the pool; after each of the three responses the minister immersed him completely in the water. The invocation of the Trinity necessary to baptism consisted in the proclamation of the Church's faith in the Trinity proposed by the minister to the candidate, and received and professed by him. In this way baptism was clearly shown to be the "sacrament of faith," as the Fathers and St. Thomas call it.

VIII. THE ANOINTING, THE WHITE GARMENTS, THE LIGHT

Immediately after the immersion or ablution, the neophyte (i.e., the newly baptized) is anointed on his head with holy chrism. While this sign is not necessary to the validity of the sacrament, it expresses one of its principal effects, identification with Christ. The prayer accompanying this anointing does not bring out its significance, since this has already been done in the Chrism Mass of Holy Thursday.

Then the neophyte is clothed in a white garment (a procedure quite feasible in our times, although it is so often reduced and distorted). When baptism was given by immersion, the old garments were left behind at the entrance to the pool and not put on again. Everything was to be completely new for the neophytes, even their clothing. The color white, which was not unusual at that time for city wear, was chosen for its biblical significance. The neophytes wore these garments all during Easter week, laying them aside only on Saturday.

In conclusion, the newly baptized are each given a lighted candle, a sign of their sharing in the light and life of Christ.

IX. AFTER BAPTISM: CONFIRMATION AND THE EUCHARIST

When the bishop is present at the baptism of adults, he gives them the sacrament of confirmation immediately after baptism. Then Mass is celebrated, the neophytes taking part for the first time in offering the Sacrifice and receiving Communion. This was the ancient Roman practice at the Easter Vigil, culminating in the first Easter Mass. The Epistle of this Mass (Col. 3:1-4) and the Tract, "Praise the Lord, all you peoples," thus assume their full significance in relation to baptism, as do all the Masses of Easter week.

After their first Communion the neophytes of ancient times were given a drink of milk and honey. Baptized, confirmed, and nourished by the Eucharist, initiated Christians are already in possession of the Promised Land "where milk and honey flow in abundance" (Exod. 3:8; Is. 7:22, etc.).

Article Three
BIBLICAL AND LITURGICAL SYNTHESIS

The meaning of Christian baptism is revealed to us by the liturgy and the Bible together. Starting from the signs of the water, the invocation of the Trinity, the anointing with the oil of struggle and with chrism, the white garments, the Fathers developed their teaching on baptism along the lines laid out by the New Testament itself.

I. WATER THAT WASHES, PURIFIES, HEALS

The meaning of water which comes immediately to mind is that of cleansing. Water washes our bodies, does away with dirt. The Bible makes us aware of the uncleanness of our hearts and eager for a water which can cleanse us of it:

> On that day there will be a spring opened up for the house of David and to those who dwell in Jerusalem, for sins and impurity (Zach. 13:1).

> I will pour out on you pure water and you shall be purified. I will cleanse you of all your stains and of all your idols, and I will give you a new heart (Ez. 36:25).

This desire for spiritual cleansing is associated particularly with the miracle of the healing of Naaman (4 Kings 5). He was a pagan, not a son of Abraham, and so Jesus interpreted Eliseus' mission to him as a sign of the calling of the Gentiles to salvation (Luke 4:27). He had been struck by leprosy, an illness which the Fathers frequently compared to sin. The simplicity of the remedy proposed by Eliseus scandalized him: why should he bathe in the Jordan when there were far more beautiful rivers in his own country? Yet he obeyed, and his "flesh became like that of a little child." It is easy to see why the Fathers delighted to comment on this episode in connection with baptism.[11]

Christian baptism is the answer to this prophetic expectation. Here is the water that cleanses us of sin. "I believe in one baptism for the remission of sins."

> Christ gave himself up for the Church, to make her holy by purifying her through the bath of water accompanied by a word, for he wished to present her to himself as wholly radiant, without spot or wrinkle or anything of the kind, but holy and immaculate (Eph. 5:26-27).

> Do you not know that the unjust will not inherit the kingdom of God? Do you deceive yourselves in this: neither the impure, nor idolators, nor adulterers, nor the depraved, nor men of evil life, nor thieves, nor the covetous, neither drunkards, or the evil-tongued or the greedy will inherit the kingdom of God. But you have been washed, you have been made holy (1 Cor. 6:9-11).

> Let us approach with a sincere heart, in the fullness of faith, our hearts cleansed from all stains of an evil conscience and our bodies washed with pure water (Heb. 10:22).

The healing effect of baptism is seen by the Fathers as symbolized particularly by Jesus' healing of the paralytic at the pool of Bethsaida (John 5:1-14).

[11] J. Daniélou, *The Bible and the Liturgy*, pp. 110-113 and 208-223, develops the thought of the Fathers on this and all the following biblical images of baptism.

This cleansing and healing effect is so essential to baptism that when St. Augustine set about proving the existence of original sin, he argued from the fact that the Church has always baptized little children as yet incapable of personal sins. Baptism is, therefore, the effect and the proof of God's mercy.

II. "THE SPIRIT OF GOD HOVERED OVER THE WATERS"
(Gen. 1:2)

These negative effects, purification and healing, as well as all the positive effects of baptism are due to the Holy Spirit, who acts by means of the water. From its very first lines the Bible associates the Spirit of God with this element; the Spirit is shown as hovering over the primeval waters. The Fathers also see Him as associated with this element in the image of the dove sent out by Noe to fly over the waters of the Flood, and the cloud accompanying the Hebrew people as they crossed the Red Sea and journeyed through the desert.

These various images sketch out the reality fulfilled in the New Testament: the Holy Spirit given in the baptism of water. John the Baptist said that Christ would baptize with the Holy Spirit (Matthew 3:11; Mark 1:8; Luke 3:16). John recognized Jesus when he saw the Spirit resting on Him in the form of a dove after the baptism in the Jordan (Luke 3:21-22, etc.). And Jesus Himself spoke of rebirth of water and the Spirit (John 3:5), and of the water that He would give to those who came to Him: "He said this of the Spirit whom they who believed in Him were to receive" (John 7:37-39).

The consecratory prayer of Easter night and the patristic commentaries might seem to imply that the Holy Spirit becomes present in a permanent way in the baptismal water. But what they are bringing out is rather the fact that it is truly the Spirit who acts, who is sent and given in Christian baptism. Baptism, receiving its efficacy from the passion of Christ, makes the Christian a "temple of the Holy Spirit" (1 Cor. 3:16, etc.).

> He has saved us by the bath of rebirth and renewal in the Holy Spirit. And this Spirit he has poured out on us in abundance through Jesus Christ our Savior (Tit. 3:5-6).

III. WATER, THE ENVIRONMENT THAT BRINGS FORTH LIFE

God said, "Let the waters swarm with a swarm of living creatures" (Gen. 1:20). In the vision of the sacred writer, life began in the waters, or, rather, water produced life at God's command. Modern science seems to echo this biblical idea. In any case, the Fathers and the liturgy see it as illustrating the fact that in the water of baptism life is received, a birth produced.

> We are little fish, and we are born in the water following after our Fish, Christ Jesus. It is only by remaining in the water that we are saved (Tertullian, *On Baptism*, 1:3).

This apparently strange sentence corresponds to the imagery of the Roman catacombs. It is one way of illustrating the statement in St. John's Gospel that we must be born anew to enter the kingdom of heaven. The baptismal pool is, as it were, the maternal womb of the Church from which are born the children of God.[12]

> In truth, in very truth, I tell you, unless he be born from on high, no man can see the kingdom of God. Nicodemus said to him: How can a man be born, once he is old? Can he enter his mother's womb again and be born? Jesus answered: In truth, in very truth, I tell you unless he be born of water and the Spirit, no man can enter into the kingdom of God. What is born of the flesh is flesh, what is born of the Spirit is spirit (John 3:3-6).

When the Christian comes out of the baptismal water, therefore, he is a "new creation" (2 Cor. 5:17). However old he may be physically, he is now new-born.

> As new-born children, crave pure spiritual milk, that by it you may grow to salvation; if, indeed, you have tasted how good is the Lord (1 Peter 2:2-3).

Begotten by God, the baptized person can now in full truth say "Our Father." He is truly a son of God (Rom. 8:15; Gal. 4:5; Eph. 1:5; 2 Peter 1:4).

IV. THE FOUR RIVERS OF PARADISE

Man was driven out of paradise by sin; he re-enters it by baptism. "You are outside of paradise, O catechumen, you share the exile of Adam our first father. Now the door opens. Enter from whence you came out and do not delay," writes St. Gregory of Nyssa (PG XLVI, 417c. See also 420c and 600a).

The book of Genesis speaks of the river that flowed from paradise and divided into four streams (2:8-17). The Fathers therefore see the baptismal water as the river of the new paradise.[13]

---

[12] The Fathers, St. Augustine in particular, and St. Thomas after them, insist on this image (*Summa* III, 67, 4). Modern psychology emphasizes its echo in the depths of the psyche.

[13] See especially Hippolytus of Rome, *Commentary on Daniel* 1:17.

This implies that since sin is destroyed in baptism, the consequences of sin must also disappear. The Christian is to regain original integrity, remake the shattered unity within himself, recover intimacy with God. The new economy is under the sign of Christ who suffered and died; consequently this integrity must be laboriously reconquered by the Christian and only completely attained in the resurrection. Nevertheless all this is already mysteriously given to him in baptism.

For the Fathers this restoration was indicated by the baptismal nakedness. "How wonderful!" says St. Cyril of Jerusalem. "You were naked before the eyes of all without feeling any shame. This is because you now carry within you the image of the first Adam who was naked in paradise without feeling any shame" (PG 33, 1080a).

The baptismal return to paradise is, therefore, the sign of the complete victory of Christ. And it is also the starting-point of the Christian spiritual life, for what has been done still remains to be done. The means of regaining the paradisal familiarity with God is "the restoration of man's primitive state as image of God. We must become what the first man was by retracing the stages by which we went out of paradise" (St. Gregory of Nyssa. Cf. *Summa* III, 64, 2).

V. THE WATER OF THE FLOOD: BAPTISM AND JUDGMENT

The relationship between the water of baptism and the water of the Flood is indicated in St. Peter's first Epistle (3:18-22):

> Christ himself died once for sins, the Just for the unjust, that he might bring us to God. Put to death in the flesh, he was made alive in the spirit, in which he also went to preach to the spirits in prison, to those who formerly had refused to believe, when the patience of God had waited, in the days when Noe was building the ark in which a small number of persons, eight in all, were saved through water. What corresponds to this (its antitype) is baptism, which now saves you, and this is not the taking away of bodily stain, but the pledging to God of a good conscience through the resurrection of Jesus Christ, he who, having gone on to heaven, is at the right hand of God, angels, dominions and powers being made subject to him.

This passage is now generally considered obscure, but many of the Fathers commented on it in connection with the eschatological character of Christian baptism. The waters of the Flood carried out God's judgment by destroying sinful mankind (Gen. 7:6), and brought salvation to the just man, Noe, who was spared to become the firstborn of the new race and the beneficiary of a covenant with God (Gen. 9:8-17). Like the Flood, the work of Christ brings both judgment and salvation. The world is already judged, the day of the Lord is coming (Matthew 24:37-42; 2 Peter 2:4-10; 3:3-10). And it is baptism which causes us to enter both into the economy of God's mercy that saves us by means of water and into the eschatological victory of Christ over iniquity and the demon.[14]

This aspect is brought out in the final exorcisms preceding baptism.

> Know well, Satan, that you must undergo the penalty, undergo your torments, and that the day of your judgment is approaching, the day of eternal punishment, the day on which you will go into the fire and in which the eternal death prepared for you and your angels will strike you.

VI. THE WATER OF THE RED SEA: BAPTISM AS THE PASCH OF THE CHRISTIAN

By far the most important theme is that of baptism as the passage of the Red Sea, the new Exodus. It is developed by all the Fathers and presented in the liturgy of the Easter Vigil along the lines laid out in the New Testament in St. John's Gospel, in the First Epistle of St. Peter and especially in the First Epistle to the Corinthians.

> Our fathers were all baptized in Moses in the cloud and in the sea, all ate the same spiritual food and all drank the same spiritual drink, for they drank from the spiritual rock which accompanied them and this rock was Christ. Yet with most of them God was not pleased, for their bodies were strewn over the desert (10:1-5)[15]

To understand the thought presented by the Apostle in such a condensed form, we need to realize that it is the mystery of Christ's exodus, His passage from this world to the Father, which associates the Exodus with Christian baptism.

1. The crossing of the Red Sea, the deliverance of God's people.

Pursued by Pharaoh's armies, the Hebrews crossed the Red Sea dryshod. Here again, water was the instrument of God's judgment, saving the Hebrews and destroying the Egyptians. This event was decisive in the existence of the People of God. The Hebrews were delivered from slavery to idolators, from oppression, from forced labor and ill-treatment. They journeyed by night, but God was their light and guide, under the sign of the cloud. God made a covenant with them: "You will be my people." He led them toward the land He had promised them. And on the

---

[14] "Baptism is a certain imitation of the judgment by means of water which causes us to participate mystically, but not corporally, in the destruction of iniquity. This is to be completed through the judgment by the fire of the resurrection, as baptism, which is supernatural conformation to Christ dead and risen, will be completed by the eschatological resurrection of the body" (J. Daniélou, "Déluge, baptême, judgement" in *Dieu vivant* 8, 1947, p. 105).

[15] See *New Testament Reading Guide,* #8, pp. 35-36.

way He fed them miraculously with manna in the desert and gave them drink from the water Moses brought from the rock.

2. The return from exile and the ransom of the captives. Many centuries after the original Exodus came the exile after the disasters of 721 and 600-587 B.C. This was the occasion for the proclamation of a new Exodus by the prophets. The captives will be delivered (Is. 43:14-21) and this will come about not by violence but by redemption.

> Thus says Yahweh: You have been sold for nothing and you will be ransomed without money. Thus says the Lord Yahweh: Of old my people went down into Egypt to dwell there, then Assur oppressed them with violence (Is. 52:3).

The psalms sing of this same ransoming, first in the night of hope and then in the joy of realization, after the return and the reconstruction. Yet this realization, like the first Exodus, was only a figure of the work of the Christ to come.

3. The Pasch of Christ. Christ's work is understood by the Fathers as the true and definitive Exodus of the People of God.

> At the Pasch the Jews escaped from slavery to Pharaoh. On the day of the crucifixion, we are freed from captivity to Satan. They immolated a lamb and were saved by its blood from the Destroyer. We are saved by the blood of the beloved Son from the works of corruption we have done. They had Moses for their guide. We have Jesus for our Head and Savior. Moses divided the sea for them and had them cross it. Our Savior opened hell and broke its gates asunder. When He went down into its depths, He opened them up and marked out the path for all those who come to believe in Him.[16]

This text by a fourth-century Persian, St. Aphraates, sums up the common teaching. It indicates the two paschal themes fulfilled in Christ's redeeming work, that of the immolated Lamb whose Blood saves us (1 Peter 1:17-19) and that of the crossing of the Red Sea. This second aspect is fulfilled in Jesus' going from this world to His Father, through His death, His descent into hell, His resurrection and ascension (John 13:1; cf. 5:24; 7:3, 14).

Christ's descent into hell, an article of the Creed, is being reemphasized in our times, for it is the focal point in Christ's victory. He descended into the abyss of death (the "Hades" of the Greek poets, and of the Septuagint and the New Testament) to give decisive battle to Satan, to conquer death and deliver the just from their bonds (1 Peter 3:19). Victorious in this struggle, He rose again on the third day, drawing after Him in His

[16] Quoted in J. Daniélou, *The Bible and the Liturgy*, p. 94.

triumph all those who were prisoners of death. "Awake, O you that sleep! Arise from the dead and Christ will enlighten you" (Eph. 5:14).[17]

4. Baptism, the Pasch of the Christian. As the Hebrews were saved from their slavery in Egypt by crossing the Red Sea, so the Christian is saved from slavery to sin and death by going through the baptismal water to become a member of the new people of God, enter into the New Covenant, and begin his journey toward the Promised Land.

But all this is a reality only by virtue of Christ's Pasch to which baptism mysteriously unites him. The water of baptism has the efficacy of the Blood of Christ. The descent into the baptismal pool, the triple immersion and the coming up out of the water signify that the Christian dies with Christ, with Him is buried and goes down into the depths, and with Him rises again on the third day. The passion of Christ is operative in baptism because it is here represented as in a symbol, according to the expression of St. Thomas (*Summa* III, 66, 12). Christ Himself spoke of a bath, a baptism, in connection with His death (Mark 10:38-39).

All this is true, obviously, whether baptism is administered by immersion or by one of the other methods sanctioned by the Church. Actual immersion is not essential for the validity of baptism, as is indicated both by the practice of the Church and the teaching of theologians (*Summa* III, 66, 7). Every Christian must take literally the statements of St. Paul:

> Do you not know that, baptized in Christ Jesus, it is in his death that all of us have been baptized? We have therefore been buried with him through baptism in death, so that, as Christ has been raised from the dead by the glory of the Father, we also should lead a new life (Rom. 6:3-4).

> Buried with him in baptism, you are also risen with him, because you have believed in the power of God that raised him from the dead (Col. 2:12).

> Now that you are risen with Christ, seek the things that are above, where Christ is seated at the right hand of God. Think of the things that are above, not those of earth. For you are dead, and your life is henceforth hidden with Christ in God. When Christ, who is your life, is manifested, then you too will be manifested with him full of glory (Col. 3:1-4).

Baptism, then, marks a complete break in a man's life, as complete a change as was brought about by the Exodus in the history of Israel. The "old man" is destroyed, the new man created according to God. Dead to the past, Christians have risen to a new life (Rom. 6:19-21; Eph. 4:23-28).

---

[17] See C. Bouman, "He Descended into Hell," *Worship*, 33 (1959), pp. 194-203; H. U. von Balthaser, *Science, Religion and Christianity*, pp. 129-135; E. Biser, "He Descended into Hell," *Theology Digest*, 8 (1960); Damasus Winzen, *The Great Sabbath Rest*.

Easter Vigil = Bapt. oriented

In this light, it is easy to understand why the glories of Christian baptism are proclaimed during the Easter Vigil, why the Vigil should include the actual administration of baptism whenever possible, and why we renew our baptismal promises before taking part in the Vigil Mass, the first Mass of Easter.

VII. THE WATER OF THE JORDAN

In the history of Israel, the crossing of the river Jordan completed the crossing of the Red Sea because it marked the entry of the People of God into the Promised Land (Jos. 3–4; cf. Pss. 113:3-6; 65:6; 73:13-15). So baptism is compared also to the crossing of the Jordan, since it puts us in possession of the true Promised Land, or at least gives us a pledge of it since it gives access to the Eucharist.

This first association of the river Jordan with baptism introduces us to a far greater mystery. Christ went into the water of the Jordan to receive John's baptism, an event so decisive that it has been considered by theologians to constitute the institution of Christian baptism (*Summa* III, 66, 2 and 10). For the source of our baptism is Christ's passion and resurrection, and the event at the Jordan was precisely the prefiguration of Christ's redeeming death.

The sign of the baptismal bath is, therefore, directly connected with Jesus' own pasch. He Himself referred to His future passion as a baptism (Mark 10:39). He received from John a baptism of penance not meant for Him since He was without sin (Matthew 3:13-15), but which was accepted because He bore the sins of the world (John 1:29). When He came out of the water, the heavens opened, the voice of the Father was heard and the Spirit was given; the messianic realities of Christ's resurrection were already inaugurated.

Christ's baptism in the Jordan is, then, the exemplary cause of our baptism and confirmation, and the Fathers delight in commenting on it as such. This is the reason why in the Eastern rites the consecration of the baptismal water takes place on the feast of the Epiphany, the day on which they celebrate Jesus' baptism.[18]

VIII. BAPTISM AS ENLIGHTENMENT

Christ's healing of the man born blind (John 9:1-38) links together the idea of the healing water of baptism with that of baptism as giving sight, true enlightenment ("I went, I washed, and now I see"). Christ works the same miracle for the baptized person as He did for the man

---

[18] In the Roman rite this feast celebrates three "ephiphanies" or manifestations of Christ to the world—the adoration of the Magi, the baptism in the Jordan, the wedding at Cana—but stresses the first on the feast itself and the second on January 13.

born blind. For after He had opened the man's physical eyes to the light of day, He opened the eyes of his soul to the light of faith.

> Jesus met him and said to him, "Do you believe in the Son of man?" He answered, "Who is he, Lord, that I may believe in him?" Jesus said to him, "You see him, it is he who is speaking with you." Then he said, "I believe, Lord," and he prostrated himself before him.

The enlightenment of the baptized, then, consists in faith. Although an adult candidate receives the message of faith before his baptism and would not be given the sacrament unless he had previously indicated by his life as a catechumen that he had accepted the faith, baptism is strictly the sacrament of faith, according to the formula of theologians. Faith has not received the seal which authenticates it until baptism has been received.[19] Baptism itself, as was explained above, involves the proclamation of faith in the three divine Persons. And, through baptism these Persons in whom we have been given the faith to believe come to dwell in our souls as in a temple.

The lighted candle given to the newly-baptized at the end of the ceremonies brings out this aspect of baptism as enlightenment. "Rise from among the dead and Christ will enlighten you" (Eph. 5:14; cf. Heb. 6:4; 10:32). The light received at baptism is the light Christ came to radiate in the darkness (John 1:4-9), the wonderful light to which the Father calls us (I Peter 2:9), the light praised in the Easter *Exsultet*. This lighted candle also emphasizes the eschatological orientation of baptism, connected with the parable of the ten virgins (Matthew 25:1-7). The Christian himself is to radiate Christ's light as he awaits His return. *"Be my Witnesses"*

IX. BAPTISM AS GIVING A SHARE IN CHRIST'S ROYAL PRIESTHOOD

The anointing of the newly baptized with Chrism immediately after the actual administration of baptism presents one of the great biblical themes, a theme developed at length in the consecratory preface of the Chrism Mass on Holy Thursday.

1. Jesus as the Christ, God's anointed. In the Old Testament, when a prophet poured oil in God's name on the head of a man God had chosen, this man became God's anointed. He was now a sacred personage on whom no one might lay hands, even if he was unfaithful to his mission (1 Sam. 9:26; 10:8; 16:1-3; 24:7; 26:9-23; 2 Sam. 1:14-16, etc.). This anointing was given to the kings of Israel: Saul, David, Solomon (1 Kings 1:39, Jehu (2 Kings 9:6), etc. The psalms frequently apply the title

---

[19] Faith is ordered to the sacrament which comes to sanction it and to consecrate it in a "corporeal" way. Above all, by the gift of grace baptism unites us with Him whom faith causes us to glimpse. Cf. *Summa III*, 65, 5.

"the Anointed" to David and his dynasty (Pss. 19:7; 27:8, etc.). But David and the royal house before the exile were only the ancestors and figures of the King to come. He was to be the Anointed of Yahweh, the Messiah, the Christ (the three terms are identical) in a special and supreme sense.

To say that Jesus is "the Christ," therefore, is to say that He has received the anointing which makes Him this long-awaited King, the founder of the kingdom of God. To Him applies full the phrase of Psalm 44: "God, your God, has anointed you with an oil of gladness." This royal anointing of Jesus was manifested by the resurrection and is brought out repeatedly in the apostles' preaching (Acts 2:36; 3:20; 4:26-27).

In the Old Testament an anointing was also given by God's command to the high priest and to other priests (Exod. 30:22-38). Jesus received this anointing as the unique High Priest of the New Law (Heb. 2:17-18 and 3 —10). The Fathers dwell particularly on this anointing, which is nothing other than the incarnation itself. The Divine Person of the Word consecrated Christ's human nature.[20]

Finally, Christ received still another anointing, that of Prophet, visibly manifested at His baptism, which we will discuss in connection with confirmation.

2. The Christian as identified with Christ through baptism.   Baptism confers on the Christian a resemblance to, an identification with Christ. This is expressed in various ways by St. Paul and St. John; all tradition witnesses to its being a real identification in the strongest sense of the term.

> You are all sons of God by faith in Christ Jesus. For, baptized in Christ, you have all put on Christ. . . . But if you are Christ's, then you are the descendants of Abraham, heirs according to the promises (Gal. 3:26,29).

> Those whom he chose in advance, God has also predestined to reproduce the image of his Son, so that he may be the first-born among a multitude of brothers . . . (Rom. 8:29).

> To all those who have received him, he has given power to become children of God (John 1:12).

The Christian is, therefore, another Christ, as St. Augustine puts it. He participates in Jesus' royal and priestly anointing.[21] Baptism marks him with an indelible sign, the "character," and the nature of this character is to give the faithful a share in Christ's priesthood. Baptism itself, which confers this spiritual anointing, and the external anointing which is

[20] See Claude Peifer, "Anointing in the Old Testament"; "Jesus the Anointed of Israel"; "The Anointing of the Christian," in *Worship* 35 (1961), pp. 577-586; 36 (1962), pp. 26-35; pp. 234-242.

[21] See, for example, the *Apostolic Constitutions* of Hippolytus III,16,3.

the sign of it are given to each person individually. But the faithful share in Christ's royal and priestly anointing by virtue of becoming, by baptism, members of a people of priests and kings, the Church.

3.. "A people of priests and kings." The Exodus from Egypt and the crossing of the Red Sea made a crowd of isolated slaves into a people, conscious of its unity and journeying together toward the Promised Land under the leadership of God and of Moses. By the covenant of Sinai this people became the People of God. "I will have you, says the Lord, as a kingdom of priests and a consecrated nation" (Exod. 19:6).

This royal and priestly character of the People of God belongs in a far more perfect way to the new Israel, the Church.

> You are a chosen race, a royal priesthood, a holy nation, a purchased people, to proclaim the praises of him who has called you out of darkness into his wonderful light, you who were not a people and are now the People of God (1 Peter 2:9-10).

> You are worthy to take the book and open its seals, for you were slain and you redeemed for God, at the price of your blood, men of every tribe and language, people and nation. You made of them, for our God, a kingdom of priests ruling over the earth (Apoc. 5:9-10).

Baptism makes us members of this holy people and therefore children of God, sharing in Christ's own royal and priestly dignity. As Christians we are fused into a unity that transcends all human divisions and inequalities; we become one in Christ (Gal. 3:28; 1 Cor. 12:13; Eph. 4:3-5).

X. BAPTISM AS COMMITMENT TO THE CHRISTIAN COMBAT

As we said earlier, the pre-baptismal exorcisms and anointing with oil both indicate the struggle against evil to which baptism commits us. The Church inaugurates this struggle for us by the exorcisms; she prepares us to take our part in it during the catechumenate, a preparation indicated by the anointing, like that of athletes, given just before baptism. The Fathers saw the immersion in the baptismal water as signifying this struggle which we undertake with Christ and in His strength, not our own. Here water is seen as the home of the biblical sea-monsters, Dragon or Leviathan, and so symbolic of the lower depths to which Christ descended in His redeeming death to give battle to the demon. At baptism the Christian goes down into these depths with Him and is victorious in virtue of His victory.

Yet this struggle against evil will continue all our lives and reach its climax at the moment of death.[22] Everything is already gained and yet

[22] See Louis Bouyer, *Introduction to Spirituality*, pp. 166ff.

is still to be accomplished. St. Paul, who stresses the connection between baptism and heaven so strongly as to say that we are "already glorified" (Rom. 8:30), nonetheless urges us to mistrust ourselves. In the desert, the place of temptation, the Israelites fell away in spite of all the wonderful works of God in their behalf. The same thing can happen to the Christian (1 Cor. 10). Paul also compares himself to an athlete aiming at victory; he describes the arms with which the Christian should be equipped (Eph. 6: 10-20).

Similarly during Lent the liturgy presents the Gospel warning of Luke 11:14-28. The demon who has been driven out will come back with "seven more evil spirits." The Easter Vigil includes the imprecations of Moses from Deut. 31:22-30, and the Masses of Easter week and the Easter season frequently ask God's aid that Christians may live up to their baptismal vocation.[23]

XI. BAPTISM AS SHARING IN CHRIST'S VICTORY

The clothing of the newly-baptized in a white garment indicates the complementary aspect, the eschatological character of baptism. Although everything is still to be done, it is already mysteriously accomplished. Our life is in heaven (Phil. 3:20). We are risen with Christ (Col. 3:1-4), the inheritance of the Promised Land is ours. In the Bible, shining whiteness is the very vesture of God (Dan. 7:9) and also of those who, living in His presence, are already in glory: the angels (Mark 16:5; Matthew 28:3; Acts 1:10), the twenty-four "ancients" (Apoc. 4:4), the innumerable multitude of the elect (Apoc. 7:9, 13). At Christ's transfiguration, "His garments became shining, all white, as no fuller on earth could make white" (Mark 9:3; cf. Matthew 17:2; Luke 9:29).

This is also the wedding garment necessary for admittance to the banquet of the Father (Matthew 22:11-12), an eschatological orientation connected with the Eucharist.

Article Four
THEOLOGICAL CLARIFICATIONS

I. THE EFFECTS OF BAPTISM: THE CHARACTER AND GRACE

From the scriptural data provided by the Church's liturgical and catechetical tradition and her practice, theologians have further clarified

---

[23] The Fathers discuss this aspect of continual struggle, continual "amendment of life" in their baptismal catecheses, since baptism commits us to it and enables us to carry it on not as isolated fighters but as members of the Church, and not in our own strength, but in that of Christ. But, under modern conditions, it seems better to discuss it in more detail in connection with the sacrament of penance.

the effects of baptism in answer to the difficulties that have arisen through the centuries.

Baptism cannot be repeated when it has been validly received (*Denz.* 867). On this point the teaching and the discipline of the Church have been fixed since the third century. This is because baptism imprints on the soul an ineffaceable character (*res et sacramentum*). It marks a man with the sign of his membership in the Church, designates him to divine worship, enables him to receive the other sacraments. This is why baptism is called "the door to the sacraments." The character is acquired even by a person who receives baptism with bad dispositions; it remains in the sinner and the apostate.

Unless the person receiving baptism has set up an obstacle by his lack of the necessary dispositions, this character in turn produces the grace of new birth (*res*). The Holy Spirit is given to the baptized person (Rom. 8:9). He brings the remission of all sins,[24] both personal sins and original sin, and this remission is so complete that it leaves none of the penalties due to sin. Unlike the forgiveness of sins in the sacrament of penance, this baptismal remission requires no work of reparation or satisfaction. The coming of the Holy Spirit makes the baptized person a child of God (Rom. 8:14-16; Gal. 4:6), a member of the Church and of Christ (1 Cor. 6:17, Eph. 3:17; 1 Cor. 12:13; Eph. 2:16, 18; 4:4). His coming brings the love of God (Rom. 5:5ff.); it is the pledge and principle of our future resurrection (Rom. 8:11) and of our heritage of heaven (Rom. 8:17).

This is what the Council of Trent calls "justification" (Sess. 7), and what modern writers call "sanctifying grace". But its true nature as the grace of baptism, as St. Paul saw it, must always be kept in mind, and all instruction on grace should take baptism as its starting-point.

When validly received baptism has not produced its effect of grace due to the subject's lack of the necessary dispositions, grace is given by means of the baptismal character when, with the gaining of these dispositions, the sacrament "revives" (*Summa* III, 69, 9-10).

II. THE BAPTISMAL "PROMISES"

When we are baptized, we are brought into the mystery of Christ, engaged in it, committed to it. We enter into it as into a life that draws us into its own dynamic flow.

> It was not you who chose me; it is I who have chosen you and have appointed you to go out to bear fruit, a fruit that remains (John 15:16).

> Let us love, since he has first loved us (1 John 4:19).

---

[24] "He is Himself the remission of all sins" (Postcommunion, Pentecost Tuesday). This phrase is inspired by St. Peter's discourse in Acts 2:38 and expresses the unanimous consensus of tradition.

This commitment is expressed by the renunciation of Satan and, even more, by the profession of faith. To say "I do believe" is not simply to express our recognition of the truth of the word received from the Church. This word is the revelation of the three divine Persons. To believe in Them implies putting all our hope in Them, loving Them, giving ourselves to Them without knowing precisely what will be asked of us—even if this profession of faith should lead to martyrdom.

Consequently, it is impossible to distinguish "profession of faith" from "baptismal commitment"—they are the same thing. The terms "baptismal promises" or "vows" are used, but not in the strict and limited sense of either term. In fact, the commitment involved in baptism is carefully distinguished from promises or vows as such by theologians. For it cannot be precisely defined, nor does violating it constitute a perjury. Its import is on a plane other than that of law. It is a seed to be developed, it is the flowering of the liberty of God's sons, a privilege, not a limitation of freedom. This is why children take on this commitment when they are baptized even though they cannot as yet personally assent to it. This is also why it does not depend on later ratification or acceptance and is not a contract that can be cancelled.[25]

III. CONDITIONS FOR THE BAPTISM OF ADULTS

To receive valid baptism (i.e., to receive the baptismal character), an adult (i.e., someone having the age and the use of reason) must, obviously, intend to receive the sacrament. Nobody can be baptized by force. And nobody truly receives the sacrament who, for one or another reason, pretends to desire baptism. The period of probation provided by the catechumenate has as one of its purposes to eliminate such cases of feigned intention which might harm the Church.

If baptism is to produce its normal fruits of regeneration, the candidate must have the required dispositions. First, he must have received the faith of the Church and adhere to it. ("What is to prevent my being baptized?" asked the Ethiopian eunuch. "If you believe with all your heart, it is allowed," answered Philip.) This is why instruction is such an important part of the preparation for baptism.

Secondly, the candidate must regret his past sins and amend his life. The radical change to be effected interiorly by the sacrament must be accepted and manifested exteriorly. The book of Jonas occupies an important place in the Fathers' catecheses and in ancient Christian iconography because the Ninivites completely changed their sinful ways and did penance at Jonas' preaching.

[25]See Cyprian Vagaggini, *Theological Dimensions of the Liturgy*, p. 45; Godfrey Diekmann, "The Church Year in Action" in *Come Let Us Worship;* P. Nearing, "Making All Things New" in *The New Man in Christ,* PNLW (1948), pp. 110-118.

The catechumenate, therefore, has as its purposes: to insure the complete sincerity of the candidate, to instruct him in the faith, and to help him cultivate the required dispositions. Therefore, today as in ancient times, the Church requires a protracted period of preparation before an adult may be baptized.

IV. THE BAPTISM OF CHILDREN

"Children" or "infants" here include all those who have not effectively attained the use of reason, whatever their age may be. The question of the legitimacy of baptizing children arose in the early centuries. How can people be baptized who have not asked for baptism, who are incapable of understanding the message of revelation, who cannot profess their faith? And from what sin do they need to be purified?

The Church has in fact always baptized infants at the same time as adults. When Paul and Silas baptized the jailer, the Acts say that "all his family" were baptized at the same time (16:33). The *Apostolic Tradition* of Hippolytus clearly witnesses to the practice around the year 200 of baptizing infants. St. Augustine draws from the universal practice of the Church his argument against the Pelagians to prove that every child is born a sinner and that, since his parents cannot transmit spiritual life to him along with physical life, he must be purified of the sin by which we are all dead in Adam. The baptism of children is, then, a striking manifestation of the complete gratuity of the gift of God. No previous initiative, no conditions are required on their part. They receive faith together with baptism.

What children cannot do for themselves, the Church supplies for them:

> Mother Church lends to children her maternal mouth so that they may drink of the holy Mysteries, since they cannot yet believe unto justice with their own heart, nor confess the faith for salvation with their own mouth (St. Augustine, *On the Punishment of Sin*, I, 25).

> To little children Mother Church lends the feet of others that they may come, the heart of others that they may believe, the tongue of others that they may affirm their faith (St. Augustine, *Sermon* 176,2).

These "others" are the godparents, who represent the Church, not the parents of the child.

However, except when a child is at the point of death, the Church does not allow him to be baptized against the will of his parents. St. Thomas says: "To baptize children against their parents' will would be as contrary to natural law as to baptize an adult enjoying the use of reason against his will" (*Summa* III, 68, 10). And even when unbelieving parents are willing to have their children baptized, this must not be done without the assurance that "they will not be exposed to the danger of lapsing into unbelief because of a natural affection for their parents" (*ibid.*, and Can. 750).

Christians should have their children baptized as soon as possible after birth. This obligation is stated in Canon Law (Can. 770) and further clarified according to local customs. It is not due directly to fear lest children die without baptism, but rather indicates the viewpoint of Christian faith. Parents ought to be in haste to have their children receive the supernatural life which they themselves cannot transmit to them. The prolonged delay of baptism is an indication of the dechristianization of a country or an environment.

V. MINISTER AND GODPARENTS

The bishop is, supremely, the minister of baptism, although he usually delegates its administration to the pastor of the candidate, who in turn may delegate it to another priest or to a deacon (Can. 744, 738-741).

In case of danger of death, baptism can be conferred by anyone—one of the faithful, a schismatic, a heretic or even a non-Christian—provided that he carries out the rite exactly and has the intention of "doing what the Church does."[26]

These conditions of carrying out the rite exactly and intending to do what the Church does are, obviously, fulfilled in the baptisms conferred in schismatical Churches; their baptism is therefore valid. The same thing is true of heretical Churches, when the minister carries out the rite exactly and intends to baptize in the sense in which the Church understands baptism. Protestants differ widely here, some conferring baptism merely as an external sign of repentance and conversion, rather like the baptism of John the Baptist. This is why the Church administers conditional baptism ("If you have not been baptized, I baptize you . . .") to converts from some forms of Protestantism.

The godparents (only one is required) have an important liturgical function as representatives of the Church. In the baptism of adults, they carry out certain of the acts of exorcism. In the baptism of children, they answer in the child's name. They also have a wider charge: in the case of an adult, of guaranteeing the sincerity of his dispositions; in the case of a child, of being responsible, together with the parents, for his religious formation. Godparents, therefore, should be selected with reference to these roles, not for family or social reasons, a fact which explains why certain possible godparents are excluded by Church law (Can. 762-769).

---

[26] The person baptizing must pour natural water on the forehead of the subject while saying, "I baptize you in the name of the Father and of the Son and of the Holy Spirit," with the intention of doing what the Church does. This suffices for valid baptism. It is good, if possible, to observe the traditional prescription of the Roman Church of pouring the water three times.

VI. THE NECESSITY FOR BAPTISM AND SUBSTITUTES FOR IT

The Gospels present baptism as the necessary means of salvation. "He who believes and is baptized will be saved; he who does not believe will be condemned" (Mark 16:16): "Unless a man be born of water and the Spirit, he cannot enter into the kingdom of God" (John 3:5).

Yet God's mercy is not bound by the sacraments. This is why the Church has always recognized the existence of substitutes for baptism: martyrdom or "the baptism of blood" (even that of the Holy Innocents), and desire for baptism on condition that this includes perfect charity (cf. *Denz.* 796).

We should avoid trying to oversimplify the complex question of the salvation of unbelievers and the still more delicate one of children who die without baptism. Theologians have not arrived at any unanimity on these matters. In religious instruction we should limit ourselves to these two essential statements: on the one hand, faith and baptism are necessary for salvation; on the other, "God wills that all men be saved and come to the knowledge of the truth" (1 Tim. 2:4).[27]

Article Five

BAPTISMAL SPIRITUALITY

I. THE BASIS OF CHRISTIAN LIVING

In setting out the demands and opportunities of the Christian life, St. Paul and St. Peter base their presentation on what has been done for the Christian at his baptism. The basic attitude of the Christian is to be thanksgiving and praise, and, as the Apocalypse shows, this thanksgiving will continue in heaven. Baptism is the visible pledge of our vocation, the realization in time of the eternal prevision of God in our regard. It gives the pledge of future life, it assures our hope.

The presence of the Holy Spirit within us as in His temple should rule our conduct. The break effected by baptism should be definitive. It has made us dead to our sins, and so day by day we should die more completely to our tendencies to evil. The Christ whom we have "put on" should manifest Himself more and more clearly in our mortal flesh, by a

---

[27] See Vincent Wilkin, S. J., *From Limbo to Heaven;* W. Van Roo, "Infants Dying without Baptism. A Survey of Recent Literature and Determination of the State of the Question," in *Gregorianum* 25 (1954), pp. 406-473; P. Gumpel, "Unbaptized infants—May They Be Saved?" in *Downside Review* 72 (1954), pp. 317-346; M. Eminyan, *The Theology of Salvation.*

more and more complete identification of our reactions, our sufferings, our actions with those of Christ. We are already established in heaven where Christ is seated at the right hand of the Father; our tastes and our pursuits, therefore, should never have the things of earth as their final aim, but those of heaven. Fused together by the bond of one faith, one baptism and one Eucharist, we all form but one body. Fraternal charity is required by the grace of baptism. Moreover, as baptized Christians we are to witness to Christ's love; through observing our good works, pagans should come to "glorify God in the day of visitation" (1 Peter 2:12).

The Christian spiritual life, then, springs from the concrete sacramental fact of baptism and develops along the lines of the paschal mystery. Here it finds its true orientation and outlook. All through our lives we live more and more fully the mystery of Christ and of our own initiation. We continue the pilgrimage in faith—the exodus inaugurated by Abraham, carried out by the People of God, fulfilled in Christ—as we look forward to the blessed parousia. Christ will come in glory to bring us into the Promised Land. Death itself is simply the "fulfillment of our baptism," as an ancient inscription admirably expresses it.[28]

II. BAPTISM AND THE PERFECT LIFE

Among the baptized, some are called by the Lord to carry out the counsels of the Gospel to the letter, and to establish themselves in the heavenly state here below by the renunciation of marriage and the good things of earth, and by life in community. It is important to stress, with St. Paul, the eschatological significance of the monastic life and, in due proportion, of the various forms of the "religious life."

> The time is short. Henceforth let those who have wives be as if they had them not; those who weep, as if not weeping; those who rejoice, as not rejoicing; those who buy, as not possessing; and those who use the world, as if they did not use it, for the figure of this world is passing away (1 Cor. 7:29-31).

This "perfect life" is founded on baptism. When a Christian undertakes it, he does so as a trustful response to a divine call which has already taken the initiative by calling him to faith and baptism. The renunciations he imposes on himself are to help him to carry out more speedily and effectively the baptismal *metanoia*, "change of heart." Even though he is already converted to the faith, he vows *"conversio morum,"* the changing of his way of life, his habits. As the neophyte is clothed with a white garment, the monk is clothed with the monastic habit to signify his special dedication to the Christian work of "putting on Christ."[29]

[28] See bibliography for Chapter 7, C, p. 313.

[29] See bibliography for Chapter 7, B, p. 314.

Article Six
REMINDERS OF BAPTISM

The liturgy includes frequent reminders of baptism as the decisive event of our life, and the foundation of both the Eucharistic assembly and of personal spirituality.

1. The anniversary of baptism. The Christians of ancient times took care to celebrate the anniversary of their baptism on the exact date of its occurence; there was even a special Mass formulary for this celebration. But they relived their baptism still more each year by taking part in the exercises of Lent and by celebrating the holy Easter night.

In our times it is again becoming customary to celebrate the anniversary of baptism. But of even greater importance is the fact that, thanks to the renewal of the Easter Vigil, Lent has regained its traditional meaning as a period of strenuous preparation for the renewal of the grace of baptism, leading up to the public renewal of our baptismal commitments at the Vigil before taking part in the first Mass of Easter. Thus Christians have regained the means of liturgically celebrating the anniversary of their baptism together with the whole Church.

2. Easter week. In ancient Rome the newly baptized assembled in a different basilica each day of Easter week to receive instruction on the sacraments they had just received. The texts of the Masses of Easter week proclaim the privileges and demands of the Christian life in relation to the mystery of Christ's pasch and our baptism. We should make every effort to take part in these Masses in order to rejoice with our risen Lord and to deepen our appreciation of the life He gives us in the Church.

3. The Sunday Asperges: use of holy water. Since Sunday is a weekly Easter,[30] Christians should call to mind on this day particularly the resurrection of Christ and their own baptism. The rite of sprinkling the congregation with holy water before the principal parish Mass is a reminder of baptism. The actions of taking holy water, particularly on entering the Church, and of making the sign of the Cross are also meant to remind us of our baptism.

4. The recommendation of the departing soul: Christian death. In the tradition of the Church and in the liturgy, the death of a Christian is presented as the fulfillment of baptism.[31]

[30] See in particular H. A. Reinhold, "The Christian Meaning of Sunday" in *The Sanctification of Sunday*, PNLW, 1949.

[31] See B. Ehmann, "Christian Death" in *Bible, Life and Worship* (PNLW) 1961, pp. 83-88; H.L. Duffy, "Death and Resurrection in Christ" in *The New Man in Christ* (PNLW) 1948, pp. 37-43.

At burials the prayer of the Church expresses the Christian's chief claim on God's mercy—the dead person has been baptized, received the faith from the Church, and been marked with the seal of the Trinity.[32]

Section Two

CONFIRMATION

Article One
THE CONNECTION BETWEEN
BAPTISM AND CONFIRMATION

A study of the liturgy and the discipline of the sacrament of confirmation makes it clear that this sacrament is closely related to baptism but distinct from it. Tradition unanimously states that confirmation "completes" or "perfects" baptism. The very name "confirmation," used for this second sacrament in the Latin Church since the fifth century (Council of Orange in 441, Can. 2), is related to the terminology used by the ancient liturgies in connection with the Eucharist. To give the species of wine to someone who had received the consecrated bread was also to "confirm," a term expressing fullness, completion.

The confirmed Christian, then, is "perfect" in the sense that he has attained, on the sacramental plane, the fullness of likeness to Christ proper to the Christian layman. Baptism caused him to be born, confirmation makes him adult, following the image of physical life which brings "a special perfection when a man arrives at the age of maturity and can carry out perfectly the acts of a man, as the Apostle says, 'When I became a man I put away the things of a child' " (Summa III, 72, 1).

The continuity of baptism and confirmation as administered in the liturgy of antiquity and of the Eastern rites today expresses the continuity of the spiritual work accomplished by these sacraments. As confirmation is administered in the West today, it gives a hierarchical stamp to the process of Christian initiation as begun by the priest and completed by the bishop.

These two sacraments, then, are complementary. But they are two different sacraments. The spiritual anointing received at baptism is not that received at confirmation. At baptism the Christian is marked with

[32] See J. Hofinger, Worship, the Life of the Missions, pp. 240-244.

the baptismal character, the indelible sign of Christ. He becomes another Christ, participating in His royal and priestly anointing. It is as a sign of this that the Roman rite has retained an anointing with chrism as part of the ritual of baptism, distinct from the anointing at confirmation. The character received at confirmation, as we shall see, configures us to Christ as Prophet and Witness, giving us a share in His prophetic anointing. The Fathers distinguish between the two by saying that Christ Himself received two different anointings, that of the incarnation and that which followed His baptism by John.[33]

Nor is the grace proper to baptism the same as that of confirmation. The Holy Spirit is given at baptism; without Him there would be no remission of sins and no grace. This gift is proper to this first sacrament which fulfills the requirements of "water and the Spirit." Then there is another giving of the Spirit at confirmation in view of our public mission as Christians to be witnesses and messengers of Christ.

In giving instruction on these two sacraments, therefore, we should be careful to indicate how confirmation completes and perfects baptism and yet is distinct from it (the Church has never considered confirmation a sacrament necessary for salvation with a necessity of means, Can. 787). We should also indicate how the process of Christian initiation leads up to and is completed by the Eucharist.

Article Two
THE SACRAMENTAL SIGN AND THE MINISTER

The rites following baptism in the early Roman Church are described in the *Apostolic Tradition* of Hippolytus, a Roman document dating from about the year 200.

> When he has come up out (of the water), (let each neophyte) be anointed by a priest with the oil that has been sanctified, with these words: I anoint you with holy oil in the name of Jesus Christ. Let them each dress themselves after being dried, then let them enter the church.
>
> Let the bishop, while laying his hand on them, pray: O Lord, who has rendered these worthy to merit the remission of sins by the bath of regeneration of the Holy Spirit, send down on them Your grace, so that they may serve You according to Your will, for to You is glory, to the Father and the Son with the Holy Spirit, in the holy Church, now and for the ages of ages. Amen.

[33] See the texts cited by Jean Daniélou, *The Bible and the Liturgy*, pp. 114-126.

Then, taking the sanctified oil with his hand and putting it on their
heads, let him say: I anoint you with holy oil, in the Lord, the Father
almighty, Christ Jesus, and the Holy Spirit.

And, having made the consignation (sign of the Cross) on their
forehead, let him give them a kiss, saying: The Lord be with you.
And let him who has been signed say: And with your spirit. Let him
do this for each person.

This ritual was also that of the early Church in Africa, as Tertullian indicates in various works (in particular *On the Resurrection* 8,3). And, in
its essentials, it has remained that of the Roman Church up to our own
times.

The present Latin rite, like that described by Hippolytus, includes two
anointings with chrism. The first is connected with baptism and is carried
out by the priest who administers baptism; the second is characteristic of
confirmation and is normally reserved to the bishop. This second anointing is accompanied by an imposition of hands and a consignation.

The imposition of hands is indicated as the essential action of the sacrament by the Code of Canon Law:

> The sacrament of confirmation is to be conferred by the imposition
> of the hand with the anointing of chrism on the forehead . . . (Can.
> 780).

The value of the consignation is indicated by the words accompanying the
action:

> N . . . , I sign you with the sign of the Cross and I confirm you with
> the chrism of salvation, in the name of the Father and of the Son and
> of the Holy Spirit.

Confirmation, then, includes three signs: imposition of the hand, anointing, consignation. The only difference from the ancient practice is that today these three signs are carried out simultaneously whereas formerly
they were successive.

These essential actions are preceded by a prayer, very similar to that
given by Hippolytus, which emphasizes the close bond between baptism
and confirmation. An imposition of hands over all the candidates together has been added and also a litany of the gifts of the Holy Spirit
(though these two ceremonies are not essential to the sacrament).

The rite concludes, as formerly, by a greeting which is a prayer for
the Lord's peace. This greeting indicates that the gesture it accompanies
is a substitute for the kiss of former times—a gesture of affection and not a
blow.[34]

[34] On the concluding prayer, see Article 3, p. 144. Each person being confirmed should
have a sponsor of the same sex, whom he has selected himself (if anyone has not done so,
the minister designates a sponsor) and who in theory should not be one of the person's
godparents, since the two sacraments are separate in their administration.

Two elements in the ritual just described appear in the Acts of the Apostles—the imposition of hands and the intervention of the highest degree of the hierarchy.

> Philip went into a town in Samaria and preached Christ. . . . When they had believed Philip who proclaimed to them the good news of the kingdom of God and of the name of Jesus Christ, they were baptized, both men and women. . . . Learning that Samaria had welcomed the word of God, the apostles who were at Jerusalem sent to them Peter and John. They therefore went down to the Samaritans and prayed for them so that the Holy Spirit would be given them. For he had not yet come down on any of them, they had only been baptized in the name of the Lord Jesus. Then Peter and John laid their hands upon them, and they received the Holy Spirit (Acts 8:5-17).

This event should be connected with that of Acts 19:1-7. The disciples of John the Baptist at Ephesus learned through Paul that they should receive a new baptism, that of Jesus:

> At these words, they had themselves baptized in the name of the Lord Jesus, and when Paul laid his hands upon them, the Holy Spirit came on them and they began to speak with tongues and to prophesy.

The Greek Fathers comment on these texts, but describe a rite shorter than that of Hippolytus, including only the anointing with chrism. Origen at Alexandria in the third century and St. Cyril of Alexandria[35] at the end of the fourth century consider the act of anointing as itself producing the effect attributed in the Acts to the imposition of hands, causing the Christian to participate in the outpouring of the Holy Spirit received by Jesus after His baptism.

The Eastern rites have generally abandoned the post-baptismal anointing, conferring only one anointing with chrism, that of confirmation. This is carried out by the priest who confirms immediately after baptism, instead of being reserved to the bishop as in the discipline of the Roman Church. (As we said earlier, this great diversity of practice with regard to this sacrament is one of the clearest proofs of the scope left by Christ to His Church in determining and using certain of the sacramental signs.)

In the West, confirmation has in principle been reserved to the bishop since ancient times. But exceptions are provided for, allowing priests to confirm either by a concession of the law or by a personal indult. For example, the decree *Spiritus sancti munera* of Sept. 14, 1946, grants pastors the faculty to confirm any of the faithful within their territory who are in grave danger of death. In doing so, these priests are the extrordinary min-

---

[35] Or his successor, John. The attribution of the *Mystagogic Catecheses* to St. Cyril himself is now disputed.

isters of the sacrament and use chrism consecrated by a bishop. Bishops alone are the ordinary ministers of confirmation (*Denz.* 967).

Article Three
THE EFFECTS OF CONFIRMATION

Only one method is valid in explaining the effects of confirmation and in distinguishing them from those of baptism: to seek an understanding of the sacramental signs and of the bond between the mysteries of Christ and the sacramental character in biblical and liturgical tradition.

I. THE TWO ANOINTINGS OF CHRIST: THE ANOINTING OF PROPHETS

The Fathers, especially the Greek and other Eastern Fathers, distinguish two anointings of Christ and two sendings of the Spirit down upon Him. The first is that of the incarnation. The Holy Spirit is the author of this mystery, as is proclaimed in the Gospel (Luke 1:35) and in the Creed. The second anointing is that manifested by the visible descent of the Holy Spirit in the form of a dove after Christ had received John's baptism (Luke 3:21-22).

This second anointing presents Christ to men as the Prophet of the New Law. It fulfills the prophecy of Isaias 61:1-2, quoted by Jesus Himself (Luke 4:16-21):

> The Spirit of the Lord is upon me because he has consecrated me by anointing. He has sent me to bring the good news to the poor, to announce deliverance to the captives and sight to the blind, to give freedom to the oppressed, to proclaim a year of the Lord's grace (*Septuagint version*).

In the Old Testament generally, the Spirit of God is always given in view of a public mission requiring strength and boldness, and, more widely, to confer on a man the function and the grace of prophecy. It is the Spirit who speaks by the prophets (Nicene Creed; Zach. 7:12).[36]

Confirmation, then, causes the Christian to participate in the prophetic mission of Christ. It reproduces in the baptized person what took place for Jesus when He came out of the water of the Jordan; the same anoint-

[36] See Louis Bouyer, *The Meaning of Sacred Scripture,* pp. 221-223.

ing, the same sending of the Holy Spirit, the same result—the coming of the Spirit. We find this stated by St. Hilary of Poitiers, St. Optatus, St. Athanasius, St. Cyril of Jerusalem, Theodore of Mopsuestia, St. Irenaeus, and St. Cyril of Alexandria. From this unanimity of tradition we conclude that the Holy Spirit is given a second time to the Christian in confirmation to make him a herald of the Gospel, a witness and messenger of Christ the Prophet.

II. THE FRAGRANCE OF THE GOSPEL

The same conclusion is drawn from the fact that it is not ordinary olive-oil which is used at confirmation, but aromatic oil. In preparing chrism, bishops of the Latin rite mingle the oil with balm from Arabia or San Salvador; the patriarchs of the Eastern rites include a great variety of essences. In the Fathers' instructions on confirmation, this perfume signifies the fulfillment in the Christian of St. Paul's words about the preachers of the Gospel:

> Thanks be to God who, in Christ, leads us in his triumph and who, through us, spreads abroad in every place the aroma of His knowledge. . . . For we are, for God, the fragrance of Christ among those who are saved and among those who are lost: to the former, a vital, life-giving fragrance; to the latter, a deathly, deadly odor. Who, then, is equal to such a task? We are not, indeed, like so many who traffic in the word of God. No, it is as sincere men, as envoys of God, that, before God, we speak in Christ (2 Cor. 2: 14-17).

This text is expressly cited in connection with confirmation by Cyril of Jerusalem, Athanasius and the *Apostolic Constitutions,* and is taken up by St. Thomas. The confirmed Christian is, then, continually to witness to Christ in his daily life among the pagans, to witness by his very presence. Furthermore, as the text indicates, "the fragrance of Christ" which we are to spread around us is not something sweet and insipid. Authentic witnessing to Christ necessarily brings about the effect of the Gospel preaching, to distinguish between those who welcome God's message and those who refuse it.

The significance of this aromatic quality of chrism also indicates the precise sense in which confirmation causes us to go from the state of infancy to that of adulthood. It is not a question of "stature" or "growth," but of a change in social situation. "When he has reached the age of maturity, the man who up to that time lived only for himself now takes his first steps in the society of his fellow-men" (*Summa III,* 72, 2). It is entirely correct, consequently, to base the work of Catholic action on the character given by confirmation.

III. THE IMPOSITION OF HANDS AND THE
SPIRIT OF PENTECOST

The Fathers see both the anointing and the imposition of hands as signifying the reproduction in the Christian of what took place for Jesus
after His baptism. Both actions are referred to in Is. 61. Both signify the
sending forth on a mission, with an interior change and the gift of the
Spirit. But the action of imposing hands adds an important note: he who
gives the Spirit has already received Him, so the power that he confers is,
as it were, an emanation of his own.[37] The Spirit given in confirmation
is precisely the "Spirit of Pentecost" received by the apostles and communicated to the faithful by them and their successors. This is brought
out in the final prayer of the ceremony in the Roman rite: "O God, as You
gave the Holy Spirit to Your apostles and willed that, through them and
their successors, this gift should be transmitted to the rest of the faithful . . . ."

This prayer echoes the apostles' preaching. "These men have received
the Holy Spirit as well as we." "God who knows hearts has witnessed in
their favor, in giving the Holy Spirit to them as well as to ourselves; he
has made no distinction between them and us." The event of Pentecost
which caused so much stir and drew the crowds was not limited to the
apostles: "The promise is for you, for your children, and for all those who
are far away" (Acts 15:8-9; 10:45-47; 11:15; 2:38-39).

The promise referred to is that of the prophet Joel and of Jesus Himself. Joel, quoted by St. Peter (Acts 2:17ff.), had foreseen the day when
"prophecy," instead of being a rare and isolated privilege, would become the inheritance of all the new People of God (Joel 2:28ff.). Jesus
had assured the apostles that He would send them the Holy Spirit so that
they would be witnesses. When they were brought to give witness before
rulers and judges, they would not need to concern themselves about
what to say, for "the Spirit of your Father will speak in you." The terms
"prophet" and "witness" thus become closely associated in the New Testament, both designating those who boldly confess the Name of Christ.
When the apostles, Stephen, Paul and many others had received the Holy
Spirit, they could no longer keep silence, even when threatened or faced
with death.

IV. THE STRENGTH OF MARTYRS

Tradition constantly states that confirmation brings a special grace of
strength for combat. The baptized Christian is already a soldier enrolled

---

[37] This may be the explanation of the change of sign in the Eastern rites. A bishop
could, like the apostles, confirm by the imposition of hands alone if the Church so decided.
A priest could not; he needs the intermediary of chrism consecrated by the bishop.

in Christ's army and equipped for the struggle necessarily involved in the Christian life. But the added trials for which we are strengthened by confirmation are those proper to prophets and apostles. Witnessing requires fortitude, the strength of the Spirit. In the Old Testament the Lord chose as prophets some who were timid by nature, but He gave them the strength to endure the persecution involved in their mission. Christ Himself died for His witnessing and His disciples are to suffer for theirs. "You will be betrayed even by your fathers and mothers and brothers and kindred and friends, and you will be put to death; and you will be hated by all because of my name" (Mark 13:12-13; Luke 21:16-17).

And so the prayer consecrating the chrism speaks of an "anointing of martyrs" as one with that of prophets. St. Thomas holds that the grace of martyrdom is never given without the sacrament of confirmation or at least the desire for it:

> A man may, without the sacrament of confirmation, receive the spiritual strength publicly to confess the faith of Christ, as one can receive the remission of sins without baptism. Yet, as no one receives the effect of baptism without the desire for baptism, so nobody receives the effect of confirmation without the desire for it (*Summa* III, 72, 6 ad 1).

The sacrament of confirmation, then, imprints in us the indelible character which configures us to Christ as the Prophet of the New Law and makes us His witnesses before men, giving us for this mission a grace of fortitude, if need be even to martyrdom.

Article Four
THE AGE FOR CONFIRMATION[38]

Here again, the practice of the Church has varied greatly in the past and still varies today. There is, of course, no question in the case of an adult. When the bishop himself presides at the baptism, he confirms the neophyte immediately afterwards, before the Mass at which the neophyte communicates for the first time. Otherwise he goes to the bishop as soon as possible to have his initiation completed.

But with regard to the confirmation of children, the practice of the Church has varied considerably in past times and continues to vary. In ancient times confirmation was given immediately after baptism, since

[38] See J. P. Kenny, "The Age for Confirmation," *Worship*, 35 (1960), pp. 4-15.

this was always presided over by the bishop himself. Similarly, in the East today priests have the faculty to give this sacrament and children receive it immediately after baptism.

In the West the rule has come to prevail that children should not be confirmed until they have reached the age of at least seven years and have received some adequate catechesis (Can. 786-788). But this is a matter of discipline, not of principle. It is a universal rule that infants in danger of death be confirmed (Can. 788), and the ancient custom of confirming infants after baptism is still observed in certain Western countries, such as Spain. Elsewhere the age varies from seven to eleven or twelve years.

It is therefore useless to attempt to base any particular usage on theological principles—as, for example, to try to make an analogy between spiritual and physical age. Even little children can be "adults" according to grace, while old persons can be reborn in baptism (*Summa* III, 72, 8). It is a mistake, consequently, to speak of confirmation as the "sacrament of adolescence." Only pastoral considerations determine which is the most appropriate age.

Section Three

THE EUCHARIST AS THE COMPLETION OF CHRISTIAN INITIATION [39]

Article One

CHRISTIAN INITIATION INCOMPLETE WITHOUT THE EUCHARIST

In the ancient liturgy the celebration of the Eucharist followed baptism, as we see in the *First Apology* of St. Justin, written about the year 150, in the *Apostolic Tradition* of Hippolytus, written about the year 200, and in the catecheses of St. Augustine, St. Ambrose, St. Cyril of Jerusalem, etc. All the baptized received Communion, whether they were adults or little children (the latter received only the species of wine).

[39] Here we are concerned with the Eucharist simply as a sacrament of initiation in connection with baptism and confirmation—a most important aspect from the catechetical viewpoint. The complete study of the Eucharist will be taken up in the next chapter.

The Fathers particularly stress the profound bond between baptism and the Eucharist, a bond so strong that the newly-baptized are in haste to take part in the Eucharist. As St. John Chrysostom says, for example:

> You have seen what is the figure and what the reality of baptism. See, now I am going to show you also the table and the mysteries sketched out here. For after the passage through the sea and the cloud, Paul (1 Cor. 10:3-4) goes on to say, "And all ate the same spiritual food and drank the same spiritual drink."

> Just as you, coming up out of the pool of water, advance in haste towards the table, so they, having come up out of the sea, went to a new and wonderful table—I mean the manna. And just as you have a mysterious drink, the Blood of salvation, so they had a wonderful kind of drink, water in abundance gushing from a dry rock (*Sermon on 1 Cor. 10*, PG 51, 248).

And St. Ambrose comments on Psalm 22:

> Having laid aside the old clothing of the ancient error, his youth renewed like the eagle's, he hastens towards the heavenly banquet. He arrives, and seeing the holy altar prepared, he cries out, "You have made ready a table before me" (*On the Mysteries*, 43).

This bond between baptism and the Eucharist consists in the unity of the paschal mystery. Baptism draws its efficacy from the sacrifice of Christ which the Eucharist makes present. Baptism incorporates us into Christ; the Body of Christ is given us as food to seal our union with Him. Baptism opens out to us the road to the Promised Land, and the Eucharist is the anticipation and pledge of our inheritance of this Land.

On the level of figures, St. John Chrysostom recalls that the manna and the water from the rock were given to the Hebrews after they had crossed the Red Sea. Other Fathers point out that the paschal lamb whose blood marked the doors and preserved from destruction (baptism) was to be eaten during a meal of departure for a journey (the Eucharist). On the level of realities, baptism and the Eucharist together constitute the paschal sacrament, participation in Christ dead and risen again.

> In the same way as we receive the birth of baptism by means of the death of Christ, so also with our food. We receive it sacramentally by means of His death. . . . To take the oblation and to participate in the mysteries is to commemorate the death of our Lord which gains for us resurrection and the enjoyment of immortality. For it is fitting that we who have received a sacramental birth through the death of our Lord the Christ should receive the nourishment of the sacrament of immortality through the same death. We must be nourished from the same source from which we were born (Theodore of Mopsuestia, *Hom.* 15,6).[40]

[40] See G. Diekmann, "Unto Full Stature" in *Come Let Us Worship;* L. Bouyer, *Liturgical Piety*, pp. 165-172.

Article Two
FIRST COMMUNION

Today, as formerly, the first Communion of an adult should follow immediately after baptism (Can 753,2; Roman Ritual, II, 4, 7 and 52). Consequently, an adult who is not considered prepared to communicate should not be admitted to baptism, and preparation for baptism must include preparation for the Eucharist. The pastoral and catechetical importance of this principle is obvious.

Up to about the thirteenth century, that is, while Communion under the species of wine was maintained in the West, infants were given Communion at the time of their baptism and from then on were admitted to the Eucharist. In the East, where the use of the chalice for the faithful has continued, Communion for infants has been maintained, not only on the day of their baptism but every Sunday.

In the West the abuse of putting off children's first Communion until fourteen or even sixteen or seventeen years of age gradually crept in. St. Pius X remedied this abuse by his decree *Quam singulari* of 1910 (Can. 854). Its chief prescriptions are as follows.

For Christians of the Latin rites, the Church still normally reserves the Eucharist to children who have reached the "age of discretion," that is, who have the use of reason, and who have also received elementary religious instruction and are capable of preparing themselves for the Eucharist with devotion. These conditions are usually fulfilled about the age of seven.

Since the age at which these conditions can be fulfilled varies so greatly, parents should be alert to discern when their child has reached the "age of discretion" so that he may be prepared for his first Communion. (In the case of a child in danger of death, the Church requires only that he be capable of distinguishing the Eucharist from ordinary food and of receiving it with religious reverence.)

In the thought of St. Pius X, it is the parents and the confessor who are to take the initiative in this matter, rather than children being arbitrarily admitted in a group belonging to one or another grade in school. In any case, parents should whenever possible be given the opportunity and the means to prepare their own children for the Eucharist, or at least to cooperate actively in this preparation.

In preparing children for first Communion, it should be brought out that they are now to take their full part in the Mass as members of the royal and priestly People of God, to which they belong by baptism. First Communion will then be seen, as it should be, in the perspective of Christian initiation, not as an isolated act. And it will be clear that this first Communion is a beginning, not an end in itself.

Chapter 4
THE EUCHARIST

Preliminary Remarks

"The mystery of the most holy Eucharist which Christ the High Priest instituted and which He commands to be continually renewed in the Church by His ministers is the culmination and center, as it were, of the Christian religion . . . the crowning act of the sacred liturgy" (*Med. Dei* 66). As such, it differs in certain respects from the other sacraments (*Summa* III, 73, 1 ad 3). These differences were so greatly emphasized in the recent past that elementary manuals and catechisms came to depart in two ways from the method of instruction on the Eucharist used both by the Fathers and St. Thomas. The doctrine of the Eucharist was divided into three parts studied quite separately: the Real Presence, the Sacrifice of the Mass (or "the Eucharist as sacrifice") and Communion (or "the Eucharist as sacrament"). Further the study of the Eucharist as sacrifice aimed to prove that the Mass, taken as an isolated act, fulfills a definition of sacrifice developed from data furnished by the study of comparative religion.

This departure from the traditional method, breaking up the unity of the Eucharist as the sacramental Sacrifice, led to certain inadequacies. Communion was not seen as participation in the Mass. Devotion to the Real Presence was separated from the Sacrifice and from Communion. And the Sacrifice was seen as only the representation of the sacrifice of Calvary from which we receive grace and as the action making Christ present for adoration and for Communion, and not as above all enabling the faithful to worship the Father "in Spirit and in truth" by, with, and through Christ our High Priest.

Again, this method separates the mystery itself from the rites which express it, and so any explanation of the prayers and actions of the Mass either seemed unnecessary or was done mainly on a purely rubrical, external plane. Moreover, since this method starts from abstract ideas and even from definitions not unanimously accepted by scholars, it discourages the contemplation which true religious instruction should open out to young and old, simple and learned Christians alike. What a sacrifice is and how the Mass fulfills the definition is largely a matter for controversy. But all the baptized, even children, ought to be able to see the Mass with the intelligent gaze of faith, to participate in it and live it.

Recent works have drawn attention to the defects of this method and have shown how it is also open to criticism on the properly theological level.[1] The Eucharist is inseparably sacrament and sacrifice, or still better, the sacramental sacrifice. Precisely because it is the center of the whole sacramental organism, it must be studied by the method proper to the sacraments. We must begin from the liturgical signs (which might be called

[1] See A. Vonier, *Key to the Doctrine of the Eucharist;* discourse of Pius XII in *The Assisi Papers*, p. 233.

the *sacramentum tantum* in an extended use of the term). We must explain these signs and so state the divine reality which they contain and signify: Christ really present and the efficacious memorial of the sacrifice of the Cross (*res et sacramentum*). Finally, we must bring out the graces of the Eucharist for the communicant, the whole Church, the living and the dead (*res sacramenti*).

We must study the Eucharist in the context of the whole Mass. Christians of every age need a type of instruction which enables them to follow the whole movement of the liturgy of the Mass. The *Directoire pour la pastorale de la messe à l'usage des diocèses de France* warns against the danger of limiting our view of the Mass to the sacrifice and Communion:

> The Mass, the principal act of Christian worship, includes two distinct parts closely related to one another: a liturgy of the Word and the Eucharistic sacrifice. Even though the current expression "Fore-Mass" seems to imply it, the rites preceding the Offertory are not to be considered a mere prelude to the celebration. On the contrary, the Word of God is an essential element of the liturgical assembly. It is nourishment for souls. It is also the proclamation in the Church of the mystery of salvation embodied in the Eucharist.[2]

When the Sunday Mass of the present day is thus properly considered as forming a dynamic whole, it resembles very closely the description given about the year 150 by St. Justin of Rome for the benefit of his pagan fellow-citizens:

> On the day which is called that of the sun, we all, both in towns and in the country, come together in one place. We read, for as long as we have time for, from the recollections of the apostles and the writings of the prophets. When the reader has finished, he who is the president of the assembly speaks, urging us to imitate these beautiful teachings. Then we all arise and pray together aloud. Then . . . bread is brought, with wine and water. The president sends up prayers and eucharists to heaven to the extent that he is able, and all the people answer with the acclamation *Amen*. Then the distribution and sharing of the Eucharistic gifts takes place, and a part is sent to those absent by the deacons (*First Apology*, 67).

Three principles should guide anyone who wishes to study the liturgy of the Mass or present it to others. First, the Mass is an action, a movement that has its own rhythms, its moments of heightened activity and of repose. Consequently, it cannot be grasped by studying each act or prayer in isolation from the whole. Actions and prayers find their meaning precisely in the dynamic context in which they are inserted. This pattern of movement itself enables us to perceive the varying importance of the succesive rites and prayers.

[2] See the conclusions formulated by the Strasbourg Congress in *The Liturgy and the Word of God*, pp. v-ix.

Secondly, the solemn Sunday parochial Mass must be the norm for our study. Certainly we must uphold the legitimacy and value of the "devotional Mass,"[3] one celebrated by a priest for reasons of personal devotion with only a server assisting. Such a Mass brings out clearly the fact that the consecration produces its sacrificial effect *ex opere operato* and that the Mass as such is the action of the Church. Yet a "devotional Mass" is in fact a reduced version, as it were, of the Sunday parochial Mass celebrated in the midst of the Christian assembly, and therefore the latter provides the best basis for instruction.

Thirdly, as the starting-point for catechesis, we should use the solemn Mass, that is a sung Mass celebrated with the assistance of sacred ministers, rather than the low Mass or the simple sung Mass, since the solemn Mass alone brings out the proper distribution of roles between the celebrant, the sacred ministers, the choir and the congregation.

Finally, in the same connection, it should be kept in mind that the Sunday parochial Mass is in turn simply the local manifestation of the bishop's Mass. This Mass alone constitutes the complete manifestation of the local Church assembled in unity around the Word of God and the Eucharist.

Obviously, then, those giving instruction on the Mass should have had the experience of participating in all these various modes of celebration.

There are many ways of celebrating the one Eucharist of the Church. It is most important to emphasize that the Roman Mass, the form to which so many of us are accustomed, is not the only legitimate rite. Every Christian should be made aware of the fact that there exist different rites both in the West and in the East, all legitimate, going back to ancient times, rich in a magnificent treasury of prayer and witnessing by their very diversity to the unity of tradition. The existence of Churches of various Eastern rites in many of our cities and the recent efforts to foster interest in their liturgies by demonstrations, lectures, etc., should be brought to students' attention, and this for two reasons: first, because an awareness of other rites promotes the sense of the unity of the one Church made up of many Churches; secondly, because a comparison of the various liturgies helps us to distinguish what is essential and primary in the Eucharistic celebration from what is accessory. What is to be found in all the rites is nearly always of the essence, while they differ in accidentals.[4] It should be noted here that while the West uses the term "Mass," the Eastern rites use the term "the Liturgy" to refer to the whole Eucharistic celebration.

[3] This term is suggested by H. A. Reinhold in *Bringing the Mass to the People* as an acceptable substitute for the term "private Mass" banned by the Instruction of Sept. 3, 1958, as implying that such a Mass is not a public act of the Church. The legitimacy of such Masses is stated by the Council of Trent (*Denz.* 944, 955) and *Mediator Dei,* 95-97.

[4] See the chart on p. 155; also the charts comparing the elements of the various liturgies in *Sacraments and Worship,* SCT I, pp. 68-71.

PRINCIPAL LITURGIES OF THE MASS

I. WESTERN (Latin) Liturgies

Ancient Liturgy of Spain (Visigothic, Mozarabic)
Ancient Gallic Liturgy
Milanese Liturgy
Roman Liturgy
Liturgy of Lyons
Dominican Liturgy

II. EASTERN LITURGIES

Egypt: Coptic Liturgy
Ethiopia: Ethiopian Liturgy
Constantinople: Byzantine Liturgy (Byzantine, Melkite,
Ruthenian, Russian, Rumanian, etc.)
1. Liturgy of St. John Chrysostom
2. Liturgy of St. Basil
Armenia: Armenian Liturgy
West Syrians
1. Syrian Liturgy
2. Maronite Liturgy
East Syrians
1. Chaldean Liturgy
2. Malabar Liturgy

Section One

THE RITES OF THE MASS

A. THE LITURGY OF THE WORD

There is good reason to distinguish two parts in the Mass: the one ending after the Creed, the other beginning at the Offertory. This distinction is founded on liturgical history. In the ancient Church on certain solemn fast-days the service included no Eucharist—only readings, psalms and prayers. Conversely, on Holy Thursday in Rome the offering of the Eucharist was not preceded by any reading-service. These, however, were exceptions. The Sunday liturgy everywhere had the complete form described by St. Justin.

But the distinction is also based on the nature of the rites. When the bishop celebrates Mass, he presides from his throne during the first part and goes up to the altar only at the time of the Offertory. In the Eastern liturgies, as formerly also in the West, a procession opens each part: the Gospel procession (the Little Entrance) opens the biblical readings, and the procession with the bread and wine (the Great Entrance) opens the Eucharistic prayer.

These two parts are best named "the liturgy of the Word" and "the liturgy of the Eucharist." This terminology is more correct than others in current use because it distinguishes the proper content of each part and also suggests the fact that they complement one another. The terms "Mass of the catechumens" and "Mass of the faithful" are inexact historically, implying that the first part of the Mass was reserved for the non-baptized, which was never true. Moreover they give an unfortunate archaic impression. And the terms "Fore-Mass" and "the Mass properly speaking" imply that the former is not really part of the Mass.

I. ESSENTIAL ELEMENTS[5]

At first sight, the first part of the Eucharistic celebration seems extremely complex as well as variegated. The Eastern rites include litanies, psalms, canticles, readings, prayers, sometimes duplicating one another or even going on simultaneously. Yet in this complexity we always find the essential elements: the proclamation of the Word of God, chants, prayers.

1. *Proclamation of the Word of God.* Every liturgical assembly includes the proclamation of the Word of God, consisting of the reading of Holy Scripture and the commentary on the inspired text, the celebrant's homily.

The number of readings varies. The Roman Mass usually has two: the second is taken from the Gospels, the first gives a privileged place to St. Paul's Epistles. This is why the first reading is usually called the Epistle, although it may be taken from other New Testament writings (especially in Easter time) or from the Old (weekday Masses in Lent). Sometimes we find three readings; in the Armenian liturgy, for example, the people hear successively a prophet, an apostle and then the Gospel. Again, the Roman Masses for Ember Saturdays include seven readings, since they formerly took up a night's vigil. Whatever their number, these readings always follow an ascending movement, expressing the economy of salvation. The Old Testament comes before the New, and the apostles are heard before the Gospel which is always the climax.

The choice of readings is in some cases motivated by the desire to have the faithful hear the books of the Bible successively in the course of the

[5] Many authorities now distinguish the Entrance Rite (through the Collect inclusive in the Roman Mass) from the liturgy of the Word properly so called. See H. A. Reinhold, *op. cit.*, pp. 47-52; J. A. Jungmann, *The Early Liturgy*, pp. 291ff.

year. This *lectio continua* was the method used in the ancient Church; it is still the method followed by the Eastern and Western Syrians. It applies to the Gospel readings in the Byzantine liturgy and we can still find traces of it in the Roman liturgy. The other basis of choice is that of proclaiming some mystery of Christ, the method followed throughout Lent and Easter week, and on feastdays. Here the readings are chosen so that the Old Testament illuminates the New, the writings of the apostles herald and explain the Gospel.[6]

These readings are to be proclaimed. It is not enough that each participant read the text with his eyes on his missal. Here the Church is presenting the Word of God to us, transmitting it orally and with authority. A minister of the Church must carry out this proclamation, chosen in accordance with the importance of each text. The Old Testament is entrusted to a lector, and so, strictly speaking, are the writings of the apostles, although in the solemn Mass of the Roman rite the Epistle is reserved to the subdeacon. But the Gospel can only be proclaimed by a member of the hierarchy of orders: a deacon, or, lacking a deacon, by the celebrant himself.

All are to listen to the readings rather than read them. If the liturgy is celebrated in a language not that of the people, the readings are to be proclaimed in a translation as well.[7] Obviously, the same respect should be accorded to the sacred text in any language.

The preaching which concludes the liturgy of the Word should, as a rule, be a commentary on the Scriptural passages just read. The sermon is meant to be organically connected with the readings, as the opening-out, the adaptation of the written Word of God by the words of Christ's minister to this particular, concrete audience. As can be seen from the homilies of the Fathers, this was how they understood its function. Consequently, the homily is not an interruption of the Mass, but a part of it, forming a whole with the readings and sharing the same liturgical solemnity. This is why it should normally be given by the celebrant.

2. The chants. The readings are interwoven with chants, varying in origin, nature and function. These are biblical for the most part, psalms or canticles from the Old Testament. But compositions in the style of the psalms are also used, for example the *Gloria in excelsis.* (This jewel of primitive Christian prayer, used in the Churches of both East and West

---

[6]See P. Jounel, "The Bible in the Liturgy," *The Liturgy and the Word of God,* pp. 1ff.

[7]The Instruction *On Sacred Music and the Liturgy,* of Sept. 6, 1958 says that it desirable that this be done by a lector at Sunday and feastday low Masses at the same time as the Latin readings are being carried out. In some countries a special indult allows a translation to be proclaimed at sung Masses immediately after the reading has been chanted in Latin. In the United States, when the readings are chanted the translation must be given at the time of the sermon. In the Eastern liturgies, even when the Eucharistic part of the liturgy is in a dead language, the readings are in the language of the faithful.

and rich in biblical inspiration, came into the Roman Mass as a hymn for special occasions, reserved at first to Easter). Hymns of a more popular type also occasionally occur, for example sequences such as the *Victimum Paschale, Stabat Mater, Dies Irae* of the Roman liturgy.

Some of these chants are meant to be heard for themselves, to be meditated, e.g., the Gradual psalm or Tract in the Mass, the canticles following the readings in the Easter Vigil, the Beatitudes in the Byzantine liturgy. Or, these chants may be a kind of response of the assembly to the Word of God, a purpose frequently motivating the choice of certain psalms.[8] One chant should be particularly mentioned in this connection, the *Credo,* the symbol of the faith fixed in its present form by the Council of 381 (except for the word *Filioque* added in the ninth century). This is the response of the Sunday assembly to the Word of God received in the readings and the homily; it is a recalling of our baptismal profession of faith.

Other chants are designed to accompany processions: the Introit psalm with its refrain is meant to be sung during the entrance of the celebrant and his ministers; the Alleluia verse, during the Gospel procession.

Finally, brief and unvarying responses and acclamations allow even an untrained congregation to participate vocally and wholeheartedly in the celebration: the "short responses," the *Kyrie,* the *Alleluia.*

All these chants, obviously, should be sung, some by the choir, some by the choir and the congregation. Singing is an indispensable means of expression for a large gathering, making possible a rhythm and harmony difficult to achieve in speaking aloud. It is imposed on the Christian assembly for still another reason—as the sign of the overflowing joy of the redeemed, the natural way of expressing thanksgiving, as St. Paul remarks so frequently in his Epistles (Col. 3:16; Eph. 5:19-20).[9]

3. The prayers. The liturgy of the Word is not to be confused with a meeting for instruction or edification. Here the Word of God is solemnly proclaimed to a people in prayer. Prayer prepares the faithful for hearing the Word. The Word is received in the prayerful silence of religious recollection. Finally, by prayer the assembly responds to God who has spoken.

Like the chants, this prayer takes on various forms. For the most part it is at once communal and personal, the prayer of the whole assembly and of each individual composing it. For example, the greeting *Dominus vobiscum* and its response unites celebrant and people for prayer. His *Oremus* is an invitation for them to formulate their own petitions, which he then gathers together and expresses in their name in the Collect prayer. Finally, all express their union with this prayer by their final

[8] See J. Gelineau, "The Church Responds to God with the Word of God," *The Liturgy and the Word of God,* pp. 84-90.

[9] See Gerald Ellard, *The Mass in Transition,* pp. 183-213; J. Hofinger, *Worship, the Life of the Missions,* pp. 157-182.

Amen. (The invitation *Flectamus genua* used on Ember Days and in the Holy Week services is meant to give the faithful the opportunity to pray silently before the celebrant expresses their petitions together with those of the whole Church in the official prayer formula.) But the liturgy also provides prayers for individuals. It gives the celebrant and his ministers the "prayers at the foot of the altar" as their immediate preparation for going to the altar of God. It gives the deacon (or priest) a prayer-formula as preparation for proclaiming the Gospel.

One characteristic of the prayer of the assembly as such is that it expresses to God our common condition as sinners and our poverty: "Lord, have mercy." This recognition of our wretchedness does not cast a shadow over the Christian gathering, for it brings with it our discovery of the God who is merciful and faithful to His promises, the redeeming God. This is why Christian prayer is fundamentally always joyful thanksgiving, contemplation and praise of God, adoration, though here on earth this praise can and should include petition.

St. Paul urges Christians to ask the Lord in their liturgical assemblies for everything needed here on earth, in particular to pray for the leaders of the earthly city:

> I urge . . .that petitions, prayers, supplications and thanksgivings be made for all men, for kings and all those in authority, so that we may lead a quiet and peaceful life in all piety and dignity (1 Tim. 2:1-2).

In following his counsel, the Eastern liturgies have the deacon on several occasions in the Liturgy proclaim intentions for prayer, the people answering to each, "Lord, have mercy." The Roman liturgy for Good Friday has preserved the magnificent series of solemn prayers which were formerly prayed at all Masses. The prayers for persons in special need and for the dead, customary today in many parishes at the time of the sermon, fulfill the same role. Traditionally, it is after the homily and before the Eucharist that this prayer for the needs of all should be located.[10]

II. THE PROFOUND MEANING OF THE LITURGY OF THE WORD

The first part of the Eucharistic celebration is not meant simply to teach or edify. The liturgy and the Fathers give us a deeper view of the realities of the faith: the Word of God carries out the work of salvation as we receive it from the Church, here fulfilling her commission to give us this Word. Holy Scripture always contains a message for each of us here and now, but this message reaches us primarily as proclaimed to us in the assembly, at the command of the hierarchy. When the Christian has received the Word of God in the liturgy, he can then meditate on it at leisure just

[10] See Gerald Ellard, *op. cit.,* pp. 226-235; H. A. Reinhold, *op. cit.,* pp. 55-58; Johannes Hofinger, *op. cit.,* pp. 53-54, 60-61.

as the Christians of ancient times used to carry the Eucharist home from the Sunday liturgy for their nourishment during the week.

Furthermore, the Gospel is considered as a special presence of Christ, its proclamation an authentic way of reliving His mysteries. For us who are far removed from the events in time and space, hearing the inspired narrative takes the place of the experience of Christ's actions. "The reading is in some way transformed into vision," to use an expression of St. Leo the Great. The sound of the words produces in our minds the image of the deeds (*Sermons* 52, 69, 70).

The Church has always surrounded the book of the Gospels with a respect comparable to that given to the Eucharist. It is carried in procession with lights and incense ahead of the bishop who is celebrating a pontifical Mass. It is kissed, placed in the center of the altar. (In the Eastern rites the procession of the Gospel, the "little entrance," is always carried out with great ceremony.) The people sing acclamations: *Gloria tibi, Domine; Doxa soi Kyria, Alleluia,* and all stand while the text is read. In the Middle Ages some churches had a kind of tabernacle for the Gospel book opposite that in which the Holy Eucharist was reserved.

The comparison between the Gospel and the Eucharist is developed in a celebrated passage of the *Imitation of Christ* (4, 11).

> Without these two I could not live, for God's Word is the light of my soul, and Your sacrament the Bread of life. These can also be called the two tables placed in the treasury of holy Church. One table is that of the sacred altar on which rests the holy Bread that is Christ's precious Body; the other is that of divine law which contains holy doctrine, teaches the true faith, lifts the veil of the sanctuary and leads us securely to the holy of holies.

But it was the sixth chapter of St. John's Gospel that first established this relationship. The Bread of life presented by Jesus is at once His Word and His Eucharist, so intimately related that exegetes have great difficulty in deciding which parts of the discourse refer to one or the other.[11]

III. INTERDEPENDENCE OF THE LITURGY OF THE WORD AND THE LITURGY OF THE EUCHARIST

The incident of the apparition of Jesus to the disciples at Emmaus on Easter evening (Luke 24:13-32) shows us the relationship between the liturgy of the Word and the liturgy of the Eucharist, the bread of the Word and bread of the Body of Christ. We are to see them, not as paralleling, but as completing one another.

[11] See *New Testament Reading Guide,* #13, pp. 40-42. "Jesus is the true Bread, both as the Word of God, vv. 32ff, and as Victim offered in sacrifice, through His Body and Blood given for the life of the world—vv. 51-58" (*Bible de Jerusalem*).

As Jesus walked along with the disciples He said, "Did not Christ have to suffer these things in order to enter into His glory?" And beginning with Moses and going through all the prophets, He interpreted what had been said about Him in all the Scriptures. Yet the disciples did not recognize Him. For their eyes to be opened, Jesus had to come in with them to supper, to break the bread over which He had said the blessing, and to give it to them. It was then, and not before, that they discovered who had been their Companion on the road.

In the Eucharist we do not see the face of Christ, we do not hear His word. Therefore, we first have to hear the voice of the Gospel. The various readings of the sacred texts preceding the Eucharistic sacrifice in the context of the whole Mass cause us to enter successively into the various aspects of Christ's mysteries in the course of the liturgical year. The Eucharist would be unintelligible without the Gospel, for it would no longer be recognizable as Christ, whose history is the unique event, whose word is revelation.

Equally, without the Eucharist the Christ of the Gospel would remain distant; His word is only fully intelligible to the Christian who has taken part in offering His sacrifice and experienced His presence and His friendship in Communion. The Eucharist alone finally seals our faith in a commitment of our whole selves to the inner mystery of Christ. In this sense the Eucharist perfects baptism, which is, as we have seen, the sacrament of faith.

B. THE LITURGY OF THE SACRAMENT

The liturgy of the Eucharist simply reproduces and developes the actions and words of Christ at the Last Supper. "He took bread. . . . He took the cup containing wine. . . . He gave thanks. . . . He broke the bread and gave it to the disciples."

The simple, functional actions of taking the bread and taking the cup have given rise to the ceremony of the "great entrance" in the Eastern liturgies, and to the various Offertory prayers in the Western.

Christ's "giving thanks" has provided the theme of the Eucharistic prayer called the *anaphora* (meaning "offering") in the Eastern liturgies, and to the various Offertory prayers in the Western. This is the prayer which effects the sacramental sacrifice, itself called the Eucharist.[13] At first its wording was left to the celebrant and then later fixed in the liturgies of various localities toward the end of the fourth century. The

---

[13] This is the Greek term used by the New Testament usually translated in English as "thanksgiving," though it has wider connotations of praise. See L. Bouyer, *Liturgical Piety*, pp. 115-120; Cornelius Bouman, "The Eucharistic Prayer as a Prayer of Praise," *Participation in the Mass*, PNLW (1959), pp. 258-265.

Eucharistic prayer was originally continuous, later undergoing developments that tend to conceal its basic unity. But it always contains both a theme of thankful praise (brought out in the Roman liturgy particularly in the Preface and Sanctus and the concluding doxology) and the narrative of the Last Supper.

Christ's breaking of the bread is reproduced in the "fraction" of the Host. His giving it to the disciples is reproduced in Communion.

It is on these basic rites, consequently, that instruction on the Eucharist and theological study should be based. We need also to consider, however, the additional elements to be found in all the liturgies which express the basic attitude of the Church toward the Eucharist and indicate the spiritual attitudes required of the faithful. In our presentation we shall therefore study first the prerequisites and rites preliminary to the Eucharistic prayer; then this prayer itself with its various elements and aspects; and lastly the "fraction" of the Host and the Communion rites.

I. THE ALTAR

In every liturgy, when the bishop celebrates the holy Sacrifice, the transition from the first to the second part of the Mass is marked by his moving from his throne to the altar.

Christ celebrated the Eucharist at a supper-table. But now, except under extraordinary circumstances, the Church prescribes that it be celebrated on an altar of stone, containing the relics of martyrs and consecrated by the bishop (Can. 822).[14] Two biblical themes are represented in the stone altar which make it an image of Christ, to be honored as such.

First, there is the theme of the rock or stone itself, indicating Christ as the life-spring and head of His Church. He fulfills the image of the rock which gave water to the Hebrews in the desert, and accompanied them on their journey ("And this rock was Christ," 1 Cor. 10:4).[15] He is the foundation-stone or keystone of the building (Acts 4:11; Ps. 117:22; Matthew 21:42; 1 Peter 2:4-7; Ps. 28:16; Eph. 2:20; 1 Cor. 3:11).

Secondly, there is the theme of the stone altar. The history of Jacob provides us with the image which has set the pattern for the consecration of Christian altars: "Jacob set up a stone as a memorial pillar and poured oil over it" (Gen. 28:18). In the primitive Mosaic legislation, an altar

---

[14] An altar-stone, in which relics are sealed, set in the middle of the altar so that the Sacrifice is actually celebrated on it, fulfills this requirement when the whole altar is not made of stone. Portable altar-stones are used by missionaries, etc., who celebrate the holy Sacrifice outdoors, in buildings not designed as churches and under other special circumstances. Only under very exceptional circumstances, such as obtained in Nazi prison camps, may the holy Sacrifice be celebrated without an altar-stone. For the development of the Christian altar, see J. A. Jungmann, *op. cit.,* pp. 119-120, 187.

[15] See *New Testament Reading Guide,* #8, p. 35.

could be of different materials, but when it was built of stones, these had to be rough-hewn (Exod. 20:25). From the time of Deuteronomy, stone was required for the altar of holocausts (Deut. 27:5-7), a principle applied at the reconstruction after the Exile (cf. 1 Mac. 4:44-46) and under Judas Maccabeus (4:47). All these altars were remote images of Christ, the unique altar of the New Law (cf. Heb. 13:10), as He is also its unique temple, priest and victim. As Origen (*Hom. on Josue* 9,6) and, following him, St. Cyril of Alexandria, say, "Christ is the altar, the offering and the priest."

> Keep this in mind, that the divine prescription requires a reverent spreading out of the holy oils for the consecration of an altar for the holy Sacrifice. . . . For since it is on Jesus Himself, the completely divine altar of our sacrifice, that the consecration is carried out according to the divine plan . . . let us regard this altar for the holy Sacrifice as something surpassing what we see here, for it is here that the holy Victim is sacrificed and consecrated (*Ecclesiastical Hierarchy* 4, 12).

This exhortation of Pseudo-Dionysius expressed the unanimous tradition of the Fathers expressively developed in the rites of consecration. The Christian altar represents Christ, and so it is marked with the signs of His wounds, it is given His anointing. Therefore, it is also given many marks of veneration during the Eucharistic celebration and is the focus of the whole church building.

II. THE KISS OF PEACE

The kiss of peace expresses the prerequisite condition for taking part in offering the Eucharist, and so it is included here. The Eastern liturgies have kept to the ancient practice described by St. Justin (*First Apology*) of giving the kiss of peace before placing the materials for the Sacrifice on the altar, thus indicating that those taking part have followed out Christ's command:

> When you present your gift at the altar, if there you remember that your brother has anything against you, leave your gift before the altar and first go and be reconciled with your brother, and then offer your gift (Matthew 5:23-24).

In the Roman liturgy the kiss of peace is given at the time of Communion and in connection with it, indicating that the Eucharist seals the unity of the body which is the Church, and so produces charity, the true peace of Christ (John 14:27; prayer before the kiss of peace in the Roman Missal).

> We all receive the same food when we receive the same Body and Blood. "We all, though many, form one body because we partake of

the one bread" (1 Cor. 10:17). Before approaching the mysteries, then, we must carry out the rule of giving the kiss of peace. By this we signify our union and our charity toward one another. It would not be fitting for those who form one ecclesial body to hate some brother in the faith (Theodore of Mopsuestia, *Catechetical Homily* 15, 40).

Modern liturgies limit the kiss of peace to the most solemn celebration of the Eucharist and reserve it to the clergy. In ancient times, however, it took place at every Eucharistic celebration and included the whole congregation. Both St. Peter and St. Paul witness to this custom as a liturgical act, if not specifically in connection with the Eucharist: "Salute one another with a holy kiss" (1 Peter 5:14; Rom. 16:16; 1 Cor. 16:20; 2 Cor. 13:12, 1 Thess. 5:26).

III. THE OFFERTORY: THE PREPARATION
AND GREAT ENTRANCE

"Bread, and a cup containing wine and water are brought to the president of the assembly." This description by St. Justin indicates the basic purpose of the Offertory.

1. Bread and a cup with wine and water. "Bread made of wheat" and "the fruit of the vine" are expressly mentioned by Christ at the Last Supper. Diluting the wine with water was customary at that time, and so, although the Gospels do not explicitly mention it, the Church has always required in practice that the wine be mixed with a small quantity of water. Certain Eastern anaphoras develop the account of the Supper as follows: "He took the chalice, mingled wine and water, and gave thanks . . ." (Syrian and Coptic liturgies).

The bread must be made of wheat to the exclusion of every other grain. In ancient times, and in the majority of Eastern rites today, ordinary raised or "leavened" bread is used. The Latin liturgy came to prefer unleavened bread, thus going back to the ritual of the Jewish Passover meal. Sacramental pedagogy has been complicated by this fact, since it has to be explained that the hosts really are bread and meant to be nourishing food.

2. Bringing up the bread and wine. In the present Roman Mass the actions of the Offertory are rather limited. The subdeacon brings the empty chalice from the credence table to the altar. On the chalice rests the paten containing the bread. He also brings up the ciboria containing the hosts for the people. At a Mass celebrated without deacon and subdeacon, the chalice, paten and ciboria are placed on the altar before Mass begins. When the celebrant has transferred the bread from the paten to the corporal, at the Offertory, the acolytes bring wine and water from the credence table and these are poured into the chalice.

In the ancient Roman practice, the faithful came in procession to the celebrant and his assistants bearing bread and wine from their own homes to be used for the Sacrifice, the present Offertory verse being the refrain used between the psalm verses chanted to accompany this procession. The collection customarily taken up during the Offertory at Sunday Mass is the modern substitute. But attempts are being made to find practical and acceptable modern versions of the ancient procession, the more vividly to bring out the active part of the faithful in offering the Sacrifice.

In the Eastern liturgies the bread and chalice are prepared before the Liturgy begins in a special ceremony which takes place in a sacristy or chapel called the *diakonikon,* or at a side altar. At the time of the liturgy of the Eucharist, they are brought up to the altar by the deacon or priest in a solemn procession called the Great Entrance.

3. The Offertory prayers. The Eastern rites have multiplied prayers to accompany the preparation of the materials for the Sacrifice. Similarly the Western rites, during the Middle Ages, developed prayer-formulas for the celebrant to say in a low voice during the Offertory. The redundancy of these prayers in all the liturgies is now deplored.[16]

Four kinds of Offertory prayers may be distinguished: (1) processional chants (a psalm in the Roman liturgy, hymns in the Eastern liturgies) accompanying the transfer of the bread and wine to the altar; (2) the formulation of particular intentions to be united with the universal intention for which the Eucharist is celebrated; (3) expressions of unworthiness and humility on the part of the celebrant prior to his acting in the very Person of Christ in celebrating the Eucharist, e.g. the *in spiritu humilitatis* of the Roman Mass; (4) prayers accompanying actions, e.g. the recitation of Psalm 25 while the priest washes his hands.

4. The meaning of the Offertory. Both in the Eastern and Western liturgies, the Offertory rites tend to give the impression that the consecration has already taken place. In the East the bread and wine are "adored" during the Great Entrance; in the Roman rites the bread and the chalice are "offered." This may be explained as expressing the sacredness of the bread and wine now set apart for the Sacrifice in which they will be changed into the Body and Blood of Christ. Thus they are called by anticipation "the spotless victim . . . the chalice of salvation."

But the Offertory is not a kind of natural sacrifice of our human gifts preliminary to Christ's sacrifice. The fruits asked for in the Offertory prayers are those which the sacrifice of Christ and it alone can gain for us.

Since the Offertory is properly defined as "placing on the altar the materials to be consecrated," it includes only one essential element: the

[16] See H. A. Reinhold, *op. cit.,* pp. 59-63.

intention which the priest forms of consecrating this bread and this wine, an intention made explicit by placing them on the altar.

IV. THE EUCHARISTIC PRAYER

The Eucharistic prayer, as we said earlier, was originally conceived as a single prayer, beginning with the dialogue between the celebrant and the faithful and ending with the *Amen* of the congregation. This prayer is called the *anaphora* in the Eastern liturgies; it includes the Preface and Canon of the present Roman rite. While this prayer has been broken up into more or less distinct formulas, we must keep in mind its underlying unity if we are to understand it rightly.

1. The Preface and its dialogue. In instruction on the Eucharist, every effort should be made to overcome the mistaken impression that the Preface is not included in the central and most solemn part of the Mass and that the term connotes a mere "introduction" or "foreword."[17] Actually the Preface begins the Canon and gives the whole its character of thanksgiving, of "eucharist." "It is truly fitting and just, right and for our salvation, always and everywhere to give thanks to You, O Lord, holy Father, almighty, eternal God."

To give thanks is to renew the prayer made by Christ at the Last Supper. The term "thanksgiving," as a biblical formula, goes far beyond the mere expression of gratitude for gifts received; rather, it becomes a joyful contemplation of the divine perfections. Philo expresses the Jewish tradition as follows:

> We affirm that the activity most characteristic of God is to give His blessings. But that most fitting to creation is to give thanks, because this is the best it can offer Him in return. For when creation tries to make any other return to God it finds that its gift already belongs to the Creator of the universe, not to the creature offering it. Since we now realize that to give due worship to God only one duty is incumbent upon us, that of giving thanks, we must carry it out in all times and in all places.[18]

St. Paul continually insists on the duty of giving thanks (Phil. 4:6; 1 Thess. 5:18; Eph. 5:19-20; Col. 3:17; 2 Cor. 1:3, etc.). The Church car-

---

[17] "*Praefatio* is indeed made up of the words *prae* and *fari,* to speak before. But it need not be taken only in a temporal sense, one speech before another. It can also be thought of in terms of space, speaking before an audience. The word was used in this sense in pre-Christian sacral language; it was the speech made before the divinity or else the speech made before the assembly. A public proclamation was also called a *praefatio.* This word was transferred to the liturgical language of Christendom and at least at Rome continued to be used in its original sense. *Praefatio* was therefore the solemn prayer and was part of the Canon; in fact, for a time, the whole Canon was, it would seem, called *praefatio*" (J. A. Jungmann, op. cit., p. 300).

[18] Cited by Odo Casel in *Le Mémorial du Seigneur* (Paris: 1945), p. 27.

ries this out supremely by celebrating the Eucharist. The Mass is the "sacrifice of praise."

In the Eastern anaphoras, and especially that of St. Basil, we find a full development of the motives inspiring our Christian thanksgiving. Two chief themes are presented: the divine perfections and the work of God in creation and redemption. Here the Eucharistic prayer continues the tradition of the psalms (Pss. 103, 134, 135, etc.), going from the praise of the eternal God to praise for His intervention in the history of Israel. This intervention attains its full purpose and meaning in the saving work of Christ, and so the proclamation of God's wonderful works leads into the narrative of the Last Supper.

All this is expressed much more briefly in the ordinary Preface of the Roman Mass: the wonderful privilege of our duty to give thanks; the titles by which God is addressed to express His divine perfections; the mediation of Christ our Lord, through whom the heavenly hosts also offer their praise; our desire to unite our praise with theirs. In special seasons and on special feasts, some particular aspect of Christ's redeeming work is included as a special reason for today's praise.

The thanksgiving opens with a dialogue between the celebrant and the people:

> Let us lift up our hearts.
> —We have raised them to the Lord.
> Let us give thanks to the Lord our God.
> —It is fitting and right.

This dialogue is considered vitally important in the Fathers' catechetical commentaries:

> The prayer of the thanksgiving is made in common. The bishop does not give thanks alone, but the whole assembly joins him. For, though the bishop speaks for the people, he does so only after they have said that it is fitting and right that he should begin the Eucharist (St. John Chrysostom, *Homily* on 2 Cor. 18:3).

2. The narrative of the Last Supper. The narrative given in our Latin Mass does not reproduce exactly any of the four texts of the New Testament (Matthew 26:26-28; Mark 14:22-24; Luke 22:19-20; 1 Cor. 11:23-26). It makes a kind of concordance of them all and adds certain details: "with His eyes lifted to heaven," a phrase found in the accounts of the multiplication of the loaves; and the phrase "the mystery of faith" (cf. 1 Tim. 3:9). In the Roman liturgy again, the narrative is acted out by the celebrant, who reproduces certain of Christ's actions while speaking of them.

3. The anamnesis and offering. *Anamnesis* is the name given to the prayer following the narrative of the institution: the celebrant refers to Christ's command at the Last Supper, "Do this in memory of Me," and at once proceeds to carry it out. "Remembering then, O Lord, the blessed passion of Christ Your Son, our Lord, His resurrection from among the dead and also His ascension into the glory of heaven. . . ."

This formula is found in all the liturgies and is witnessed to in all the early documents. To "remember" Christ is to recall the whole paschal mystery: His death, descent to the world of the dead, resurrection, ascension to the glory of the Father. His enthronement at the Father's right hand and His glorious return, included implicitly in this mystery, are also explicitly mentioned in some liturgies.

The anamnesis leads into a formula of offering, also found in one or another form in all rites:

> . . . we Your servants (i.e. the celebrant and his ministers) and also your holy people offer to Your sovereign Majesty this offering chosen from the blessings You have given us: the pure Victim, the holy Victim, the unblemished Victim, the holy Bread that gives eternal life and the chalice that gives everlasting salvation. Be pleased to look down on them kindly and favorably. Accept them as You accepted the gifts of our father Abraham and that which Melchisedech, Your high priest, offered to You, a holy sacrifice, a spotless victim.

The formulas so far mentioned within the Eucharistic prayer of the Roman rite—the Preface, the narrative of the Last Supper, the anamnesis and offering—are witnessed to in the *Apostolic Tradition* of Hippolytus and have been practically fixed in the Roman usage since the time of St. Ambrose. These are primary in studying the theology of the Mass, and should guide the spiritual activity of the Christian as he takes part in the Eucharist. Consequently, they should form the basis of instruction.

The other formulas are less ancient and are not found in all liturgies. Their study, therefore, should come as a secondary stage in teaching, to deepen our understanding of the mystery.

4. The epiclesis. The *epiclesis* is the invocation in which the celebrant asks God Himself to effect the changing of the bread into the Body of Christ and the wine into His Blood. This prayer of invocation witnesses to the entire gratuity of the gift of the Eucharist, a gratuity which we should gratefully recognize even though we know that the gift is infallibly connected with the carrying-out of the sacramental sign by the celebrant. In the Roman Mass it precedes the narrative of the Last Supper and leads into it.

In the Eastern liturgies this prayer invokes the coming of the Holy Spirit, and to Him is attributed the changing of the bread and wine into Christ's Body and Blood, since all the great works of salvation require the intervention of the Spirit, the Author of the incarnation and of all grace. The rites in which the epiclesis mentions the Holy Spirit place this prayer after the narrative of the Supper and after the anamnesis; yet the epiclesis asks for the changing of the bread and wine. There is no inconsistency in this, since the whole Eucharistic mystery is entirely accomplished in the consecration of the bread and wine. The various prayer-formulas bring out one or another aspect of the one mystery, but not necessarily in what seems to us logical order.

> When we ask God now to change the bread into His Body, now to receive with favor the oblation that we make of it, now to have His holy angel present it on the heavenly altar, now to have pity on the living, now to grant that this oblation may give solace to the dead: do we believe that God waits to do each of these things for the moment in which we speak to Him about them? Certainly not.
>
> All this is a consequence of human language, which can only explain itself part by part; but God, who sees in our hearts with one single glance everything we have said, are saying, and wish to say, hears all and accomplishes everything at the fitting times known to Himself, without our needing to trouble ourselves as to the precise moment in which He does so; it is enough that we express everything by fitting actions and words, and that the whole, even though it is carried out and proclaimed step by step, represents to us in unity all the effects and, as it were, the whole face of the divine mystery.[19]

5. The Eucharist: participation in the heavenly liturgy.   The liturgy of the Eucharist takes various means to relate the act carried out on our earthly altar to the liturgy of heaven. In the Eastern liturgies this is brought out in the hymns accompanying the Great Entrance:

> We who in a mystical way represent the Cherubim and who sing "Holy, holy, holy" to the life-giving Trinity are now to put aside all temporal care, so as to welcome the King of heaven and earth whom legions of angels invisibly accompany *(Byzantine Liturgy)*.
>
> Let all mortal flesh be silent and stand with fear and trembling and nothing earthly raise its voice here. For the King of kings, the Lord of lords is advancing to be sacrificed and given as food to the faithful. . . . He is preceded by choirs of Archangels with all their power and might, by many-eyed Cherubim and six-winged Seraphim who veil their eyes, singing . . . *(Greek Liturgy of St. James)*.

In the Roman rite the *Sanctus* invites us to make our own the chant of the Cherubim (Is. 6:3). Again, the prayer *Communicantes* indicates the Church of heaven as one with the Christian assembly on earth. And, finally, there is the formula following the anamnesis and offering:

> Almighty God, we humbly beg You to have these offerings carried by the hands of Your holy angel to Your heavenly altar in the presence

---

[19] J. B. Bossuet, quoted by A. M. Roguet in "The Whole Mass Proclaims the Word of God," *The Liturgy and the Word of God,* p. 70. The whole context, pp. 68-71, should be read in this connection.

of Your divine Majesty. Then we who take part in the sacrifice at this altar and are to receive the most sacred Body and Blood of Your Son shall be filled with all the blessings and grace of heaven.

The iconography of the churches of Ravenna and the Byzantine East reproduces the image of the heavenly liturgy. This is also an important aspect of the Eucharistic catecheses of the Fathers.[20] What takes place on the altar puts us into contact with heaven. It brings us into the very presence of God, and so is a pressing invitation to adoration, to the holy fear felt by the heavenly witnesses to the divine transcendence, the pillars of God's majesty. It is an obscure but real anticipation of our future state as citizens of heaven.

6. Prayers of petition or intercession.   In the Eucharist, as in Jacob's vision of the ladder (Gen. 28:11-12), there is an ascending and descending movement. The Church causes the sacrifice of praise to "ascend" to the heavenly altar, to the Father; the Father causes His graces and blessings to "descend" on those present.

The Eastern rites arrange petitions for these blessings in a continuous prayer of intercession, usually prolonged in a litany directed by the deacon.

The Eucharistic prayer of the Roman Mass includes, before the consecration, formulas of petition for the Church spread throughout the world and for her hierarchy, for those present at the assembly and those absent (*Te igitur* and *Memento* of the living), for peace in our earthly life. After the consecration, anamnesis and offering, comes prayer for those who are to receive Communion, for the faithful departed (*Memento* of the dead), and for those celebrating the Mass (*Nobis quoque peccatoribus*), asking that all may attain the life of heaven of which the Eucharist is the anticipation and pledge. These petitions that God may complete His wonderful works in our behalf indicate once more how our Eucharistic prayer follows the original Jewish pattern of "giving thanks,"[21] as they lead up to the final doxology:

By Him, with Him and in Him is to You, God the Father almighty, in the unity of the Holy Spirit, all honor and glory for ever and ever. Amen.

7. The response of faith.   The formulas of the Eucharistic prayer, with the exception of the narrative of the Last Supper which includes the consecration, are said by the celebrant in the name of the whole assembly. It is not he alone who "gives thanks" and "recalls"; the holy People of God do likewise. The offering is not that of the clergy alone, but of the "whole household" of the Lord. The Christian should therefore unite

[20] See J. Daniélou, *op. cit.,* pp. 135-137.

[21] See L. Bouyer, *Liturgical Piety,* pp. 115-128.

himself interiorly with these prayers in silent adoration. To arouse this act of faith in the Real Presence of Christ and His Sacrifice, all the liturgies contain a showing or elevation of the consecrated gifts at some point during the liturgy.

But this silence is not enough. In the Roman rite the members of the congregation indicate their faith and their participation in the sacrifice of praise by joining in the dialogue at the Preface, in the singing of the *Sanctus,* and in the final *Amen* at the end of the doxology (cf. *Mediator Dei,* 104; the significance of the people's *Amen* is repeatedly brought out in the Fathers' catecheses).

In the Eastern rites, the Coptic in particular, *Amen* is sung after each of the formulas of consecration or even after each detail of the narrative of the Last Supper. The East also gives the faithful a more active external part in the Eucharistic prayer by means of hymns called troparies which constitute a kind of echo of the celebrant's prayer.

V. BREAKING THE BREAD

Breaking the bread reproduces the action of Christ at the Last Supper, an action mentioned in all four of the New Testament accounts. Moreover, it was when the disciples at Emmaus saw their Guest carrying out this action that they recognized who He was (Luke 24:30-31). In itself, the act of breaking bread is not peculiar to the Eucharist; it was traditionally the role of the master of the house, of the father at the family table. As such it is typical of a meal, and a meal taken in common.

As carried out by Christ, breaking bread took on a messianic significance brought out by the evangelists in connection with the multiplication of the loaves (Matthew 14:19; 15:36; Mark 6:41; 8:6, 19; Luke 9:16). The accounts indicate through many details the biblical theme of Christ as the Good Shepherd who leads His flock to the pastures of the Promised Land. This sign of breaking bread attained its highest and definitive realization when Christ instituted the Eucharist. The Eucharist is already the meal of the Promised Land, the Land to which Christ is leading us.

"The breaking of bread" was the term first used by the apostolic community to refer to the Eucharist (Acts 2:42, 46; 20:7, 11; 27:35;[22] 1 Cor. 10:16-17). To its eschatological meaning St. Paul adds another. "The bread that we break, is it not communion in the body of Christ? Since there is but one bread, we all form one body, for we all partake of the one bread" (1 Cor. 10:16).

In Roman antiquity the rite of the "fraction" was given great ceremonial importance. Unfortunately this was greatly diminished as a con-

---

[22]This use of the term "breaking of bread" by St. Luke in the Acts gives exegetes greater certitude in seeing the Eucharist indicated in the episode in St. Luke's Gospel (24:30-31) of the disciples at Emmaus.

sequence of the frightening rarity of Communions in the Middle Ages and the influence of unfortunate allegorical notions.[23]

VI. THE COMMUNION RITES

1. Preparation for Communion. In all rites, the *Pater* is the supreme prayer of preparation for Communion because of the petitions, "Give us this day our daily bread" and "Forgive us our trespasses as we forgive those who trespass against us." In the Roman Mass the "fraction" comes after the *Pater* and is included in the rites preparatory to Communion. Other prayers have been added to ask for the graces proper to the sacrament and to express faith, adoration and desire.

2. Communion. The celebrant bends over the altar, eats the Bread which has been broken and then drinks the chalice. In every liturgy he must communicate, and do so under both species. If he should become too weak or otherwise unable to finish celebrating the Mass, another priest normally must take his place so that the Sacrifice may be complete, "perfected."

Customs regarding the Communion of the faithful have varied in the Roman rite. In the ancient Church and at least up to the twelfth and thirteenth centuries, they received first the species of bread from the priests and the species of wine from the deacons. They held out their hands crossed, palms upward, to receive the Bread and then communicated themselves, saving some of the Eucharistic Bread to take home for Communion during the week. In giving each sacred species, the priest or deacon said, "The Body of Christ!" "The Blood of Christ!" and the communicant answered, "Amen." To receive Communion, the faithful came up to the steps of the sanctuary in procession, singing a psalm, most frequently Psalm 33. Such a procession accompanied by communal song is a very meaningful sign, bringing out both the communal and the paschal character of Communion, and is happily being restored today in many parishes.

The Eastern rites have kept to the ancient customs in this as in other matters, except that in some cases the two species are given together: the Bread cut up into little cubes is dipped in the wine, or put into the chalice and then given with a special spoon. But the West has ceased to give Communion under the species of wine to the faithful since the Middle Ages. This may have come about simply for some practical reason such as hygiene or danger of profanation. But the heresies of the fifteenth and sixteenth centuries attacked the suppression of the cup for the laity with such vigor in the name of an erroneous theology that the Church re-

---

[23]On the rite and its development, see J. A. Jungmann, *The Mass of the Roman Rite*, II, pp. 303ff. Even St. Thomas shows the influence of this allegorism (*Summa* III, 83, 5, ad 7), already exemplified in the Gallican liturgy of the seventh century.

fused to return to Communion under the species of wine where this custom had been abandoned. Nevertheless, the pronouncement of the Council of Trent on this question was disciplinary and not dogmatic (Sess. 22).

3. After Communion. The Roman Church has composed Postcommunion prayers to be sung by the celebrant in the name of all present. Austere and brief, like the majority of the orations in the Roman Missal, they express thanksgiving for the gift received, stress the sacrifice just celebrated, and lead our thoughts to our daily life as it is to be transformed by the Eucharist and to the eternal life of which the Eucharist is the pledge.

The assembly is dismissed by the deacon with the simple words, "Go, it is the dismissal," to which the faithful reply, "Thanks to God!," thus giving an explicitly eucharistic conclusion to the celebration of the Eucharist. No allegorical meaning is to be attached to this dismissal;[24] it is inspiring in its obvious sense. The Eucharistic celebration is finished; we are to go out from it to witness to Christ.[25]

Section Two

THE EUCHARISTIC MYSTERY

THE RE-PRESENTATION OF THE LORD'S SUPPER

The liturgy of the Eucharist might be summed up in this brief formula: it re-presents the Last Supper. The developments in the various rites through the ages have only one purpose—to bring out and clarify Christ's actions and words and their meaning.

For the validity of the Eucharist, the Church counts it sufficient that a priest, who has received a share in the apostolic priesthood through ordination, pronounce the narrative of the Last Supper over the bread and wine, following the intention and conditions required by the

[24] See J. A. Jungmann, *op. cit.,* II, pp. 432ff.

[25] See *Liturgy and Social Order,* PNLW 1955; J. Lécuyer, "Happy are They Who Hear the Word of God and Put It into Practice," *The Liturgy and the Word of God,* pp. 157-171.

Church.[26] Communion is not required for the validity of the sign, although the Eucharist is meant to be eaten in a meal.

Christ Himself commanded that the Last Supper be renewed and He entrusted this renewal to His apostles.

> For I myself received from the Lord what I in turn have handed on to you. The Lord Jesus, on the night in which he was betrayed, took bread and, having given thanks, broke it and said, "This is my body which is delivered up for you, do this in memory of me." In the same way, after the meal, he took the cup saying, "This cup is the new covenant in my blood; whenever you drink it, do it in memory of me" (1 Cor. 11:23-25).

St. Paul stresses this command in order to oppose the confusion he found in the assemblies of Corinth. The gatherings had become like ordinary meals and no longer the Supper of the Lord (1 Cor. 11:20). Following St. Paul's example, all the liturgies mention Christ's command to renew the Last Supper, realizing that it is because of this command that the Eucharist is celebrated. Moreover, the Council of Trent sees in Christ's command the institution of the Christian priesthood (*Denz.* 949).

The priest celebrating the Eucharist is identified with Christ in this action to such a degree that he efficaciously acts in the Person of Christ and in him Christ is present. "He lends his tongue to Christ, he offers Him his hand," says St. John Chrysostom (*Homily* 86 on John, 4).

> Everything that has been said up to this point is said by the priest himself; we offer praise to God, we pray for the people, for rulers, for everyone. But as soon as we come to reproduce the holy sacrament, the priest no longer uses his own words, but makes use of the words of Christ. It is, then, the word of Christ that produces this sacrament (St. Ambrose, *On the Sacraments,* 4,14).

> The priest carries out the role of Christ, doing what Christ did. In the Church he offers the true and complete sacrifice since he offers it just as Christ Himself offered it (St. Cyprian, *Letter* 63,14).

Because it efficaciously reproduces the Last Supper, the Eucharist gives us the Real Presence of Christ as our food and drink. It is a true sacrifice, the memorial of the passion of Christ. It is the proclamation of His return: "Each time that you eat this bread and drink this cup, you proclaim the death of the Lord until he comes" (1 Cor. 11:26). It is by starting from the Last Supper, then, that we discover the truth of these statements about the Eucharist and their meaning for our faith.

---

[26] We say "the narrative of the Last Supper" and not simply "This is My Body . . . ," following de la Taille, *Mysterium Fidei* (Paris: Beauchesne, 1921), pp. 459-467. This is in fact the practice of the Church. In case of defect in the celebration, she always has the whole narrative repeated. St. Thomas states that the words "This is My Body . . ." are pronounced "in a narrative" (*Summa* III, 18, 5).

Article One
THE REAL PRESENCE OF CHRIST

All the other aspects of the Eucharist are based on the fact of the Real Presence of Christ. If He were not really present, there would be no sacrifice and no anticipation of future blessings. Furthermore, serious heresies concerning the Eucharist have arisen in connection with the Real Presence, and so the Church has been obliged to explain her doctrine in precise terms while the faithful have been stimulated to a more ardent manifestation of their faith in Christ's Presence.

Yet it is a mistake, either in our spiritual attitude or in our teaching the Eucharist, to separate the fact of the Real Presence from the other aspects of the Eucharist: the memorial of the passion, Communion and the pledge of heavenly glory. The Office of Corpus Christi brings them all together in the verse:

> O sacred banquet! Here Christ is received; here the memory of His passion is recalled, our spirit filled with grace, the pledge of future glory given us.

The Real Presence is a mystery which we must accept, experience and pass on to others first in the simple way it is expressed in the Gospel and the liturgy. On this basis, our understanding of the mystery may then progress and develop into a theology, making use of the new lights and more exact formulations provided through the centuries by the practice of the Church, the contemplation of the saints, Christian devotion and disputes against heresies.

I. THE STATEMENT OF THE MYSTERY

In its essential affirmation, nothing is simpler than Christian faith in the Eucharist. Christ said, "This is My Body . . . this is My Blood"; the Church says, "The Body of Christ!" The faithful answer, "Amen, it is true."

> It is not without reason that you say "Amen" since you recognize in your spirit that you are receiving the Body of Christ. For when you present yourself, the priest says to you, "The Body of Christ!" and you answer "Amen," that is, "It is true." What your tongue professes, your conviction must also retain (St. Ambrose, *On the Sacraments*, 4, 25).

The ancient Fathers in their catecheses and modern educators use the same method. They take the words of Christ at the Last Supper; they explain the meaning of these words by the teaching which Christ gave on the Eucharist; they insist on the efficacy of the Word by whom all things were made.

1. The words of Christ at the Last Supper.   The four accounts of the Last Supper all agree on essentials. This is the more remarkable since they present many differences as to details and can be divided into two distinct traditions: Paul and Luke on the one hand, Mark and Matthew on the other (see the chart on p. 204).

The words of Christ, "This is My Body," "This is My Blood" or "This cup is the New Covenant in My Blood," cannot be taken in an allegorical sense. They are not to be understood as a parable or a comparison, but literally. There are several reasons for this assertion. In the first place, there is the fact that these words accompany and are connected with material, bodily actions using the concrete elements of a meal. "He took bread, broke it, distributed it. . . . Take . . . eat." Again, the sacrificial context of the Last Supper and particularly the establishment of the New Covenant require the reality of the Presence. Moses had said, "This is the blood of the covenant" when he was pouring out the blood of the slain animals (Exod. 24:8). Jesus said, "This is My Blood, the Blood of the covenant." There is also the paschal character of the Last Supper which prescribed the eating of the lamb. Here again, we see that faith in the Real Presence attains its full development only in relation to sacrifice and Communion.

St. Paul understood the Eucharist in this way:

> The cup of blessing that we bless, is it not communion in the Blood of Christ? The bread that we break, is it not communion in the Body of Christ? Since there is but one bread, we all form one body, for we all partake of the one bread. Consider Israel according to the flesh. Were not those who ate the victims in communion with the altar? . . . You cannot drink the cup of the Lord and the cup of demons. You cannot partake at the table of the Lord and at the table of demons (1 Cor. 10:16-21).

Most important of all, Christ Himself had spoken of the Eucharist before He instituted it, bringing out both its realism and its sacramental significance. This last point is important because bread and wine as such would not necessarily signify His Presence.

2. The signs of bread and wine.   At first sight, the Gospels might not seem to indicate any relationship between wine and the Eucharist, but when we examine them more deeply, we find that they do. They mention the "new wine" which must not be put in old wineskins (Mark 2:22). "New wine" is also mentioned in the accounts of the Last Supper as the drink of eschatological times. In this light, the miracle of changing water into wine at Cana shines out as a most expressive sign of the Eucharist, especially since it took place at a wedding-feast. Jesus also spoke on several occasions of the "cup" which He was to drink, a symbol of sacrifice. All these references, then, aid our understanding of the Eucharist in its sacrificial and eschatological context.

Most enlightening of all is Jesus' reference to wine as "the fruit of the vine" in the Synoptics' accounts of the Last Supper, a reference which takes on its full meaning in the light of the discourse connected with the Supper in St. John's Gospel. Throughout the Old Testament the vine is a symbol of the People of God.[27] And so, when Jesus says

> I am the true vine and my Father is the vine-dresser. . . . Live on in me as I in you. As the branch cannot bear fruit of itself unless it lives on in the vine, so neither can you unless you live on in me (John 15:1ff).

He is telling us that we enter into the new People of God by union with Him, a true union of life. Here, then, He attaches a symbolism to wine corresponding to the symbolism He had already given to bread in an even more explicit way.

When He announced His imminent passion at the time of the last Passover, Jesus compared Himself to a grain of wheat: "If the grain of wheat does not fall to the ground and die, it remains alone; if it dies it bears much fruit" (John 12:24). But shortly before an earlier Passover, He had given a complete instruction on bread, beginning with a miracle. In the desert the Hebrew people had eaten manna, that is "bread come from heaven" (Ps. 77:24). So Christ fed His people in a wonderful way by multiplying the loaves (John 6: 1-16), showing Himself as the new Moses, the expected prophet (v. 14). This "sign" was the starting-point of His teaching. He Himself is the Bread of heaven, the true Bread that gives life to the world: "I am the bread of life, he who comes to me will never hunger." Like the manna, He comes from heaven: "I have come down from heaven not to do my will but the will of Him who sent me" (vv. 34, 38). While the Hebrews who had eaten the manna had died, the Son of God gives eternal life to those who believe in Him (vv. 40, 49). But believing is not enough—the manna was to be eaten. In the same way:

> This is the bread that comes down from heaven so that whoever eats of it will not die. I am the living bread come down from heaven; he who eats this bread will live forever, and the bread that I will give is my flesh, for the life of the world (vv. 50-51).

The idea of sacrifice is here connected with that of the food of im-mortality. As in the other catecheses transmitted to us by St. John (to the Samaritan woman, to Nicodemus), Jesus goes about His teaching step by step, presenting the mystery gradually, each time waiting for the

---

[27] See J. Guillet, *Themes of the Bible*, pp. 211-217.

reaction of His hearers. As they ask Him questions and bring up difficulties, Jesus makes His meaning clearer and causes His hearers to enter more deeply into His revelation. In this case, the Jews are baffled by the realism of Christ's way of speaking and ask one another, "How can this man give us His flesh to eat?" Far from softening His words, Jesus repeats and accentuates His statements:

> In truth, in very truth, I tell you, unless you eat the flesh of the Son of Man and drink his blood, you shall not have life in you. He who eats my flesh and drinks my blood has everlasting life, and I will raise him up on the last day. For my flesh is true food and my blood true drink. He who eats my flesh and drinks my blood lives on in me and I in him. As I live by the living Father who sent me, so he who eats me will live by me. This is the bread that came from heaven. It is not like the bread that your fathers ate. They are dead, but he who eats this bread will live forever (John 6:53-58).

This teaching provoked murmuring and defections among His disciples. But Jesus did not take it back (6:60, 61, 66-67), proof that we must understand His announcement of a new manna in the sense of a real eating of His flesh. The Twelve remained, including Judas, and after Peter's profession of faith ("You have the words of eternal life"), Jesus immediately predicted His betrayal: "Have I not chosen you twelve, and one of you is a devil?" (vv. 68-72), a striking anticipation of His statement at the Last Supper: ". . . one of you will betray me" (John 13:21). Here, then, the Bread that is Christ's flesh, the Last Supper and the passion are intimately connected.

3. The efficacy of Christ's word. The Church has always taken literally Christ's words at the Last Supper repeated in the celebration of the Eucharist (*Denz.* 874, 883). To this testimony of her liturgical life is added that of the Fathers' pastoral works and apologetic treatises.[28]

The Fathers present only one motive for belief in the mystery of the Eucharist, and this is the Word of Christ, not only because it is truthful, but because it is efficacious.

> It is the word of Christ that produces this sacrament. What word of Christ? That by which all things were made. The Lord commanded and the heavens were made. The Lord commanded and the seas were made. The Lord commanded and creatures were brought forth. You see how efficacious is Christ's word. If then the word of the Lord Jesus has such power that what was not began to be, how efficacious it must be in causing that which already exists to become something else (St. Ambrose, *On the Sacraments*, 4).

The Word of God who made all things by His word is the same Christ who commanded the winds and the sea, who cured human ills and raised

[28] See *The Sacraments and Worship* (SCT I), pp. 132ff.

the dead to life by His word. In the Eucharist, "the Word-made-flesh makes bread His flesh by His word and wine becomes Christ's Blood" (St. Thomas, *Pange lingua*).

II. THE THEOLOGY OF THE MYSTERY

1. Transubstantiation. The Presence of Christ in the Eucharist is produced by the changing of bread into the Body of Christ and the wine into His Blood. Before the consecration there was bread and wine; when Christ has pronounced the words (at the Last Supper and through the ministry of the priest in the Mass), the bread and wine are His Body and Blood.

What takes place is not a substitution, but a change. This is clearly stated in the epicleses of the various liturgies, for example the invocation that precedes the consecration in the Roman canon:

> Be pleased to make this offering blessed in every way. Accept it, accord it Your full favor, make it perfect and pleasing to You in every way, so that it may become for us the Body and Blood of Your well-beloved Son.

Or this Syrian formula:

> Send forth Your holy Spirit . . . so that by His coming He may make this bread the Body of Christ, the Body which is the author of life, the Body which brings salvation to our souls and our bodies, the Body of the Lord . . . and that He may make this mixture in the chalice into the Blood of Christ, the Blood that purifies our souls and our bodies, the Blood of our Lord and our Savior, Jesus Christ.

As St. Ambrose says:

> Perhaps you say, "This is just ordinary bread." It was bread before the sacramental words. As soon as the consecration takes place, the bread is changed into the flesh of Christ (*On the Sacraments*).

Or St. John Chrysostom:

> How can you say, "I wish I might see how He looks, His face, His clothing, His sandals." It is He Himself whom you see, whom you touch, whom you eat (*Homily on Matthew*, 82,4).

This last quotation brings out the fact that in the Eucharist Christ is truly present but that there is a difference between His natural presence and His sacramental presence. Those who knew Him in His earthly life could hear Him and see Him. But His sacramental presence does not come within the range of our senses. Instead we have the taste, color, weight, etc., of the bread and wine—the species, to use the theological term—remaining as the sign of His Presence.

> You know that wine and water are put into the chalice, but that the consecration effected by the heavenly word changes them into Blood. Perhaps you say, "I do not see the appearance of blood." But this is the symbol of it. As you took the symbol of death, so you also drink the symbol of blood (St. Ambrose, *On the Sacraments*).

In the above quotation, the word "symbol" is the exact equivalent of "sign" or "species." The fact that the species remain after the consecration should not, therefore, lead us to imagine them as a kind of veil hiding Christ, or as a container in which He is to be found. Christ is not *in* the bread, or *with* the bread, as certain Protestant theologians held at the time of the Reformation. The bread is changed into the Body of Christ with the species of bread remaining as the sign. This is what the Council of Trent calls "transubstantiation" (*Denz.* 877, 883-884).

Consequently, the changing of the bread and wine into the Body and Blood of Christ is a reality apart, belonging to the sacramental order. It is not a creation from nothing; the Eucharist presupposes bread and wine. Nor is it a new incarnation of Christ; only very roughly can the Eucharistic consecration be compared to the coming of Jesus on earth. As St. John Damascene remarks:

> The Body is truly united to the divinity, and it is the Body that was born of the Virgin. But it is not as though the Body that He took came down from heaven. The bread and wine themselves are transformed into the Body and the Blood of God" (*On the Orthodox Faith*, 4, 13).

Nor, strictly speaking, is transubstantiation a miracle, since it follows the law of the sacramental order. Moreover, miracles are signs for unbelievers, while transubstantiation is an object of faith.[29]

In our way of thinking about the Eucharist and speaking of it, therefore, we must avoid applying to Christ what is true only of the species. For example, Christ is not "a prisoner in the tabernacle" although the reserved Host is kept locked up for the sake of safety. Again, while great care should be taken to guard the Host against profanations, they do not touch Christ directly; they are an offense against Him only by reason of the guilt of those committing them. We should, then, avoid the pious imagery and type of hymns which cause confusion in the Eucharistic piety of the faithful[30] and always keep in the foreground of our minds the principle that the Eucharist is food and drink: "Take and eat . . . take and drink."

[29] See *Christ in His Sacraments*, in *Theology Library*, 6 (A. M. Henry, ed.), pp. 117-120.

[30] See A. M. Roguet, "Popularizing Mystery" in *Orate Fratres* 21 (1946), pp. 546-555.

2. The continuing presence of Christ in the Eucharistic species.

The Church has always taken for granted the fact that Christ remains present in the Eucharistic species as long as the species last. This is indicated, for example, by the practice since the earliest times of reserving the Eucharist for the Communion of the sick, or that of allowing the faithful to take some of the sacred species home with them for Communion during the week. Again, the earliest writers point out the care that must be taken to avoid any disrespect, even involuntary, in the service of the Eucharist:

> We take good care that nothing from our chalice or our bread should fall to the ground (Tertullian, *On the Crown*, 3,4).

> You who are accustomed to assist at the divine mysteries know with what respectful care you guard the Body of the Lord when it is entrusted to you, for fear lest any crumb should fall and any part of the consecrated treasure be lost (Origen, *Homily on Exodus*, 13).

From these facts the Council of Trent concluded that the Eucharist is constituted by the consecration previous to its being eaten and drunk, and remains as long as the species subsist; only their decomposition brings about the cessation of the Presence of Christ. Here the Eucharist differs from the other sacraments which are constituted in the act of being administered to a subject.

> If anyone says that after the consecration the Body and Blood of Christ are not in the sacrament of the Eucharist, but are present only when a person actually receives Communion and not before or after, and that the true Body of Christ does not remain in the consecrated particles left over after Communion, let him be anathema (*Denz.* 886).

3. Consequences of the sacramental mode of Christ's presence.

His flesh is food, His blood is drink,
But under each species
Christ remains whole.

Uncut, unbroken, undivided
By our communicating,
Each receives Him wholly.

Whether one receives Him or a thousand,
Each one receives the same,
Nor is He diminished by being received.

The Host, then, can be broken—
Have no doubt, realize that in each fragment
Christ is present as in the whole Host.

The reality is not divided,
Only the sign is broken up;

He who is signified
Is not diminished in state or stature.

These lines from the hymn *Lauda Sion* used in the Mass of Corpus Christi summarize the Church's teaching on certain consequences of the sacramental mode of Christ's Presence. A great amount of consecrated bread or wine is not needed in order that Christ is really received. Breaking the bread does not divide the Body of Christ. Communion under one species gives the whole Christ.

Communion under both species is obligatory only for the celebrant. In the practice of the early Church, Communion was given to the faithful under the species of wine only, for example to infants; and under the species of bread only, for example when the faithful communicated in their own homes. The complete abandonment in the West of the cup for the faithful was recognized as valid by the Church, particularly at the Council of Trent *(Denz.* 876, 885), since Christ is present whole and entire under each species.

The risen Christ dies no more; consequently, the Body and Blood of Christ cannot really be separated. When we consider the effect indicated by the words, the consecration of the bread is an efficacious sign only of the Body of Christ. But since His Body is now inseparable from His Blood, His Blood is made present with His Body by what is called "concomitance." (This is the term used for the Presence under one of the Eucharistic species of what is not signified by the words of consecration but is inseparable from what they do signify, because of the risen state of Christ.) In the same way, the species of wine by reason of the words of consecration is the efficacious sign only of the Blood of Christ, but His Body is present by concomitance. Under each species Christ is present whole and entire with His soul inseparable from His living body, and His divinity united for ever with His humanity *(Denz.* 883); therefore we owe the Eucharist a cult of adoration.

4. Adoration of the Eucharist. Together with faith, adoration is the spiritual attitude imposed in the presence of the Eucharist. Under the sacramental signs, here is the Lord, the Son of the living God. It is a universal tradition in the liturgies to elevate or show the consecrated bread and the chalice at some point after the consecration to arouse the assembly to this faith and adoration.

The Latin Middle Ages acquired a special taste for these "ostensions," leading to the development of rites such as the Corpus Christi procession or the solemn public adoration of the Blessed Sacrament, as during the "Forty Hours."

The Church emphasizes, however, that these accessory rites should remain clearly related to the Mass and to Communion. For example, the Corpus Christi procession should follow the Mass, and the Host venerated should be one consecrated at that Mass. Again, the sacred Host is to be reserved in a tabernacle on an altar.

The cult of the Eucharist, therefore, must safeguard both the reality of the personal Presence of Christ and the sacramental mode of that Presence. The Eucharist is the supreme sign, the "Blessed Sacrament," not only because of its content, but also because of the dimensions of its symbolism. The sacred species have been consecrated in the course of a Eucharistic celebration and are meant to be our food and drink in Communion. Thus the Real Presence of Christ here today under these species refers us to the whole of sacred history, centered in Christ's sacrifice, and to the life of the world to come, of which the Eucharist is the anticipation.

Article Two
THE EUCHARISTIC SACRIFICE

I. THE EUCHARIST A TRUE SACRIFICE

The definition of the Council of Trent simply formulates what Christians have always believed about the Eucharist:

> If anyone say that in the Mass there is not offered to God a real sacrifice properly so called, let him be anathema (*Denz.* 948).

The character and prayers of the Eucharist liturgy clearly indicate the Church's conviction that she is offering a sacrifice to God. This conviction is shown by her terminology: the altar-bread to be consecrated is called *hostia* (victim) or *amnos* (lamb). It is brought out by the prayers accompanying the preparation of the bread and wine and also, in the Roman Mass, by the Postcommunions. Above all, the prayers that follow the consecration give the oldest and most universal expression of this conviction, and the richest from the viewpoint of instruction:

> We offer to Your sovereign Majesty this offering chosen from the blessings You have given us, the pure Victim, the holy Victim, the unblemished Victim, the holy Bread that gives everlasting life and the chalice that gives everlasting salvation.
>
> Be pleased to look on them kindly and favorably. Accept them as You accepted the gifts of Your holy servant Abel and the sacrifice of our father Abraham, and that which Melchisedech Your high priest offered to You, a holy sacrifice, a spotless victim.[31]

[31] See the corresponding prayers in, e.g. *The Divine Liturgy of St. John Chrysostom*, ed. Basil Shereghy, pp. 46-50.

The Mass is a sacrifice because Christ is offered, the only Victim pleasing to God, who offered His sacrifice once for all on the Cross. The prayers of the liturgy therefore direct our attention to Christ by mentioning the sacrifice of Melchisedech (since Jesus is priest according to the order of Melchisedech [Heb. 7:11]) and to His Cross by referring to the sacrifices of Abel and Abraham. For the Mass is not an independent sacrifice, taking away from the unique character of the sacrifice of the Cross:

> It is one and the same Victim; it is the same (Christ) who offers Himself today through the ministry of priests and who once offered Himself on the Cross; the only difference is in the mode of the offering (*Denz.* 940).

This mode is sacramental, the mode of the Real Presence; the Mass is the effective memorial of the sacrifice of the Cross. Consequently, in order to understand how the Mass is a sacrifice and our sacrifice, we must first see the death of Christ as a sacrifice and then the connection between the sacrifice of the Cross and the Last Supper, reproduced in the sacramental sacrifice of the Eucharist.

II. THE SACRIFICE OF THE CROSS, THE ONE SACRIFICE OF THE NEW LAW[32]

As we said earlier, to make a definition of sacrifice from the study of comparative religion and anthropology and to apply it to the Mass is not a satisfactory approach. It is only through studying concrete biblical history—the biblical figures and the development of the idea of sacrifice in the Old Testament—that we gain a perception of the richness and purity of the idea of sacrifice and see how Christ's death on the Cross is *the* sacrifice. This is the method followed, for example, by St. Augustine.

1. The primordial models: Abel, Abraham, Melchisedech.

> Abel become a keeper of flocks and Cain cultivated the soil. Time went on, and it happened that Cain presented his fruits of the soil in an offering to Yahweh, and Abel, for his part, offered the first-born of his flock and their fat. Now Yahweh was pleased with Abel and his offering. But he was not pleased with Cain and his offering (Gen. 4:2-5).

In the world of sin inaugurated by his parents, Abel is just, even "the Just" as he is called in all the books of the New Testament (Matthew 23:35; Heb. 11:4; John 3:12). The offerings of the two brothers were not evaluated in terms of material worth; Yahweh sees into the depths of hearts and is not content with an insincere gesture. He is free to accept or reject what we offer Him.

[32] See F. X. Durrwell, *The Resurrection*, pp. 59-77.

Abel was also the first of the just men and prophets whose blood was poured out. His line extends to Zacharias, son of Barachias, and finally includes Christ Jesus and His disciples (Matthew 23:35). God had Cain hear the blood of his brother crying out to Him from the earth. But the Blood of Christ speaks more eloquently than that of Abel (Heb. 12:24). It brings judgment upon those who reject Him (Matthew 23:35; 27:25), but it cleanses and saves those who believe in Him.

Like that of Abel, the sacrifice of Abraham is mentioned in almost all the oldest liturgies, and it figures also among the traditional readings for the Easter Vigil. This sacrifice has a special place in the economy of the promises of the Old Testament and in Christian typology. Abraham was tested by Yahweh in his faith itself (Gen. 22:1-19). He was told to take Isaac, his only son and only heir of God's promise, to a mountain which would be shown him and to offer him as a holocaust, setting up a pyre of wood and sacrificing him upon it. It seemed as though God wished to annul His own promises. Nevertheless, in faith and obedience Abraham offered his son, "considering that God is mighty enough to raise even the dead to life" (Heb. 11:17-19). God spared Isaac; the sacrifice was not carried out because it was only a figure, to be fulfilled in Christ's obedience even to the death of the Cross.[33]

Melchisedech, finally, is one of the most important figures in the typology of the New Testament and the Church:

> When Abram returned after conquering Kedor-Laomer and the kings who were with him, the king of Salem went out to meet him. . . . Melchisedech, king of Salem, brought bread and wine; he was the priest of the Most High God. He pronounced this blessing: Blessed be Abram by the Most High God who created heaven and earth, and blessed be God the Most High who has delivered your enemies into your hands. And Abram gave him a tenth of everything (Gen. 14:17-20).

The "Most High God" is the true God, the God of Abraham (Gen. 14:22); Melchisedech is king of Salem, the city with a name meaning "peace," and later to be identified with Jerusalem (Ps. 75:3; cf. Jud. 4:4). He was king and also priest. This twofold function united in one man will be the privilege of the Messiah, Son of David. But the Messiah will not offer thanks for the victory of someone else; He will Himself be victorious over His enemies and will also be the priest who, according

[33] "This episode, connected with a place of worship (v. 5), the name of which is explained (v. 14), divinely establishes a ritual prescription: the substitution of a single animal victim for the first-born of men; these belong to God as do all first fruits (Exod. 22:29), but they are not to be sacrificed, but redeemed (Exod. 13:13; 34:19-29), as Jesus was (Luke 2:23-24). God can ask for everything, but He condemns the sacrificing of children, those heroic and barbaric offerings of the Canaanite cults which even Israel practiced with a kind of frenzy at certain periods (2 Kings 16:3; 21:6). But this account gives a higher spiritual lesson also. God asks above all for obedience in faith. (1 Sam. 15: 22ff; Ps. 51:18ff.) (*Bible de Jerusalem,* note on Gen. 22).

to the Lord's decree, will offer the sacrifice of thanksgiving: "You are a priest forever according to the order of Melchisedech" (Ps. 109:4).

Jesus claimed this office prophesied in this psalm (Matthew 22:24; Acts 2:34-35). The Epistle to the Hebrews continually repeats that His priesthood is "according to the order of Melchisedech." Christ is like Melchisedech because the Father appointed Him priest, a glory Christ did not take on Himself (5:5-10); because His priesthood is superior to that of Aaron and has abrogated the Levitical priesthood (7:1-10); and because it is an eternal priesthood (7:3; 20-28) .

But Genesis simply says that Melchisedech "gave thanks" and "brought up bread and wine," which does not have the appearance of a sacrifice. Only the Eucharist, then, completely fulfills the idea of Christ's priesthood as being according to the order of Melchisedech.[34]

2. The sacrifice of the paschal lamb. The deliverance of the Hebrews from Egypt and their journey to the Promised Land were inaugurated by a sacrifice. Each family was to slay a lamb, then take the blood and put it on the two doorposts and the entrance to their house. The Lord would spare the houses thus marked when He passed by to strike the land of Egypt (Exod. 12:1-7; 12-13).

This sacrifice was to lead up to a meal, a family meal at which the lamb was to be completely eaten. This meal was also to be the first act of the departure from Egypt; they were to eat standing up, in haste, clothed and shod for travel. As soon as they left the table, they started out on the journey through the night toward the Red Sea and the Promised Land (Exod. 12:7-11). Moreover, this sacrifice and meal were to be renewed each year as a commemoration. This day was to be "commemorated and solemnized as a feast in honor of Yahweh; for all generations, you shall prescribe it as a feast forever" (Exod. 12:14; 13:3-9).

All these elements taken together are extremely important for our understanding of the sacrifice of Christ and the Last Supper, and particularly of the profound unity between them.[35]

---

[34] On the Fathers' use of Melchisedech as a type of Christ, see J. Daniélou, *The Bible and the Liturgy*, pp. 143-145; cf. *Summa* III, 73, 6.

[35] As S. Lyonnet points out in *Introduction à la Bible II* (A. Robert and A. Feuillet, ed.), the Passover rite is important as indicating the true biblical meaning of sacrifice, not as "appeasing" God but as uniting men with Him, consecrating them to Him. "In the rite of the first Pasch, the blood of the lamb, which the Apocalypse mentions twice (7:14 and 12:11) and St. Paul implicitly evokes (1 Cor. 5:7), certainly did not have, in the mind of the biblical narrator, the function of appeasing Yahweh but of indicating to the destroying angel the houses of those who belonged to the people, the first-born son of Yahweh, like the sign of the Tau in Ez. 9 with which the 'man in white' marked the foreheads of the faithful Israelites (4:6), while in the Apocalypse the servants of God thus marked are said to 'wear on their foreheads the name of the Lamb and of His Father.' This was therefore a rite of consecration, separating Israel from the pagan world, constituting it a people apart. And the Bible does not hesitate to call the ceremony of the Pasch a sacrifice . . . commemorating the day when Yahweh delivered Israel from a servitude that it was increasingly to regard as the very type of slavery to sin" (p. 880).

3. The sacrifices of Leviticus. The sacrificial prescriptions of Leviticus astonish us by their complicated and detailed ritual and their crudity. Yet they were "a shadow of the good things to come" (Heb. 10:1), and three of them in particular have an important spiritual significance for us: (1) the evening sacrifice, the "offering of fine aromatic incense" (Exod. 29:39; 30:8; Ps. 140:2), which became the sign of the prayer of praise; (2) the holocaust, that is the complete transformation of a victim into smoke by being burned after its blood had been poured out (Lev. 1, etc.); (3) the yearly sacrifice of expiation, carried out by the high priest, who on this occasion only entered into the Holy of Holies and sprinkled the blood of a bull and a he-goat "in expiation for him and his house, for the impurities of the children of Israel, for their transgressions and for all their sins" (Lev. 16).[36]

But the same Lord who prescribed these sacrifices in the Law warned the people through the voice of the prophets that He rejected them and held them in abomination because they had become mere external gestures.

> I hate, I detest your feasts,
>   I have only disgust for your solemnities.
> When you offer me holocausts
>   I do not desire your oblations,
>   I do not look down on your sacrifices of fat beasts (Amos 5:21-22).
> Of what use to me is incense brought from Sheba,
>   or sweet-smelling reeds come from a far land?
> Your holocausts do not please me,
>   your sacrifices find no favor (Jer. 6:20).

---

[36] "For the Bible, expiation consists in effacing sin wherever it is found, that is to say, in the people of Israel and then in man as such. And as this sin is not conceived as a mere soiling which it is in the power of man to remove, but is identified with the rebellion of Israel and man against God and what theologians were to call the *aversio a Deo*, expiation 'effaces' sin precisely by giving Israel the 'presence' of God in the midst of His people by once again uniting man with God. This is further confirmed by the meaning the Bible attributed to blood in the sacrifice of expiation with which it is indissolubly united—according to the rabbinical saying, no expiation without the shedding of blood (cf. Heb. 9:22, which speaks of 'remission'). Contrary to the other religions of the ancient Orient in which the immolation of the victim generally occupied the central place, in Israel the rite of spreading the blood certainly constituted the central act. . . . According to the description of Lev. 16:15-19, the purpose of the blood was to 'purify' and 'sanctify' the sanctuary. Here again, the Bible shows us that the Hebrews attributed to blood this role of purification and consecration 'in virtue of the life that is in it,' still more literally, 'inasmuch as it is life' (Lev. 17:11). . . . Bearer of life, identified with life, and so an essentially divine reality for the Bible, blood is eminently fitted to consecrate to God, that is to purify (Robert—Feuillet, *ibid.*, pp. 869, 874).

"With regard to holocausts, "the victim whose blood was poured out was said to be 'for Yahweh' (Lev. 16:8-9). It alone was immolated, 'sacrificed,' that is to say, according to the Bible, it 'passed over to Yahweh.' Obviously, it could not do so without being first transformed; so in the holocaust it was not destroyed—for God is never pleased with death—but made capable of ascending to Yahweh. . . . In the sacrifice of expiation, the effusion of blood, which was necessarily preceded by the immolation, expressed in the same way the same desire for union with God, or more precisely for re-union with God from whom the sinner had been separated by sin" (*ibid.*, 874).

The most emphatic statements are those of Isaias (1:10-16) and the Psalms (39:7; 49:7-13; 50:18; 69:32). The Lord detests these sacrifices He has prescribed; He does not need these goats or bulls or incense or anything He has created; everything is already His. What He desires is what these sacrifices should have signified: man's heart, his sincere interior prayer, his profound cry of sorrow and desire for reunion with God, his love, fidelity to God's Law, thanksgiving. If Yahweh is to accept a sacrifice, the gift must be perfect and pure, both as regards the offering and the intention of the offerer (Osee 6:6; Mich. 6:5-8).

4. The prophecy of the pure oblation. But the children of Israel were not always to be thus constrained to offer the Lord sacrifices that He rejected, while remaining incapable of offering themselves to Him with the complete purity of heart which alone would be pleasing to Him. The divine oracle which proclaimed that God detested these sacrifices was accompanied by the prophecy of another sacrifice, this time a pure and perfect one. The house of God would become a house of prayer for all nations; Yahweh would then accept the holocausts of strangers (Is. 56:1-8). "From the rising of the sun to its setting My Name is great among the nation and in every place a sacrifice of incense is presented to My Name as a pure offering" (Mal. 1:11). This pure and universal liturgy is to be, it would seem, the work of a single man:

> You wished neither sacrifice nor oblations:
>   You have formed a body for me.
> You have required neither holocaust nor victim,
>   then I said: See, I come.
> At the head of the book it is written concerning me
>   that I would do your will (Ps. 39:7-9, from the Greek version used
>   by the Epistle to the Hebrews).

This man will not offer a token sacrifice—he will offer himself. This theme is connected with the development of the theme of the Servant of Yahweh in the book of Isaias:

> All we, like sheep, have gone astray,
>   each one following his own path.
> And Yahweh has caused to fall upon him
>   the crimes of us all.
> Greatly misused, he humbled himself,
>   he did not open his mouth.
> Like a lamb led to the slaughter,
>   like a dumb sheep before the shearers,
>   not opening his mouth (Is. 53:6-7; see also Jer. 11:19).

5. The death of Christ, fulfillment of all sacrifices. All these incomplete and imperfect sacrifices were replaced by the death of Christ, which fulfilled all prophecies and realized all figures. The offering of

Christ on the Cross is the true sacrifice of the New Law, the perfect and efficacious sacrifice.[37]

The psalmist sang of Christ's entrance into the world in Psalm 39, just quoted (Heb. 10:1-10). He is the priest according to the order of Melchisedech. He fulfills the holocaust of Abraham (Rom. 8:32), the sacrifice of expiation (Heb. 7:26-28; 9:1-14; 10:1-4), the evening praise, the inauguration of the new Temple (Matthew 21:13; John 2:21, etc.), the pure oblation predicted by Malachias. This last statement is not found explicitly in the New Testament, but is traditional in the teaching of the Church (*Denz.* 939).

More clearly still, the death of Jesus fulfills the sacrifice of the Servant in Isaias, the lamb of expiation (Acts 8:32-33; cf. Matthew 26:63 and parallels). Christ is the Lamb of God who bore the sins of the world (John 1:29). In heaven He appears as the Lamb who was slain (Apoc. 5:6). His immolation is a paschal feast, the true Pasch: "Christ our Pasch has been sacrificed" (1 Cor. 5:7); the very circumstances of the passion fulfill the ritual of the Exodus (John 19:36). And the tradition of the Church adds the fulfillment of the sacrifices of first fruits: Christ is offered to the Father as the first-born, the beginning of the new creation (St. Irenaeus, *Against Heresies*, 4, 17-18).

6. Christ's sacrifice accomplished once for all. The offering of Christ is the perfect sacrifice because of His dignity as Son of God, because of the obedience and self-abandonment to the Father expressed by this sacrifice, because of its efficacy: "He has made perfect forever those whom he has sanctified" (Heb. 10:14). By the very fact of its perfection, it is unique, offered once for all (Heb. 10:10-12). It marks the final age. There can be no other sacrifice because He has made expiation for all sins (Heb. 7:27; 9:12, 26-28). To suppose that Christ could repeat His sacrifice would be to doubt its efficacy (Heb. 10:1-12; the whole Epistle, with the commentary given in *The New Testament Reading Guide*, #11, should be read in this connection).

How, then, can a pure oblation be celebrated over the whole earth, when Christ's sacrifice took place on one day in one place "outside the gate" of Jerusalem? How can we Christians take part in the sacrifice which Christ offered as our Head and Mediator, our High Priest? How can we offer Christ so that He will be our sacrifice? All this is possible because Christ inaugurated His Pasch by the Last Supper. He encompassed the whole of the next day's sacrifice in a sign, and provided for the renewal of this sign.

---

[37]"As the victim of the holocaust changed into smoke 'ascended' to God, so Christ by His act of love and obedience returned effectively to His Father. His 'sacrifice' is precisely His return to God" (Robert–Feuillet, *ibid.*, p. 876).

III. THE LAST SUPPER, THE SIGN OF CHRIST'S SACRIFICE

The inspired writers and the liturgies give special emphasis to the context of the institution of the Eucharist and the actual words pronounced. We should do the same in giving instruction on the holy Sacrifice, bringing out how this context and these words guide and enrich our Christian faith. For we come to an understanding of a sacrament through its sign and particularly through the words spoken, and this is eminently true of the sacramental sacrifice of the Eucharist.

1. The inauguration of Christ's Pasch.   In St. Paul's epistles the institution of the Eucharist is connected with a precise date, "the night on which He was betrayed." Following Paul, all the liturgies recall this fact by using the same or a similar phrase, "the eve of His passion." In the Gospels the connection between the Last Supper and the passion is indicated still more clearly. The treason of Judas in leaving the Supper to go and betray Jesus is presented as fulfilling the Scriptures (Pss. 40:10; 54:13 in the Greek version). Jesus went directly from the Cenacle to Gethsemane to suffer His agony and be arrested. Liturgical tradition has, therefore, always begun the readings of the accounts of the passion with the narrative of the Last Supper (it has been omitted for pastoral reasons by the recent reform of the Holy Week rites, to shorten the ceremonies).

The Last Supper, then, is part of the passion. We are meant to see more than a chronological link; the unity between them belongs to the mystery itself. The death of Christ on the Cross was the immolation of the paschal lamb. The Last Supper was the paschal meal in which the paschal lamb was eaten. From this meal Christ and the disciples went out into the night for the New Exodus. While in the figurative Pasch the immolation preceded the meal, here the meal precedes the immolation.

Exegetes discuss the question whether Christ and His apostles actually observed the Passover ritual at the Last Supper. The difficulty arises from St. John's statement that the Passover began on Friday evening (John 18:28; in this case the lambs for the Passover meal were being sacrificed at the time when Jesus was dying on the Cross). Yet in the Synoptics, Jesus says that the meal He took with His disciples before He suffered was the paschal meal (Matthew 26:17-20; Mark 14:12-17; Luke 22:7-13, 15-16: "With great desire have I desired to eat this Pasch with you before I suffer, for I say to you, I shall not eat it again until it is fulfilled in the kingdom of God").

Various solutions have been proposed. But whether it was a paschal meal or a "meal with Passover overtones" (*New Testament Reading Guide*, #13, p. 67) matters little, for the old Pasch was replaced by the new, the Eucharist. This has been constantly stated by tradition since the end of the second century (J. Daniélou, *op. cit.*, pp. 168-172; *Summa* III, 66, 9, 5; the Mass and Office of Corpus Christi; *Denz.* 938).

In religious instruction, the theme of the Pasch stands out as the best way to convey an understanding of the Eucharistic mystery. Here sacrifice and meal can be seen expressly united and the deep significance of both most easily grasped.

2. Bread and wine as signs of the passion of Christ. We have already seen how Jesus indicated bread and wine as signs of His Presence and something of their sacrificial signification. The grain of wheat is cast on the earth and dies so as to bear much fruit (John 12:24; cf. *Summa* III, 74, 3; St. Augustine, *Treatise on John*, 51, 9). The bread promised by Jesus is His flesh that He will give "for the salvation of the world" (John 6:51). Wine is the drink of the covenant between God and man; here we come back to the principal biblical theme of the Last Supper expressed in several of Christ's parables and particularly by the miracle of Cana prefiguring Calvary and the birth of the Church.

But here again, the various biblical indications of the sacrificial significance of bread and wine can be understood only in the light of Christ's own words at the Last Supper. It is these which we must consider in order to enter the Eucharistic mystery.

3. The words of Christ signifying His passion. The words Christ said over the bread are, as reported by Mark and Matthew and many of the liturgies, very brief: "This is My Body." St. Paul and St. Luke add "given for you." Some divergence is found in the manuscript tradition of St. Paul's account given in the Epistle to the Corinthians; instead of "given," we find "broken" or even "crushed" in some versions, and the Eastern liturgies make use of these different terms.

In contrast, the Gospels give longer forms for Christ's words over the chalice, expanded still further in the liturgies, and we need to consider the Scriptural implications of each of the terms used:

"This chalice," "this cup," "this is the chalice of My Blood." Cup or chalice is the term Christ used on several occasions precisely to indicate His passion. He asked the sons of Zebedee: "Can you drink the cup that I am to drink?" (Matthew 20:22; Mark 10:38), a question directly connected with His announcement of His coming passion. At Gethsemani He prayed: "My Father, if this cup cannot pass without my drinking it, may thy will be done" (Matthew 26:39, 42). At the moment of His arrest, He told Peter, "Put your sword back in its sheathe. Should I refuse the cup the Father has given me and not drink it?" (John 18:11; cf. *Summa* III, 78, 3, 1).

"The blood shed for a multitude in remission of sins" (Matthew 26:28), *"the blood shed for a multitude"* (Mark 14:28), *"shed for you"* (Luke 22:20). This phrase anticipated what John was to see the next

day, to which he solemnly testifies (John 19:34-35). At the Last Supper the Blood of Jesus is His Blood outpoured. The phrase echoes the prophecy of Isaias:

> . . . because he has laid down his soul in death
> and has been reckoned among sinners,
> while he carried the faults of the multitudes
> and interceded for sinners (53:12) .

The "blood poured out for the remission of sins" is, again, the sacrifice of expiation which the Epistle to the Hebrews sees accomplished in Christ's death on the Cross. In this connection, we should note the phrase added by the Roman liturgy, "the mystery of faith," inspired by 1 Tim. 3:9, in which St. Paul may have had in mind the distribution of the Eucharist under the species of wine (*New Testament Reading Guide,* #10, p. 24).

"This chalice is the new covenant in My Blood," "this is My Blood, the blood of the covenant." Here we have the most important and significant biblical theme of all. The establishment of the Old Covenant is described in Exod. 24:3-8:

> Moses came and told the people all the ordinances of Yahweh and all the customs. To these the people with one voice answered: All the laws that Yahweh has decreed we will carry out. Moses put into writing all the laws of Yahweh and early the next day he built an altar at the foot of the mountain and twelve pillars for the twelve tribes of Israel. Then he commissioned certain young Israelites to offer holocausts and to immolate young bulls and communion-sacrifices to Yahweh. Moses gathered up half the blood and put it in basins and he cast the other half on the altar. He took the book of the covenant and read it to the people, who declared: We will carry out and obey everything that Yahweh had said. Then Moses took the blood, sprinkled it on the people and said: This is the blood of the covenant that Yahweh has concluded with you on these conditions.

Henceforth Yahweh was bound to Israel by a covenant: "I will be your God and you shall be my people." The Promised Land was to be the reward for fidelity to the Law that had just been promulgated and accepted. This covenant was ratified by the outpoured blood, poured on the altar and sprinkled on the people to signify their community of life with Him who was now their God.[38]

But Israel was not faithful. As a result they did not remain in possession of the Promised Land, but suffered the Exile with its deportation. But in

[38]"As in pacts of friendship, the blood exchanged by the contractants 'produced psychic community between the two parties,' in the sacrifice of the covenant concluded by Moses in the name of Yahweh, 'the blood which is the soul was spread on the altar, which represented Yahweh, and on the people, that is on the two contracting parties; by contact with one and the same soul they became a single soul'" (P. Imshoot, *Théologie de l'Ancien Testament,* I, p. 244 as cited in Robert—Feuillet, *ibid.,* pp. 870-871).

the depths of their misfortunes God sent them the prophetic announcement of a new covenant, a covenant of pardon, of mercy, of interior salvation.

> Behold the days are coming—oracle of Yahweh—when I will make with the house of Israel and the house of Juda a new covenant, not like the covenant that I made with their fathers on the day when I took them by the hand and led them out of Egypt. That covenant, my covenant!—it is they who have broken it. And so I have made them feel my mastery—oracle of Yahweh.
>
> But this is the covenant that I will make with the house of Israel after those days—oracle of Yahweh. I will put my Law within them and I will write it on their heart. Then I will be their God and they shall be my people. They shall no longer have need to teach one another, saying to one another, "Have knowledge of Yahweh!" But they shall all know me, from the littlest to the greatest—oracle of Yahweh—for I will pardon their crime and no longer remember their sin" (Jer. 31:31-34).

This text, one of the high points of the Old Testament,[39] taken up by the later prophets (Ez. 36:25-28; Is. 55:3; 59:21; 61:8, etc.), was fulfilled in Christ on the Cross and at the Last Supper. On the Cross He actually poured out His Blood, realizing, as the Epistle to the Hebrews says, the prophecy of Jeremias and abolishing the Mosaic covenant (8–9). Yet it was at the Last Supper that Christ celebrated the liturgy of the New Covenant, already presenting His Blood outpoured. The rite of Holy Thursday gave its meaning to the event of the next day, but the meal itself would have had no meaning if the immolation of Christ had not already been present in the sign.

This New Covenant, like the Old, is accompanied by the gift of the Law. "A new commandment I give you" (John 13:34); "This is my commandment that you love one another as I have loved you" (John 15:12; cf. 17); "If you keep my commandments . . ." (John 15:10). Again, the New Covenant, like the Old, is a work of gathering together, of constituting a people, now the new People of God. Christ died "to gather into one the children of God that were dispersed" (John 11:52). And He prayed at the Last Supper: "That all may be one, as You, Father, in me, and I in you" (John 17:21). The new Promised Land is also indicated: "I will that where I am, they also may be with me" (17:24). The Last Supper in its entirety is clearly, therefore, the celebration of the New Covenant, established by Christ's effecting a sacramental identity between the Eucharist and His death on the Cross. "By instituting the Eucharist, the sacrifice of the new covenant, our Lord committed Himself, freely

---

[39] See A. Gelin, *Key Ideas of the Old Testament,* pp. 37-40; L. Bouyer, *The Meaning of Sacred Scripture,* pp. 15-22, 88-90.

gave Himself up to His coming death, already sacramentally present and anticipated in His Eucharist."[40]

IV. THE MEMORIAL OF THE LORD'S DEATH

Christ intended the Last Supper to be renewed: "Do this in memory of Me." Thanks to its renewal, the passion of Christ is not merely a memory which the Church recalls simply by thoughts or words or images. It is a presence. The sacrifice offered once for all by Christ on the Cross is the sacrifice of the Church which she makes present in all times and all places, "the pure oblation" announced by Malachias.

It is a true sacrifice, enabling all Christians to adore and praise God by, with, and through Christ, our Head and High Priest, "free to enter the Holies in virtue of the Blood of Christ (Heb. 10:19ff.); enabling them to present God with the first fruits of creation that He has given us, Christ Himself, and to join Him in offering His own sacrifice. Because Christ is our sacrifice, we know that God accepts this offering. Because this sacrifice is sacramental, it is not something added to the sacrifice of Calvary. This remains always unique, accomplished once for all: the sign is multiplied, not the reality.

1. **The sacramental sacrifice.** The Last Supper was a sacramental sacrifice, since Christ anticipated in sign the unique sacrifice of Good Friday. The Church's celebration of the Eucharist in a sense is even more fully sacramental because Christ celebrates it through the minister who acts in His Person. At the Last Supper, on the Cross, and in the Church's celebration of the Eucharist it is always the same sacrifice of Christ offering Himself to the Father. At the Supper as in the Mass, the immolation is sacramental. But in the Mass the offering also is sacramental, effected through the ministry of the priest. As the Council of Trent put it:

> In the divine sacrifice which is offered in the Mass, it is Christ who is present and immolated in an unbloody manner, the same Christ who offered Himself once for all in a bloody manner on the altar of the Cross. . . . There is one and the same Victim. He who offers Himself today through the ministry of the priests is the same who then offered Himself on the Cross. Only the manner of offering is different (*Denz.* 940).

Consequently, everything about the Eucharist is sacramental: the Victim present under the signs of bread and wine; the Priest who carries out the sacrifice through His minister; the altar, of which the stone table is only the symbol. Victim, Priest and altar are Christ (*Summa* III, 83, 1).

The Eucharist is not a new sacrifice on Christ's part, offered today in heaven and on earth and distinct from the sacrifice offered under Pontius

[40] C. Bouman, *Key to the Missal*, p. 57.

Pilate. It is the very sacrifice of the Cross which is "rendered present," according to the expression of the Council of Trent (*Denz.* 930). The Mass is an efficacious sign because it is a memorial and because the Christ who suffered and rose to glory is here present.

Therefore, we should not try to ascertain how the Mass fulfills one or other definition of sacrifice. The sacrifice of the Cross is the unique sacrifice. What we need to see is how the Eucharistic celebration signifies the Cross and so discover how it is sacramental. But we find this out from the practice of the Church, not by means of logical reasoning.

The practice and legislation of the Church teach us that the consecration alone constitutes the sacrifice. For validity, it is necessary and sufficient that a priest pronounce the narrative of the Last Supper over the bread and wine. The consecration of only one species is not sufficient to signify the sacrifice; the Church requires that in case of accident the missing consecration must always be supplied (Roman Missal, *De defect. in celeb.* III-IV; X, 3). Deliberately to consecrate only one species would be a sacrilege; whether it would be a valid consecration is seriously disputed, since the intention of the priest to do what the Church does would be missing (Can. 817). No urgency, however serious, dispenses from this prescription.

The separate consecration of the two species is, therefore, the sign of the sacrifice, "seeing that Jesus Christ is symbolically shown by separate symbols to be in a state of victimhood" (*Med. Dei,* 70). "In the passion of Christ, the Blood was separated from His Body. This is why the bread is received separately as the sacrament of the Body and the wine as the sacrament of the Blood" (*Summa* III, 74, 1).

2. The sacrifice of the Church. The sacramental mode is what distinguishes the Mass from the Cross. And it is this sacramental mode that enables us to understand how and in what sense the Mass is the sacrifice of the Church.

St. Thomas says that "it is in the Eucharist that divine worship chiefly consists because it is the sacrifice of the Church" (*Summa* III, 63, 6). The Council of Trent makes a similar statement (*Denz.* 938, 940). In the Eucharist, the Church, Christ's Bride and Body, offers His sacrifice with and through Him. She offers the Victim of Calvary, the Body and Blood of Christ. She offers the sacrifice of the Cross, the only offering pleasing to God.

This offering of Christ by the Church is sacramental: she does it through signs. Christ offers Himself through the priest who consecrates, and this priest represents the Church because he takes the role of Christ, the Head of His Mystical Body. Consequently, the Church cannot offer the sacrifice without the consecrating priest. This sacerdotal act cannot be shared in by the faithful. They can unite themselves with the consecrator, they can truly offer the sacrifice, but only on the condition that a priest has carried out the consecration.[41]

Thus the consecrating priest has a place apart in the Eucharist as a sign of Christ the Priest as the one consecrator. This sacramental character of the priesthood is brought out very strikingly when the Eucharist is celebrated by concelebration, i.e., when several bishops or priests consecrate the same Eucharist at the same time and at the same altar. (This takes place in the Latin rite at the ordination of bishops and priests [Can. 803] and more frequently in the Eastern rites.) For here it clearly appears that all the priests together are a single sign of the unique Priest, Christ (*Summa* III, 82, 2).

2. The participation of the faithful. The act of the consecrating priest is an act of Christ's *ex opere operato*. This means that Christ offers Himself and is offered by the Church by the sole fact that the consecration is carried out. The participation of the faithful is not required for the validity of the Eucharist or to make it truly the sacrifice of the Church (*Denz.* 944, 945). But

> by its very nature the Mass requires that all who are present take part in it, each in the way proper to him. This participation should above all be interior—consisting in devout attention of mind and the affections of the heart. The faithful thereby enter into closest union with their High Priest . . . and together with Him offer the sacrifice, surrendering themselves in union with Him. The participation of those present becomes more complete, however, when in addition to this interior attention there is outward participation manifesting itself in outward acts (*Instruction on Sacred Music and the Sacred Liturgy* III, 22: cf. *Mediator Dei*, 78-128).

With the celebrant, the faithful give thanks, they make the remembrance of the passion of Christ and offer the immaculate Victim. Hence the great importance of the Preface with its dialogue and the *Sanctus*, and of the prayers that follow the consecration, especially of the anamnesis and offering which the celebrant says in the name of all. By taking part interiorly in all these prayers, the faithful carry out Christ's own command clarified by St. Paul: "As often as you eat this bread and drink this cup, you proclaim the death of the Lord until He comes" (1 Cor. 11:26).

> Do we not offer the sacrifice daily? We offer it, but by making the remembrance (anamnesis) of His death. And this sacrifice is unique, not multiple. It was offered once, just as He entered once into the Holy of Holies. The anamnesis is the figure of His death. It is the same sacrifice that we offer, not one today and another tomorrow. Only one Christ everywhere, entire everywhere; only one Body. As everywhere there is one Body, so everywhere there is one sacrifice. This

---

[41] See *Mediator Dei*, 92-93; Pius XII in *The Assisi Papers*, pp. 228-230.

is the sacrifice that we still offer now. This is the meaning of the anamnesis; we carry out the remembrance (anamnesis) of the sacrifice (St. John Chrysostom, *On the Epistle to the Hebrews*).

The faithful also offer themselves in union with Christ, an aspect stressed in *Mediator Dei* (80, 98-104) and again in the *Instruction* quoted above. This offering is a spiritual sacrifice, "not confined to the liturgical sacrifice" (*Mediator Dei*, 99) but, as it were, focusing the whole effort of the Christian life to offer ourselves with Christ in order to carry out the will of the Father, to be transformed into the likeness of Christ dead and risen.

But this recalling of the death of Christ and our self-offering with Him do not mean sadness. We do not stop short at the remembrance of Christ's death. The Eucharist is the whole Pasch of Christ, making present "the victory of His death and His triumph" (*Denz.* 878), in which we share as His members.

This active internal participation needs to be expressed externally. The faithful form a community round the priest and the altar. And because they are a community they must express in words, silence, song and posture the part they are taking in the Eucharist, and this external expression in turn fosters and facilitates their internal participation.

Normally this participation should also be sacramental. The faithful provide the bread and wine and everything needed for the Sacrifice as the sign of their desire to take part in offering it.[42] Above all, full participation includes receiving Communion, which imparts the fruits of the Sacrifice to the communicant (*Mediator Dei*, 118, *Instruction*, 22c). This is why the Church, since the impetus given by St. Pius X, has done so much to promote and facilitate frequent Communion.[43]

Article Three
THE ANTICIPATION OF THE HEAVENLY KINGDOM

When St. Paul says that in the renewal of the Last Supper, we "proclaim the death of the Lord," he adds immediately, "until He comes" (1

---

[42] The direct offering of the bread and wine may not be possible today as it was in the early centuries. But the faithful still supply the materials for the Sacrifice, the support of the priest, and the needs of the Church by Mass stipends and contributions of money. The custom of taking up the collection during the Offertory brings out this aspect of participation to a certain extent, especially when the collection is deposited in the sanctuary. But it becomes much more meaningful through some external act involving the actual altar-breads, e.g., when on entering the church each person who is to communicate transfers an unconsecrated host from a cup or basket to the ciborium, which is then carried to the altar at the Offertory. See *The Liturgy and the Word of God*, pp. 177-178; G. Ellard, *The Mass in Transition*, pp. 236-255 with their references.

[43] See G. Ellard, *op. cit.*, pp. 256-298 with their references.

Cor. 11:26). Similarly, the liturgical anamneses never stop at the passion. They go on to remember the resurrection (in all the rites), the ascension (in all except the East Syrian); certain rites recall Christ's enthronement at the right hand of the Father and His return in glory. For example, the Syrian anamnesis reads:

> Do this in memory of Me. For each time that you eat this Bread and drink this chalice, you commemorate My death and confess My resurrection until I return. We commemorate Your death, Lord, we confess Your resurrection and we await Your second coming. . . . While we are commemorating, Lord, Your death, Your resurrection after three days, Your ascension into heaven, Your enthronement at the right hand of the Father, Your terrifying and glorious second coming when You will judge the living and the dead and render to each according to his works, we offer You this dread sacrifice.

The Eucharist is indeed the memorial of the passion, but the Christ present is the risen Christ. This Presence of the glorified Christ makes the Eucharist the announcement and anticipation of the blessed parousia. The Eucharistic mystery is already the heavenly liturgy and the efficacious sign of the Church of the world to come. But it is the Eucharistic meal which is in a special way the sign of this eschatological aspect.

I. THE PRESENCE OF THE GLORIFIED CHRIST

In contrast to the Last Supper, which looked forward to the resurrection, the Eucharist actualizes it; Christ is risen, His Body is glorious. The Eucharistic immolation can only be sacramental, since "Christ having risen from the dead dies no more, death has no further power over him" (Rom. 6:9). The Christ who suffered is present, but the Christ who is present can no longer suffer. He is present in glory.

Thus the Eucharist realizes the paradoxical vision of St. John in the Apocalypse: in the glory of heaven, the Lamb appears as though He were slain and yet He stands erect (Apoc. 5:6). The Eucharist renews what took place on Easter evening and again the following Sunday. In the midst of the assembled disciples, Jesus appeared and showed them His hands and His side, the marks of His passion, as proof of His resurrection (John 20:19-20).

It is precisely because the Christ of the Eucharist is Christ risen and glorious that the liturgies and patristic catecheses so often present the Mass as a heavenly sacrifice, a worship taking place in the very temple of heaven.

> It is in heaven and not on earth that He now exercises His priesthood. For He died, rose again and ascended to heaven to raise us all with Him and to have us ascend to heaven.

. . . Each time then that the liturgy of this awesome sacrifice is carried out we must imagine that we are in heaven. For this liturgy is clearly patterned on the heavenly realities and obtains for us the grace to take hold of these realities through eating and drinking the Eucharist. By eating and drinking we truly participate in the blessings to come. By faith we sketch out in our minds the vision of the heavenly realities; we consider that the Christ who is in heaven, who died for us and rose again and ascended into heaven, is still the Victim through these signs. And so as we look with the eyes of faith on what is now recalled, we see again that He died, rose and ascended to heaven, all of which once took place for us (Theodore of Mopsuestia, *Homily* 15, 15 and 20).[44]

Here again, the theme of the Pasch shows us the way to a deeper understanding of how the Eucharist gives us at once the death of Christ and His triumph. For the Eucharist contains the whole Pasch of Christ, His passage from this world to the Father.

The reality of the presence of the risen Christ and His Pasch in the Eucharist is what makes the celebration of the holy Sacrifice essential to Easter and to Sunday, "the day of the Lord," in the sense of the day on which Jesus, in His glorified human nature, became the Lord at the right hand of the Father.[45]

But while the Eucharist is a presence, it is at the same time a proclamation and an expectation of the Kingdom to come. Here and now in the Eucharist the Body of Christ can only be reached through the signs, and so by faith. Christ is at the right hand of the Father and we are not yet with Him in heaven. Yet the Eucharist is at once the anticipated possession and the sign of the Kingdom to come, since it is the messianic banquet.

II. THE ESCHATOLOGICAL MEANING OF THE EUCHARISTIC MEAL

The Church has had to state against some Protestant errors that the presence of Christ and His sacrifice are realized by the consecration so completely that Communion is neither essential nor required for the validity of the Mass. But we must also stress the fact that the Eucharist is meant to be completed in a meal, and that this meal is required both by

[44] M. de la Taille in *Mysterium Fidei* assembled the various witnesses to this tradition, but the theological explanation which he deduced from them is not satisfactory. There is no heavenly sacrifice on the ritual level. The risen Christ is present; He offers Himself sacramentally; but it is the one sacrifice of the Cross which is reproduced, and the offering is ministerial. In one unique act, Christ consummated His sacrifice in the temple which is His Body. "It is the same priestly action which took place in a precise moment of history, which is eternally present in heaven, and which subsists under the sacramental species" (J. Daniélou, *The Bible and the Liturgy*, p. 138).

[45] See *The Sanctification of Sunday*, PNLW (1946).

the words of Christ ("Take and eat . . . take and drink") and by the very nature of the signs, bread and wine. The meal is "an integral part," necessary to the "integrity" of the Eucharistic sacrifice. And this remains imperfect without Communion even though the sacrifice has really been accomplished.

For this reason, by divine command, the celebrant must communicate—and under both species. If he should be unable to finish Mass, another priest must complete the sacrifice by communicating. This is also why, although it is not necessary, the faithful are urged by the Church to take their part in the banquet. For, even more important than its bringing a personal grace to each communicant, Communion is a sign of the Church and the anticipation of the heavenly banquet.

We might add here that the species of wine most clearly signifies the banquet in the Kingdom, as Jesus indicated: "I will not drink henceforth of the fruit of the vine until the Kingdom of God is come" (Luke 22:18 and parallel texts, Matthew 26:29, Mark 14:25).

1. Meals in the Bible.[46] The book of Deuteronomy prescribes a liturgical meal connected with the offering of sacrifices and including the joyful acknowledgment of all Yahweh's gifts, to be taken in His own dwelling (Deut. 12:4-18). The prophets raised the minds of God's people from earthly blessings to the greater gifts He had in store for them by presenting the happiness of messianic times again as a meal:

> All you who thirst, come to the waters,
>   even if you have no money, come!
> . . . Hear me, and you will eat good things,
>   you shall delight in rich viands (Is. 55:1-3).

In the sapiential writers, this meal is offered by Wisdom (Prov. 9:1-2; Eccles. 24:19-21). It is prepared by the Shepherd in Psalm 22 (cf. also Ps. 21:27). It will be a sign of the last times, gathering all peoples together on the mountain of Yahweh (Is. 25:6).

Christ takes up and develops these same themes in His proclamation of the Kingdom:

> Many shall come from the east and from the west to take part in the feast with Abraham, Isaac and Jacob in the kingdom of heaven (Matthew 8:11).
> I give you possession of the kingdom as my Father has given it to me; you shall eat and drink at my table in my kingdom (Luke 22:29-30).

Jesus' meals during His earthly life as described in the Gospels also have something sacramental about them. The miracles accompanying them and Christ's attitude and words signify that all men are to have ac-

---

[46] See J. Daniélou, *op. cit.*, pp. 152-161, 215-222.

cess to the messianic community and to the abundance offered by the Good Shepherd.

The wedding feast has a special place among meals in the Bible and in Christian tradition. In the Canticle of Canticles Yahweh celebrates His espousals with His people, inviting His friends to take part in the wedding-feast (5:1). Christ made use of this theme in many parables, and the Fathers comment on some of these parables precisely in connection with the Eucharist. The wedding feast at Cana, with the miracle accompanying it, is especially rich in eschatological significance and is seen by the Fathers as a type of the Eucharist.

These various themes are brought together in the celebration of the Eucharist: it is the meal of messianic times and the wedding feast of the Kingdom, a joyful feast, incompatible with penitential fasting, for we are aware that here the Bridegroom is present with us (Matthew 9:14-15). It is at once the announcement of the life to come and the present enjoyment of it. From this point of view, we must note particularly the continuity between the meals of Jesus after His resurrection and the Eucharist.

2. The meals of the risen Christ. In the accounts of the resurrection, when Christ appeared to the disciples, He ate together with them. It was at the table at Emmaus that He broke bread, enabling the disciples to recognize Him (Luke 24:30). He showed Himself to the Eleven when they were at table (Mark 16:14; Luke 24:42). He prepared a meal for them on the lakeshore at Tiberias (John 21:12-14). It was at table that He gave them His last instructions before ascending visibly to heaven (Acts 1:4). The stress the sacred writers put on these meals and Peter's insistence that he had eaten with the risen Christ (Acts 10:41) indicate their special value as signs. These meals fulfill the promises and show that the Kingdom has begun. "Is there not a continuous chain from the Last Supper to the final messianic banquet going through these meals with the risen Christ? For these meals were the pledge of that final banquet as well as of the Eucharistic meals of the Christian community, which prolong those meals with the risen Christ."[47]

3. The meals on the journey to the Promised Land. In Judaism, the paschal meal of Exodus was considered a figure of the kingdom to come, a messianic feast. And so the paschal journey was seen as a continuous procession from the Exodus out of Egypt to the arrival in the Promised Land. This outlook was drawn from Scripture itself. A paschal feast inaugurated the journey through the desert and the Pasch celebrated in Canaan concluded it (Jos. 5:10-11). The continuity between these two meals is found in the food taken on the journey, the manna with which God fed His people in the desert. Christ specifically

---

[47] Y. de Montcheuil, *Mélanges théologiques,* (Paris: Aubier, 1946) p. 36.

relates the Eucharist to the manna both as food for the journey and as a pledge of the Promised Land (John 6). As we saw earlier, ancient liturgical tradition brought out this eschatological aspect of the Eucharist by giving the newly-baptized a drink of milk and honey, the foods of the Promised Land, immediately after their first Communion.

Here again, the paschal symbolism is the most fruitful, showing the Eucharist as being at once the starting-point, the way and the goal: hope and possession.

III. THE EUCHARIST, SIGN OF THE CHURCH

St. Thomas repeats that the Eucharist "makes" the Church. Following the patristic tradition, he insists on the analogy of the grains of wheat together making one bread, and the crushed grapes making one cup of wine. This living unity is the *res sacramenti* of the Eucharist, because it is the effect of Christ's sacrifice on the Cross. By dying, He won His beloved Bride, the Church; He offered His life to "bring together into one the children of God who were dispersed" (John 11:52).

Yet the Church will be completely whole and one only when sin and death have finally been destroyed, when charity is perfect, when union is definitive and without intermediary, when God is all in all. Consequently, the Eucharistic mystery (*res et sacramentum*) is the announcement of, and preparation for, the return of Christ and the Kingdom to come, particularly because it causes Eucharistic grace (*res sacramenti*). But because here and now it gives the presence of the risen Christ and intimacy with Him, and because it is completed in a meal, it is the anticipated enjoyment of the good things of heaven.

Section Three

THE GRACE OF THE EUCHARIST

The grace of the Eucharist is twofold. There is the grace flowing from the offering of the sacrifice and the grace connected with sacramental participation through Communion. Liturgical tradition distinguishes between the two. It emphasizes the first in the prayers preceding the consecration and the actions connected with the bread and wine. It brings out the second after the consecration, in view of God's giving us as His gift the Christ whom we have offered to Him:

> . . . We humbly beg You to have these offerings carried by the hands of Your holy angel to Your heavenly altar in the presence of Your

divine Majesty, so that we who take part in the sacrifice at this altar and receive the most sacred **Body** and Blood of Your Son shall be filled with all the blessings and grace of heaven.

But since every grace calls for man's response to God, we cannot study the grace of the Eucharist without at the same time studying what the Eucharist requires of us, the method followed by St. Paul (1 Cor. 10: 16ff.).

Article One
THE FRUITS OF THE SACRIFICE

Since the Eucharist makes sacramentally present the sacrifice of the Cross, it always offers the same grace to the Church. Yet the grace of the unique sacrifice of Christ, acquired once for all, becomes our own to the extent to which this sacramental renewal of His sacrifice permits us to participate in the offering of Christ.

I. CHRIST OUR SACRIFICE

The Eucharist is our thanksgiving and praise, our adoration. Since it is Christ's "sacrifice of praise" and we are His members, we can come into the Father's presence with Him, offering His perfect holocaust. And so, in the Eucharistic prayer the Church includes formulas of praise and thanksgiving, continuing those of Christ at the Last Supper, and also formulas of offering Christ as her perfect Gift. The Church truly adores, gives praise and thanks whenever the sign is carried out. Consequently, every Eucharistic celebration as such is of value for the whole Church. The fact that the celebrant acts as the minister of the Church, because he is the minister of Christ, assures this efficacy.

But if we consider the celebrant, his ministers and the congregation, the fact that the Sacrifice is infallibly accomplished and that they take part in the rite and the prayers still leaves in uncertainty the approval that God may give to their personal activity. This is the bearing of the priest's personal expressions of unworthiness at the Offertory and the end of the Mass. It also explains the attitude of humble pleading that our sacrifice be accepted, voiced by the priest for the whole congregation in many of the Secret prayers and in the Canon.

The praise and adoration which we offer to God in the Eucharist is effective and pleasing to Him only because Christ is offered also as the Victim of expiation. It is also because we offer this Victim that we ef-

ACCOUNTS OF THE LAST SUPPER

I Corinthians 11:23-25	Luke 22:13-20	Mark 14:16-25	Matthew 26:19-29
For I myself received from the Lord what in turn I have handed on to you			
	And they prepared the Pasch	And they prepared the Pasch	And they prepared the Pasch
The Lord Jesus, on the night he was betrayed,	When the hour had come, he sat at table with his apostles and said to them: (cf. vv. 21-23)	When it was evening, he came with the Twelve, And while they were at table and were eating, Jesus said: In truth I say to you, one of you will betray me, one who is eating with me. . . .	When it was evening, he was at table with the Twelve, And, while they were eating, he said: In truth, I say to you, one of you will betray me. . . .
	Eagerly have I desired to eat this Pasch with you before I suffer; for, I say to you, I will not eat it again until it is fulfilled in the kingdom of God (vv. 17-18 below).		
took bread and, having given thanks, he broke it and said: This is my Body which is (broken) for you. Do this in memory of me.	Then, taking bread and, giving thanks, he broke it and gave it to them saying: This is my Body which is to be given for you. Do this in memory of me.	And, while they were eating, Jesus took bread and, having said the blessing, he broke it and gave it to them saying: Take, this is my Body.	And, while they were eating, Jesus took bread and, having said the blessing, he broke it and gave it to his disciples saying: Take and eat, this is my Body.

1 Corinthians	Luke	Mark	Matthew
In the same way, after the supper, he took the cup, saying:	After the supper, he did the same with the cup, saying:	Then, taking a cup, he gave thanks and gave it to them and they all drank of it, And he said to them:	Then, taking a cup, he gave thanks and gave it to them, saying:
This cup is the new Covenant in my Blood,	This cup is the new Covenant in my Blood which is to be shed for you.	This is my Blood, the Blood of the Covenant which is to be shed for a multitude.	Drink of this, all of you, for this is my Blood, the Blood of the Covenant which is to be shed for a multitude, unto the remission of sins.
Whenever you drink of this, do so in memory of me. Each time, then, that you eat this bread and drink this cup, you proclaim the death of the Lord, until he comes.			
	(vv. 17-18) Then, taking a cup, he gave thanks, and said: Take this and share it among you:		
	for I say to you, I will not drink henceforth of the fruit of the vine Until the kingdom of God has come.	In truth I tell you, I will drink no more of the fruit of the vine until the day when I drink new wine in the kingdom of God	I tell you, I will not drink henceforth of this fruit of the vine until the day when I drink new wine with you in the kingdom of my Father.

fectively ask graces for ourselves and for the whole Church. The four ends or effects of the Sacrifice—adoration, praise and thanksgiving, expiation, and impetration—are thus intimately interwoven and cannot be dissociated.

II. FROM THE SACRIFICE OF CHRIST TO THE SPIRITUAL SACRIFICE OF CHRISTIANS

Christ died on the Cross to bring mankind back to the Father; to win His Bride, the Church, and make her spotless and holy; to constitute the new People of God in unity. This is the final effect of Christ's sacrifice, its *res sacramenti*—that the Church be holy, that she appear on the day of the parousia in all her splendor. Then our identification with Christ will be complete, then the Body of Christ will have attained its full stature and perfection, then God will be all in all. This eschatological grace is present in the Eucharist because it is the *res* of the Sacrifice. So the Eucharist is in a special way the sacrament of the Church; it makes the Church. Thus "in the oblation that she presents, the Church herself is offered" (St. Augustine, *The City of God*, 10, 6). This offering is expressed by the liturgy as an eschatological expectation:

> As this broken bread, once scattered over the mountains, has been gathered together to become one single whole, so may Your Church be gathered together from the ends of the earth in Your Kingdom (a phrase from the *Didache* used in several liturgies).

In this sense, then, the Church as offered is not the Mass, but the effect of the Mass.[48]

---

[48] The precise sense in which the Church and the faithful participating in the holy Sacrifice are offered with Christ is a subject of discussion today. In "Rights of the Baptized" (*Theology Digest*, 10:2, pp. 106-112) Anselme Robeyns summarizes the positions taken on this and other aspects of lay participation in the Mass by several outstanding writers and adds some very practical comments of his own. B. Botte says, for example: "The Mass is the sacrifice of the whole Church as well as that of Christ, for the whole Church offers it with Christ. It has both an interior and an exterior reality, and the faithful participate on both levels. They participate in the interior invisible sacrifice both as offerers and as included in the secondary victim (the Church). The exterior sacrifice, the sacramental oblation, is reserved strictly to Christ and is performed by the celebrant. But even here the faithful have a part, in that they ratify and make their own the act of the celebrant, although this does not make them either mediators, priests or sacrificers." And B. Capelle states it as follows: "Both on Calvary and in the Mass, Christ is not only priest and victim but also offerer, the primary offerer. On the Cross, Christ offered His sacrifice in the name of the human race, of which He was the genuine representative. Today we offer, as far as we can, the oblation that was made in our name on Calvary. Our actual offering of the Mass is the realization in time of our vicarious offering of the sacrifice of Calvary. The ritual offering of the Mass is a symbol of the devotion of the offerer. But it is more immediately a sacrificial action by which the victim is offered, in the precise sense that this term takes in the language of sacrifice. The Church is quite clear: The primary victim is not ourselves but Christ alone. Still, because Christ and the faithful are united in one Body as Head and members, at Mass the entire Body offers the victim to God. The entire Body in each of its members gives life to this action with attitudes of perfect obedience and love, which are those of the victim offered. All are, in this sense, offerers with Christ. This does not alter the fact that Christ alone is the agent of the mystic immolation, the propitiatory and salvific action of the Cross. It is the Head alone who, being made victim, saves the whole Body."

Baptism gives us a share in the effects of Christ's sacrifice and makes us members of the Church, thus drawing us into this current of holiness. What has been realized in us in mystery is to permeate our whole being and shine out in our lives. We must continually die with Christ and rise with Him; we must live in heaven (Col. 3:1-3). And so the Christian is invited to present his body as a holy victim, to offer his spiritual sacrifice, the transformation of his life (Rom. 12:1-2; Heb. 13:15; 1 Peter 2:5). In doing so, he corresponds with the grace of Christ's sacrifice, and so, in offering Christ at Mass, the Christian is urged to offer himself. This transformation of life, this "spiritual sacrifice" of our whole lives is an effect of the Mass, a grace:

> We pray You, Lord, in Your goodness to sanctify these gifts and, receiving the offering of this spiritual victim, fashion us into an eternal gift to You (*Secret for Pentecost Monday*).

III. THE MASS OFFERED FOR THE LIVING AND THE DEAD

The Church has always offered prayers of petition during the Eucharistic sacrifice—for the hierarchy and the faithful all over the world; for those surrounding the altar, for those who offer gifts, for those who have "gone before us with the sign of faith and who sleep the sleep of peace." Petition is not only formulated in connection with the liturgy of the Word; it is also taken up into the very heart of the Eucharistic prayer and connected with the offering of the sacrifice. This prayer of petition or intercession is exemplified in the Roman Mass in nearly all the prayers leading up to the narrative of the Last Supper and, after the consecration, in the prayer for those who are to communicate, the memento of the dead and the *Nobis quoque*.

As the Council of Trent states it:

> Since in the divine sacrifice which is carried out at the Mass, it is Christ who is present and immolated in an unbloody manner and since it is the same Christ who offered Himself once for all on the altar or the Cross in a bloody manner, the holy Council teaches that this sacrifice is truly propitiatory. . . . It is offered not only in behalf of the sins, punishment, satisfaction and other needs of the faithful living on earth, but also for those who have died in Christ and are not yet fully purified; this is in conformity with the tradition of the apostles.
>
> If anyone say that the Mass is only a sacrifice of praise and thanksgiving, or that it is a simple commemoration of the sacrifice accomplished on the Cross without any effect of propitiation, or that it is effective only for him who communicates, and that it should not be offered for the living or the dead, or for sins and their chastisement and satisfaction, or for other needs, let him be anathema (*Denz.* 940, 950; see also 942 and 943).

The teaching was expressed in the most ancient liturgical formularies, and other liturgical acts were later introduced bringing out still more clearly this aspect of supplication and petition. In the East, litanies led by the deacon were developed to accompany the celebrant's formulas of intercession. Of special importance here is the presentation of the pieces of bread at the preparation of the bread and wine, while the prayer intentions indicated by this action are announced. In the West, the multiplication of Masses of devotion, the stipend given to the celebrant and the formularies for votive Masses have answered the same need.

The efficacy of such prayer is based on the sacrificial identity between the Cross and the Eucharist (*Denz*. 940). It is therefore valid only to the extent to which it is finally directed toward the blessings acquired by the sacrifice of the Cross. Thus it takes away nothing from the sacrifice of the Cross. It is subject to the same economy; the Savior who calls us freely will not save us without our cooperation.

IV. MASS INTENTIONS

The Church recognizes the legitimacy of the contract by which a priest engages himself to celebrate the Eucharist for the intention of one of the faithful who gives the priest an alms or "stipend" in return (Can. 824). Historically, this alms may have been substituted gradually for the bringing of the bread and wine for the Eucharist. In any case, it expresses the Christian's intention to take a special part in making possible the carrying-out of the sacramental sign, and his conviction that such a special connection with a particular Mass is the source of a special grace, termed by theologians the "special fruit."

These intentions are subject to the same conditions and liable to the same abuses as prayer in general. Christians have to be taught to look beyond their immediate preoccupations, to realize more clearly the meaning of the sacrifice of Christ and its effects of grace, to make their own the intentions of the Church and of the Lord.

Article Two
EUCHARISTIC COMMUNION

I. COMMUNION AS PARTICIPATION IN THE SACRIFICE

From what has been said already, it is obvious that it is a serious spiritual and pedagogical mistake to consider Communion apart from its connection with the Sacrifice. For Communion by its nature is a sacrificial meal at which we partake of the offering that has been accepted by God and so enter into His intimacy and life, as was foreshadowed by the figurative rites of the Old Covenant. It is also the paschal meal: "Christ our Pasch is sacrificed."

In Communion, then, we receive "Christ dead and risen, the Victim which has been offered and accepted. Holy Communion is communion in the Victim of the sacrifice; its essential role is to unite us actively with this Victim and so cause us to enter into the movement of the sacrifice."[49]

So the *Instruction* of September, 1958, states that "complete active participation is achieved only when sacramental participation is included. By this means the faithful who are present take part not only by spiritual desire but also by sacramental reception of the Eucharist" (22c; cf. Council of Trent, Sess. 22, 6).

Consequently Communion is to be distributed to the faithful at the proper time during the Mass, and not outside of Mass except for some reasonable motive. Pius XII insisted that "the people approach the holy table after the Communion of the priest," and recommended that the faithful be given hosts consecrated at the Mass in which they are taking part (*Mediator Dei*, 121). This last prescription is obligatory for the evening Mass of Holy Thursday. And the General Decree of July 6, 1960, on the Rubrics of the Roman Breviary and Missal states:

> The proper time for distributing holy Communion to the faithful is within the Mass, after the Communion of the celebrating priest, who himself distributes it to those who seek it, unless it is appropriate by reason of the great number of communicants that he be helped by another priest or priests. It is altogether improper, however, that the holy Communion be distributed by another priest, outside of the proper time of Communion, at the same altar at which the Mass is being celebrated. On the other hand, it is also permissible for a good reason to distribute holy Communion immediately before or after Mass, even outside the time of Mass (502).

But this must be a really good reason. The French *Directoire pour la pastorale de la Messe*, for instance, severely censures the abuses still existing in certain places and even in religious communities where Communion is not given during the celebration and the faithful are forced to receive it either before or afterwards (113-118).

Even when it is received outside of Mass, Eucharistic Communion is always communion in the Sacrifice. The effects we expect from it are those of the redemption: there is only one Eucharistic grace. In the ages when the faithful communicated in their homes during the week, they realized clearly that they had received these consecrated loaves at the

---

[49] Y. de Montcheuil, *op. cit.*, p. 54.

Sunday celebration in which they or other members of their family had participated. To make this same connection clear, the Church today requires that the Eucharist be reserved on an altar. This connection should always be brought out in instruction on Communion outside of Mass, particularly in connection with Communion for the sick and Viaticum.

II. CONDITIONS FOR COMMUNICATING

The following are excluded from Communion: (1) the non-baptized. Baptism is the "door to the sacraments"; traditionally the catechumens were sent away from the assembly before the Eucharistic liturgy; (2) the baptized who are not in communion with the Church. In all ages the Eucharist has been considered as the manifestation of the bond between the faithful and the Church. To establish the fact that a Christian has never ceased to receive Communion is to prove that he has remained in the communion of the Church;[50] (3) public sinners (e.g., divorced persons who have remarried, Can. 2356).

The following are not given Communion in the Latin Church: (1) little children who have not yet reached the age of reason or who have not received the required preparation, except in danger of death; (2) those who have never had any use of reason. (It is respect for the sacrament that causes hesitation as to giving the Eucharist to persons suffering from some types of mental illness.)

The faithful who are conscious of having committed a mortal sin and who have not yet submitted it to the power of the keys by sacramental confession must of their own accord abstain from Communion (Can. 856). It is not enough, except in most exceptional circumstances, to have recovered the state of grace by perfect contrition (cf. *ibid.*). Communion is the act of union with the Church. Consequently, the very nature of the sacrament (and not merely a precept) demands that the sinner first receive pardon from the Church for sins requiring that pardon (*Denz.* 880, 893).

It is true that Eucharist is the redeeming sacrifice, but participation in it should follow the remission of serious sins, not precede it. As St. Paul severely warned the Corinthians: "Whoever eats the bread or drinks the cup of the Lord unworthily will have to answer for the Body and Blood of the Lord. Let each one, then, prove himself . . . for he who eats and drinks, eats and drinks his own condemnation if he does not discern the Body" (11:27-29). The Eastern liturgies inaugurate the distribution of Communion with a solemn warning: "The holy things, for those who are holy!"

The Church also insists that the Christian have the right intention in receiving Communion. It is a communal act, but also the act which most

---

[50] See, for example, the text of Dionysius, bishop of Alexandria in the third century, given in Eusebius' *Ecclesiastical History*, 7, 9.

fully engages the person and the personality of the Christian, since it is a mystery of faith and love. Special care should be taken lest Christians be led to the holy table by any kind of social pressure or for motives foreign to the faith.

Present discipline forbids anyone from communicating more than once a day. The exception to this rule is the reception of Viaticum by a Christian who has already communicated and suddenly finds himself in danger of death (Can. 857).

A long discipline prescribes a certain period of fasting before communicating. This Eucharistic fast has been the subject of new legislation in our times in the *Motu Proprio, Sacram Communionem* of Pius XII, March 19, 1957. For those in good health, it consists in abstaining for three hours from all solid food and from alcoholic drinks (beer, wine, hard liquor, etc.) and for one hour from non-alcoholic drinks. Natural water, mineral water and water that has been chlorinated or otherwise treated for safe drinking do not break the Eucharistic fast. For the faithful, the time for beginning to abstain is calculated from the moment when they are to communicate; for the celebrant, from the moment when Mass is to begin. The sick, even those who are not bed-ridden, are bound to the three-hour fast from solid food and alcoholic drinks, but they are not bound to fast from non-alcoholic drinks or from medicines (in the strict and pharmaceutical sense of the term) even if these are solid or contain alcohol.

III. THE GRACE OF COMMUNION

The Fathers and theologians bring out both the personal and the communal character of the grace of Communion. It is at once incommunicable intimacy with Christ and more complete engrafting into His Body, the Church. These two aspects are of the essence of God's plan for our salvation. Great care should be taken, therefore, not to neglect either of them in our spiritual life or in our teaching (*Denz.* 875).

1. Intimacy with Christ. The Fathers particularly recommend Psalm 33 as a Communion hymn, in accord with the liturgy of their time: "Taste and see how good is the Lord." They also comment on the Canticle of Canticles in connection with Communion, drawing from it images and expressions of deeply intimate love. This intimacy was offered by Jesus Himself in His teaching on the Bread of life: "He who eats my flesh and drinks my Blood lives on in me and I in him" (John 6:56). Moreover, the marriage union between Christ and the Church, in which each Christian participates, was prefigured in the marriage at Cana and is realized in the Eucharist. And so the Fathers also apply to Communion the parable of the wedding feast (Matthew 22:3), which by its eschatological and communal character expresses the idea of gladness as well as intimacy.

Eucharistic gladness is symbolized especially by the species of wine: "Wine rejoices man's heart" (Ps. 103:15). To the critic who might be disturbed because wine can cause drunkenness, the Fathers explain that it is a true but "sober" inebriation that the Eucharist produces in the faithful soul:

> But the inebriation that comes from the chalice and the Blood of the Lord is not like that produced by common wine. Thus when the Holy Spirit says in the psalm, "Your inebriating chalice," he adds, "It is truly wonderful." For the chalice of the Lord inebriates in such a way that it leaves us our reason; it leads souls to spiritual wisdom; through it, each person goes from the taste for profane things to the understanding of the things of God. Finally, just as ordinary wine frees the spirit, sets the mind at ease and banishes all sadness, so the use of the Blood of the Lord and of His saving chalice takes away the memory of the old man, gives forgetfulness of the profane life of former times and sets us at ease, pouring the joy of the divine goodness into the sad and gloomy heart which previously was overwhelmed by the load of its sins (St. Cyprian, *Letter* 63, 11).

This passage is one of the classic texts of patristic literature. It expresses the principle found in all the catecheses: Communion is the inauguration of the mystical life.[51]

2. Identification with Christ as victim. While wine brings gladness, bread is the food that gives strength (Ps. 103:15; Gen. 18:5). It sustains and develops life. By assimilating food the organism renews its own substance. The Eucharist acts as a food and produces the effect it signifies: "My flesh is truly food. . . . If you do not eat the flesh of the Son of Man and drink his Blood, you shall not have life in you. . . . He who eats me shall live by me" (John 6:56, 54, 57). But this food assimilates us to Christ.

> I am the food of the strong; believe and you shall eat of Me. You will not assimilate Me to yourself like the food of the body; it is you who will be assimilated to Me (St. Augustine, *Confessions*, 7, 10).

> Participation in the Body and Blood of Christ effects nothing less than our passing into what we receive. It causes us to carry in our spirit and in our flesh He in whom and with whom we are dead, buried and risen again (St. Leo, *Sermon* 63).

3. The pledge of the resurrection. "Christ wished the Eucharist to be the pledge of our future glory and of eternal happiness." This formula of the Council of Trent (*Denz.* 875) summarizes well the teaching of the Gospel and of tradition.

---

[51] See J. Daniélou, *op. cit.*, pp. 177-190; *Summa* III, 79, 1, 2.

Jesus' comparison between the Bread that He will give and the manna of the desert has a twofold meaning. Like the manna, this Bread comes from heaven;[52] it is also the foretaste of the Promised Land and the food that gives us the strength to arrive there. But the Eucharist is much more: it is the very cause of immortality and the pledge of the resurrection.

> Your fathers ate the manna in the desert and they are dead.
> This bread is that which comes down from heaven
>   so that he who eats it may not die. . . .
> He who eats this bread will live forever. . . .
> He who eats my flesh and drinks my blood has everlasting life
>   and I will raise him up on the last day. . . .
> This is the bread come down from heaven;
>   it is not like that which your fathers ate: they are dead;
>   he who eats this bread will live forever (John 6:49-58).

Because this Bread is the Body of the risen Christ, it constitutes the pledge of the resurrection. Assimilating us to the glorified Christ, it places in us the seed of our own glory (cf. 1 Cor. 15:1-28). This aspect is particularly marked in the Greek Fathers.

> What, then, is this medicine? It is precisely that glorious Body which showed itself stronger than death and which became for us the source of life. As a little leaven, as the Apostle says, makes all the dough like itself, so the Body (of Christ) raised by God to immortality, once it is introduced into our body, changes it and transforms it wholly into its own substance (St. Gregory of Nyssa, *Catechetical Oration,* 37, 3).

> What man seeks in food and drink—the satisfaction of his hunger and thirst—he truly finds only in this food and drink which render him immortal and incorruptible in the society of the saints (St. Augustine, *Treatise on John,* 26).

The characteristic of the Eucharist is what makes Viaticum so necessary for the dying. The Christian facing the last stage of his journey to God finds his strength and security in the Eucharist. Thanks to the Bread provided by God he can, like Elias, arouse himself from his weakness and "sustained by this food, journey forty days and forty nights even to Horeb, the mountain of God" (3 Kings 19:4-8). This final Communion takes on a particular solemnity and also a special urgency, since it is the object of a divine command. It is the supreme pledge of salvation. The happiest death for a Christian, then, is to give up his soul to God after receiving Viaticum.

[52] We should be careful to remember the true meaning of the expressions "bread of heaven" and "bread of angels." These are biblical terms connected with the manna (Pss. 77:23-25; 104:40; Wis. 16:20-21) and not applicable to the Eucharist except by way of the manna.

4. Effects of the Eucharist on our bodies. But even here and now the Eucharist brings a grace of strength for our bodies, as the prayers in the liturgy frequently state:

> May the heavenly mystery bring about the restoration of soul and body (*Postcommunion,* 8th Sunday after Pentecost).

> Be pleased, O Lord, to purify and renew our souls by Your heavenly sacraments, so that thereby even our bodies may also draw help for the present and the future (*Postcommunion,* 16th Sunday after Pentecost).

St. Thomas explains that "while man's body is not the immediate subject of grace, the effects of grace nonetheless flow from the soul to the body. For in the present life our members are arms of God's justice, as St. Paul expresses it (Rom. 6:13), and in the future life our body will partake of the glory of our soul and its incorruptibility" (*Summa* III, 79, 1, 3).

5. The unity of the Church and brotherly love. The Body of Christ in the Eucharist is the sign of the Mystical Body;[53] the Blood of Christ was shed to win His Church and to gather together the scattered children of God. As the sign of this eschatological goal, the Eucharist brings to each participant the grace which hastens its attainment: a closer union with the Church and a gift of brotherly love. The Eucharist is the sign of unity, since we receive it from the Church in a family meal in which all partake of the same Bread. It brings the grace of unity as communion in the sacrifice by which Christ established the Church. At the same time that the Eucharist produces unity it calls for it; we must show forth in our lives the mystery in which we have participated. These various aspects are brought together and clarified in the liturgy, the teachings of St. Paul and the Fathers, and the studies of theologians.

The liturgy has generally required that there be but one chalice on the altar, however numerous the partakers. Some rites also emphasize the breaking of the Bread, giving it the meaning brought out by St. Paul in 1 Cor. 10:16-17. The prayers also accentuate the theme of unity: for example, the *Domine Jesu Christe* of the Roman Mass and the hymn of the Eastern liturgies, "There is but one holy One, one Lord, Jesus Christ."

The Fathers develop St. Paul's teaching and follow St. Ignatius of Antioch in showing the Eucharist as the supreme sign of the Church and the bond of charity. This doctrine attained its greatest development with St. Cyril of Alexandria and St. Augustine. Through the influence of the latter, it reappears in all the theologians of the Middle Ages, who clar-

---

[53] This expression is used by the Council of Trent (*Denz.* 875). It condenses a rich tradition explored by H. de Lubac in *Corpus Mysticum* (Paris: Aubier, 1944).

ify the *res sacramenti* of the Eucharist as being the unity of the Mystical Body and charity.[54]

> In this sacrament as in all the others, what makes the sacrament what it is, is the sign of the effect it produces. Now the sacrament of the Eucharist has two effects. The first is to unite us with Jesus Christ, for it contains His Body as well as signifying it; the second is to unite us with His Mystical Body, the society of the saints, which it signifies but does not contain (*Summa* III, 80, 4).

This charity is the very "love of God poured out in our hearts by the Holy Spirit" (Rom. 5:5). It enables us to love God with His own infinitely generous love and our neighbor with that same love:

> "Herein we know that we love the children of God, when we love God" (1 John 5:2). What does this mean, my brothers? The preceding verse referred only to the Son of God, not to the children of God. It presented one Christ to us and told us: Whoever believes that Jesus is the Christ is begotten of God; and whoever loves the begetter (that is, the Father) loves also the begotten of Him (that is, the Son, our Lord Jesus Christ). Then John continues: "Herein we know that we love the children of God." He had just said "the Son of God," and now he says "the children of God."
>
> The reason is that the children of God are the body of the only Son of God, and, since He is the Head and we the members, there is but one Son of God. Therefore he that loves the children of God loves the Son of God, and he that loves the Son of God loves the Father. Nor can anyone love the Father unless he love the Son; and he that loves the Son loves also the children of God. (St. Augustine, *Letter to Parthos*, PL35, 2059).

This traditional and vital aspect of the Eucharist, somewhat neglected in the recent past, is in our times once more being restored to its vital place.[55]

IV. THE NECESSITY OF THE EUCHARIST

The practice of the Latin Church since the Middle Ages of not allowing Communion to infants proves that the Eucharist is not necessary to salvation in the same way as baptism. This was defined by the Council of Trent (*Denz.* 933, 937). This definition, guaranteed by the infallibility of the Church, is reconciled with Jesus' teaching: "If you do not eat the flesh of the Son of Man and drink his Blood you will not have life in you" (John 6:53), by the distinction between the *res* and the *res et sacra-*

[54] *Summa* III, 73, 1 and 2. See the references to the Eucharist in E. Mersch, *The Whole Christ*, listed in the bibliography.

[55] See, e.g. *The Liturgy and Unity in Christ*, PNLW (1960).

mentum of the Eucharist. St. Bede, writing at a time when Communion was still given to infants in the West, brought out this distinction: the *res* of the Eucharist, union with Christ and His Church, is indispensable to salvation, but the actual reception of the sacrament, of the Body and Blood of Christ, may be lacking without compromising salvation.[56] Later theologians added the distinction between actual reception, which is in itself not necessary for salvation, and the desire for the Eucharist, which is indispensable but sufficiently expressed by the fact of baptism (*Summa* III, 73,3; see M. de la Taille, *op. cit.,* Elucid. 49).

But St. Thomas adds: "This desire for the sacrament would be an illusion if it were not carried out when opportunity allows. Therefore it is evident that each of us has an obligation to receive it, not only because of the precept of the Church, but as a consequence of the command of Jesus Christ" (*Summa* III, 80, 11). Thus Viaticum is required by divine command (*Denz.* 51).

Because of the decrease of Communions in the Middle Ages, the Church had to prescribe under pain of mortal sin that every Christian who has reached the age of reason must receive the Eucharist at least once a year, at Easter time (*Denz.* 437; Can. 859). This is the indispensable minimum without which the individual's bond with the Church is no longer manifested; with less than this there is no possibility of a normal spiritual life.

But the popes of this century have continually urged that Christians should not be content with this minimum. Since St. Pius X boldly took the initiative, the hierarchy has continually encouraged frequent and even daily Communion. We are to think of the Eucharist not as the reward of the perfect, but as the nourishment of the weak. To facilitate the reception of the Eucharist, Pius XII modified the age-old law of the Eucharistic fast in his constitution, *Christus Dominus* of 1953 and his *Motu Proprio, Sacram Communionem* of 1957.

The expression "spiritual Communion" is found in *Mediator Dei* (117), but in a context that avoids all danger of misunderstanding it. Actually a sacrament cannot be received merely spiritually; the desire for a sacrament has value, but only if it leads toward receiving it, unless some insurmountable obstacle stands in the way. Thus it is good to encourage people who cannot go to Mass to read the Mass texts and join in their parish Mass by desire; and it is good also to encourage those who for some reason cannot communicate when they are taking part in the Mass to make a "spiritual Communion" in the sense that the term is used in *Mediator Dei.* But we should never give the impression that this is in any way an acceptable substitute for actually receiving Communion for those who could do so.

[56] In Gratian's *Decretals, On Consecration,* d. 2, C. 36; this may be a quotation from St. Augustine.

V. CORRESPONDENCE WITH THE DIVINE GIFT

1. After receiving Communion. The Christian should respond with an effort of personal prayer to the intimacy with Christ offered him in Communion.[57] Then, in the name of all the celebrant prays the Post-communion prayer, in which he gathers together and voices the prayers of all. After the dismissal the faithful who have the opportunity to do so are urged to prolong their conversation with the Lord (*Mediator Dei*, 123-124).

2. In daily life. "The current of love with which Mass and Communion have enriched the members of the Christian assembly must pass into their daily life as members of the human city and through them reach out and permeate the community."[58] The whole New Testament and Christian tradition teach us that this love of God must include love of neighbor and must be expressed not only in words but in deeds:

> Love all men, even your enemies; love them, not because they are your brothers, but that they may become your brothers. Thus you will ever burn with fraternal love, both for him who is your brother and for your enemy. . . . Even the man who does not as yet believe in Christ . . . love him and love him with fraternal love. He is not yet your brother, but love him precisely that he may become your brother (St. Augustine, *op. cit.*).

If we truly meet Christ and go with Him to the Father in the Eucharistic sacrifice, we shall be able truly to practice the love of neighbor which Christ has commanded, in the "love of God poured out in our hearts by the Holy Spirit." So we shall witness to Christ's love for all men as we take our share in the work of the Church and in the work of the human city.[59]

The Postcommunions of the Roman Mass frequently remind us of this daily effort which the Eucharist, perfecting the grace of baptism, calls for throughout our daily lives, an effort toward complete conversion and growing likeness to Christ in cooperation with His grace, so as to be instruments and witnesses to His love.

[57] The traditional practice of congregational singing during the distribution of Communion—a paraphrase of the Communion antiphon with a psalm, or some suitable hymn—is happily being widely restored. Some people find difficulty at first in reconciling such singing with their own personal heart-to-heart prayer. But when it is pointed out that such singing can be a most personal prayer and at the same time a sign of the unity of the Church and of brotherly love, the difficulty is seen to be unreal. Obviously, the hymns must be chosen, both as to text and music, so that all present, and not only the sensationally "pious," can fully mean what they are singing.

[58] L. Terrier, "Après l'assemblée," *La Maison Dieu*, 40, p. 116.

[59] See H. U. von Balthasar, *Science, Religion and Christianity*, pp. 142-145; M. Burbach, "The Eucharist as the Sacrament of Unity," and T. Carroll, "True Christian Spirit at Work in Today's World," in *The Liturgy and Unity in Christ*, PNLW (1960).

Pour into our hearts, O Lord, the spirit of Your love, and so by Your loving kindness make one in heart those whom You have fed by these paschal sacraments (*Easter Sunday*).

May the working of the heavenly gift take possession of us body and soul, so that not our own impulse but its effect may always be foremost within us (*15th Sunday after Pentecost*).

CONCLUSION

In concluding our study of the Eucharist, we need to stress once more the vital importance of the theme of the Pasch. It does not exhaust the wealth of the Eucharistic mystery, but it enables us to understand its unity. And it is in this living unity that the Eucharist must primarily be understood. It is at once the memorial of Christ's saving death, the Presence among us today of the risen Christ, and the anticipation and pledge of His return. It is sacrifice and banquet, intimate meeting with the Lord and supremely communal action. All these interwoven aspects are those of the paschal mystery. Here, above all, by following God's education of His people through the Old Testament, we reach a rightful understanding of the realities of the New.

And when the Eucharistic mystery is lived and contemplated in its living unity, it becomes the principle of unity for the Christian's thought and life. It gives him the insight that reconciles the apparent paradoxes in God's plan for our salvation. The celebration of the Eucharist is the supreme act of unselfish love, directed to God in adoration and thanksgiving. At the same time, it is propitiation for our sins and intercession for all our needs. It is at once the gift of God to man and man's supreme response to God in Christ. What is already realized in Christ our Head is what we hope for. Its realization is Christ's work and yet He wills to accomplish it with our cooperation. The Eucharist is union with Christ and equally union with the Church.

Thus "the catechesis (of the Mass) offers us the way to regain a Christian vision of the universe centered on the liturgy and so to refashion the unity of those disparate ideas which too often are those of our Christians today."[60]

[60] J. Daniélou, in *La Messe et sa catéchèse*, p. 72. See also C. Vagaggini, *Theological Dimensions of the Liturgy*, pp. 84-87.

Chapter 5

PENANCE

Preliminary Remarks

The sacrament of penance has two characteristics which should be noted from the outset. First, it bears the name of a virtue. The virtue of penance is necessary to every man and was so even before the coming of Christ. Man's need to repent is one of the major themes of the Old Testament. We need to see, then, how it is that this virtue can be specifically Christian. We also need to see how it is that, though the sacraments are by their nature free gifts of God to man, acts of Christ, the virtue of penance —by its nature a disposition in man himself—can be so characteristic of a sacrament as to give it its name.

Secondly, the changes in the discipline and use of this sacrament witness to a development, a refining and interiorizing of the Christian conscience through the centuries and to a deepening understanding of the riches of God's forgiveness. The historian, working only by the lights of his science, is astonished at these changes. He is tempted either to minimize or to exaggerate them. The difficulty of research on this subject is increased by the fact that the documentation for the patristic period is very sketchy. But, in the light of faith, this development can be attributed, not simply to changes in human mentality and customs, but to the Holy Spirit always present with the Church.

Article One
GOD'S PEDAGOGY

The progressive discovery of the true nature of penance to which the Lord led His people in the Old Testament may be summed up in three key-words: sin, mercy, conversion or repentance.

I. THE DISCOVERY OF SIN

1. *The discovery of God and the discovery of sin.* When St. Peter had welcomed Jesus into his boat and witnessed the miraculous catch of fish, his sudden discovery of Christ forced him to say: "Depart from me, Lord, for I am a sinner" (Luke 5:8). His almost instinctive cry echoes those of all the seers of the Old Testament. For example, Isaias, gazing at the theophany of Yahweh the thrice-Holy lamented: "Woe is me, I am lost, for I am a man of impure lips" (Is. 6:5).

Only the discovery of God makes possible a true discovery of sin.[1] Sin certainly involves the degradation of man, the loss of integrity; it is the cause of shame, suffering and death (Gen. 3). But it is, essentially, wilful abandonment of God, estrangement from God. The cry of guilty man resounds from one end of the Bible to the other: "I have sinned against God." As Psalm 50 sings: "Against you, you alone, have I sinned. I have done what is evil in your eyes"; and Isaias says: "We have greatly sinned in your sight."

"In your sight" means that we find ourselves in the presence of the divine One who speaks to us. This presence, which leaves us no possible hidingplace (Ps. 138), is not that of a judge spying on us to catch us in a fault, but of a Father who loves us and is saddened by our disobedience and lack of love. The God in whose presence we have sinned is the God who has revealed Himself, who called Israel, who made a covenant with His people and was pleased to dwell in their midst. This is why sin is a revolt against God (Exod. 23:21). But more than a revolt, it is adultery, prostitution, unfaithfulness to the love between God and His people which the inspired writers express in terms of the love between husband and wife: "The prostitute heart that has abandoned me, and the adulterous eyes that have attached themselves to idols" (Ez. 6:9).[2]

It is not, then, primarily to ourselves that we must admit our sins, but to God.

> I was silent and my bones wasted away
> in sighing all the day.
> Night and day your hand lay heavy upon me,
> my heart was changed into stubble
> in the full heat of summer.
> Then to you I confessed my fault,
> I no longer hid my guilt.
> I said, I will go to Yahweh
> and confess my sin (Ps. 31) .

Religious instruction should very carefully bring out the precise character of this act of admission as something quite different from introspection, from any kind of philosophic judgment and, still more, from any guilt complex. The masters of the spiritual life have always paid great attention to it;[3] an understanding of it is essential to the formation of a truly Christian conscience. We are to think of our sins in relation to God, in the light of His presence; we are to admit them, confess them to

---

[1] "The idea of sin is as it were the reverse side of the idea of God" (A. Gelin, *Key Ideas of the Old Testament*, p. 84).

[2] See the development of these themes in L. Bouyer, *The Meaning of Sacred Scripture*, pp. 52-90.

[3] For example, St. Ignatius' *Spiritual Exercises;* C. Marmion, *Christ, the Life of the Soul.*

Him who has revealed Himself to us, whose gaze rests on us, who loves us, who is eager to forgive us and have us return to intimacy with Him.

2. The interiorization of the idea of sin. Taking the Chosen People in a very rudimentary stage of moral conscience, divine revelation led them step by step to a discovery of personal responsibility and to the true nature of the interior combat. The Mosaic legislation laid down a code of impurities which could be cleansed by means of legal expiations. But it led the people immediately from this crude conception to the idea of wrongdoing as taking place in the heart and intention even before it is translated into action. "You shall not lust after the house of your neighbor, nor his servant, nor his maid-servant, nor his cow, nor his ass, nor anything that is his" (Exod. 20:17).

Many centuries later Jesus would have to re-establish this true idea of sin, while deepening it (Matthew 5:27-28). It is what comes out of the heart of man that can soil him, not what touches him from without (Mark 7:14-23; Matthew 15:1-20). The ritual prescriptions of the Law concerning purity were to be abolished or, rather, fulfilled by the Christian law of love.

Next, as Ezechiel proclaimed at the time of the great chastisements of the whole people for their sins, there is no sin without responsibility. The Lord will judge each person according to his own right and wrong actions, not those of his father or his children, and He will judge according to each one's final turning to Him or away from Him (Ez. 18).

But sin affects man so profoundly that it cannot be covered over or simply "forgotten" by God. It constitutes such a stain that no earthly cleansing agent can do away with it. Yahweh Himself must cleanse us (Jer. 2:22). Our very hearts (that is, the inmost core of our whole intellectual-volitional life) are spoiled and need to be replaced—something that only Yahweh can do (Jer. 4:4; Ez. 12:19; 36:26; Ps. 50:12-14). The New Testament will go even further and say that "sin is death" (cf. Rom. 6:21; Heb. 10:28-29).

3. Sinners one and all. We need God's revelation to show us the true nature of sin and our own sinfulness. Yet, in the vision of the world given us by the Bible, sin has invaded everything. At the time of the Flood only eight persons were free of the general corruption and were saved by God in the ark (2 Peter 2:5). In the days of Abraham, not even ten just men could be found in Sodom and Gomorrah (2 Peter 2:6). The Egypt from which the Lord delivered His people was a land of idolatry and cruelty (Exod. 1-2).

And Yahweh's own people, His elect, for whom He worked so many wonders, heaped up faults and betrayals: "For forty years this race disgusted me" (Ps. 94). After their settling in Palestine, things were no better. The Lord's anointed ones, the kings of Israel—even David—were sinners. Although David was raised up by penance and Ezechias and Josias were exceptionally good men, the royal line as a whole is presented in a very harsh light by the Bible. And the people were no better than their leaders. All Israel was unfaithful to God. A chosen vine, lovingly cultivated by the vine-tender, it produced nothing but grapes unfit for anything.[4]

Even good men experience how sinful they are in God's sight. "All our acts of justice are like soiled linen" (Is. 64:6); "No living man is justified in your sight" (Ps. 142:2); "Evil was I born, a sinner did my mother conceive me" (Ps. 50:7). The New Testament further clarifies this realization. "If we say that we are without sin, we deceive ourselves and the truth is not in us" (1 John 1:8). St. Paul sees all mankind as enclosed in sin (Rom. 3:20; Gal. 3:22, etc.), for all men are children of Adam, the first sinner (Rom. 5:12).

Therefore the only valid attitude in God's presence is total self-abandonment: "My God, have mercy on me a sinner" (Luke 18:13). This attitude was that of the *anawim,* the "poor" of Israel, those who, in the final stages of God's preparation for Christ's coming, fully corresponded with His education of His people.

> In their upward ascent, these holy souls realized increasingly their own incapacity. They longed for God to lean over them more closely and pour His grace into them, to establish a mysterious new source of light and energy at the very root of their religious and moral activity. . . . When the bridge had been made between the Old Testament and the New, Mary greeted the messianic age with her *Magnificat,* which repeats words and themes dear to the *anawim.*[5]

The Old and New Testaments only bring out the reality and the universality of sin in order to reveal God's mercy, His loving-kindness which both calls and enables sinful mankind and every individual sinner to repent and return to Him.

---

[4] See J. Guillet, *Themes of the Bible,* pp. 211-217.

[5] A. Gelin, *op. cit.,* p. 93. See also B. Ahern, *Mary, Queen of the Poor;* J. Danielou, "Blessed are the Poor" in *Cross Currents* 9 (1959), pp. 379-388; J. Tillard, "Mary's Faith and Israel" in *Sponsa Regis* 32 (1961), pp. 233-242.

II. THE REVELATION OF GOD'S MERCY[6]

God revealed the infinite depths and extent of His mercy step by step, from the historical books of the Old Testament to the full light of the Gospel.

1. "And Yahweh refrained from bringing down upon His people the misfortune He had threatened." The first experience of God's mercy given us in the Bible is as the reward of faith and suppliant intercession. Abraham was allowed to plead the cause of Sodom and Gommorah (Gen. 18:16-33). Moses intervened effectively in arresting the just vengeance of God against His people. In his prayer he argues with touching simplicity that it is the honor of Yahweh himself in the sight of the nations which is at stake (Exod. 32:11-14 and Deut. 9:25-29).

2. "God delights in having mercy." With the prophets appears the loving spontaneity of the divine forgiveness:

> Who is the God like to you, taking away iniquity,
> > pardoning crime,
> > not forever inflaming his wrath,
> > but delighting in having mercy?
> Once more have pity on us.
> > Trample on our iniquities,
> > cast into the depths of the sea
> > all our sins (Mich. 7:18-19).

Osee is perhaps the greatest witness to mercy, being called to manifest it in his life as well as his prophecies. Yahweh is a husband who loves his wife even when he sees her degrade herself by unfaithfulness and prostitution. His love is capable of transforming her and giving her back her first innocence; it is a creative power:

> I will allure her and lead her into the wilderness
> and there I will speak to her heart. . . .
> I will espouse you to myself for ever,

[6] Recent Scriptural studies bring out this dynamic and positive notion of God's merciful love, His *hesed,* as being not opposed to His justice, but rather having His justice as one of its aspects. Speaking of St. Paul's use of these biblical terms and categories, S. Lyonnet says that in the context of the Old Testament, "justice seems to refer to an activity (not an attribute) of God which accomplishes the restoration of Israel by means of divine truth, fidelity and constancy. . . . The biblical terms Paul uses differ radically from the terminology of modern theology. The theologian envisages salvation as the restoration of order. Justice therefore applies to punishments meted out for sin, whether their effect is to purify or condemn. Equally, in this theological perspective, mercy must be the attribute that spares sinners. But St. Paul sees salvation as the restoration of *man.* God's response to sin is either anger—historical anger (Rom. 1:18ff.), which is the result of man's separating himself from God by personal sin, or eschatological anger, by which man is fixed definitively in his estrangement—or justice, goodness, mercy, fidelity, which, as so many aspects of the efficacious love of God for man, effect his restoration to grace, his justification" ("The Saving Justice of God," *Theology Digest,* 8:2 1960).

> I will espouse you in justice and judgment,
>   in tenderness and in love:
> I will espouse you to myself in faithfulness
>   and you shall know Yahweh (2:16, 21-22).[7]

The Lord is also a Father overcome with emotion at the guilt of His children:

> How should I abandon you, O Ephraim,
>   give you over, O Israel? . . .
> My heart is moved within me,
>   I am stirred to the depths.
> I will not give rein to the heat of my wrath,
>   I will no longer destroy Ephraim
>   for I am God and not man (Osee 11:8-9).

Continually He calls to "rebellious Israel," lovingly watching out for her return (Jer. 3:12-13). He takes pleasure only in the conversion of the wicked man, not in his death:

> By my life—oracle of the Lord Yahweh—I take no pleasure in the death of the wicked, but in the return of the wicked, changing his ways to have life. Return, return from your evil way. Why will you die, O house of Israel? (Ez. 33:11-12; see also 18:21-23).

3. The message of the book of Jonas. The book of Jonas was a favorite with the Fathers, who often commented on it and used it in their baptismal instruction. It proclaims the value of repentance. Still more, it shows God's mercy as not limited to the Chosen People, but offered to all men (cf. Luke 11:30-32). The prophet proclaimed only the divine punishment; but the Ninevites still hoped for pardon, and they obtained it.

> Who knows whether God will not turn and relent, if he will not hold back the heat of his wrath so that we may not perish? God saw what they did to turn away from their evil ways. And God repented of the prophecies of misfortune that he had made to them, he did not carry them out (Jonas 3:9-10).

This divine way of acting scandalized the prophet. The scene of the bush growing with miraculous speed to shade him (ch. 4), described with the humor that permeates the whole book, is designed to make us understand the thoughtfulness of God's care for all His creatures:

> You, you are troubled over the bush that cost you no labor, that you did not make grow, which grew up in a night and withered away in a night. And shall I not be troubled for Nineve, that great city, in which there are more than a hundred and twenty thousand people who cannot tell their right hand from their left, as well as a mass of animals? (Jonas 4:10-11).

[7] See L. Bouyer, *The Meaning of Sacred Scripture,* pp. 61-67.

4. The proclamation of the mystery of the divine forgiveness. While

a deepened idea of sin was developing in the People of God, the desire
and expectation of a truly radical forgiveness grew clearer also. It is
not enough that God should take away threatened punishments—scourges,
sickness, catastrophes; it is not even enough that God should "forget"
our sins. The divine forgiveness must bring about a complete transformation of our whole being, since sin itself is a degradation and a death. Eze-
kiel proclaimed that God could and would effect this interior change:

> I will take you from among the nations and gather you together from
> all strange countries, and I will lead you back to your own land. I will
> pour out on you pure water and you shall be purified. And I will give
> you a new heart, I will put a new spirit within you. I will take away
> from your flesh the heart of stone, and I will give you a heart of flesh;
> I will place my spirit within you (Ez. 36:25-27).

This change will be a resurrection: "The bones that were crushed
shall dance" (cf. Ez. 37:1-14). And it will be connected with the new
Covenant proclaimed by Jeremias, when the Lord will put His law in
the very depths of His people's being and write it in their hearts (Jer.
31:33).

God will bring about this renewal by a redemption, like the first redemption of the Israelites from their slavery in Egypt.[8]

> I have dispersed your sins like a mist
>   and your wrongdoing like a cloud.
> Return to me, for I have redeemed you (Is. 44:22).

This redemption will be effected by the sufferings and death of the Servant of Yahweh, which will bring about "atonement" (at-one-ment)
i.e., the reunion of mankind with God.

> It was our sufferings that he bore,
>   our sorrows with which he was laden.

---

[8]"In the Old Testament, the deliverance from slavery in Egypt was only the first
phase of a saving event completed on Sinai. Israel was delivered from Pharaoh only to
become God's people. So the idea of 'redemption' has an essentially positive content,
as the etymology of the Latin term presupposes. The question is one of an 'acquisition'
(*emere*), of a purchase, of a taking possession by God which 'delivers' (*red-*) us from
slavery in order to 'acquire' (*emere*) us for God. In the Jewish mentality, the two notions
of redemption and acquisition are so closely akin that the one can replace the other.
In Exod. 15:16, Codex B of the Septuagint version has 'the people that You have acquired
(*ekteso*),' a literal translation of the Hebrew, but Codex A has "the people that You have
delivered (*elutroso*)'" (S. Lyonnet in *Introduction à la Bible*, A. Robert and A. Feuillet,
ed., pp. 866-867). Fr. Lyonnet also remarks in the same connection, speaking of St. Paul's
notion of our redemption, that "We have therefore become, as St. Paul sees it, God's
property, in virtue of a contract that has had all its conditions fulfilled, including that
which has been often noted: the sum has been paid (1 Cor. 6:20; 7:23). But as Fr. Prat
very rightly remarks (in *The Theology of St. Paul*), 'the metaphor is not meant to be
carried too far and no one is mentioned as claiming and receiving the price'" (*op. cit.*,
p. 864).

> . . . he was pierced because of our sins,
> crushed because of our iniquities.
> The chastisement that gives us peace fell upon him
> and by his bruises we are healed (Is. 53:4-5).

5. The psalms. The psalms distil into prayer both God's revelation and man's response, itself inspired by God. They continually praise God's *hesed,* His merciful love. The liturgy invites us to make these prayers our own, our response to God's love now revealed and given to us in Christ. For example, Psalm 50 echoes Ezechiel's prophecy:

> Cleanse me with hyssop and I shall be clean,
> wash me and I shall be whiter than snow.
> Give me back the sound of joy and feasting,
> let the bones that you crush dance again.
> Turn away your face from my sins,
> and blot out all my guilt.
> O God, create a pure heart for me. . . .

Psalm 102 proclaims:

> As high as are the heavens above the earth
> So mighty is his love for those who fear him;
> As far as the East is from the West,
> so far from us does he put our sins.
> As a father is tender to his children,
> so is Yahweh tender to those who fear him;
> He knows of what we are fashioned,
> he remembers that we are dust.[9]

Psalm 129 brings together forgiveness and redemption:

> For with the Lord is kindness,
> redemption in abundance,
> It is he who will redeem Israel
> from all his iniquities.

6. The mercy of God as revealed by Jesus. Jesus proclaimed the good news to the "poor," salvation and deliverance to sinners, and so revealed the merciful love of the Father. Publicans and prostitutes will reach the Kingdom of God before the high priests and elders of the people Matthew 21:31). "There is more joy in heaven over one sinner who repents than over ninety-nine just men who have no need of repentance" (Luke 15:20). Three parables in particular—the lost sheep, the lost drachma, the prodigal son (Luke 15:1-32; Matthew 18:12-14) — express God's fatherly love and the affectionate solicitude of His mercy.

The prayer of Jesus' disciples, therefore, should be like that of the publican who "went home justified" when he had deeply experienced

---

[9] See J. Guillet, *op. cit.,* pp. 76-82.

his sinfulness and expressed it in God's presence: "The publican stood far off, not daring to raise his eyes to heaven, and he struck his breast saying: 'My God, have mercy on me a sinner' " (Luke 17:13).

The disciples must imitate the Lord's mercy if they desire to receive it themselves: "Forgive us our sins, for we forgive our debtors" (Luke 11:4; Matthew 6:12).

> Be merciful as your Father in heaven is merciful. Judge not and you shall not be judged; condemn not and you shall not be condemned, forgive and you shall be forgiven . . . with the measure that you measure out, it shall be measured to you in return (Luke 6:36-38; Matthew 7:1-2; Mark 4:24).

Here again, the precept is illustrated through the teaching of a parable: the servant who is unmerciful toward his companion finds himself in turn refused by his master (Matthew 18:23-35).

Christ revealed God's mercy by His actions. To the great scandal of the pharisees, He "ate with sinners":

> The pharisees and their scribes murmured and said to his disciples: Why do you eat and drink with publicans and sinners? But Jesus answered them, saying: It is not those who are in good health who need a physician, but those who are sick; I am come not to call the just but sinners to repent (Luke 5:30-32; Matthew 2:15-17).

> Go, then, and learn the meaning of the word: I desire mercy and not sacrifice (Matthew 9:12).

He invited Himself to stay in the house of Zaccheus:

> Seeing this, all murmured and said: He is gone to stay with a sinner. But Zaccheus stood up boldly and said to the Lord: Yes, Lord, I will give half of my goods to the poor, and if I have wronged anyone. I will repay him fourfold. And Jesus said to him: Today this house has received salvation, because this man also is a son of Abraham. For the Son of man has come to seek and to save what was lost (Luke 19:7-10).

Christ actually exercised God's mercy by forgiving sins. At the house of Simon the Pharisee, He welcomed a sinner, and when He had explained His attitude toward her by a parable, He declared:

> This is why, I say to you, her many sins are forgiven her, because she has shown much love. . . . Then he said to the woman: Your sins are forgiven you. And those who were at table with him said among themselves: Who is this man who goes so far as to forgive sins? But he said to the woman: Your faith has saved you, go in peace (Luke 7:47-50).

Jesus often made the healing of bodily ills the sign and even the proof
of spiritual healing, as in the case of the paralytic at Capharnaum:

> Which is easier to say: Your sins are forgiven you, or to say: Arise
> and walk? So that you will know that the Son of man has power on
> earth to forgive sins, I command you—he said to the paralytic—arise,
> take your pallet and go back to your house. And instantly he got up
> as they watched, took up what he was lying on, and went home
> glorifying God (Luke 5:23-25; cf. Matthew 9:1-8; Mark 2:1-12).

One of Jesus' last words was spoken to the "good thief" crucified with
Him, who asked: "Lord, remember me when you come into your kingdom"; and Jesus answered: "In very truth I say to you, this day you will
be with me in paradise" (Luke 23:42-43).[10] And after the resurrection
Jesus set Peter over His whole Church, Peter who had denied Him three
times and had been converted by His glance (John 21:15).

Thus the revelation of God's merciful love throughout the Old Testament leads up to Jesus, the incarnate revelation of the Father's redeeming love, of His design to free men from their slavery to sin and bring
them back to share His life, the design carried out by Christ's life-giving
death.

III. THE CALL TO "CONVERSION," "REPENTANCE"

But "God who created you without you will not justify you without
you" (St. Augustine, *Serm.* 169). He could not do so without violating
the liberty with which He has endowed us. We must desire to turn away
from sin and return to God and so cooperate with His redeeming mercy.
Hence the permanent necessity for "conversion," for turning away from
sin and back to God; the Greek term *metanoia* used in the Bible means a
complete change of direction, a transformation of ourselves and our
way of life.

1. *The constituents of repentance.* God's invitation to repent, to be
converted, had already been proclaimed in the Old Testament and the
constituents of this repentance made clear. The external signs of repentance indicated are precisely those of deep grief: tears and cries
(Joel 1:8, 13; 2:12, 17, etc.); rending garments and sprinkling ashes
on the head (2 Sam. 13:19; Est. 4; Job 42:6, etc.); dressing in sackcloth
(3 Kings 21:27; Jonas 3); laying aside all insignia of human dignity
(Jonas 3; Est. 4); and above all fasting (Joel 1:14; 2:12; Jonas 3; Is.
58), which was also prescribed for sacrifices of expiation (Lev. 16:1;
23:26-32). And to these signs of mourning were added those of shame:
bowing the head (Is. 58) and striking the breast (Jer. 31:19). But these
external signs have no value unless they are the spontaneous and sincere

---

[10] See George MacRae, "With Me in Paradise" in *Worship,* 35 (1961), pp. 235-240.

expression of corresponding interior sentiments: "You must tear your hearts and not your clothing" (Joel 2:13); the true fast consists in practicing justice and charity (Is. 58).

Having done what is evil in God's sight calls for a sadness as great as the loss of an only son (Jer. 6:26); the greatest misfortune is to have turned away from the Lord. Shame penetrates the repentant sinner to his very depths:

> After turning away, I repented;
> I understood and I struck my breast.
> I was filled with shame and confusion,
>   yes, I bore the shame of my youth (Jer. 31:19).

But this shame is "glory and grace" (Sir. 4:26). Repentance is a sorrow, to be changed into joy (*Summa* 3, 84, 9). "When you shall seek me, says the Lord, I will let myself be found by you" (Jer. 29:13). For the sinner who truly repents does not enclose himself in the consciousness of his guilt, but at once sets out to seek God.

> Return to Yahweh, your God,
>   for he is tenderness and pity (Joel 2:13; cf. Osee 14:2-4).

> I will give them a heart to know that I am Yahweh . . .
>   they will return to me with their whole heart (Jer. 24:7).

This return to God requires the complete abandonment of sin, a process as clear-cut as changing the direction and goal of a journey.

> Be converted and turned away from all your sins. . . . Rid yourselves of all the sins you have committed against me and fashion for yourselves a new heart and a new spirit (Ez. 18:30-31).

> I take no pleasure in the death of the wicked, but in the return of the wicked who changes his way to have life. Return, return from your wicked way (Ez. 33:11).

Finally, repentance includes acknowledging our sins to God. This acknowledgment is the almost spontaneous expression of interior transformation: "I have sinned against Yahweh," cried David (2 Sam. 12:13). It is a prayer in which we seek to resume our dialogue with the Lord: "I will go to Yahweh to confess my sin" (Ps. 31:5).

But, as we have already seen, this conversion, this change of heart needed to return to God must itself be God's work.

> Yahweh Sabaoth, let us return; let your face shine out on us and we shall be saved (Ps. 79:4).

> Make me return, that I may return, for you are Yahweh my God (Jer. 31:18).

We need God's help even to recognize our sinfulness, as shown when He sent Nathan to open David's eyes: "That man is yourself" (2 Sam. 12:7).

To awaken His people to their sins and need of repentance, God sent calamities: exile, deportation and their previous military defeats—all were meant to make Israel recognize that they had violated the covenant, to remember Yahweh and return to Him.

> Therefore behold, I will close up your road with thorns,
>   I will build a wall, and she shall no longer find her paths.
> She shall follow after her lovers and not overtake them;
>   she shall seek them, and not find them.
> Then she shall say: I will go and I will return
>   to my first husband,
>   for I was happier then than now (Osee 2:6-7).[11]

2. Repentance and the "last times." The later prophets, particularly Joel, proclaimed more and more clearly, beyond individual misfortunes and historical calamities, the coming of the Day of Yahweh, the Day when the Lord's justice would shine out. They called for repentance and conversion as the only possible preparation.

The New Testament opens with the same proclamation. John the Baptist preached repentance in view of the imminent coming of the Kingdom of God (Matthew 3:1-11; Mark 1:1-4; Luke 3:3-8). Jesus began by preaching the same message, while indicating more and more clearly that in His Person the Kingdom had already come, bringing salvation to those who truly turned to the Lord with their whole hearts and rejection to those who closed their ears to His message.

The same call to repent, to be "converted," must always form part of the Church's proclamation of the Good News, as it did on the day of Pentecost when St. Peter quoted Joel's prophecy to show that the "last times" had already arrived. Jesus Himself entrusted this preaching of repentance to the apostles, and it is itself a fulfillment of prophecies concerning Christ (Luke 24:47). Everyone must be willing to turn from his evil ways and turn to God if he is to receive Christ's salvation.

---

[11] In the context of Osee's life and prophesying, "this idea of a medicinal punishment, already introduced by Amos, naturally reappears. It now figures as a supreme proof of love, of that virile love which does not resign itself to the fall of the beloved, which imposes the necessary suffering on her, but always first enduring suffering itself, in order to bring her back, to raise her up" (L. Bouyer, *op. cit.*, p. 63).

Article Two

OUR SINS CLEANSED IN THE BLOOD OF CHRIST[12]

All the divine preparations to free mankind from sin and bring them back to God thus lead up to Christ. He is at once the incarnate revelation and agent of God's redeeming mercy, and the new Adam in whom mankind returns to God.[13] In Him and Him alone is there forgiveness of sins.

I. CHRIST'S REDEEMING DEATH

Jesus Himself gave this meaning to His death: "My Blood that will be poured out for a multitude for the remission of sins" (Matthew 26:28). As we have already seen in studying the sacrifice of the Cross, Christ's death is the effective sacrifice of expiation, that is, of purification and consecration to God. Christ is the "Lamb of God who takes away the sins of the world," the Lamb of the paschal sacrifice, the Servant of Isaias' prophecy. The death of Christ is the atonement (the at-one-ment) "reconciling us with God" (Rom. 5:10-11; 2 Cor. 5:18-19) and "delivering us from the wrath to come" (1 Thess. 1:10).[14]

Christ's redeeming death is thus the great act and proof of God's love for us: "God so loved the world as to give His only Son, so that every man who believes in Him should not perish but have life everlasting" (John 3:16).[15] It is also the great work and proof of Christ's love for His

[12] In the light of the meaning the Bible attaches to blood as meaning "life", and its use in the various sacrifices of the Old Testament to purify, consecrate and unite man with God, such expressions as "He has cleansed us from our sins in his own Blood" (Apoc. 1:5) take on their full and proper sense. Christ's Blood is the sign of His human life offered to God in His death on the Cross, taken up and transformed by God's glory at the resurrection. We are purified, consecrated and united with God by becoming, as it were, immersed in Christ's life through faith and the sacraments.

[13] See Jean de Fraine, "Adam and Christ as Corporate Personalities," *Theology Digest,* 10 (1962), pp. 99ff.

[14] See especially J. Guillet, *Themes of the Bible,* pp. 87-89, giving the eschatological aspect of Christ's death and the remission of sins.

[15] "So as to lead back to Himself mankind whom sin had irremediably separated from Him, God the Father, by an excess of love and of respect for the liberty of man—respect being the very delicacy of love—, found a way of redemption according to which it would somehow be man in person who would effect this return and, like the prodigal son . . . come back himself to the Father who awaited him. And so God sent His own Son to become one of us and, by His solidarity with us, to take on Himself, not our sin certainly, but what St. Paul calls 'the likeness of a flesh of sin' (Rom. 8:3), that is, precisely the condition of the prodigal son . . . or, more precisely, that of men reduced by the sin of Adam to their natural condition, not only capable of dying but condemned to die. If God were to pardon man's sin, it would obviously be by submitting Himself to the conditions of man's nature that man could return to his Father. . . . Thus, in order that in Christ it would be our sinful humanity which in all truth returned to God, it was

Father: "That the world may know that I love the Father and that I do as the Father has commanded me" (John 14:31), and of His love for us: "Greater love than this no man has, that he lay down his life for his friends" (John 15:13). We should never cease praising the love God has shown us in Christ and witnessing to it by obeying His commandment to love one another as He has loved us.[16]

II. ALL FORGIVENESS OF SINS FLOWING FROM CHRIST'S SACRIFICE

Both before and after Christ's coming, men can obtain forgiveness for their sins only through Christ's sacrifice: "There is no other name under heaven given to men whereby they may be saved" (Acts 4:12). To have our sins forgiven and to be "justified," that is, to be "made right," as God wants us to be, restored to His likeness and sharing His life, we must be united with Christ by faith and the sacraments.

1. Faith in Christ. Faith could save those who lived before Christ's coming; it is essential to justification. "Without faith it is impossible to please God. For he who comes to God must believe that God exists and

temporal death which constituted the mediation of that supreme act of love by which He leads us back to His Father . . . the death of the Cross.

". . . in His flesh, as He assumed it, was inscribed a true necessity, an obligation to die. Such an obligation can be compared to a 'debt' with regard to God and His Law, a debt incumbent on mankind, which Christ, as one with mankind, fully discharged in such a way as to profit us: He discharged it 'in our favor.' But this could only profit us because it was the expression of a supreme act of love and, in consequence, something quite different from the mere paying of a debt. What might be considered as the debt which mankind owed to God and the divine Law was not death itself, either biological or eternal . . . but rather that supreme act of obedience and love which Christ—and all mankind in Him—returned to God, the act mediated by His death and all the circumstances surrounding it. Christ fully and superabundantly discharged this debt; He fully and superabundantly 'made reparation' for man's sin. Later theology was to formulate this truth by saying that He 'satisfied' for us, made satisfaction for us to His Father, satisfaction being precisely opposed to juridical punishment—as the classic saying puts it, *aut poena aut satisfactio.* . . . In any case, the juridical level is certainly transcended. For it was not by a mere reparation of the moral order—still less some 'juridical fiction'—that, in St. Paul's thought, Christ effected this return of mankind to God. It was by assuming our flesh and dying in it to that 'body of flesh' (cf. Col. 2:11) in order to rise with a 'spiritual body' (1 Cor. 15:44), becoming 'life-giving spirit' (v. 45); in other words, in being the first to pass, thanks to His death by obedience and love, from our carnal condition and the sphere of sin to the spiritual and divine state" (S. Lyonnet, *op. cit.,* pp. 882-884).

[16] Holy Scripture also gives us a glimpse, for example in the Epistle to the Corinthians, of how the mystery of our redemption evidences the Father's love for His Son, through whom and for whose sake, "unto whom," all things were made. "And he is the head of his Body, the Church: he who is the beginning, the firstborn from the dead, that in all things he might have the first place. For it has pleased the Father that in him all his fullness should dwell and that through him he should reconcile all things to himself . . . making peace through the Blood of his Cross" (Col. 13-21 and its context). We find the same orientation in the Epistle to the Hebrews: ". . . his Son, whom he appointed heir of all things, by whom also he made the world; who, being the brightness of his glory and the image of his substance, and upholding all things by the word of his power, has effected man's purgation from sin and taken his seat at the right hand of the Majesty" (Heb. 1:2-4; cf. 14-17, etc.).

is a rewarder to those who seek him" (Heb. 11:6). Through this faith men could be united to Christ and His redeeming sacrifice. Christian faith is man's response to the proclamation of the Good News, a response that is itself a grace and the fruit of Christ's sacrifice, leading by its nature to baptism, which engrafts a man into Christ's Body, the Church.

2. The sacraments. Baptism is the primary sacrament of repentance and the remission of sins, as the teaching of the apostles and Fathers shows. By it Christ brings us into His paschal mystery, causing us to die to sin and to live for God. The Holy Spirit is given in baptism, and "it is he who is the remission of sins." As we have seen, no one can have his sins forgiven and be saved without at least implicit desire for baptism. But the question then arises: how are sins committed after baptism to be forgiven?

III. FORGIVENESS OF SINS COMMITTED AFTER BAPTISM

1. The possibility of sinning after baptism. The break with his past life made by the Christian at his baptism is presented by the Epistles as decisive. Yet the same Epistles describe the first Christian communities as struggling with the mediocrity of human nature and obliged to deal with abuses, errors, sins. The Christian must examine his conscience before coming to the Eucharistic table and not approach it if he is unworthy (1 Cor. 11:27-34). When sins constitute a grave public scandal, the Church is to pronounce judgment against the guilty person (1 Cor. 5:5; 1 Tim. 1:19; 2 Cor. 2:2-11; 2 Thess. 3:14; Gal. 6:1).

The baptismal break with sin, then, may not have been final. In any case, it is not complete, for all Christians must admit to daily sins:

> If we say, "We have no sin," we deceive ourselves, the truth is not in us. If we confess our sins, he is faithful and just enough to forgive us our sins and to purify us from all injustice. If we say, "We have no sin," we make him a liar, his word is not in us (1 John 1:8-10).

2. The possibility of forgiveness. These "daily faults" which do not exclude us from the Kingdom of God do not involve the grace of baptism. But there are certain sins which destroy the work of redemption in the Christian. Recall how the Israelites fell in the desert in spite of the wonderful works God wrought for them and did not enter the Promised Land (1 Cor. 10:1-13). This is the greatest misfortune that can happen to anyone:

> If, after having escaped the defilements of the world through the knowledge of the Lord and Savior Jesus Christ, they are again entangled in them and are overcome by them, their last state has become worse than the first. For it would have been better for them never

to have known the way of justice, than, having known it, to turn
away from the holy commandment that had been given to them.
What has happened to them is what the true proverb says: "The dog
has returned to his own vomit," and, "A sow, even after washing,
wallows in the mire" (2 Peter 2:20-22).

Yet it is still possible for such unhappy persons to revive their initiation, to be "renewed a second time and led to repentance." Phrases in
the Epistles such as the above and Heb. 6:4-8; 10:26-31 are to be understood as referring to final impenitence. For the New Testament states,
and the practice of the Church has always recognized, that sins committed after baptism can be forgiven.

> The Lord uses patience toward you, willing that no man should
> die, but that all should be led to repentance (2 Peter 3:9).

> Little children, I write you so that you will not sin. But if anyone
> does sin, we have as our advocate with the Father, Jesus Christ the
> just (1 John 2:1).

Moreover, Christ Himself made God's mercy toward us the measure of
the mercy that we should extend to our neighbor; and we must pardon
our neighbor "not seven times, but seventy times seven times" (Matthew
18:22).

3. The sacraments of forgiveness after baptism.
The tradition of
the Church has always made a distinction between "daily faults" that do
not take away life and "sins that cause death," even though the concrete
evaluation of this distinction has never been easy to make and has been subject to a development paralleling that of the Christian conscience.

The forgiveness of daily faults may be obtained by "daily penance,"
sacramental or non-sacramental:

> Is it not for this that each day we strike our breasts? This is what
> we bishops also do each day in going up to the altar. This is also
> why we entreat in that prayer we should recite throughout our lives,
> "Forgive us our offenses as we forgive those who have offended us."
> Here we do not ask forgiveness for those sins that we believe to have
> been washed away by baptism; but we pray for the daily faults for
> which each Christian unceasingly offers, according to his means, the
> sacrifice of his alms, his mortifications, his prayers and supplications.[17]

But when the life of the spirit has been lost by mortal sins, it cannot
be regained nor the divine forgiveness bestowed except by certain sacraments, or at least the desire for them. Even though the Eucharist contains the very source of the remission of sin, Christ's sacrifice, it is not the
sacrament through which we are to receive forgiveness of mortal sins. He

---

[17] Sermon attributed to St. Augustine, (PL 38, 1541). Present scholarship considers
this sermon possibly not authentic.

who has not yet been forgiven his mortal sins is excluded from the Meal of the Lord; in eating unworthily, he would eat to his own condemnation (1 Cor. 11:27-29). There are two sacraments designed precisely for spiritual healing: principally and normally the sacrament of penance; secondarily, the anointing of the sick.

Article Three
THE STRUCTURE OF THE SACRAMENT OF PENANCE

"The passion of Christ acts in the sacrament of penance" (*Summa* III, 84, 5). "The sacrament of penance is, according to the teaching of the Fathers, like a second baptism, but a *laborious baptism*" (*Denz.* 895). It is therefore both like and unlike baptism.

> The infinite mercy of God goes so far to meet human sins that the hope of eternal life is given not only by the grace of baptism but also by the remedy of penance, so that those who have lost the gifts of regeneration can attain the remission of sins by freely accusing themselves. The divine goodness, however, has thus disposed of its blessings by ineluctably connecting them with the prayers of priests. The Mediator between God and men, the Man and Lord Jesus, has indeed given to the ministers of the Church this power, by which they impose the exercise of penance on those who confess their sins and, when they are healed by a salutary satisfaction, admit them by reconciliation to the communion of the sacraments.

This text of St. Leo's (*Denz.* 146) well sums up the characteristics of this sacrament; however, its discipline and its liturgy may vary in different times and places.

I. THE LITURGY AND DISCIPLINE OF PENANCE IN THE HISTORY OF THE CHURCH

Two principal usages are found in the practice of the sacrament of penance, at least in the West. First, there is solemn penance, with which the reconciliation of the dying should be connected. This is the only form which seems to have been practiced in the early Church. It was still extant in the thirteenth century, but has now fallen into complete disuse, although it is included in the liturgical books.

Secondly, the existence of private penance since the seventh century is clearly attested by the "penitential books" composed to assist priests in administering it. After coexisting with solemn penance for some time, private penance finally supplanted it completely. It has developed considerably both in its discipline and its rites.

1. Solemn penance in the early Church. Even at the beginning of the third century, the Church had a developed rite of penance, conceived in great part along the lines of the baptismal rite. Details varied in different countries and centuries, and the rite assumed an ever greater amplitude. But the characteristics and discipline of solemn penance remained basically the same up to the time of St. Thomas Aquinas in the thirteenth century (*Summa, Suppl.*, 28).

Solemn penance was designed only for Christians who had committed the gravest sins. Whatever the horror felt by the community at certain crimes (apostasy, adultery, homicide), the Church never consented to follow the rigorists. She taught that every sin could be submitted to penance, even though she sometimes required a very long period of penance. But penance was not available to clerics, and it was given to other Christians only once in a lifetime. As there was only one baptism, so there could only be one penance.[18]

The sinner separated himself of his own accord from participation in the holy Mysteries. In the case of a public crime, he could be excluded by an act of authority on the part of the bishop:

> He who fears that he will be separated from the Kingdom of heaven by the final condemnation of the supreme Judge must be separated here on earth from the sacrament of the heavenly Bread by the discipline of the Church (sermon attributed to St. Augustine, PL 38, 1542-1543).

Then he presented himself to the bishop to tell him his sin and to be assigned his penance.

Throughout the period of their trial, the penitents constituted a group apart, like the catechumens. Like the latter, they were entrusted to some member of the hierarchy who took charge of them. They participated in the first part of the liturgy, but at the time of the celebration of the Eucharistic sacrifice they were sent away, after the celebrant had said a prayer over them and blessed them. They were obliged to give alms, to fast and pray, to abstain from pleasures and feasts. In a word, they lived in a state of sorrow like the penitents of the Old Testament. In certain churches they were given sackcloth to wear.

Finally, they came to be reconciled by the bishop, who imposed his hands on them with appropriate prayers; then they took part in the Eucharist and received Communion. In Rome, from the end of the fourth

[18] In the present state of our historical knowledge, we cannot say how the Church behaved toward those who could not receive the sacrament of penance or could not receive it again. But one thing stands out clearly from the teaching of the Fathers and the Councils: there is no sin God refuses to forgive except the state of impenitence.

century, the reconciliation of penitents was carried out on Holy Thursday, thus marking the bond between penance and the paschal mystery.[19]

But even after reconciliation, penitents were subject to certain prohibitions; for example, they could not be ordained and they had to live in continence. Fear of these consequences therefore led many Christians to put off penance until the moment of death.

In time the rigor of these conditions was toned down, the duration of the period of penance was reduced and made the same for all. It then coincided with Lent: the entry into the state of penitence was assigned to the Wednesday inaugurating the forty-day fast.

This entry into the state of penance included receiving a garment of sackcloth and being sprinkled with ashes. Later an act of great symbolic importance was added: the penitents were expelled from the church while antiphons were sung recalling Adam's expulsion from Eden. "See," said the bishop, "how you are driven away from the threshold of holy Mother Church because of your sins and your crimes, as Adam the first man was driven out of paradise because of his disobedience."

The reconciliation of the penitents on Holy Thursday, as presented in the texts of the eighth century and even today in the Roman Pontifical, was one of the great liturgical acts in the life of the Church, on the same level as baptism, ordinations, and the consecration of virgins. The deacon's proclamation opening the ceremony stresses the parallel between baptism and penance:

> Here is the moment when . . . the vine of the Lord will be increased by those who come to be baptized and will be enlarged by those who return. Water cleanses and so do tears. Here, where we rejoice to receive those who are called, we rejoice also in absolving the penitent.

Among the bishop's prayers were the following:

> Most kind Lord, call back with Your accustomed goodness these Your servants whose sins have separated them from You. For You did not disdain the humiliation of the wicked Achab, but spared him his due punishment. You heard Peter's weeping and then entrusted him with the keys of the Kingdom of heaven. And to the thief who confessed his sins, You promised the rewards of that same Kingdom.
>
> Welcome back, then, O most kind Lord, these men for whom we offer You our prayers, and give them back to the bosom of Your Church, so that the enemy can in no way triumph over them. Rather, may Your Son who is equal to You reconcile them with You and purify them from all sin, so that they may be worthy to be admitted to the Eucharistic banquet. Thus may He restore them by His Flesh and His Blood, and so lead them, after this life, to the Kingdom of heaven.

[19] Holy Thursday is the last day on which the Eucharist is celebrated before the holy night of Easter. In Spain, where the reconciliation of penitents was not connected with the Mass, it was carried out on Holy Saturday.

> O God, since in Your goodness You created the human race and in Your mercy restored it; since by the Blood of Your only Son You have redeemed man fallen from eternity by the hatred of the demon, give back life to these Your servants, whom You do not wish to see die. You have never abandoned them in their sin, now receive them after their correction. Let Your goodness, O Lord, be moved by the sighs and tears of Your servants. Heal their wounds; reach out to them your health-giving hand so that they may arise . . . so that they who have received a second birth at baptism may not fall into a second death. . . ."

When a penitent was at the point of death, he was reconciled by a priest who came in the name of the bishop to pray over him, using a shortened rite. This happened the more frequently since certain sins were forgiven only at the moment of death, and also since many of the faithful put off until their final moments the entry into the state of penitence because of the obligations it entailed for the rest of one's life.

When solemn penance gave place to private penance, which was less rigorous and could be repeated, the prayer of the Church at the moment of death still retained some elements of the penitential liturgy. In our times, the apostolic blessing is, in a certain way, a reminder of this tradition; but, it does not merely witness to the ancient discipline. This blessing brings out the important fact that death, the supreme act of the Christian combat, calls for a contrite glance over our whole past, which the Lord is soon to judge. This moment is the crucial time to receive from the Church the signs of the divine pardon.

2. Private penance. Unlike solemn penance, private penance could be repeated. It did not include any *sequellae* after reconciliation. The time of expiation was very much reduced and it did not take place in a celebration with the full liturgical assembly, but simply between the penitent and a priest.

The development of the discipline of private penance has involved a two-fold clarification of the role of this sacrament. Instead of being reserved for sins of exceptional gravity, it has become the normal means for receiving forgiveness for all sins. By this very fact, it requires of the penitent an effort to examine his conscience and an ever greater precision in confessing his sins. All this could lead to an interiorization of penance. As the mercy of God, which antiquity never questioned even with regard to those who were refused the repetition of solemn penance, became ever clearer, so also did the extent of human weakness (cf. *Summa* III, 84, 10; one of the texts of St. Augustine on which St. Thomas relies here is not authentic.)

Although any private administration of the sacrament of penance was apparently unknown to St. Augustine and his contemporaries, it appeared in Ireland in the fifth century, as a development of the traditional monastic practice of acknowledging one's faults to an experienced guide as a means of progress toward perfection. But the kind of penance that now appeared was truly sacramental. The confession of sins was made to a priest; he imposed works of expiation, the gravity and length of which were to be proportioned to the number and gravity of the sins. When satisfaction had been made, the penitent came back to be reconciled.

To facilitate the priest's task in imposing these works of expiation, "penitential books" were composed. These books spread over Europe and, with them, the practice of private penance which they regulated.

The *Ordo Romanus Antiquus* of Mayence (about 950), which became widely disseminated in Europe, required the faithful to come to the priest to receive penance at the beginning of Lent. The confession of sins was preceded by a profession of faith and followed by psalms and prayers. The reconciliation of the penitent also took place in a liturgical context; it included verses of psalms, prayers of reconciliation and, frequently, a Mass with appropriate texts.

In the eleventh century, due to various causes, it became generally customary to reconcile the penitent when he made his confession, without waiting for him to carry out the works of expiation imposed. From then on private penance lost more and more of its similarity to solemn penance. It came to require only one meeting with the priest: he heard the confession, imposed the penance, and reconciled the penitent immediately. The penitent later carried out the imposed works of reparation, but could receive the Eucharist at once.

The last change produced in the Latin Church in connection with the sacrament of penance affected the form of reconciliation. Up to the thirteenth century the bishop or priest exercised the ministry of reconciliation by means of solemn prayers addressed to God, the impetratory form used at ordinations. In the thirteenth century a formula for penance came to be used which expressed in an indicative form an act of authority on the part of the minister of the Church. Instead of asking the Lord to forgive, it stated:

> According to the authority we have received from God in spite of our unworthiness, we release you from all your sins, so that you may merit eternal life.[20]

Or, more simply, according to present usage:

> I absolve you from all your sins, in the name of the Father, of the Son and of the Holy Spirit.

From the term "release" or "absolve" (in Latin, *absolvere,* to "loose from") this formula is called "absolution". The impetratory and the

[20] Found in a manuscript of the eleventh century, Paris, Bibl. Nat. 820.

indicative form each has its value: in the Latin liturgy, the second has come to be preferred because of the importance it gives to the sacramental sign of the judgment and the power which the Church exercises in the name of Christ.

II. THE MINISTRY OF THE DIVINE FORGIVENESS

1. The ecclesial character of penance.   Whether we consider penance in the solemn form of the early centuries or in its present usage, it always has the same essential characteristics.

First, reconciliation with God is reconciliation with the Church. It is true that the bond attaching the Christian to the Church is actually broken only by sins directly opposed to the unity of the Church, such as schism, heresy or apostasy (*Mystici Corporis*, 23). But all sin affects the community, since we are all one Body in Christ (1 Cor. 12:12-31). Thus reconciliation with the Church is the efficacious sign of reconciliation with God.[21]

In ancient times this aspect was emphasized by the fact that the reconciliation took place in the midst of the full liturgical assembly, with frequent prayers for the penitents. Today the rite appears to concern only the penitent and the priest, but it is no less ecclesial.

The second essential characteristic of penance is that the Church reconciles the sinner with God. The Church continues the work of redemption. It is she who puts men in contact with the mystery of salvation in Christ. It is she who brings forth the Christian at his baptism, and it is she who brings him back to life in penance. She bases her ministry of penance on the words of Jesus Christ after the resurrection:

> Receive the Holy Spirit. Those whose sins you shall forgive, shall have their sins forgiven them; those whose sins you shall retain, shall have their sins retained (John 20:22-23).

Tradition has unanimously taken these words literally (*Denz.* 894, 913). They must be understood in relation to two other Gospel texts, the one concerning the ministers of the Church as a whole ("Whatever you bind on earth shall be held as bound in heaven, and what you loose on earth shall be held as loosed in heaven"—Matthew 18:18), the other concerning the Apostle Peter ("I will give you the keys of the Kingdom of heaven; what you bind on earth shall be held as bound in heaven, and what you loose on earth, shall be held as loosed in heaven"—Matthew 16:19).

---

[21] See George McCauley, "The Ecclesial Nature of the Sacrament of Penance," *Worship*, 36 (1962), pp. 212-222; Edgar Hardwick, "Penance and the Church," *Life of the Spirit*, 14 (1959), pp. 3-12; "The Sacrament of Penance in Parish Life," PNLW (1941), pp. 126-134.

Christ gave His Church a governing power that goes beyond the earthly condition of men, since what she binds or looses on earth is bound or loosed in heaven. This power is strictly sacramental when it is exercised on sins, since the sins forgiven by the apostles really are remitted. This is the "power of the keys." When the apostles pardon, it is God who pardons and the redeeming work of the passion of Christ which is exercised. The power of jurisdiction, therefore, is not sufficient to absolve sins; the minister must have received the Holy Spirit, without whom there is no remission of sins. Moreover, the power is given not only to remit sins but also to retain them. (This clearly proves that the words of Christ did not refer only to the first remission of sins granted through baptism, for at baptism the Church cannot "retain" sins—they are forgiven if the rite is administered to a man who has the required dispositions.)

The reconciliation of penitents or, to use the modern term, absolution, is therefore a ministry which is at once a sacrament and an act of jurisdiction; we must even say that it is a sacramental act of government, and therefore requires both the power of orders and the power of jurisdiction. Because of this we say that absolution is given in the form of a judgment.

2. The ministry of the sacrament of penance.   It is the bishop above all who is the minister of the sacrament of penance, (that is, a bishop who is legitimately at the head of a diocese; titular bishops do not have any jurisdiction). He possesses the apostolic succession of ordination and of jurisdiction; he has received the Holy Spirit; he participates in the promise made to the apostles on Easter evening. This power is affirmed in the prayers of his consecration. The most ancient consecratory formula still preserved, that of the *Apostolic Tradition* of Hippolytus, prays: "May he have the power to remit sins by virtue of the Spirit of the high priesthood, according to Your commandment."

The priest shares in the priesthood of the bishop. At his ordination he received the power of orders necessary for the ministry of penance, as is indicated by the ceremony following Communion in the ordination Mass. But he cannot absolve validly if he has not also received the power of jurisdiction. This is given him only by the bishop, to the degree to which the bishop makes him a participant in his own pastoral charge (Can. 872). The bishop can also reserve to himself the power to absolve from certain grave sins "reserved sins" and sins involving an ecclesiastical censure). Thus all priests do not have the power to hear confessions and, when they are given it, it is a power which is by its nature limited to a territory, a period of time, or to certain persons. (Obviously, the Pope also, because he has a true episcopal power, can give priests the necessary jurisdiction.)

Neither deacons nor the faithful can in any way administer the sacrament of penance, because they do not possess the priestly character. It is true that certain cases can be adduced, from the practice of some churches in early times, of deacons sometimes conveying to the sick the reconciliation imparted by the bishop. Again, in the Middle Ages more or less frequent incidents of confessions made to laymen might give occasion for erroneous interpretations.[22]

Yet St. Cyprian early laid down the principles later recalled by the Council of Trent (*Denz.* 920). It is not to holy persons but to the apostles and their successors that Christ has given the Holy Spirit for the remitting of sins. It is not an exercise of fraternal correction which is expected from the minister, but a sacrament producing justification.

3. The sign of judgment. In pronouncing absolution, the bishop or priest does not merely declare to the penitent that God has forgiven him his sins—this word is efficacious; it effects what it signifies, interiorly transforming the penitent. Its efficacy comes from the fact that the minister is the instrument of Christ.

> God alone, by His authority, can absolve and remit sins. Priests, however, do both as ministers. The words of the priest act as the instrument of the divine power, which works interiorly in all the sacramental signs, whether they are acts or words (*Summa* III, 84, 3 ad 3).

But there is more to absolution than a word—it is an *act*. The minister does not pardon sins unconditionally, in the same way as he baptizes. Nor does he say that sins are forgiven because he has received an interior revelation from the Lord to this effect (*Summa* III, 84, 3 ad 5). He pronounces a judgment. Consequently, the sign includes more than the simple act of repeating a formula. The whole attitude of the priest is that of a judge seated at his tribunal, judging the nature of the sins and dispositions of the guilty person, pronouncing forgiveness. Hence we see why the sacrament requires for validity not only the power of orders but also that of jurisdiction; a judge can summon, question and judge only those who belong to his jurisdiction. The Council of Trent, in at least three places, stresses the proper character of the sacrament of penance as a judgment.

> If anyone say that the sacramental absolution of the priest is not a judiciary act, but only the service of pronouncing and declaring that the sins of the man who confesses are forgiven on the condition

---

[22] Confessing sins to someone who is not a priest is still carried out today as an ascetic practice, prescribed in certain monastic rules, but this is not sacramental confession. Such a confession might be suggested to (but not imposed on) a dying Christian if no priest were available to absolve him. Here again, this confession would obviously not be sacramental, but it would aid the Christian to gain dispositions of perfect contrition and desire for the sacrament.

> that he believes himself absolved . . . let him be anathema *(Denz.* 919; cf. 895, 902).

This judgment is at once a condemnation and an acquittal. It is a condemnation because penance is "painful"—the interior sorrow of the guilty person, the avowal of sins, and expiation. But the sinner is reconciled by this judgment and condemnation, for the sentence pronounced is ultimately the destruction of the sin: "I absolve you from all your sins." It does not consist in excusing the guilty, but in delivering him from his sin by giving him the grace of the Holy Spirit together with the divine forgiveness.

Here we come back to the eschatological character of penance already noted in the preaching of the prophets, of John the Baptist, of Christ and the apostles. In the sacrament of penance the judgment that Christ will render when He returns is already exercised:

> When the Son of man comes in his glory, escorted by all the angels, then he will take his place on his throne of glory. All the nations will be assembled before him and he will separate the people as a shepherd separates the sheep from the goats. . . . He will say to those on his left: "Depart from me, you cursed, into the eternal fire prepared for the devil and his angels. For I was hungry and you did not feed me; I was thirsty and you did not give me drink. . . . And they will go away—these to everlasting punishment and the just to everlasting life (Matthew 25:31-46).

In the sacrament of penance the priest is the minister of the glorified Christ. But here it is the guilty person who presents himself of his own accord and himself proclaims his sins, while at the Last Judgment the nations will be assembled. Here sins remain secret; the sentence pronounced condemns the sin, but saves the sinner from the wrath to come because he changes his life and is interiorly transformed.

In the present Latin rite the priest says: "I absolve you from all your sins in the name of the Father, and of the Son, and of the Holy Spirit." This invocation of the Trinity recalls that of baptism. It affirms that penance, as a second baptism, consecrates the Christian anew so that he may once again be the temple of the Holy Spirit and so that the three divine Persons may come and make their dwelling within him. He has come like the prodigal to say, "Father, I have sinned against heaven and against you, I am no longer worthy to be called your son," and he receives the embrace of his Father and is clothed in "the best robe" (Luke 15:21-22).

III. THE ACTS OF THE PENITENT AS
PART OF THE SACRAMENTAL SIGN

All the sacraments require that the recipient participate freely and voluntarily, except in the case of infants without the use of reason. The adult must prepare for his justification in baptism by faith and hope, by a beginning of love of God, and by a transformation of life. Love of God and transformation of life imply sorrow and detestation for past sins. We see why the Fathers, in their instructions to candidates for baptism, comment on the biblical texts calling to repentance. But there are two fundamental differences between the repentance of the candidate for baptism and that of the Christian presenting himself for absolution.

First, baptismal repentance does not include, as we have already noted, any expiatory and sorrowful character. The catechumen does not have to confess his sins, he is not assigned any work of satisfaction. It is enough that he tear himself away from his past and amend his life. He profits from the passion of Christ to which he is configured by the sacrament, but does not yet experience the sufferings of Christ. By contrast, the Christian who has sinned after his baptism must, to be reconciled, "be configured to the suffering Christ through a punishment or a suffering that he himself undergoes" (*Summa* III, 49, 5 ad 2).

Secondly, the conditions required of the catechumen for the fruitful reception of baptism are preliminary to the sacrament, but do not form part of it; they do not enter into the structure of the sign itself. But in the sacrament of penance the acts of the penitent form part of the sacramental sign.

For, as we have seen, in penance the minister exercises an act of judgment, and this judgment is concerned precisely with the acts of the penitent. These are either oriented toward the absolution which is pronounced on them (confession, expression of contrition), or proceed from it because they constitute the execution of the sentence (satisfaction). They are not, then, simply a preliminary condition; they are the very matter of the judgment, and thereby they enter into the sign. A part of the sacramental sign is thus supplied by the penitent,[23] so that, according to the view of St. Thomas, if the acts of the penitent are not expressed perceptibly, at least in an elementary way, there can be no sacrament properly speaking.

The acts of the penitent in examining his conscience, repenting, admitting his sins and making expiation are thus consecrated by the absolution. Of themselves they cannot gain remission of sins, since God alone can forgive. But the absolution makes them efficacious in such a way that

---

[23] *Summa* III, 84, 1 (cf. *Denz.* 896). "The very acts of the penitent—contrition, confession, satisfaction—constitute as it were the matter of the sacrament." This formulation refers to the medieval usage of distinguishing "matter and form" in the sacraments.

from the outset they are sacramental. Wholly interior and personal acts expressing the situation of a man before God, they become acts of the Church because of the sacramental action of her minister over them. The call to conversion and repentance, first heard in the Old Testament, still resounds in the Church. But the New Testament goes beyond the Old; if the sinner orients himself toward absolution, from the beginning of his change of heart he is in the sacramental order. The gratuity of God's gift is still complete. It is expressed by the priest's absolution at the end of the journey which has led the penitent to the tribunal of penance; but faith can recognize it from the outset. While in most of the sacraments it is the minister who prepares the matter which is to serve as the sign, here it is God Himself who, by His interior action in a man's heart, arouses the acts of the penitent which constitute the matter (*Summa* III, 84, 1 ad 2).

The sacramental sign, therefore, expresses at once the interior, personal aspect and the ritual and communal aspect which are "the two complementary aspects of Christian penance" and "as it were, the two poles between which is extended the complex reality of the sacrament of penance."[24]

IV. THE NECESSITY OF THE SACRAMENT OF PENANCE

As we have already observed, tradition has always stated clearly the distinction between the "daily sins" which do not destroy the life of the spirit, and the "sins that cause death." The difficulty consists in trying to lay down precisely the dividing-line between these two categories of sins, for, while they are radically different from the theological point of view, they are in psychological continuity. As a result, the differences between them have been variously evaluated in various ages. And, in any case, the concrete actuality of souls often vests in mystery the degree of guilt in any act.

But, considering these reservations, the Church has always recognized that daily sins, at least those which now are called "venial," can be forgiven without recourse to the sacrament of penance because they do not destroy the state of grace and charity. Yet they can be submitted for absolution, constituting optional but sufficient matter for it. Confessing them is recommended by the Church and has been practiced by the saints (*Denz.* 899).

For sins which have destroyed the state of grace and charity, the sacrament of penance is absolutely necessary for salvation. This is the teaching of the Council of Trent:

> This sacrament is necessary for salvation for those who have fallen
> after baptism, as baptism itself is necessary for those who have not

[24] P. Anciaux, *The Sacrament of Penance.*

yet been regenerated *(Denz.* 895) . . . . If anyone say that confession is not, by divine law . . . necessary for salvation . . . let him be anathema *(Denz.* 916).

Mortal sins committed by baptized persons can therefore never be forgiven without at least an implicit desire for this sacrament. Perfect contrition gives the grace of justification even before absolution because such contrition includes at least implicitly the intention of receiving the sacrament. Thus the obligation always remains to submit to the power of the keys of the Church sins which have already been forgiven in another way. In particular, the divine law itself is opposed to a Christian's receiving the Eucharist if he has not submitted his mortal sins to the power of the keys, even if he thinks that he has perfect contrition for them, unless there is special urgency to communicate and no confessor is available *(Denz.* 880, 893; Can. 856). This prohibition does not apply to sins forgotten in confession which one remembers afterwards.

The Church makes it a precept that every Christian who has reached the age of reason must approach the tribunal of penance at least once a year if he has grave sins of which to accuse himself. This precept is stated in Canon 906 of the Code of Canon Law, which reproduces almost exactly the text of Canon 21 of the Fourth Lateran Council of 1215 *(Denz.* 437). This great reforming Council connected the obligation of penance with that of Easter Communion; this was the sanction of an immemorial discipline, since the penitential books of the eighth century required that all the faithful receive penance at the beginning of Lent. Today the precept of yearly confession is independent of Easter and the Easter Communion, at least theoretically. But in practice the link remains, since one cannot communicate without first receiving absolution for mortal sins.

We must not forget, however, that laws prescribe only the minimum and that in teaching the commandments of the Church we should avoid a presentation that would beget any formalism. In connection with this commandment of yearly confession, we should bring out the necessity of the sacrament of penance for regaining intimacy with God when we have fallen, and its efficacy in helping us make spiritual progress.

This efficacy is the reason why the Church requires that certain classes of the faithful particularly given to the Lord in the search for perfection, and thus not ordinarily having any grave sins to make confession obligatory, should nonetheless approach the sacrament of penance once a week. This is true of religious (Can. 595, 1:3) and of seminarians (Can. 1367, 2). The Church also insists on frequent confession for all clerics, without specifying exactly how often (Can. 125).

Article Five
THE ACTS OF THE PENITENT

The Council of Trent teaches that three acts are required of the penitent:

> If anyone denies that for the complete and perfect remission of sins there are three acts required of the penitent, which are, as it were, the matter of the sacrament of penance, namely: contrition, confession and satisfaction, which are called the three "parts" of penance . . ., let him be anathema (*Denz.* 914).

The discipline of the early Church emphasized satisfaction above all, requiring that it be carried out before reconciliation. Later evolution towards a greater and greater interiority of penance developed the role of the avowal or confession as an important part of expiation for sin. But contrition, which is essentially interior though expressed exteriorly, is always the primordial element. While certain circumstances can dispense from the other acts, no forgiveness of sins is possible without contrition.

I. CONTRITION

Contrition is also the first act in the process of repentance and pervades all the others, engaging the human personality and determining the activity of the sinner on his way to forgiveness. It is the central act of the virtue of penance. The Council of Trent describes it as follows:

> Contrition, which holds the first place among the acts of the penitent, is sorrow of soul and detestation of the sin committed, together with the determination to sin no more in the future. This movement of contrition has always been necessary to obtain forgiveness of sins; it is this precisely that renders the baptized sinner ready to receive the remission of his sins, so long as it is accompanied by confidence in the divine mercy and the determination to carry out everything required for the good reception of this sacrament.
>
> The Council declares that contrition includes not only breaking with sin, determining to lead a new life and beginning to do so, but also a hatred of the past, in accordance with these words: "Do away with all the sins you have committed against me, and make yourselves a new heart and a new spirit" (Ez. 18:31). If we consider the cries of the saints: "Against you, you alone, have I sinned, I have done what was evil in your sight" (Ps. 50:6) . . . and similar passages, we can easily understand that they spring from a strong hatred of a past life and a profound detestation of sins (*Denz.* 897; cf. *Summa* III, 85, 5).

1. *The richness and dynamism of contrition.* We are not concerned here directly with contrition for venial sins, which do not change the basic situation of a man with regard to God; it is only in an analogous way that we can apply to them what is said about contrition for mortal sins. Justification is what contrition both prepares for and consents to. The biblical perspectives presented above (Art. 1) are its best nourishment.

Contrition is sorrow of soul. The saints have often asked the Lord for "the gift of tears." But we must not look for contrition on the level of the emotions, nor on the obscure level of the complexes of anxiety and guilt studied by depth psychology. It is determined at the most profound depth of the self and with complete freedom. Sin has hardened the heart of man, according to the classic biblical image, because sin is pride, the destruction of love. Contrition comes to "break," to "crush" this hardness: the sinner yields, humiliates himself, finally opens himself out and suffers. This suffering is not concerned with abstractions, with sin as such, but with the sin in *my* life, with *my* sinful state. Thus it already requires the interior acknowledgement: *I* have sinned.

This sorrow of soul is directed to the past and to the future. The state of sinfulness is perceived as present. But, in this present, contrition takes hold of the past, that is, of the sin committed. Contrition thus truly bears on this past so as to detest it; this is a point based on biblical truth, on which the Council of Trent had to insist against the Protestants. But from this past which is to be destroyed, contrition orients the Christian toward the future—not only must he change his way of living, he must also make reparation. Contrition, therefore, contains satisfaction in embryo and also the firm intention not to sin again. Without this firm intention, contrition would not be real. It involves the virtue of hope, coexisting with the experience of our wretchedness and weakness.

Contrition does not stop at man, but seeks God. Judas experienced humiliation and sorrow over his crime but, for all that, did not possess contrition. This requires a movement of faith, discovering and welcoming God's justice and mercy and reaching the mystery of Christ: "I will go to my Father." Here the supernatural character of contrition is manifested on the level of the conscience. The sinner goes to God because in reality God has come to meet him with His grace: "The first principle is the operation of God converting hearts" (*Summa* III, 85, 5).

From fear contrition raises itself to love. While our psychological acts are often so instantaneous as to defy analysis, it is normal for the sinner to regret his sin initially out of egoistic fear before going on to seek God. The prodigal son was first aware of the destitution and discomfort of his situation, and then went to find his father (Luke 15:16). So the sinner may first be moved by fear of the divine punishments; this movement already proceeds from God, since the eschatological proclamation throughout the Bible is essentially a call to repentance. But, from the fear of punishment the sinner should rise to regret for sin itself, by faith in God's justice.[25] And from this regret he should advance to the filial fear which leads him to offer satisfaction to God, not out of any form of constraint, but freely, with his whole heart.

Contrition is not only interior, but must also be "ecclesial" and sacramental. Contrition exists in the "heart," in the biblical sense of the nexus of human liberty; it does not, as such, come within the range of consciousness. It is primarily an interior disposition with regard to God. Nevertheless, it cannot be authentic without tending toward reconciliation with the Church and toward the sacrament in which it is manifested and perfected. Contrition must, then, be expressed in the penitential acts of confession and satisfaction, and also include the desire for absolution since it seeks God's forgiveness. Since it is sacramental in its goal, absolution, it is rendered sacramental from the outset.

Thus contrition appears as a movement, a progress. The divine pedagogy has laid out the stages of this journey; pastoral care should aid this progress. When contrition is arrested in its development, it becomes sterile and risks encouraging psychological regression.

2. Requirements of contrition.   We usually speak of the qualities or properties of true contrition as interior, supernatural, universal, and sovereign. The first two aspects have already been analyzed.

Contrition must be universal in that the sinner regrets all the mortal sins he has committed, without exception. Since contrition is concerned primarily with the situation of man before God, it is obvious that there can be no true repentance that does not embrace all the sins that destroy friendship with God, as there can be no pardon for some sins and not for others (*Summa* III, 86, 3).

It must be sovereign in the sense that sin is the greatest of evils, and nothing must be more greatly regretted. Contrition places man before his final goal and engages his personality at the very root of his freedom. But St. Thomas (*Summa*, Suppl., 3, 1) and all spiritual writers warn us against the confusion, which can have very serious psychological and moral effects, of looking for some manifestation of the sovereign character of contrition on the level of feelings and sensibility.

3. Perfect and imperfect contrition.   Following the theologians of the Middle Ages, but without completely accepting their viewpoint, the Council of Trent distinguishes two degrees in contrition:

> It happens sometimes that contrition may be perfect through charity and reconcile man to God before the actual reception of the sacrament; nevertheless the reconciliation cannot be attributed to such

[25] This is the process presupposed by St. Ignatius in his *Spiritual Exercises,* First Week, Ex. 1-3.

contrition itself without the desire for the sacrament that it contains.

As to *imperfect contrition,* also called attrition, it is generally born from the consideration of the ugliness of sin, or the fear of hell and punishments. If it rejects the will to sin and if it includes the hope of pardon, far from rendering man a hypocrite or a greater sinner, it is a gift of God and an impulse of the Holy Spirit. He certainly does not yet dwell in the soul but He moves it so that the penitent sets himself on the road toward justification. It cannot, true enough, of itself lead the sinner to the state of grace, but it disposes him to obtain the grace of God in the sacrament of penance. It is this fear which so beneficially overwhelmed the Ninevites who, on hearing the terrible prophecy of Jonas, became penitent and obtained the mercy of God (*Denz.* 898).

There are not, therefore, as has sometimes been said, two different ways leading to the remission of sins: perfect contrition on the one hand and the sacrament on the other. Perfect contrition cannot be valid without desire for the sacrament (explicit or implicit; here is the whole mystery of the salvation of those who are not in the Church of Christ). Such contrition is part of the sacrament toward which it is oriented, for the sacrament is composed, as we have seen, of a twofold element, the word of the Church that absolves and the acts of the penitent.

But the grace of forgiveness which justifies can precede the absolution, which is part of the sign of this grace. Then the sinner receives, together with justification, complete and perfect contrition, which is charity, union with God. The normal process, however, consists in the sinner's preparing himself for absolution by a contrition which is imperfect since he does not as yet possess sanctifying grace. Absolution comes to make perfect this contrition. In giving the divine forgiveness and grace, it gives charity.

Perfect and imperfect contrition are, therefore, to be defined primarily and above all in relation to the supernatural principle from which they proceed. Contrition which disposes man for God's forgiveness is imperfect; perfect contrition is under the influence of supernatural charity and sanctifying grace; it is the human participation in the act of justification. But on this level the nature of the contrition is not experienced psychologically, since both grace and the basic disposition of the will are outside the range of such experience.

However, a psychological effect is normally produced which can be experienced; hence the classic method of classifying contrition according to its motives. Perfect contrition, proceeding from the "charity poured out in our hearts by the Holy Spirit" (Rom. 5:5) and from the sight of Christ on the Cross, who "loved us and delivered Himself for us," detests sin as an offense against God whom we love for Himself and above all things. Imperfect contrition, while still in the light of faith, does not yet reach the level of charity; it is inspired by the realization of the ugliness of sin or the fear of hell and punishment.

Imperfect contrition is still legitimate and true contrition and an authentic road toward forgiveness. Certainly it is not a goal, but it is a normal stage on the way to the goal; the Bible presents us with a valid example of it in the repentance of the Ninevites. On the other hand, perfect contrition is possible. The Church proposes it to all Christian sinners, especially those in danger of death who cannot receive the sacrament. And she urges all who have lost the life of the spirit by mortal sin not to wait until they can go to confession, but to strive by perfect contrition to regain this life immediately.

II. CONFESSION

Confession is the acknowledgment that the sinner makes of his faults in order to receive absolution for them from a priest having the required jurisdiction. The necessity for such confession flows from the very nature of the sacrament of penance, since its sign is a judgment.

> From the fact of the institution of the sacrament of penance, the Church has always concluded that the Lord also prescribed the confession of all sins, and that confession is necessary by divine law for all those who have sinned after baptism. For our Lord Jesus Christ, before ascending to heaven, left priests to be His vicars, as rulers and judges to whom all the mortal sins of the faithful should be submitted, so that they might pronounce, in virtue of the power of the keys, a sentence of remission or of retention of sins. Now it is evident that priests cannot render this judgment without knowing the case, nor observe equity in the penalties to be inflicted if the avowal remains in general terms instead of enumerating the sins one by one (*Denz.* 899).

1. Characteristics of sacramental confession. While the whole attitude of the Christian approaching the tribunal of penance is a public acknowledgment of his condition as a sinner, the confession remains secret. In fact, it was essentially secret even when penance was publicly administered. In any case, this aspect became clarified as confession took on more and more importance among the acts of the penitent and as the priest's role of physician was emphasized as well as his role of judge. Not only is confession secret, but it binds the priest who hears it by the sacramental seal. This is even stricter than the obligations of professional secrecy, since it admits no exceptions of any kind for any reason (Can. 889-890).

But confession is not a confidence made to a spiritual physician in view of receiving a psychological cure and counsel. We should, certainly, emphasize the benefits even from the psychological point of view when confession is rightly practiced. But this is not its primary purpose; it is sacramental and ecclesial. It is an avowal made to the Lord and to the Church—the priest to whom we confess our sins is the minister of Christ and the Church. We confess in order to be reconciled with the Church and so to receive the divine forgiveness.

Confession is part of the sacramental sign, so that there can be no sacrament unless there is some avowal of sin, at least in a rudimentary fashion, on the part of the penitent. Like the whole sacrament of which it is a part, confession has an eschatological significance. The sinner accuses himself, anticipating the final manifestation of hearts which the Lord will make at His return in glory (Matthew 12:36; 25:31-46; 1 Cor. 4:5).

Confession expresses the contrition from which it originates. Consequently, it is a humble action. The avowal is animated by detestation of sin; it signifies conversion. It has nothing in common with those literary confessions in which someone seeks himself by looking back on his past, nor with the confidences which we pour out to a friend in a moment of emotional expansion.

Confession is by its nature sorrowful, like the contrition from which it proceeds, since it rejects and detests the past which it acknowledges. But sorrowful does not mean anguished. Luther's mistake was to project onto confession the torments of his own conscience. (The difficulties experienced by scrupulous persons require treatment by psychotherapy.) True confession is essentially trustful; the sinner acknowledges his sin to the Lord who forgives. His activity demands faith in the mercy of God revealed to us in Scripture.

Confession involves greater and greater demands as the Christian conscience develops, and therefore can become the chief work of penitential expiation "through the overcoming of shame, the expression of self-condemnation, the externalizing of the will to renewal."[26]

2. The progress of the Christian conscience and the development of the discipline of confession. In the present discipline of the Western Church, the penitent should normally state all the mortal sins committed after baptism which have not yet been submitted to the power of the keys and forgiven, so as to present them to the judgment of the Church. (Sins committed before baptism are excluded from sacramental confession; baptism itself remits them, so they are not matter for the sacrament of penance.) This means that mortal sins which are already forgiven but have not yet been submitted to the power of the keys should be confessed (for example, a sin forgotten in the preceding confession which one remembers later on). The same is true of sins already confessed

[26] P. Anciaux, *op. cit.*

which have not yet been forgiven, either because absolution was not given or because the bad dispositions of the subject rendered the sacrament ineffective.

In confessing his mortal sins, the penitent is required to provide all the elements necessary to enable the confessor to make a right judgment regarding them: their number, their exact nature, and circumstances which change their species (Can. 901; *Denz.* 899, 917).

Mortal sins committed after baptism which have already been remitted by the power of the keys and also venial sins committed after baptism are "free" but sufficient matter for confession (Can. 902). Being optional, the confession of venial sins need not be "integral." Although mortal sins already confessed and forgiven can be validly submitted once more for absolution as an act of the virtue of penance, recalling them may be psychologically inadvisable in some cases; the Christian should carefully observe the advice of the priest on this subject.

The precision in confessing sins now required by the Western Church is in apparent contrast to the summary character of confession as practiced today in certain of the Eastern Churches and in the Church of the high Middle Ages. But there are circumstances in the Western Church today when confession is reduced to a simpler form, e.g., when a dying person cannot express himself because of his condition, when soldiers on the battlefield receive general absolution, etc. In other words, the requirement of confession is proportioned to the needs of each human group and of each era, and takes account of impossibilities. But what is always necessary is the fundamental will to make a complete confession.

In the same way, the requirements of confession are to be adapted to the psychological possibilities of each individual. They will consequently be quite different in the case of a child and an adult, and will vary according to differences in memory, power of introspection, keenness of moral judgment. Moreover, emotional difficulties can considerably impede a person's power to state his sins correctly. A healthy pedagogy of penance will carefully take all these factors into account as the Church herself has always done.

The confession required by the Church presupposes an examination of conscience; its forms and even the awareness of the gravity of sins have varied with the progress of the Christian life. St. Paul's enumeration of the sins that exclude from the Kingdom of God (1 Cor. 6:9; Gal. 5:19-21; Eph. 5:5; Col. 3:5-6; see also Apoc. 21:8 and 22:15) or the list provided by Tertullian (*De Pudicitia,* 7:15) have undergone many developments. Our own age is now beginning to stress inquiry into sins of omission and sins against social justice.[27]

---

[27] See L. Lebret and T. Sauvet, "Examination of Conscience for Catholics," *Cross Currents,* 7 (1957), pp. 289-293.

III. SATISFACTION

Formerly, as we have seen, the state of a penitent, with its asceticism, its deprivations, its public humiliations, was imposed upon sinners for a varying period of time. It was only after they had undergone this ordeal that they were reconciled. Today the priest gives absolution at once to the Christian whose confession he has heard and whose dispositions he judges to be good. But he enjoins on him what is called a "penance", that is, a work of satisfaction, which is always a very easy one in comparison with the hashness of the early penitential discipline.

This development is justified, as we have also seen, by the fact that the confessing of sins has taken on more importance, even seeming to be the chief act of expiation and requiring an increasingly refined interiority of penance. But whatever the external form of satisfaction, its nature has not changed. Its milder forms perhaps indicate more clearly the dynamism which ought to move the penitent toward the permanent state of the virtue of penance.

1. The true nature of satisfaction. Like confession, satisfaction is sacramental, forming part of those acts of the penitent which constitute, together with the priest's absolution, the sacramental sign. It is therefore imposed by the Church, acting through her minister. It forms part of the sentence. The penitent accepts it; if he were unwilling to fulfill it, the sacrament would not be valid.

The object of satisfaction is twofold. It has a medicinal aspect, strengthening both the penitent's weak love of God and the dispositions which he should have expressed in receiving the sacrament, urging him to watchfulness in the future and to the development of virtues opposed to the sins he has committed. At least this is what it should produce according to the teaching of the Council of Trent (*Denz.* 904, 905), if the minister knows how to adapt the satisfaction he imposes to the needs of each penitent, and if the Christian does not content himself with a routine performance of his penance but truly enters into the spirit of the work imposed on him.

However, this medicinal aspect is the less essential. Satisfaction has the value of a punishment for sin, since it carries out the sentence that has condemned the sin. It is, therefore, expiation.

This last aspect was denied by the Protestants who feared a misunderstanding of the gratuity of God's gift and a diminishing of the value of the redemption. Christ has indeed made complete and adequate satisfaction to His Father's justice for all the sins of the world. We should, therefore, as the Council of Trent suggests (*ibid.*), incorporate sacramental satisfaction into our total response to God's grace. It is only in Jesus and through our union with Him that we can carry out a valid work of satisfaction; of itself the satisfaction has no value. It is the Lord's generosity which imposes it on us through the sentence of the priest. It makes us like to Christ "doing penance" for the sins of the world, crucifies us with Him, making us "carry out in our own body what is wanting to the passion of Christ "(Col. 1:24). It belongs to the order of love, not the order of justice.

2. From satisfaction to the virtue of penance. The works of satisfaction imposed by the priest can be of *three kinds*: (1) prayer and acts of the virtue of religion (in the Middle Ages, pilgrimages were the great work of satisfaction), (2) the exercise of fraternal charity, on the material level of almsgiving and doing good as well as on the spiritual level; (3) bodily deprivations (fasting and various mortifications). Only the works imposed by the minister are sacramental.

We may be surprised nowadays that penances are so light, reduced to a token. But the fact is that expiation has already begun by the confession itself and by the effort to examine one's conscience and the contrition it presupposes. But expiation should also develop beyond the work imposed, by the penitential significance which the whole life of the Christian should assume and by his discovery of the intimate bonds uniting him with the Church on earth and in heaven. After having pronounced the absolution, the priest adds the following prayer:

> May the passion of our Lord Jesus Christ, the merits of the blessed Virgin Mary and of all the saints, all the good you have done and whatever you have suffered, gain for you the remission of sins, an increase of grace and the reward of life everlasting. Amen.[28]

On the one hand, this sacrament gives us or increases in us the virtue of penance, which the sacrament consecrates and of which it is the chief expression. The insignificance of the work imposed by the confessor brings out more clearly, by way of contrast, the importance of this more general disposition, including progressive liberation from sin, union with Christ suffering by the acceptance of trials (*Denz.* 906), deeper rooting in charity. This work of purification and expiation will be completed in a passive, "mystical" way in purgatory if it is not fully carried out on earth.

On the other hand, faith in the Church and union with her give access to the riches of the Mystical Body. The Church is the dispenser of the merits of Christ and of the saints. By means of this community of grace she alleviates the severity of penitential satisfaction, in particular by offering indulgences to the faithful.

3. Indulgences.[29] Indulgences are properly studied as an extension of the sacrament of penance, even though they are not sacramental. They are works of satisfaction, but they are proposed to all the faithful in gen-

---

[28] See the excellent commentary on this prayer in C. Marmion, *Christ, the Life of the Soul*, ch. 4, 6.

[29] See P. Palmer, *Sacraments and Forgiveness*, pp. 321-368; 398-401.

eral, outside the sacrament, by the authority of the Church. The very way in which they are presented suggests that they are truly a form of satisfaction meant to supplement or complete the satisfaction imposed in the sacrament. They are always regarded as shortening the duration of public penance by some definite period of time (one year, seven "quarantines" or periods of forty days like that of Lent, etc.).

For the faithful today as for those of the Middle Ages, indulgences offer special opportunities for discovering the mystery of the Church and for reviving the virtues of penance and charity, provided that they are viewed as the Church herself presents them, far removed from egoistic formalism or a kind of magic.[30] When they are applied to the dead, they are no more than a prayer, for the Church has no power over those who have died.

Article Five
PENANCE: SACRAMENT OF SPIRITUAL PROGRESS

In the early Church the sacrament of penance seemed reserved as an exceptional remedy for dreadful crimes. But the experience of the saints and the faithful, sanctioned by the teaching of the Church, has made it one of the sacraments of ordinary life, designed by its proper grace to aid spiritual progress, and consequently capable of being received frequently. The dispositions and the attitude of penance are not, in the view of Christian revelation, something accidental, but a virtue necessary to all, since we all are sinners. This virtue, which leads us to discover by contrast the holiness of God, finds in this sacrament its consecration, its focus, and its fruitfulness in grace.

I. PERFECTING THE RECEPTION OF GOD'S GIFT

The Christian can draw greater benefit from receiving the sacrament of penance by the fidelity with which he responds to the divine advances.

The blessing of the divine forgiveness calls for thanksgiving; following the example of the psalmist and of St. Paul, we ought to sing the mercy

---

[30] "It is when this practice is isolated from the whole context of Christian penance in its ecclesial dimensions and its sacramental value, that it becomes an aberration and even leads to most regrettable abuses. Without faith in Christ and the Church, without the ardor of devotion and charity, without a sincere effort toward conversion and mortification, the practice of indulgences is nothing more than a sterile caricature and a senseless kind of arithmetic" (P. Anciaux, *op. cit.*, pp. 157-158).

of God. The psychological effort required to prepare for confession and acknowledgement of our faults should not make us forget this duty to give thanks and praise, which ends in the joy of love: he to whom many sins have been forgiven will show great love (Luke 7:47).

In the tribunal of penance the priest is not only a judge but also a shepherd and a physician. As a shepherd, he gives instruction in the sacrament, offers words of faith and strives to educate consciences. As a physician, he tries to heal wounds, to indicate appropriate remedies, to aid the wavering will, to prevent causes of relapse. Docility to the priest's action does not consist in the penitent's listening passively, even if attentively, but in planning with the priest the effective use of the means of progress he proposes.

The satisfaction imposed, as we have seen, is primarily a sign of a sincere disposition to make reparation. The penitent should therefore try to carry it out, not only as to its letter, but also its spirit. For example, he might meditate on the prayer given him for a penance and use it as an ejaculation.

II. THE CONFESSION OF VENIAL SINS

It is not necessary, as said above, to submit venial sins to the power of the keys, since they do not make us lose the life of the spirit and they are not psychologically incompatible with a basic disposition of love of God. Confessing them is consequently not an obligation but a free undertaking; they are called "free matter" for absolution, while mortal sins not yet confessed are called "necessary matter." In the same way, serious sins already confessed and forgiven constitute "free matter" for absolution; we may accuse ourselves of them again, at least if this is done in a healthy way, both psychologically and spiritually.

The penitent with only venial sins (or past sins already forgiven) may legitimately present himelf to the priest for absolution, and this practice should be encouraged.

> If anyone say that it is not allowed to confess venial sins, let him be anathema (Denz. 917).

For, although venial and mortal sin are radically different in their nature, both on the level of the supernatural organism and of the basic disposition of the soul, both are an offense against God, and therefore matter for penance. In spite of their basic difference, they can be in such psychological continuity that there is danger of passing almost imperceptibly from venial to mortal sin as the soul becomes paralyzed by its attachment to deliberate or habitual sins. Furthermore, when venial sins are not merely daily faults of weakness, which the saints themselves acknowledged, but are lucidly consented to or entertained, they cause great damage both from the spiritual point of view, rendering any search for perfection impossible, and from the psychological, for they are at the origin of many regressions and difficulties.

However, the confession of venial sins is made not only to obtain forgiveness for these faults; such confession is also an act of humility and a means of improving. We should accuse ourselves especially of humiliating venial sins and those which it is important for us to correct. Frequent confession, practiced by the saints and recommended by the Church, is important for genuine spiritual progress.

III. FREQUENT CONFESSION

1. *From penance to compunction of heart.* The sacrament of penance consecrates a virtue, a disposition of soul which should be permanent, by making it sacramental. As St. Thomas says:

> There are two kinds of penance: exterior and interior. The interior is that which makes us weep for the sin we have committed, and this should continue until the end of life. For man should always regret having sinned. . . . But regret causes sorrow in him who is capable of sorrow, and this is the case with man in this life (*Summa* III, 84, 8).

This disposition of soul which causes it to remain in a state of habitual contrition is called "compunction" by spiritual writers. St. Benedict prescribed that the monk should each day confess his past sins to God in prayer, with tears and sighs, including this among his efforts to correct himself of evil.[31] Frequent confession inserts this disposition into the economy of salvation.

2. *The sacrament of the struggle against Satan and sin.* According to the apt remark of L. Rétif, the sacrament of penance continues after baptism the work begun before baptism by the exorcisms and realized essentially in baptism itself.[32] A battle in which our souls are at stake is in progress between Christ and Satan. This struggle will endure as long as life endures. What was done at baptism remains to be fulfilled; anyone who takes the Christian life seriously continually discovers new domains of his thinking and acting which have not yet been brought under the

---

[31] *Rule of St. Benedict,* ch. 4. On compunction, see C. Marmion, *Christ, the Ideal of the Monk,* ch. 8.

[32] "In connection with the renouncement of evil, stated several times in the course of the baptismal rites, it is through a serious initiation into the sacrament of penance that the candidate becomes aware of it, at the same time as he becomes conscious of his condition as a sinner. He renews his desire to keep struggling at each sacramental confession" (*La Maison Dieu,* 28, 1951, p. 98).

dominion of the Holy Spirit. Every fervent Christian examines his conscience, makes resolutions of conversion, and experiences periodic defeats.

Sacramental confession continually renews us with the strength of Christ to carry on this struggle throughout our lives. The inclusion of the acts of the penitent in the sacramental sign enables us to understand the difference between the combat of the Christian and the moral effort of the pagan sage, between the Christian discovery of conversion always in process and an examination of conscience turned back upon itself.

3. The sacrament of penance and the pattern of daily life. As to how often we should approach the sacrament of penance, the prescriptions of the Church themselves suggest patterns of varied frequency: "at least once a year" for everyone; "once a week" for religious and seminarians. Between these two limits, each Christian must determine for himself the pattern which will be most appropriate to his state of fervor, his needs and his opportunities; this pattern will be a safeguard against negligence and forgetfulness.

But other patterns are superimposed on this regular one. The great stages of life give occasion for "solemn" Communions and also for confessions to be prepared for in a special way: marriage, religious profession or ordination, illness, the moment of death. And the same is true of great trials, crises, important decisions. Finally, the events of the spiritual life, and those connected with our families, our professional and civic life, bring with them new experiences of our responsibilities and our failings, of our wretchedness and our duties, and these may deeply modify our examination of conscience and renew our contrition. Through all this the sacrament of penance is ceaselessly rediscovered as a new well-spring; it accompanies and thus purifies the changes, the undertakings, the activities in which our human life is continually engaged.

In this way we may avoid defects in the use of this sacrament: routine (adult penitents who have important responsibilities in the world confessing like children), scrupulosity (destroying the scale of moral values and exaggerating certain details to the detriment of the essential), emotional transference (the penitent does not see Christ's minister but stops short at the man who hears confession and gives absolution). All these defects are more or less clear forms of infantilism or of regression in religious psychology.

4. The sacrament of penance and the liturgical life. The sacrament of penance is presented in our times with practically no liturgical externals. It is administered as if in secret, and may be reduced to nothing more than the confession of sins and absolution. Hearing the confessions of men does not even require a sacred place. If the priest is in a church he ordinarily puts on the surplice and violet stole, but this is not obligatory. In spite of this simplicity, the sacrament is truly an act of worship and an act of the Christian community, "an act of faith and an act of praise on the part of the Church and of the sinner, a celebration of the mystery of Christ in view of the reconciliation of the sinner."[33]

Furthermore, the public and communal character of penance is frequently observable. For, while we can go to confession anywhere and at any time in conformity with our needs, spiritual desires, or convenience, the fact remains that on certain days the faithful gather together in the place of worship to receive the sacrament of penance. Although they approach the tribunal of penance individually, all present themselves as sinners, prepare for absolution, enter the confessional and go out, prolong their prayer after confession, carry out their "penance" or satisfaction. Might it not be possible to have, besides the irreplaceable and incommunicable personal examination of conscience, silent and secret by its nature, some common expression of repentance on the part of all by means of the reading and singing of some appropriate biblical texts?

Moreover, one liturgical season, Lent, is more particularly a season of penance, because penance is a second baptism and a new participation in the paschal mystery. (The bond between Lent and the sacrament of penance is stressed by the Council of Trent—*Denz.* 901, 918.) Lent is inaugurated by an act of entry into the penitential state, the imposition of the ashes. The disappearance of the catechumenate for adults in sixth-century Rome helped to develop this penitential character of Lent, overshadowing its baptismal aspect. For many of the faithful, the confession at the end of Lent is still the only one in the year. But for those who have heard the call of the Church to frequent confession, Lent provides the opportunity to prepare liturgically for a more solemn confession, just as the Easter Communion is more solemn than daily Communions.

Certain sacramentals recall and extend in the liturgy the expression of the dispositions of repentance and the mediation of the Church who absolves. In addition to the great sacramental of the season of Lent with its ceremony of the ashes there is the general confession of sins (the *Confiteor*) with its prayers of absolution (*Misereatur, Indulgentiam*). This forms part of the preparation of the priest and his ministers for Mass and may also form part of the preparation of the faithful. It is included also in the evening prayer of Compline.

We should also note here the Apostolic Blessing, given, under certain circumstances, in the name of the Pope. This is a truly penitential rite,

[33] P. Anciaux, *op. cit.*

which requires a preliminary sacramental confession and presupposes a deepening of contrition.[34] Finally, certain particularly expressive psalms are grouped together in liturgical books and prayerbooks under the heading of Penitential Psalms.

[34] The bishop of a diocese gives this blessing after the pontifical Mass on great feasts; every priest may give it at the moment of death; missioners, etc., may be entitled to give it after missions and retreats.

Chapter 6

THE ANOINTING OF THE SICK

Preliminary Remarks

This sacrament is generally called extreme unction, the "last anointing," a term adopted by the theology of the Middle Ages and accepted by the Council of Trent in its enumeration of the seven sacraments (*Denz.* 844) and in the decree of the fourteenth session (*Denz.* 907-910). This anointing is called "extreme" or "last," says the Catechism of the Council of Trent (II, 6, 3), "because it is administered last, after the other anointings entrusted by Christ to His Church," anointings which are the sign, efficacious or not, of the sacramental characters.[1] This may well be how the expression came to be adopted. Yet in the Middle Ages it had been explained differently, many authors understanding it to mean "the anointing of those about to die" (Peter Lombard, St. Thomas). Because of this ambiguity it is desirable to return, following Cardinal Mercier, to the original name of "anointing of the sick," a choice which obviously implies a certain theological, pastoral and pedagogical orientation.

In its doctrinal presentation the Council of Trent connected the anointing of the sick with penance, calling it the culmination of penance (cf. *Denz.* 907). For the anointing has a penitential effect, distinct from that of absolution but completing and sometimes substituting for it.

However, it is a sacrament which can be given only to the sick; and the whole tradition of the Church affirms that it has a healing effect on the body. This anointing is unique, for all the others are given to the body in order to produce a spiritual effect.[2] But the spiritual and bodily effects are not independent of each other; the bond between them, as stated by the rites and by the teaching of the magisterium, following the Epistle of St. James, expresses the significance which the Bible gives to sickness in the economy of salvation.

Article One

SICKNESS IN THE ECONOMY OF SALVATION

The Old and the New Testament give an important place to sickness and its healing, teaching us to see the relationship of both to the economy of salvation. Sickness is connected with sin and the devil; when God heals

---

[1] The anointing of baptism is not essential to the sacrament; that of ordination certainly is no longer essential; that of confirmation alone forms part of the sacramental sign.

[2] Although there is a bodily effect of the Eucharist, this is not so closely connected with the sign.

bodies, it is to care for souls as well; healing the sick, together with freeing those possessed by demons, is one of the signs of the reign of the Messiah.[3]

I. THE CONNECTION BETWEEN SICKNESS AND SIN

It is by sin that sickness came into the world, with the pain of drudgery, the sufferings of childbirth, and death (Gen. 3:15-19). Although sickness is not expressly mentioned in the curse of Adam and Eve, theological tradition has always rightly seen it as included.

Sickness is even more closely connected with sin than the other effects of the Fall. Christ, who took upon Himself for our sakes all the consequences of sin, "who bore our sufferings and was weighed down with our sorrows" (Is. 53:4), never experienced sickness. "This defect (sickness)," writes St. Thomas, "is among those that are not common to all. Sometimes it is a man's fault, as through an ill-regulated diet; or it may result from some malformation. Now, neither of these causes applies to Christ, for His flesh was conceived of the Holy Spirit, whose wisdom and power are infinite . . . moreover, Christ Himself never introduced any disorder into the conduct of His life" (*Summa* III, 14, 4).

Sickness, then, may sometimes be the effect of personal sin. Human wisdom can prove this in many cases; the inspired sages merely echo common experience when they proclaim the chastisement of debauchery (Sir. 6:2-4) or of intemperance (Sir. 31:19-22). Sickness can also be the effect of a special punitive intervention by Yahweh, e.g., Saul seized by an "evil spirit" (1 Sam. 16:14), Ozias stricken by leprosy (4 Kings 15:5). As a consequence, oversimplified common opinion concluded that every sick person must be paying the penalty of his sins. This was the reasoning of Job's friends and the spontaneous observation made by the disciples of Jesus: "Master, who has sinned, this man or his parents, that he was born blind?" (John 9:2).

This false generalization was unjust with regard to Job, and Christ rejected it in the case of the man born blind: "Neither he nor his parents have sinned; but in him the works of God were to be made manifest" (John 9:3). The just man also can be stricken with sickness. This fact, though, makes sickness no less the image of sin, for sin is the true sickness, a leprosy, a malignant fever, a paralysis.

Finally, sickness gives the evil spirit a special opportunity to get at the soul through the body, tempting us through weakness and pain to despair or unbelief.[4]

---

[3] Here we depend on J. Leclercq: "Du sens chrétien de la maladie," *Vie spirituelle*, 53 (1937), pp. 136ff., and H. Duesberg, *Le psautier des malades*, Maredsous (1953), pp. 1-80.

[4] See *The Liturgy and the Word of God*, pp. 151-153.

II. THE HEALING OF THE BODY, A SIGN OF GRACE

1. *Healing in the Old Testament.* In the cures of the Old Testament St. Thomas sees the sacrament of anointing prefigured from afar (*Summa,* Suppl., 29, 1 ad 2). Charismatic cures, astonishing works of God, were performed through His prophets, from Moses to Isaias. But a place is given to medicine as well as to prayer (Sir. 38:9-15). Moreover, the healing of bodies becomes a sign that Yahweh heals souls: "It is I, Yahweh, who give you health" (Exod. 15:26; cf. Ps. 102:3, Deut. 32:39).

2. *The healing of the sick, a sign of the coming of the Messiah.* While Jesus was going through the towns and villages of Galilee to proclaim the Good News, He cured the sick and cast out demons. The evangelists consider this twofold miraculous ministry a single work connected with the Good News in an essential, not merely in an accidental or temporary way, as its sign.

> He went about through the whole of Galilee, teaching in the synagogues, proclaiming the Good News of the Kingdom and healing every sickness and every disease among the people. His fame spread throughout all Syria, and there were brought to him all the unfortunates stricken with illness and various torments, those possessed by demons, lunatics, paralytics, and he cured them (Matthew 4:23-24; cf. Luke 6:17-18; Mark 3:7-11).

In fact the Gospels contain something like a litany, repeated over and over again, of the human miseries that Christ relieved (Matthew 9:35; 15:29-31; 12:15; 14:34-36; 21:14; Mark 6:53-56) .

Jesus Himself called attention to the healing of the sick and freeing the possessed, not only because they were miracles which accredited His mission but also because they carried our Isaias' description of the messianic era (26:19; 29:18; 35:5-6; 61:1) .

> Go say to John what you have seen and heard: the blind see, the lame walk, the lepers are cured, the deaf hear, the dead arise, and the Good News is announced to the poor; and blessed are those for whom I shall not be a stumbling-block (Matthew 11:4-6; cf. Luke 7:21-23).

> Go, say to that fox (Herod): Behold I drive out demons and perform cures today and tomorrow, and on the third day I shall be consummated . . . (Luke 13:32).

3. *With the healing of the body Christ gives grace to the soul.* In the context of the New Testament, healing the sick and casting out demons are two forms of the same victory over sin. Christ granted health of soul to the sick along with health of body. The paralytic looking for deliverance from his disease was first given forgiveness of his sins (Luke 5:18-20). The sick man healed at the pool of Bethesda after thirty-eight years of immobility was exhorted to amend his life: "See, you are healed; henceforth sin no more, or still worse shall befall you" (John 5:14). To the man born blind Jesus offered both the light of day and the even brighter light of faith (John 9:35-37). In most cases, faith was demanded as a preliminary, and those who were miraculously cured were told to give glory to God. Christ is a healer indeed, but it is sinners above all whom He wishes to cure by calling them to repentance (Luke 5:31-32; Matthew 9:12-13; Mark 2:17).

4. Cures accomplished with sacred signs. At times Christ cured simply by a word, by the expression of His will: "I will it; be healed," "Your servant is cured." At other times, health was granted as if unknown to the Master, through merely touching the hem of His garment (Mark 3:10; 6:56; Luke 8:44-46). But more frequently He made gestures over the sick person: He touched him (Mark 1:41; Matthew 9:29); He took hold of him (Luke 14:4); He put His fingers in the ears of the deaf-mute and touched his tongue with His saliva (Mark 7:33); He made mud to anoint the eyes of the man born blind (John 9:6), above all, He put His hands upon those whom He healed (Mark 8:23-26; Luke 13:13).

5. The power of healing communicated to the apostles. This same gesture of the laying on of hands is to be performed by the apostles to heal the sick. In the thought of St. Mark, it is always a miraculous power, forming part of the messianic proclamation.

These are the wonders which will accompany those who believe: in my name they shall cast out devils, they shall speak in tongues. They shall lay their hands upon the sick and these shall be cured (Mark 16:17-18).

The same mission and the same charism had been given them when they were first sent out, in a provisional way and as an apprenticeship, during the public life of Jesus. But at that time they healed the sick by means of another sign.

Having called the Twelve together, he gave them power and authority over all demons, with the power to heal diseases. And he sent them to proclaim the Kingdom of God and to heal. . . . They set out then, going from village to village, announcing the Good News and making cures everywhere (Luke 9:1-2, 6).

They went out preaching repentance; and they cast out many demons and anointed many sick persons with oil, and healed them (Mark 6:12-13).

The Epistle of St. James, as we shall see, also attributes the healing of the sick to the actions of laying on hands and anointing with oil. But instead of being a miraculous power intended to manifest the coming of the Kingdom and to accredit its messengers, it is now a true sacrament, the work of the divine Healer of bodies and souls administered by His priests without any of the astonishing characteristics of miracles.

III. THE NEW MEANING OF SICKNESS
AFTER THE REDEMPTION

Though Christ healed the sick and gave His Church power over disease, He did not abolish sickness. Neither has He abolished death, pain or drudgery. However, like death, sickness has been conquered; the messianic era has been established once and for all. In the heavenly Jerusalem these ills will have no place; here below they still exist. But Christ has overcome sin and Satan, the cause of sin. Sickness has therefore lost its quality of being a curse. It can become redemptive, enabling the Christian to become like Christ in His passion and at the same time to witness to the power of the risen Christ in him.[5] When Paul begged to be delivered from the sting that attacked his body, the Lord answered: "My strength will find scope in your weakness" (2 Cor. 12:9). In his own flesh Paul is to accomplish for the Church "what is lacking to the sufferings of Christ" (Col. 1:24). "We bear at all times in our body the sufferings of the death of Jesus, that the life of Jesus also may be manifested in our body" (2 Cor. 4:10).

Article Two
THE WITNESS OF ST. JAMES' EPISTLE

The Epistle of St. James ends in a series of exhortations, including the following:

> Is someone among you suffering? Let him pray. Is someone joyful? Let him sing a canticle. Is someone among you sick? Let him call in the presbyters of the Church and let them pray over him after anointing him with oil in the name of the Lord. The prayer of faith will save the sufferer, and the Lord will raise him up again. If he has committed sins, they will be forgiven him. Confess, then, your sins, to one another, and pray for one another that you may be healed (5:13-16).

This text and its apostolic directives are referred to explicitly by all the liturgies of the sacrament of the sick, by all the legislative documents concerned with regulating its administration, and by all the commentators formulating its theology (with the sole exception of Cardinal

[5] See F. Durrwell, *The Resurrection*, pp. 343ff.

Cajetan in the sixteenth century). This is a remarkable case of agreement on the interpretation of a text; the Council of Trent made it the subject of a dogmatic definition:

> By these words, as the Church has learned from the deposit of the apostolic tradition, (James) teaches the matter, form, proper minister and effect of this sacrament (*Denz.* 908).

> If anyone says that extreme unction is not a true sacrament, in the proper sense of the word, instituted by Christ our Lord, and promulgated by the holy apostle James, but a rite that originated with the Fathers or a human invention, let him be anathema (Can. 1; *Denz.* 926).

The "presbyters" mentioned in the various writings of the New Testament are members of the hierarchy of orders instituted by the apostles. Their task involves a visit to the sick person, extending Christ's work for the sick in a sign recalling the compassionate love of the Lord: "God has visited his people" (Luke 7:16).

In the course of this visit they "pray over" the sick person—a phrase which suggests the imposition of hands—and they anoint him with oil. That this is a sacramental rite is clear from the words and actions involved and its completely ordinary nature; this is no miraculous charism. This sacramental act is directed toward obtaining a twofold favor from God: healing and the remission of sins. And it is exactly these two favors which are asked in the different rituals of the Eastern and the Western liturgies for the anointing of the sick.

Article Three
THE LITURGY FOR ANOINTING OF THE SICK

The rite includes two actions: the blessing of the oil and its application, with prayer, to the sick person.

I. THE BLESSING OF THE OIL FOR THE SICK

The oil for the sick, *oleum infirmorum,* is at present blessed in a very different way in the Latin Church and in the Eastern Churches.

In the Eastern liturgies, at least in those that have not come under Latin influence, the oil is ordinarily blessed by the priest himself in the course of the visit to the sick person and at the moment when it is about to be used. This is the usage of the Byzantine, the Melchite and the Coptic rites.

But the Latin Church now reserves the blessing of the oil of the sick to the bishop, who blesses it during the Chrism Mass of Holy Thursday, though exceptions are possible (Can. 945). In the ancient Roman liturgy no special day was assigned. Whenever the faithful brought flasks of oil, these were given the blessing at the end of the Canon of the Mass, and this blessing was pronounced both by the bishop and by the priests.

The text used by the bishop today has remained the same in almost every detail as that used at the end of the sixth century. It is simply a development of the prayer given by Hippolytus in the *Apostolic Tradition* about the year 200:

> May Your holy blessing make of it a divine remedy for all who will receive its anointing, a remedy which protects soul and body and dispels all sadness, all sickness, all suffering of mind or body. . . .[6]

However, it seems that the prayers for health of soul were added only gradually. Moreover, "all who will receive its anointing" replaced the broader formula: "all who will make use of the oil in the form of an anointing, a beverage, or an application."

II. THE ANOINTING AND PRAYERS OVER THE SICK

In the Roman usage customary up to the ninth century, the faithful took flasks of blessed oil to their homes and applied it to the sick person in different ways or gave it to him to drink, just as they brought the Eucharist to their homes for Communion during the week.

Elsewhere, however, priests went personally to the home, carrying out completely the prescriptions of the Epistle of St. James. Today the application of the holy oil by someone not a priest would not be a sacrament.[7]

In the present Roman rite, the priest begins with the prayers for visiting the sick, which are not connected with the sacrament itself, being used in all liturgical ministrations to the sick. Following Jesus' instruction (Luke 10:5) he gives a greeting, saying as he enters: "Peace be to this house." He sprinkles holy water and adds: "Lord Jesus Christ, though I am a mere man, as I enter this house may there enter with me happiness without end, the blessings of God, peaceful joy, active charity, health that will last forever." If the sick person is to receive the sacrament of

---

[6] The complete text is given in *The Chrism Mass of Holy Thursday*. The present Chrism Mass gives a great deal of importance in its readings and hymns to the oil of the sick.

[7] We say "today." The development of liturgical knowledge does not allow us to dismiss the sacramentality of the use of oils in Roman antiquity, as theologians did at a time when historical knowledge was less adequate. We cannot resolve it on the authority of Can. 4 of the Council of Trent, to be discussed later, because the Council did not concern itself with this problem.

penance, the priest then hears his confession; in any case the *Confiteor* is said as a public reminder of penance.

The method of anointing the sick has varied in the course of the centuries. At present, the priest successively anoints the eyes, the ears, the nostrils, the mouth, the hands and the feet, accompanying the action with a prayer: "May the Lord forgive you, through these anointings and His mercy, all the sins committed by" (naming each of the senses).[8] In case of urgency, a single anointing may be made on the forehead. The anointing of the feet can be dispensed with for any good reason. In ancient times, however, the anointings were performed on all the principal parts of the body and "on the place where the sick person feels most pain."

Since 1925 the anointings have been preceded by an imposition of hands (obviously not essential to the sacrament) with a traditional prayer, used as early as the twelfth century:

> In the name of the Father and of the Son and of the Holy Spirit. May all power of the devil be annihilated in you through the laying-on of our hands, and through calling upon the protection of the glorious and holy Mother of God, the Virgin Mary, and of her illustrious spouse, St. Joseph, and of all the saints.

The ancient rituals surrounded the anointing of the sick with an elaborate liturgy which allowed those present to take an active part in the ceremony. Psalms were generally sung with their antiphons, followed by versicles and prayers. In the West, these prayers were penitential, stressing primarily the remission of sins. In the East, when the sacrament is given solemnly, a real vigil is held, complete with readings from the Bible[9] and hymns. Such lengthy ceremonies would seem to be especially appropriate for monastic communities, or at least for Christian communities of no great size, able to devote considerable time to the rare cases of illness among them. These rites serve to remind us that all sick persons should be aided to the greatest possible extent by the common prayer of the family and even of neighbors and friends.

The formula accompanying the anointings and the prayers suggested for those assisting are both oriented almost exclusively toward the penitential aspect of the sacrament. But the prayers which the priest must offer after the anointings are all directed to the healing of the sick person, his return to active life and participation in the Christian assembly: "Deliver your servant from sickness, bring him back to health." It is on the Epistle of St. James that this hope is founded: "Lord God, You have

[8] The Syrians have a formula accompanying the anointings which is particularly interesting: "By this anointing, may your infirmities be relieved, your sins be forgiven, and all evil thoughts be driven away from you, in the name of the Father and of the Son and of the Holy Spirit unto life everlasting. Amen."

[9] For the very interesting list of readings in the Byzantine rite, see *The Liturgy and the Word of God*, p. 12.

said through the mouth of Your Apostle. . . ." It is particularly note-
worthy that in these prayers health of body and soul are intimately connected and are both the work of the Holy Spirit.

III. IMPLICATIONS OF THE SACRAMENTAL SIGN

The sacrament of anointing requires olive oil blessed for the sick. In
the West at present, this blessing, as we have said, is reserved to the
bishop; but it does not belong to him exclusively, as does the consecration of the chrism. In any event, the blessing of the oil is necessary for
the sacrament (*Summa,* Suppl., 29, 5).

Intended for the treatment of sick persons, the blessed oil is a remedy (*Summa,* Suppl., 30, 1). The anointings are a kind of healing min-
istration; even modern medicine still uses liniments with an oil base.

We find the significance of this sacrament gradually developed throughout the Bible. Anointing with oil was carried out, as we have seen, by
the disciples whom Christ sent out during His public life (Mark 6:13),
and oil is one of the remedies applied by the Good Samaritan to the
wounds of the man he found lying by the wayside (Luke 10:34).

It is the remedy desired by "the virgin, daughter of Egypt" (Jer. 46:
11), the remedy lacking to Israel and Juda for their incurable wounds
(Jer. 30:12-13, and more expressly, Is. 1:6; Jer. 8:22). Used alone or with
balm, oil is praised by the prophets in images in which bodily illness is
the symbol of a profound spiritual evil beyond the range of earthly
medicine. This symbolism and use of oil are obviously very different from
those of chrism or the oil of catechumens. In teaching the sacraments,
then, it is very important to point out that the act of anointing and the
use of oil can have very different meanings. The anointing of kings,
priests and prophets has nothing in common with the anointing of the
sick, and the anointing for athletic struggles is of still another nature. It
is necessary, therefore, to describe each sacramental action in its whole
context as a sign and to refer it to its proper biblical symbolism. The
Church distinguishes carefully between the holy oils which she has consecrated or blessed (cf. *Summa,* Suppl., 30, 3).

The intervention of the priestly prayer is necessary, as St. James states
in his Epistle—"priestly" in the sense that it is not strictly reserved either
to the bishop alone or to priests alone. Because St. James speaks of "presbyters," some attempts have been made to exclude the bishop. Pope In-
nocent I protested against this in 416 (*Denz.* 99). Although in the Latin
rite the blessing of the oil is reserved to the bishop, priests administer the
sacrament. Concelebration by seven priests is still practiced in the
Byzantine rite of anointing, as it used to be practiced elsewhere, but
this is not required for valid administration today.

The Council of Trent has defined that the minister of extreme unction is exclusively the priest, and that the presbyters of whom St. James speaks were not laymen but priests ordained by a bishop (*Denz.* 929).

Article Four
THE TWOFOLD EFFECT OF THE ANOINTING OF THE SICK[10]

I. THE CORPORAL EFFECT: HEALING OF THE BODY

We deal first with the effect of healing the body because it is the one first emphasized in liturgical tradition and especially because it is first in the order of sacramental significance: anointing is a remedy applied to a sick body. This is the starting-point used for teaching this sacrament in the sermons of St. Caesarius of Arles, the Church Father who spoke the most about the anointing of the sick.

> When a sickness occurs, let him who is sick receive the Body and Blood of Christ; let him ask the priests, with humility and faith, for the blessed oil, and let him oil his body with it, so that what is written will be fulfilled in him. (Here St. Caesarius quotes the text of St. James.) You see, my brothers, that the sick person who has recourse to the Church will merit obtaining both health of body and forgiveness for his sins. Since, then, the good that we can find in the Church is twofold, why do unfortunate men go to consult oracles, springs, trees and wreaths of false gods, magicians, sooth-sayers, diviners, sorcerers, except to bring down upon themselves countless evils?[11]

Healing the body, however, is not the most important effect of anointing. It is subordinated to the good of the soul as to its end, and it is, as it were, the physical overflow to the body of a spiritual healing grace. Nevertheless, it is truly an effect proper to this sacrament, though the benefit of healing is a favor which God grants when He sees fit. It does not follow necessarily, but it does occur frequently and gives the sacramental sign its complete signification (cf. *Summa,* Suppl., 30, 2).

[10] See Jean-Charles Didier, *Death and the Christian,* pp. 53-66; Zoltan Alszeghy, "The Bodily Effects of Extreme Unction," *Theology Digest,* 9 (1961), pp. 105-109.

[11] *Sermon* 13:3. Almost the same passage is found in *Sermon* 19:5, if the latter is really distinct from the former. "False gods" is here substituted for "diabolical," to indicate the kind of abuse the Bishop of Arles is protesting against. The same ideas are to be found in *Sermon* 50:1 and in 184:5.

It is, then, not a magical effect infallibly produced by the use of some divine secret. Nor is it a charismatic healing due to the spiritual gifts of the minister, as was the gift of healing mentioned by St. Paul (1 Cor. 12:30). Again, it is not a miracle produced instantaneously by an obvious break with the laws of the human organism, like the cures at Lourdes. It is a truly sacramental effect, the work of the Lord through a sign, for the sake of salvation.

A false spirituality has tended to make us forget the bodily effect of this sacrament, to treat it as someting to be passed over in silence. This is not the attitude of the Church in her prayer or in her teaching. The Council of Trent hurls anathemas at anyone who denies that the anointing of the sick relieves them, or who would try to avoid the teaching of St. James under the pretext that the Apostle was here speaking of the charisms of the early Church which have since disappeared (Denz. 927).

Since this physical effect of healing is not miraculous, the sacrament should be given, when possible, at the beginning of a serious illness or at a time when the sickness is still curable.

II. THE PENITENTIAL EFFECT: THE HEALING OF THE SOUL

That the sacrament of the sick also effects the remission of sins is one of the clearest statements in the tradition of the Church. It is found in the Epistle of St. James and in the prayers for blessing and applying the oil. The Council of Trent has made it an article of faith (Denz. 927). There is nothing astonishing in this, since we have seen the connection existing in the biblical perspective between sickness and sin, and in the attitude of Christ between healing and forgiving.

However, the anointing of the sick does not normally take the place of the sacrament of penance. Before receiving the holy oil, the sick person makes his confession, if he is able to do so, and receives absolution. Theologians explain that anointing is a "sacrament of the living," which should be received in the state of grace.

The penitential effect of the anointing of the sick complements the effect of penance, but not in precisely the same way in which confirmation completes the initiation begun at baptism. For, although penance is meant for every baptized sinner, the anointing can be received only by the sick. Sickness is a providential occasion for a more profound discovery of our wretchedness, of which it is both a sign and an effect, and the sacrament of anointing proclaims the compassion of the Lord in a very special way (Summa, Suppl., 29, 9).

In seeking to define the penitential grace of anointing as distinct from that of penance, theologians have proposed many problems and more or less controversial solutions. In catechetical instruction it is better to avoid such questions and to keep strictly to the viewpoint which clarifies the specific character of the sacrament of anointing: the penitential effect it produces is that proper to the state of sickness.

For the sick person who has lost the use of his senses and cannot receive the sacrament of penance, the anointing of the sick substitutes for it, since the grace proper to the anointing includes the remission of sins. Interior contrition always remains necessary, since without such conversion a man cannot receive the divine forgiveness. The sacrament of the sick does not demand an exterior manifestation of this contrition as does the sacrament of penance; but a minimal intention, at least virtual, is indispensable.

III. THE COMFORTING AND STRENGTHENING OF THE SICK

The twofold effect of anointing is, therefore, actually one and the same grace of the Holy Spirit: the comforting and strengthening of the sick on the spiritual and the bodily level. On the spiritual level, moreover, this grace is not limited to the forgiveness of sins; it is also an aid in the difficulties characteristic of sickness, and its sanctification.

The Council of Trent, in the second chapter of its doctrinal explanation, expresses this unity and richness:

> This sacrament is a sign of the grace of the Holy Spirit; it is He whose anointing washes away sins, if there are still any in need of forgiveness, and the consequences of sin, gives comfort and strength to the soul of the sick person, awakening in him great trust in the divine mercy. Uplifted by this trust, the sick person bears more easily the inconveniences and sufferings of his state, resists more easily the temptations of the devil . . . and often receives health of body when this is useful for the salvation of his soul (*Denz.* 909).

In the present discipline of the Church, the sacrament of anointing can be given only once for the same illness (Can. 940, 2). However, in the ancient Church it could be repeated and was considered a medication to be applied throughout the sickness. Present usage invites us to see the sacrament's effect as an enduring one, connected at least basically with the duration of that particular sickness or crisis of health—hence as a *res et sacramentum* which is not affected by a relapse into sin.

In a sense, therefore, and with reference to the present discipline regarding the sacrament, we can speak of a "consecration" of the state of illness. However, the sign is a remedy for the sick rather than a consecratory anointing like that of baptism and confirmation. Finally, the Church prays for that healing toward which the sacrament is oriented.

IV. THE ANOINTING OF THE SICK AND CHRISTIAN DEATH

Illness, at least serious illness, is a sign of death and an apprenticeship for it. It takes a man away from his activities and his associates, and reduces him to some degree of helplessness and dependency. Serious illness means that the danger of death is close at hand. It is, therefore, an urgent invitation to the sick person to realize this and prepare for it. Just as all earthly calamities are a sign of the Lord's return, although we cannot tell whether or not they are the immediate preparations for it, so illness is the sign of death even when it does not actually result in it.

This is the perspective in which we should view the present discipline in the Western Church that the anointing of the sick is to be given only to sick persons in danger of death. We must remember that this anointing is meant for sick people *in danger* of death, not necessarily at the point of death. For example, a person who finds out that he has a serious heart condition may receive this sacrament, even though he is not bedridden and may live for many years. When the priest anoints a sick person whose recovery is despaired of, he does so not because the person is going to die, but because he is dangerously ill and this sacrament is a grace meant for the sick.

We should, therefore, guard against a view, rather widespread during the Middle Ages and even in our own times, which makes the sacrament of the sick into a sacrament for the dying. As a result, its administration is frequently delayed until the last extremity of an illness. One of the reasons for this view in the Middle Ages was that the penitential character of the anointing had led to its becoming associated with certain of the consequences of public penance and so to deferring it, like public penance, until the moment of death. The Council of Trent reacted strongly against this conception in its decree on extreme unction. Moreover, the prayers of the ritual have always expressed the faith of the Church in praying for healing. These prayers are sadly incongruous when the priest, called too late, administers the sacrament of healing to a person who is obviously dying.

It is Viaticum, not the anointing, which is designed to give the Christian the grace of a happy death. This is obvious from the fact that a person may be in imminent danger of death and yet not be a fit subject for the sacrament of the sick, e.g., a soldier about to launch an attack or a prisoner about to be executed. Such persons may receive Viaticum but not the anointing, since this presupposes a state of sickness. But Viaticum is required for all who are about to die, whether sick or not, by virtue of a divine precept.

V. SUMMARY

1. The sacrament of the sick is not necessary for salvation as is baptism (and penance in some cases), nor did the Lord make it the subject of a binding precept like the Eucharist. But it is a special grace neither to be disdained nor slighted.

2. To receive it validly, it is necessary for the recipient to be capable of profiting from its twofold effect, that is:

He must be sick, otherwise the sign itself would be lacking (*Summa*, Suppl., 32, 1 and 2). This is why the Church does not approve the practice of certain of the Eastern Churches of anointing people who are in good health with the oil of the sick.

He must be capable of having committed personal sins. This excludes children who have not yet reached the age of reason and the mentally deficient who have never been capable of sin.

3. The Western Church requires in addition that the sickness should be serious, constituting a danger of death—this latter condition being taken in a broad sense.

4. The sacrament can be given only once during the same illness. But if, after a crisis, there is some true recovery, then the sacrament can be given anew when another acute attack occurs; even though the cause is permanent, these states have been successive and distinct.

5. The Church insists that, whenever possible, the sacrament should be given at the beginning of a serious illness so that the sick person may receive it lucidly and fervently, and because it is a sacrament of healing.

Article Five
THE SACRAMENTALS OF THE SICK

The Church's care of the sick is not limited to the sacrament of anointing. This care includes Eucharistic Communion, but with no special formula except when given as Viaticum. The missal provides, however, the text of a Mass for the Sick which expresses admirably the Church's attitude with regard to sickness.

Moreover, the ritual gives us a very rich treasury of prayer for the successive visits which the priest makes to the sick. For each occasion there is a text from the Gospel, a psalm, a collect prayer, which allow him "to break the bread" of the Word of God and to offer the comfort of the Church's prayer. Finally, the various blessings for the sick in general and for certain categories of sick persons should be known and used. If the priest cannot come to visit the sick as often as he would wish, it is the duty and privilege of their families and friends to open up to them this treasury of the Church's prayer.

Chapter 7
MARRIAGE

Preliminary Remarks

The study of Christian marriage cannot be separated from that of consecrated virginity. Marriage and virginity are so closely related in the plan of salvation that we can understand virginity adequately only in reference to marriage, and clarify the Christian mystery of marriage only by recognizing the superiority of consecrated virginity. For both are essentially ordered toward the eschatological union of Christ and the Church; marriage is the sign of that union, virginity gives up the sign in order the more speedily and directly to attain the reality signified.

Christian marriage differs essentially from pagan marriage because the marrying partners are baptized. Though Christ did not create a new institution peculiar to Christians, as is the case with the other sacraments, He raised the institution of marriage to the dignity of a divine mystery. This is true even when there is no apparent difference between the marriage of Christians and non-Christians, as was the case in some periods of the past and may still happen in exceptional cases. For Christians, marriage is henceforth a sacrament—so they cannot enter marriage with one another without receiving the sacrament. Moreover, it is the very act by which the marriage is contracted which constitutes its sacramental sign.

Article One
MARRIAGE AND VIRGINITY IN THE ECONOMY OF SALVATION

Marriage is a human, earthly reality complete in its own order. But for the baptized it is a sacrament in the strict sense of the word, a sacrament just as the six others are, even though its celebration does not necessarily require rites expressing its signification. This is true because of its connection with the economy of salvation. This connection is so close that marriage has been modified in its structures at every stage of this economy, and has become, through the divine pedagogy of Holy Scripture, the most expressive sign of our redemption through Christ.

I. MARRIAGE AND VIRGINITY AT DIFFERENT STAGES OF SACRED HISTORY

The solemn blessing pronounced by the celebrant at a wedding Mass invites us to contemplate marriage at different periods of the history of salvation. "O God, as You . . . give to this union, the first to be established, the sole blessing which was not taken away in punishment for original sin nor in the sentence of the Flood. . . ." It is Christ above all who, in His Gospel, obliges us to adopt this "historical" view of the condition of marriage as being different at creation ("in the beginning," says Jesus in Matthew 19:8); after the fall, and especially under the law of Moses; in the Law of Christ ("And I say to you . . ."—Matthew 5:32); and at the resurrection.

1. *"In the beginning."* The book of Genesis gives us two accounts of creation, the first representing the tradition called "priestly," the second called "Yahwist." Both state that God instituted marriage at the same time that He created man and woman:

> God created man to his image, to his image he created him, man and woman he created them. God blessed them and said to them: Be ye fruitful, multiply and fill the earth and govern it; rule over the fish of the sea, the birds of the air and all the animals. . . . God looked on all that he had made; it was very good. It was evening and morning: the sixth day . . . (Gen. 1:27-28, 31).

> Yahweh said: It is not good that man should be alone. It is fitting that I give him a helpmate like unto himself. . . . Then the Lord God had man fall into a profound slumber, and he slept. He took from him one of his ribs and closed the flesh at that place. Then, of the rib which he had taken from the side of man, the Lord God fashioned a woman and brought her to man. Then he cried out: She now is bone of my bone and flesh of my flesh! She shall be called "woman" since she was drawn from man. This is why man leaves his father and his mother and unites himself to his wife, and they become but one flesh . . . (Gen. 2:18-24).

The figurative nature of these texts, primitive and oriental as they are (especially the second), should not blind us to the importance they have in revelation. It is to them that Malachias (2:10-16) refers in a message quite close to that of the Gospel. It is to them that St. Paul constantly returns in explaining the laws of Christian marriage (1 Cor. 6:16; 11:7-9; Eph. 5:28-32; 1 Tim. 2:13). Finally, they are expressly referred to by Christ, who presents His own law as a return to "the beginning." Following the New Testament, liturgical prayer always refers to these texts.

> O God, who by Thy mighty power hast made all things where before there was nothing; who, having put in order the beginnings of the universe, didst form for man made to Thy image an inseparable helpmate, woman, so that Thou didst give woman's body its origin from man's flesh and teach that it is never right to separate her from the one being whence it has pleased Thee to take her . . . (Nuptial Blessing, Roman Missal).

Several doctrinal statements are to be found in these passages from
the book of Genesis. Marriage comes from God, not from man. It is an
institution placed above human conventions, since it is founded on the
very nature of man as God created it. "Man and woman he created them,"
at once equal in dignity but different and complementary; woman being
subject to man, but not so as to be diminished in anyway by this submission. Notice the way in which St. Paul develops these views in 1 Cor.
11:2-12.

The Lord has blessed marriage, even pagan marriage, with a special
blessing which makes clear its goodness. This blessing has led theologians
to an optimistic view which neither moral depravity, nor Manichaean tendencies, nor the harsh rigorism of certain admirers of St. Augustine has
succeeded in affecting.

The original law of marriage which comes from God is that one man
unite himself to one woman to form a couple so joined that death alone
can separate them. This is what Jesus states very clearly (Matthew
19:4-6).

We should note that in the earthly paradise there was no place for virginity. So long as sin had not entered the world, there was perfect harmony between human life and the plan of God; there was no danger of
man's forgetting that everything comes from God and returns to Him.
Moreover, Adam and Eve would have transmitted divine grace to their
children along with life. In "filling the earth" in accordance with the divine command, they would by that very fact have filled heaven with
children of God.

**2. "The sole blessing which was not taken away in punishment
for original sin nor in the doom of the flood."** For her sin Eve received
a punishment which affected marriage in its fruitfulness as well as the
harmony of love.

> To the woman, Yahweh said: I will multiply the sorrows of your
> childbearing, in sorrow shall you bring forth children. You shall long
> for your husband, and he shall dominate over you (Gen. 3:16).

Sin seems to multiply on earth more quickly than do the children of
men; because of ever-increasing shamelessness (Gen. 6:1-4), the anger of
God brings down the Flood. And yet, in the midst of this general decline
there appear a few just men. Their wives are movingly described by the
sacred writer; their conjugal love triumphs over all doubts and all crises.

These descriptions in the book of Genesis look towards the Promise, the
offspring of Abraham, the work of God in founding His people and in
preparing for Christ. And so the liturgy of marriage, in the East and the
West, draws attention first to the homes of the patriarchs.

The Christian wife should "follow at all times the example of the
holy women. May she be the beloved of her husband as was Rachel" (from

the fact that Jacob was willing to serve Laban for seven years to win Rachel, "seven years, which seemed to him like a few days, so much did he love her"—Gen. 29:20).

May she be "wise, like Rebecca" (who knew how to preserve her twins from fratricidal hatred—Gen. 27:41-46—after having procured for Jacob, by deception and trickery it is true, the blessing which his father was saving for Esau; here she was unwittingly the instrument of God, whose choices are free—Gen. 27:6-17).

May she be "faithful throughout the course of a long life, like Sara" (a tender faithfulness, since Sara "obeyed Abraham, calling him her lord"—1 Peter 3:6; a fidelity based on supernatural faith, since, though she had remained barren until old age, she believed Him who promised a son "because she judged Him faithful" to His promises—Heb. 11:11).

Other books of the Bible present an ideal, even idyllic, picture of the happiness of couples who love, marry, and as an incontestable proof of His blessing, receive from God, children who crowd about the family table. We should note particularly the following: the story of Tobias, which attains to an ideal of conjugal chastity close to that of the New Testament; the Introit of the wedding Mass, repeating the wishes of Raguel for the newly-married couple; Psalm 127, which is a classic part of the Christian nuptial liturgy; the acrostic poem on the perfect woman which concludes the collection of the Proverbs (Prov. 31:10:31); and the book of Ruth, which is a model of fidelity to the Law, within which grew up a conjugal love at once tender and moving.

Marriage therefore retained, in the eyes of the sacred authors, a blessing of such quality from God that the New Testament and the Church have never ceased to look to the ancient history of the people of God for lessons and valuable models for Christian married people. Yet, in spite of these beautiful examples, it seems that the institution of marriage even in the heart of the patriarchal families lost its early characteristics.

3. "It is because of your hardness of heart that Moses permitted you to put away your wives" (Matthew 19:8). Deuteronomy (24:1) wrote into the Law of Moses a procedure for divorce allowing a man to put aside his wife "if she has not found favor in his eyes and if he has discovered a defect that he may impute to her." The rabbis were later on to discuss the extent of this sad privilege. In the Gospel they try to make Jesus judge their controversy; He then imputes the concession of the Mosaic divorce to the "hardness of heart" of the Israelites (Matthew 19:8; Mark 10:5).

But it must be admitted that long before Moses the unity and indissolubility of marriage had already become precarious. We admire the wives of the patriarchs through whom God fulfilled His promises; but these patriarchs at the same time had sons by other wives. The kings, even David and Solomon, the anointed of the Lord, had harems, following the custom of their pagan neighbors. There was, then, a regression at least in morals, although at the same time the divine plan of salvation was unfolding, the plan of which marriage had already become the sign. However, on the return from the exile, the prophecy of Malachias stresses a new spirit:

> Yahweh is witness between you and the wife of your youth to whom you show yourself to be unfaithful, even though she was your companion and your wife by oath. Has he not made a single being, with flesh and breath of life? And this one being—what does he seek? A posterity given by God Have regard, then, to your life, and be not unfaithful to the wife of your youth. For I condemn him who goes back on his word, says the Lord God of Israel. Let him not flaunt injustice as an outer garment, declares the Lord of armies. Have regard, then to your life and commit not this perfidy (Mal. 2:14-17).

Neither among the patriarchs nor in the Law of Moses, nor among the prophets is there any consideration given to virginity. On the contrary, the woman who does not find a husband is unfortunate; the wife who is barren is humiliated. For the People of God of the Old Testament were perpetuated and increased by generation: the Promise was for posterity, for the race. Yet it was to a barren woman like Sara that God gave the son of the Promise. And we find the "barren one" amongst those "poor" whom Yahweh is pleased to load with favors (Cant. of Anna; 1 Sam. 2:5; Ps. 112:9; Is. 54:1). Here again, then, the Old Testament prepares for and looks forward to the New, which nonetheless is new with the creative newness of Christ.

4. Marriage and virginity in the law of Christ. Jesus' teaching proclaimed two important changes in the condition of marriage. Abolishing the concession granted by the Law of Moses, Christ re-established the indissolubility and unity of marriage, restoring it as it was in the beginning.

> It has been said: Whoever puts away his wife must give her a bill of divorcement. But I say to you: Whosoever puts away his wife, outside the case of prostitution,[1] destines her to become an adulteress; if anyone marries a wife who has been put away, he commits adultery (Matthew 5: 31-33; cf. Luke 16:18).

[1] We prefer to translate the Greek word *porneia* by the word "prostitution," since this suggests an inadmissible union which could in no case become a true marriage. This is how J. Bonsirven (*Le divorce dans le Nouveau Testament*: Desclee, Paris, 1958) interprets the text, basing himself on the rabbinical tradition: "One may not set aside one's wife unless there was a false marriage." On the other hand, the translation, "outside the case of fornication," supported by the Vulgate, has suggested the possibility of a separation in case of adultery. At all events, the Church, the authentic interpreter of the thought and words of Christ, refuses to see in this an exception to the indissolubility of marriage (Council of Trent, *Denz.* 977).

The Pharisees came to Jesus and said to him, to put him to the test: Is it permitted to put away one's wife for any reason whatever? He answered: Have you not read that the Creator in the beginning made them man and woman and that he said: So, then, shall a man leave his father and his mother to unite himself to his wife, and the two will become but one flesh? Therefore they are not two, but one single flesh. Well, then, what God has united let man never separate. Why, then, they say to him, did Moses lay it down that a man should give a bill of divorce when he puts his wife away? It was by reason, he said, of your hardness of heart that Moses permitted you to put away your wives; but in the beginning it was not so. Now, I say to you: whosoever puts away his wife—I am not speaking here of prostitution— and marries another, commits adultery (Matthew 19:3-9; cf. Mark 10:2-12).

St. Paul also witnesses to this precept of the Lord:

As for married persons, this is what I ordain, or, rather, not I but the Lord: let not the wife separate from her husband in case of separation, let her not marry or let her be reconciled with her husband; and let not the husband put away his wife (I Cor. 7:10-11).

Faced with such a law, the disciples protest (notice that it is the disciples, not the Pharisees; cf. Mark 10:10): "If this is the condition of a man in relation to his wife, it is not expedient to marry" (Matthew 19:10). This immediate reaction is valuable as expressing the difficulty felt by men of all periods since the Fall, and not only by the Israelites. The answer Christ gives shows that to regain the original meaning of marriage and accept the natural law as willed by God since the creation, we must rise to the level of faith: "Not everyone understands this saying, but only those to whom it is given" (Matthew 19:11). And then Jesus announces something entirely new—continence.

There are in truth eunuchs who were born so from their mother's womb; there are eunuchs who have become so through the action of men; and there are eunuchs who have made themselves so for the sake of the Kingdom of Heaven. Let him understand who can (Matthew 19:12).

In contrast to the Old Testament, in which the Kingdom was a hope based on the flesh, the New Testament gives a primary place to voluntary celibacy, to virginity for the sake of the Kingdom of heaven. Its position is superior to that of marriage, and it is the possibility of such virginity which makes clear the possibility of a marriage that is one and indissoluble. Here, again, St. Paul explains clearly Christ's teaching:

The man who is not married is solicitous about the affairs of the Lord, for the means of pleasing the Lord. He who is married is solicitous about the affairs of the world, about the means of pleasing his wife, and he is divided. So, too, the unmarried woman, like the young girl, is solicitous about the affairs of the Lord; she seeks to be holy in body and spirit. She who is married is solicitous about the affairs of the world, about the means of pleasing her husband. I say this in your own interest, not to set a trap for you, but to lead you to what is fitting and what unites you to the Lord without distraction (1 Cor. 7:32-35).

The complete answer to the disquiet shown by the disciples of Jesus, as also the full light on virginity, is provided by the revelation which the Lord made, not to the crowd, but to his apostles and the Church. Marriage has become a "mystery" in the Pasch of Christ. From now on it is the sign of the love of Christ for His Church, a love of which Christian man and wife receive not only the example but also the grace, the love which virgins attain without having to go by way of the sign.

5. In the resurrection. St. Paul gives another motive for celibacy. "The time is short. . . . Let those, then, who have wives live as if they had none . . . those who use this world as if they used it not For the figure of this world is passing away" (1 Cor. 7:29-31).[2] Virginity is an anticipation here on earth of eternal life. Marriage will no longer exist in heaven, as Jesus teaches and as St. John forsees in the Apocalypse.

> The children of this world take husband or wife; but those who have been judged worthy to take part in the other world and in the resurrection from the dead take neither wife nor husband. Also, they can no longer die, for they are equal to the angels and they are sons of God, being sons of the resurrection (Luke 20:34-35; cf. Matthew 22:30; Mark 12:25).

> Behold a Lamb appeared to my sight; he was standing on Mount Sion and with him a hundred and forty-four thousand having his name and the name of his Father written on their foreheads. . . . These are they who were not defiled with women, they are virgins; they follow the Lamb wherever he goes" (Apoc. 14:1-4).[3]

II. "A GREAT MYSTERY IN CHRIST AND THE CHURCH"

A wholly new condition of marriage proceeds from the Pasch of Christ; the marriage of Christians is its sign and brings its grace.

[2] L. Legrand, "The Prophetical Meaning of Celibacy," *Review for Religious* 20 (1961), pp. 330-346 (reprint from *Scripture,* Oct. 1960, Jan. 1961).

[3] "This expression is to be taken in a metaphorical sense. Lewdness and debauchery are a participation in the worship of idols. The one hundred and forty-four thousand are virgins in the sense that they never gave themselves over to the worship of the Beast: they could be espoused to the Lamb" (note on this passage in the *Bible de Jérusalem*).

1. The love of Christian man and wife, sign of the mutual love of Christ and the Church.

When St. Paul wishes to give married Christians the rules of conduct suited to their state, he proposes that they imitate the mutual attitude of Christ and the Church.

> Let wives be subject to their husbands as to the Lord. Indeed, the husband is head of his wife as Christ is head of the Church, he the savior of the body. Now, the Church is subject to Christ. Wives, should then, and in the same way, be subject in all things to their husbands.
> Husbands, love your wives as Christ has loved the Church. He gave himself up for her, to sanctify her by the bath of water which a word accompanies; for he wished to present her to himself all radiant, without spot or wrinkle nor anything of the kind, but holy and immaculate. In the same way, husbands ought to love their wives as their own bodies. To love one's wife—is this not to love oneself? Now, no one hates his own flesh; rather he nourishes it and is careful of it. It is just this that Christ does for the Church: are we not members of his body? See, then, why the husband will leave his father and his mother to cleave to his wife and the two will form but one flesh. This is a mystery of great import—I mean that it applies to Christ and the Church (Eph. 5:22-32).

This text, which serves as the Epistle of the Nuptial Mass, is of great significance not only for what it says but also for its relation to the Old and New Testaments. The work of Christ in founding the Church is a work of love: "He gave himself up for her." But it is a married love; Christ and the Church form but one flesh since the Church is the Body of Christ, identified with Him. Baptism, the "bath of water that a word accompanies," has an analogy in the Oriental custom of the bride's ceremonial bath before her marriage; it is a rite of espousal.[4] The holiness Christ gives to the Church is the ornament given to the wife as a marriage gift.

Christians are, then, to reproduce in their married lives the model set before them. It is not through a mere desire to edify or to foster family spirituality that St. Paul thus introduces the nuptial union of Christ and the Church, for he also deals with this latter theme separately, particularly in Gal. 4:21-31, where the Church, the Jerusalem from on high and our Mother, is compared to Sara, the wife of Abraham.

2. The marriage of Christ and the Church in the witness of St. John.

The Jerusalem from on high, Bride of Christ and our Mother, appears again in the Apocalypse, coming for the marriage, beautiful and adorned as in the text of the Epistle to the Ephesians.

---

[4] Cf. Ezechiel 16:9. This point is particularly stressed by St. John Chrysostom in his first baptismal catechesis. See J. Daniélou, *The Bible and the Liturgy*, pp. 205-207; F. X. Durrwell, *The Resurrection*, pp. 168-169.

Let us be joyful and glad, let us give glory to God; see, it is the marriage of the Lamb, and his spouse is made beautiful. She has been clothed in linen of shining whiteness—the linen that is the good deeds of the faithful. Then he said to me, Write: Happy are those who are invited to the marriage feast of the Lamb (Apoc. 19:7-9).

And I saw the Holy City, New Jerusalem, coming down from heaven, from God; she is made beautiful as a young bride adorned for her husband (Apoc. 21:2).

The Spirit and the Bride say: Come! Let him who hears say: Come! (Apoc. 22:17).

Again, the fourth Gospel presents Jesus as the Lamb and also as the Bridegroom.

The bridegroom is he who has the bride, but the friend of the bridegroom, who is standing by and hears it, is overcome with joy at the voice of the bridegroom. This is my joy, and it is now perfect (John 3:29).[5]

In studying the marriage of Cana (2:1-11) and the death of Jesus (19:25-37) as presented in the fourth Gospel, modern scholars have reached conclusions which agree in many respects with the interpretation already given by liturgical and patristic tradition. The literary method of St. John indicates his intention of treating the founding of the Church as a marriage ceremony. The miracle of Cana is the inauguration of this mystical marriage: "He manifested his glory, and his disciples believed in him" (2:11). The death on the Cross is its fulfillment: "One of the soldiers pierced his side and immediately there came forth blood and water" (19:34).

The Syriac liturgy thus summarizes this mystery in its marriage chant:

Glory to the heavenly Bridegroom who, through His love, was betrothed to the Church that was soiled by the peoples and, by His crucifixion, purified her, cleansed her and made her His glorious Bride. . . . There had never been a bride like her whom the First-born espoused. He won her for Himself before all things and in His death He gave her a marriage feast. He mounted the wood and she was near to Him; He opened His side and she was washed in His blood.

3. The "mystery" of Adam and Eve in the light of the New Testament.
Above all, we should take account of the way in which John recalls the account of the creation of Eve in describing Jesus' death. In creating the first man and the first woman, God already had Christ in view; all the details mentioned in Genesis are matched in the Gospel of John.

---

[5] We should note that in the Synoptics Jesus called Himself the Bridegroom; while He is present there should be no fasting (Matthew 9:14-15; cf. Matthew 22:1-14; 25:1-13).

"From the side of Christ asleep in death flowed the sacraments, that is to say, the blood and water by which the Church was instituted" (*Summa* III, 92, 2 and 3), just as from the side of Adam plunged in sleep God created Eve. This is why marriage was, from the beginning, a sign of the Christ to come (*Summa* III, 61, 2 ad 3).

This is far deeper than allegory, since the redemption was to come from Eve's posterity. "I will establish," says Yahweh to the serpent, "enmity between you and the woman, between your seed and her seed; he shall crush your head and shall lie in wait for his heel" (Gen. 3:15). The maternity of Eve is, therefore, not only an image, but also the beginning of the history of salvation which will end in Christ, born of a woman.

4. The mystery of marriage in the Old Testament. The language of the New Testament did not seem at all surprising to those who had the benefit of the divine preparation in the Old. Before John and Paul presented and mystery of salvation as the marriage of Christ and the Church, and even before John the Baptist spoke of Christ as the Bridegroom, the prophets, the Canticle of Canticles, and the psalms had accustomed God's people to see the covenant as a marriage-covenant, the love of God for His people as the love of a husband for his wife.

It was Osee who first brought home this message, not only by his words, but also by his own married life, intended as a sign by Yahweh. Experiencing his own wife's infidelity, Osee discovered and witnessed to the sentiments of Yahweh for His unfaithful people. Osee took his wife back, guilty as she was, and gave her his love again as on the first day of his marriage; so he showed that Yahweh took pity on Israel and was able to save her from her sin (Osee 1:2; 3:1-5).

Jeremias developed this message. Using the same image of conjugal love, he insisted on the tenderness of God for the "virgin Israel":

> With an eternal love have I loved you, and I have kept you in my favor. I will rebuild you; you will be rebuilt, virgin Israel. . . . Come back, virgin Israel, return to the cities that are yours. How long will you turn, now here, now there, unfaithful daughter? For God creates a new thing on earth: the wife seeks out her husband (Jer. 31:3, 21-22).

This prophecy should be related to the first chapter of Lamentations; Is. 54:1-14 (cf. Gal. 4:27) ; Ez. 16; and finally Is. 60—61, which looks forward to chapter 21 of the Apocalypse.

The Canticle of Canticles and Psalm 44 sing the marriage-song of Yahweh and His people in terms so woven of colorful imagery that exegetes have frequently been tempted to see them as "occasional" pieces composed exclusively for earthly marriage celebrations. In the light of the whole prophetic revelation, however, these descriptions of the mutual love of Bridegroom and Bride express the depth of love with which God cherishes Israel and every faithful soul.

5. From sign to reality. Marriage is therefore the biblical sign above all others of the redemptive covenant, prefigured and announced since Genesis and accomplished by Jesus on the Cross. And Christian marriage, the sign of the union between Christ and His Church, is one of the seven sacraments of the New Law.

Since marriage is only a sign, it is to give way to the reality at the time of the "eternal marriage-feast of the Lamb," when the "return of the marriage-feast" will take place, i.e., at the parousia. So the Syriac marriage liturgy prays: "Make us worthy, Lord God, to share in the joy of Your feast which has no end, in the happiness of Your marriage-chamber, the happiness which never diminishes."

This is why Christian marriage is inferior to virginity or celibacy undertaken in view of the Kingdom of heaven. As the Roman preface for the consecration of virgins says:

> Nothing forbids marriage or lessens its dignity, nor has the nuptial blessing ceased to sanctify this bond. Yet there are loftier souls who turn away from the union of marriage, desiring ardently the divine reality which it represents. Dispensing with what is carried out in marriage, they unite themselves with what is there symbolized. . . . In You may she possess everything that she wishes to love, and to love above all. Through You may she keep what she has promised. Made pleasing not through the body but the soul to Him who looks within the heart, may she be numbered among the wise virgins and await the heavenly Bridegroom, with the lamp of virtues alight and filled with the oil of vigilance. May she not be troubled by the sudden arrival of the King; but confident, carrying her light and one with the choir of virgins who have gone before her, may she joyfully go to meet Him.[6]

Article Two

THE SACRAMENT OF MARRIAGE

I. ONE OF THE SEVEN SACRAMENTS

> If anyone says that marriage is not truly and properly one of the seven sacraments of the law of the gospel and instituted by Christ the Lord,

[6] For a fuller history of this ceremony, its significance and present use in the United States, see L. Muenster, *Christ in His Consecrated Virgins.*

but introduced into the Church by men, or that it does not confer grace, let him be anathema (Council of Trent; *Denz.* 971).

This condemnation was directed against Calvin and Luther. But there is no doubt that these innovators had found support in the disputes of preceding centuries. From early times an inveterate mistrust of things carnal had led both Gnostics and Manicheans to deny the sanctity of marriage. Moreover, certain theologians of the thirteenth century had refused to include marriage in the list of the sacraments instituted by Christ to produce grace, some denying that it had the quality of a sacred sign, others that it could produce sanctification.[7] Even more than the witness of the Fathers in combating these errors, liturgical practice is the proof of the faith of the Church; all the rites of East and West celebrate marriage and attribute grace to it.

St. Thomas insists that this sacrament has its own character; he discourages oversimplified analogies with the other sacraments. He sketches out a doctrinal synthesis with elements already provided by St. Augustine. This synthesis, which has become classic, is found in the marriage encyclicals of Popes Leo XIII and Pius XI.

II. THE LITURGY OF THE SACRAMENT OF MARRIAGE

From the liturgical aspect also, the sacrament of marriage has a position all its own. Its celebration is less tied to the general laws of Christian worship and allows local customs and practices, provided these are legitimate and praiseworthy (Can. 1100). In case of necessity, the liturgical aspect of marriage can be minimized to such an extent that, in certain exceptional circumstances, not even the presence of the priest is required (Can. 1098, for the Latin Church).

1. *Traditional principles.* Two traditional principles, seemingly contradictory, regulate the celebration of Christian marriage. The first is that "Christians marry like everyone else," according to the phrase of the *Letter to Diognetus* written in the second century or at the beginning of the third. Pope Nicholas I, in 866, explained this more precisely: "The consent of those who are marrying is sufficient according to the laws . . . if this is lacking, everything else is worthless" (*Letter to the Bulgarians, Denz.* 334).

The Church has made other requirements which have become so binding that they ordinarily involve the validity of the contract, e.g., the priest's blessing in the Eastern Churches, the presence of the pastor in the West. But these additional requirements do not affect the essence of the sacrament, nor do they affect married people who receive baptism after their marriage. The Church can ignore them when she sees fit, and they were imposed only gradually.

[7] For a summary of their objections and answers to them, see *Summa*, Suppl., 42, 1 and 3.

The first Christians followed the customary family rites of their city, while making a profound attempt to christianize them and to break with everything idolatrous or licentious. Such an effort is necessary at all periods, since the establishment of a fitting social context and customs helps to maintain the proper character of marriage.

But the marriage of Christians is also a reality which transcends human society; its celebration should clearly indicate that it is a sacrament and an act of worship. As early as the beginning of the second century St. Ignatius of Antioch states:

> It is fitting that men and women who are going to marry should contract their union with the counsel of the bishop, so that their marriage will take place in accordance with the will of the Lord and not according to passion. Let everything be done for the honor of God (*Letter to St. Polycarp,* 5: 2; this refers to a preliminary step, not to the marriage itself).

St. Ambrose adds at the end of the fourth century: "Marriage should be sanctified by the priestly veil and blessing" (*Letter* 19:7, PL 16, 984).

Without in any way contradicting the principle set forth by Nicholas I, a liturgy of marriage was established in which three developments can be distinguished. (1) Human social acts associated with marriage were transposed to the liturgical plane, the bishop or his representative assuming the role of the father of the family. (2) The bond between marriage and the Eucharist was emphasized either by the actual celebration of the Eucharist or by Communion alone. (3) The contract itself, a juridical act, was concluded in front of the Church (*in facie ecclesiae*); it was required that the consent of each party be given aloud before witnesses and in a public place. Then the act of making the contract was brought into the sanctuary itself and surrounded with prayers; and, finally, the Church in the West required, under pain of nullity, that the pastor or his delegate be a qualified witness.[8] In the East, the priest's blessing is required even for the validity of a marriage, at least in modern legislation.

2. The liturgy of marriage in the Eastern Churches. The liturgical aspect of marriage is more developed in the East than in the West. We find elements in it, of course, that are common to the whole Church: the blessing by the priest, with the allusions to the holy women of the Bible; Psalm 127; the blessing of the rings; the joining of hands, etc.

But the East has one characteristic element unknown in Latin rituals—the crowning of the bridegroom and bride. Originally a family rite and then later performed by the bishop or his priests, this crowning was given its classic explanation by St. John Chrysostom: "A crown is placed

---

[8] The requirement that it be public and that the priest be present is fairly recent. Though formulated by the Council of Trent in 1563 (Decree *Tametsi*), it was published only in certain countries, and was not extended to all marriages of Catholics until the time of St. Pius X (Decree *Ne temere,* 1907).

on the heads of the bridegroom and the bride as a symbol of victory, for they are advancing unconquered towards the haven of marriage, they who have not been conquered by pleasure" (*Homily* 9 on 1 Tim.). The victory of Christian marriage over the passions is likewise emphasized, at least among the Byzantines, by texts borrowed from the liturgy of the martyrs.

Moreover, the Churches of the East willingly grant a liturgical character to the human ceremonies of a wedding. Among the Syrians for example, it is customary to go in procession to the wedding-feast, which is frequently presided over by the priest. There are also ceremonies to be carried out in the home, e.g., the blessing of the wedding garments and the cup among the Armenians.

Finally, in places where marriage does not include the celebration of the Mass, it is nevertheless accompanied by readings from the Bible, hymns and prayers, which constitute a living and very rich catechesis.[9]

3. The liturgy of marriage in the Latin Church. With the exception of Gaul and Spain, where the priest used to go to the house and bless the marriage bed, the West never developed any marriage rites other than those taking place within the church building or its portico. The Roman liturgy, which spread throughout practically the whole Latin Church, at first included only the ceremony of the veil accompanied by the priestly blessing. The veil ceremony disappeared, but the blessing was inserted into the Mass itself and acquired greater solemnity.

Up to the Middle Ages the exchange of vows took place outside the church and without the assistance of the priest. But it was then put under the protection of the hierarchy and celebrated, first before the door of the church, and later before the altar. Finally, certain acts which had originally been part of the betrothal ceremony took on new meaning when they were transferred to the exchange of vows, e.g., giving the ring.

The exchange of vows must now take place, under pain of nullity, in the presence of the pastor or his delegate, who questions the bridal couple as to their mutual consent, and in the presence of two other witnesses. Except in unusual circumstances, the ceremony takes place in church and is preceded by some instruction given by the priest. The formula varies according to local customs; the following are examples taken from rituals of other centuries:

> N . . ., You are taking N . . ., here present, as your promised wife; and you promise that you will grant her a good and unfailing claim on your body and your possessions. You will care for her healthy or sick and you will never change her for another, as God has decreed and ordained and our Holy Mother Church maintains and commands (*Meaux,* Statutes of 1493).

[9] See *The Liturgy and the Word of God,* p. 12.

N . . ., say after me: I take you as my promised wife and I swear to you by the loyalty I owe to God and my share in Paradise that I will be a faithful husband and will keep loyalty to you of my body and my possessions, and I will do whatever I can to aid you in your every necessity, so long as it pleases God to let us remain together, as He Himself has commanded and Holy Mother Church ordains (*Meaux, Ritual of 1617*).

After the exchange of vows comes the joining of hands, a gesture which now symbolizes the mutual self-donation of bridegroom and bride.[10] The formula spoken by the priest affirms and ratifies the marriage which has just been contracted, but this formula has no effective force of itself: "I unite you in marriage, in the name of the Father and of the Son and of the Holy Spirit."

The priest then blesses the ring(s). A ring is the sign of fidelity, as well as of mutual love. Originally it was a simple ring of iron, given at the time of the betrothal; Germanic custom made it into the wedding-ring. The names it has been given in different languages express the bond which it signifies: *alliance,* in French; *fede,* in Italian, etc. The Roman Ritual provides for only one ring—that of the bride—whereas custom has the bridegroom wear one also. The German and Spanish rituals provide for blessing both rings.

Prayers composed of verses from the psalms and a Collect offered by the celebrant conclude the rite. If these lack originality, it is because they should not trespass on the marriage blessing normally given during the Mass.

The Nuptial Mass constitutes the normal climax of a Christian wedding. The celebrant gives the marriage blessing in the course of the celebration; only under exceptional circumstances may it be received outside of Mass. The readings from the Epistle to the Ephesians and Matthew 19, and the chants from Tobias and Psalm 127 constitute the Church's official instruction on the sacrament. With the Collects, the whole community joins in prayer for the new home. At one time this Mass had its own Preface, thanking God that "the fruitfulness of marriage increases the fruitfulness of the Church, and . . . the union of man and wife, strengthened by the gentle yoke of harmony and peace, serves for the multiplication of the sons of adoption."

The bridal couple should receive Communion at this Mass.[11] The Church recommends that the priest consecrate the necessary hosts at this

---

[10] The ancient Romans used it to express an entirely different meaning. The father placed the hand of his daughter in that of the bridegroom to indicate that she was to be no longer under his paternal authority, but under that of her husband.

[11] This does not mean that communicating should be limited to the bridal couple, or to the bridal party. Every Catholic present, so far as possible, should receive Communion at a wedding Mass as an aspect of participation in the sacrifice. Many couples now express in the wedding invitations the desire that their Catholic friends will join them at the holy table.

particular Mass (cf. *Mediator Dei*, 118, 121). This Communion has a two-fold importance. First, all the important acts of life, especially sacramental acts, should include the Eucharist (the various stages of Christian initiation, ordination, religious profession, danger of death). Secondly, "marriage is connected with the Eucharist by its symbolism insofar as it represents the union of Christ and the Church, the unity which the Eucharist itself signifies" (*Summa* III, 65, 3). The source of the grace of Christian marriage is the paschal mystery; marriage is the sign of this mystery which is really contained in the Eucharist. As a Byzantine author says: "The Church rightly prepares the divine gifts for the marriage blessing. Thereby He who both gives and is given becomes present at the marriage and He is there also for the peaceful union and harmony of bride and bridegroom."

At present, the celebrant of the Nuptial Mass blesses the bride and groom twice—after the *Pater* and after the *Ite, missa est*. This last blessing, Mozarabic in origin and introduced rather late into the missal, repeats the wishes of Raguel and Gabriel for the young Tobias and Sara (Tobias 7:15 and 9:11 in the Vulgate).

The traditional Roman prayer is the blessing which follows the *Pater* and which originally preceded the kiss of peace. Though it is simply read today, it was formerly sung to the solemn chant of a consecratory Preface. We have already cited several extracts from its first part, referring to different stages in the economy of salvation. Following St. Paul, it recalls the fact that the Lord has "consecrated the marriage union, making it a sign so profound as to prefigure in the marriage covenant the mystery of Christ and the Church."

The wishes expressed in this blessing are exclusively concerned with the bride, a fact which should not cause surprise because in the secular ancient world it was the bride who was the center of the family ceremonies of marriage. Again, this blessing has in view her future motherhood, and bringing forth children is the primary end of the institution of matrimony. Undoubtedly sacramental symbolism plays a part here too: the woman is blessed since she is the image of the Church, but not the man since he is the image of Christ. "Let the law of her life be love and peace; let her marry in Jesus Christ . . . in the knowledge which comes from heaven." For both bride and bridegroom the prayer asks that they may have a long life, "may they see their children's children."

The traditional discipline of the Church discourages the celebration of marriages during the penitential periods of Advent and Lent (*Denz.* 981; Can. 1108). At least, all solemnity should be avoided in these seasons. A marriage celebration by its nature calls for rejoicing and festivity, and so is incompatible with the penitential way of life.[12]

[12] The Nuptial Mass in the Roman missal gives the outline of an exhortation to be given after the second blessing.

III. THEOLOGICAL FORMULATIONS

Theologians have had difficulty in defining the exact nature of the sign of the sacrament of marriage, as well as in determining the connection between this sign (*sacramentum tantum*) and the reality which it signifies (*res sacramenti*) for the latter is twofold: the union of Christ and the Church, and the grace given to the bridal couple.

1. The sacramental sign. It is certain, in spite of the hesitancy of certain ancient authors, that the blessing of the priest, even in the East where it is required for validity, does not form part of the sacramental sign. This blessing is a sacramental that develops and emphasizes the sign, but it is of ecclesiastical institution (*Summa*, Suppl. 42, 1 ad 1; 42, 45, 3).

It is not necessary for the validity of a marriage that it be consummated by the conjugal act, as some medieval canonists believed.[13] To be sure, a marriage that has not been consummated has not become irrevocably indissoluble, and it is true that bodily union is the object of the marriage contract. But the marriage of Mary and Joseph was a true marriage even though it was not consummated; however exceptional their vocation was, Christian spirituality has always held that it could be imitated (*Summa*, Suppl. 42, 4 and 48, 1).

The sign, then, resides in the contract, the exterior and sensible manifestation of the mutual consent of the bridal couple. Without this exterior manifestation, there would be no sign, which normally consists of words (Can. 1088, 2). "Consent" here means the free act of will whereby the couple give to one another here and now the mutual right to the physical act of union. It would be pointless to try to distinguish between act and word here, as we do in the other sacraments; the word is the whole sign since it expresses and creates the state of marriage.

Since it is the bride and groom who make this contract and since it is sacramental in virtue of the baptismal character of the contracting parties, they are said to be the ministers of the sacrament. They confer it on each other in the sense that the sacramental sign is constituted by their mutual consent as a single entity.

Because the contract, the exterior manifestation of this mutual consent, constitutes the sign of the sacrament, there is such identity between the contract and the sacrament that there can be no marriage between two Christians which is not at the same time a sacrament.[14] Anything that vitiates the contract makes the sacrament invalid; anything that invalidates the sacrament renders the contract null. This principle has not

---

[13] See John C. Ford, S. J., *The Validity of Virginal Marriage*.

[14] It is seriously disputed whether the marriage of a Christian and a non-baptized person is a sacrament for the Christian, even though it is a valid marriage. For validity, a Catholic marrying a non-baptized person must obtain a dispensation for "disparity of cult."

been solemnly defined, but it is emphatically stated in the encyclical *Arcanum* of Leo XIII, in the Code of Canon Law (Can. 1012), and in the encyclical *Casti connubii* of Pius XI.

It would be a grave error, therefore, to think of Christian marriage as having two stages, the first consisting in the contract as a purely human action in the domain of the earthly city, the second in the consecration of this contract by the sacrament of the Church. In states which deny civil validity to marriages contracted before the Church, Catholics are obliged to express their consent before a civil officer to have their marriage legally recognized, before doing so in the presence of their pastor. But for them this civil ceremony is not a true marriage, since they can contract marriage validly only before the pastor or his delegate. This is equally true when a Catholic marries a non-Catholic Christian or a non-Christian.

This is true only for Catholics—a fact which complicates instruction. When a couple are baptized Christians who have never been members of the Catholic Church (Protestants, for example), their marriage is both valid and sacramental, whether it takes place in the presence of their own minister or a civil officer. Again, if a couple are not Christians, their civil marriage is a valid marriage, though not sacramental since they have not been baptized. And when two non-Christians who have been validly married receive baptism, their marriage does not need to be renewed; it becomes sacramental in virtue of their baptism.

A marriage may be null—that is, what appears to be a marriage may prove not to be one—because of interior defect of consent (if it was not given freely, if it was not based on the true object of marriage, if it excluded certain of the essential elements, if it was dependent on conditions not realized). It may also be null because of exterior defect of consent (if the consent of each party was not externally manifested). Again, a Catholic marriage may be null by defect of the solemnity required by the Church (the presence of the pastor or his delegate and two other witnesses, or through the existence of some diriment impediment).

Since the Church has received from Christ the mission of administrating and regulating the sacraments, she has the right to prescribe the conditions for solemnizing the marriage of baptized persons, (such as the blessing of the priest in the Eastern rites, the presence of the pastor or his delegate in the Western) and to do so under pain of nullity. She also has the right to decree impediments and to dispense from them. Finally, she has the right to teach which of these impediments are based on natural and divine law.[15]

However, the Church does not "annull" a marriage. She may examine a marriage in court, discover that a true marriage never existed, and then declare the marriage null. Ecclesiastical tribunals alone are competent to deal with cases of nullity of marriage (*Denz.* 982).[16]

2. The matrimonial bond.   It is, then, the exchange of vows, the mutual consent establishing the contract (*sacramentum tantum*) which creates the bond of matrimony (Can. 1110), the state of marriage, which of its nature is perpetual and exclusive. This bond is the *res et sacramentum,* the effect of the consent and, in turn, the symbol of the ultimate reality, the love of Christ and the Church and the sacramental grace (*res sacramenti*). It is this bond which gives mutual conjugal rights and duties. It is the source of grace and the symbol of the love of Christ for the Church.[17]

3. The reality signified (res sacramenti).   The reality signified is, as was said above, twofold: the sacramental grace contained in the conjugal bond; and the Pasch of Christ giving Himself up out of love for the Church, symbolized by the bond but not contained in it. While this latter reality is not contained in the bond, it is the source of the grace given in marriage through the efficacy of the sign (*Summa,* Suppl., 42, 1 ad 4 and 5).

This sacramental grace assures indissolubility (*Denz.* 969) and transforms human love into the love of charity.

> Christ has willed that man and wife, assisted and strengthened by heavenly grace, the fruit of His merits, draw holiness from marriage itself. In this union which has become wonderfully conformed to the model of His mystical union with the Church, He has rendered natural love more perfect and bound together still more closely by the bond of divine charity the indivisible society of man and wife (Leo XIII, *Arcanum*).

The sacrament of marriage enables the married couple to imitate the divine model set before them in the Epistle to the Ephesians and to fulfill their mission as parents, not only in view of the earthly city but

---

[15] The impediments to marriage are of two kinds: *diriment* impediments rendering marriage null and *prohibitive* impediments rendering it illicit. Certain of the former are based on the very nature of things and so cannot be the subject of any dispensation, e.g., impotence, the existence of a previous matrimonial bond, kinship in the direct line. Others are bans laid down by the Church, e.g., the bonds of ordination and of solemn profession. Certain impediments express the danger implied in certain kinds of unions. In these cases, precautions must be taken or guarantees given (e.g., in mixed marriages) before marriage can be permitted.

[16] On this whole subject see F. J. Sheed, *Nullity of Marriage.*

[17] This *res et sacramentum* of marriage is not, however, a "character," as in the case of baptism, confirmation and orders.

also of the heavenly Kingdom. "Wherever they are, these two, there also is Christ," says Tertullian (*To His Wife* 2:8).

IV. THE THREE BLESSINGS OF CHRISTIAN MARRIAGE[18]

In explaining the ends and laws of Christian marriage in his encyclical *Casti connubii,* Pius XI took two texts of St. Augustine as basic:

> All these things are good and make marriage good: children, conjugal fidelity, the sacrament (*De bono conjugali* 24, 32; PL 40, 394).

> In conjugal fidelity we see the obligation of married persons to abstain from sexual relations outside the marriage bond. With regard to children, they have the obligation to treat them with love, to nurture them with care, to bring them up in a religious way. Finally, with regard to the sacrament, they have the duty not to disrupt their common life or break the law which forbids those who separate to contract another union, even for the sake of children. Such is the law of marriage, where the fruitfulness of nature finds its glory and the dissoluteness of incontinence its check (*De Genesi ad litteram* 9, 7, 12).

Peter Lombard and St. Thomas both borrowed from St. Augustine his list of the three goods of marriage—conjugal faith, children, the sacrament (*Summa,* Suppl., 49, 2ff.). This method has become classic and can be used profitably in catechesis with certain clarifications.

1. Children. "The first end of marriage is parenthood and the formation of Children" (Can. 1013, 1). This is the traditional teaching of the Church, formulated by St. Thomas (*Summa,* Suppl., 40, 2), adopted by *Casti connubii* and proclaimed by the liturgy: "Lord, be pleased to assure Your presence in the institution of marriage, by which You have willed to regulate the transmitting of human life."

This was the command given by the Creator in the beginning: "Be fruitful, multiply, fill the earth and govern it" (Gen. 1:27). It constitutes the natural law of marriage, valid for men both before and after Christ. But Christian revelation raises this law to a supernatural level; from the heavenly Father "all fatherhood in heaven and on earth takes its name" (Eph. 3:15). The children of men are destined to become children of God and citizens of heaven.

However, there is danger that the teaching of the Church on this point may be misinterpreted or misrepresented. A non-consummated marriage may be valid and legitimate. Sterility does not render marriage null. Again, various motives of Christian prudence and mutual consid-

---

[18] Our study is primarily concerned with the sacrament and is not intended as a complete discussion of the state and vocation of marriage. See the bibliography, p. 312f., for a list of titles giving a fuller development from various aspects.

eration may set limits to the procreation of children. But these limits are to be set by man and wife in freedom and dignity, not imposed from without by society.[19]

The precise object of marital consent is the "mutual giving of rights to acts leading to procreation" (Can 1081, 2), a definition that leaves room for the exceptions just mentioned. To exclude this right would be to exclude marriage. The procreation of children is, then, the primary end of marriage in the sense that married persons would sin seriously in directing the conjugal act away from this end.[20]

But, as Pius XI says in *Casti connubii,*

> The good of the child does not end with his having been procreated; we must add another, that is, the good education of the child. For all His wisdom, God would have provided very poorly for the fate of children and of the whole human race if those who have received from him the power and the right of procreating children had not also received the right and the responsibility of bringing them up. No one, in fact, fails to recognize that a child cannot take care of himself in matters connected with his natural life; and there is all the more reason why he cannot do so in matters connected with the supernatural life. For a good many years he needs the help of others, he needs instruction and education.
>
> It is evident, moreover, that in conformity with the requirements of nature and the divine order, this right and this task belong primarily to those who began the work of nature by generation, and who are absolutely forbidden to leave incomplete the work they have undertaken and thus to expose the child to certain destruction.

2. Conjugal fidelity. Parenthood and the formation of children presuppose and require the mutual love of husband and wife—a self-giving love, and hence one that endures. The happiness and reciprocal development of the partners comprise the second end of marriage in the traditional formula. But it is so far from being a negligible end as to be necessary for the attainment of the primary one (cf. *Summa,* Suppl., 49, 2 ad 1).

Conjugal fidelity consists above all in the mutual faithfulness of the couple in observing the marriage contract.

> Let the husband render to the wife her due and so the wife to her husband. The wife has not authority over her body, but the husband; the husband also has not authority over his body, but the wife. Do not deprive each other, except perhaps by consent, for a time, that you may give yourselves to prayer. Then return together lest Satan tempt you because you lack self-control (1 Cor. 7:3-5).

[19] See A. Zimmerman, *The Catholic Viewpoint on Overpopulation.*

[20] See Paul M. Quay, "Contraception and Conjugal Love," *Theological Studies,* 22 (1961), pp. 18-40.

Fidelity rules out any carnal relationship with a third person and demands absolute conjugal unity, "of which the Creator has Himself given us the first example in the marriage of our first parents, when He willed this marriage to be between but one man and one woman" (Pius XI, *Casti connubii*). This original law of unity was, as we have seen, definitively restored by Christ.

> If anyone says that Christians are permitted to have more than one wife at one time, and that this is not forbidden by the divine law, let him be anathema (Council of Trent; *Denz.* 972; cf. 969).

Not only actual adultery but even sins of thought or desire are contrary to conjugal fidelity: "And I, I say to you that whoever looks upon a woman lustfully has already committed adultery in his heart" (Matthew 5:28).

Conjugal fidelity is more than faithfulness to a commitment in the order of justice:

> It requires that man and wife be united by a special love, by a holy and pure love. They are not to love each other in the manner of adulterers, but as Christ has loved the Church; and Christ has surely enclosed his Church in a boundless love, not for His personal advantage, but solely for the good of His Bride. We are speaking, then, of "charity," not something founded on a purely carnal inclination and quickly spent, nor limited to affectionate words, but residing in the deepest sentiments of the heart and also—for love proves itself in deeds—manifested in external action (Pius XI, *Casti connubii*).
>
> It is a sharing in common of the whole life, a habitual intimacy, a society *(ibid.)*.

The dignity of woman, so misunderstood in pagan societies, is fully affirmed in Christian marriage. Husband and wife have an equal eternal destiny, a personal vocation, an equally strict obligation with regard to conjugal duties. "Among us," says St. Jerome, "what is not permitted to wives is not permitted to husbands; they have the same obligations, but also the same status" *(Letter* 77). However, in the society of the family there should flourish what St. Augustine calls the "order of love."

> Let wives be subject to their husbands as to the Lord, for the husband is head of the wife as Christ is head of the Church (Eph. 5:22-23; cf. 1 Cor. 11:7-9; 1 Tim. 2:13).

Pope Pius XI states this in another way: "In the body that is the family . . . if the husband is the head, the wife is the heart; and as the first possesses primacy in ruling, the second can and should take over as her own the primacy of love" *(Casti connubii)*. These principles emphasize the complementary character of the sexes originally stated in Genesis, as well as the mutual support that married people are to find in marriage. This mutual support provides a fulfillment of sexual desire, and an aid in earthly life. But it is also to be a source of spiritual progress, in "the forming of the inner life of each by the other," according to the phrase of *Casti connubii*. This aspect of Christian marriage is increasingly being studied and developed in our times.

3. Sacrament and indissolubility. Following Christ Himself, the Church teaches the indissolubility of sacramental marriage:

> The marriage of baptized persons, if this has been validly contracted and consummated, cannot be dissolved by any power nor for any reason other than death (Can. 1118).

This principle has been always recalled in the canonical legislation of the West, in papal documents, and in the acts of the solemn magisterium at the Councils of Florence and of Trent.

It must be admitted that certain separated Churches of the East have hesitated on this point. It was to avoid condemning them openly that the Council of Trent used indirect expressions in drawing up the second of the following prohibitions:

> If anyone says that the matrimonial bond can be broken by one of the partners because of heresy, domestic incompatibility, or deliberate desertion, let him be anathema.
>
> If anyone accuses the Church of being in error for having taught or for teaching, in accordance with the teachings of the Gospel and of the Apostle, that the bond of marriage cannot be dissolved because of the adultery of one of the partners; and that neither one nor the other, even if innocent, and having given no ground for adultery, can, while the other partner is still alive, contract another marriage; and that he or she who remarries after having sent away the adulterer, is in turn guilty of adultery, let him be anathema (*Denz.* 975, 977).

To remarry while a partner is alive is, in the language of canon law, a "crime." It puts those who do so in the category of public sinners, and consequently bars them from the sacraments and from ecclesiastical burial, and renders them incapable of validly exercising offices in the Church (among others, that of being a sponsor at baptism or confirmation—Can. 2356, 2294, 2). These punishments should not be regarded as the Church's sanctions to protect her own laws. The divine order of things is concerned here, of which the Church is the guardian, but not the mistress. It is the Lord who rejects divorce; and the divine law is not, like human law, subject to substantial changes.

It should be noted here that in certain well-defined cases the Church may grant a decree of separation of spouses. Such a separation leaves the conjugal bond intact. It may be necessary to give such a separation civil sanction by obtaining a legal divorce. In such a situation, a Catholic is, obviously, not subject to the sanctions mentioned above unless he attempts to remarry.

Instruction on marriage should, certainly, point out the great good that indissolubility assures to the partners, to children and to society, and, on the other hand, the ravages wrought by divorce. To the evidence presented by the encyclicals *Arcanum* and *Casti connubii,* we can add that presented in our day by sociology and psychiatry. It is natural that such abuse of God's law should lead to many evils, since this law is designed to show man how to be truly human.

But we must rise above this purely human level and appeal primarily to faith. Only the grace of Christ and the discovery of His love can raise men from their weakness, the weakness expressed so movingly by the disheartened reflections of the disciples in Matthew 19:19. Christians, then, must be made aware of the fact that the ideal presented in the Gospel calls for a struggle, a break with pagan ways of thinking and acting. During the early centuries, Christians learned to think and to live in accordance with the Christian idea of marriage in a hostile society, with customs foreign to the spirit of Christ. "The laws of the Caesars are of one kind," says St. Jerome, "the laws of Christ another; the interpretations of the jurist Papinian are of one kind, those of our Paul of another" (*Letter* 77). Even when the Church's laws have coincided with those of the state, the Christian idea of marriage and of sexual morality has seldom been fully accepted by any society. Today there is again an obvious conflict. Christians must be shown where to find the strength to live in accordance with God's law—not in a merely negative morality, but in the Christian life fully lived in its true realism and dynamism. They need to be shown also their responsibility with regard to the reform of the social order, to fight against the conditions that foster sexual immorality and the degradation of marriage.

In the view of the Fathers and theologians, the indissolubility of marriage is bound up with the fact that it is a sacrament. The marriage of Christ and the Church constitutes the new and eternal covenant; the love of Christ for the Church is "to the end" (John 13:1). Christian marriage, then, the sacramental sign of this reality, is indissoluble.

Hence we see why a valid and consummated marriage contracted by two baptized persons is the only marriage which is absolutely indissoluble. A marriage that has not yet been consummated can be dissolved, notably by a dispensation from the Pope. Canon law provides for a preliminary procedure to be followed in such a case. Similarly, the solemn profession of one of the partners in a religious order would break the bond of a nonconsummated marriage—an exception stated by the Council of Trent (*Denz.* 976), though a rather chimerical one in the context of existing canon law.

There are also cases in which the marriage of non-baptized persons can be dissolved. This can happen on the occasion of the later baptism of one of the couple by use of "the privilege of the faith," which includes "the Pauline privilege" stated by St. Paul as follows:

> If a brother has an unbelieving wife who consents to live with him, let him not put her away. And if a woman has an unbelieving husband, and he consents to live with her, let her not put away her husband. For the unbelieving husband is sanctified by his believing wife, and the unbelieving wife is sanctified by her believing husband. . . . But if the unbeliever wishes to depart, let him or her do so; in such a case, neither the brother nor the sister (i.e., the Christian partner) is bound: God has called you to live in peace. And how do you know, O wife, whether you will save your husband? And how do you know, O husband, whether you will save your wife? Except for this case, let everyone continue to live in the condition in which the Lord has placed him and where the call of God found him (1 Cor. 7:12-17).

Second marriage, i.e., the marriage of the partner who survives the death of the other, raised a theological problem for the Fathers and the Doctors of the Church. But in spite of certain rigorist groups, the Church has always admitted its legitimacy, following St. Paul:

> The wife remains bound to her husband so long as she lives; but if the husband dies, she is free to marry whom she wishes, only in the Lord (1 Cor. 7:39; cf. 1 Tim. 5:14).

This second marriage is sacramental, and really symbolizes the union of Christ and the Church.

Yet the liturgy, canon law (1142) and Christian spirituality assume that remarriage is second best, at least as judged objectively and independently of concrete situations.[21] The liturgy of the West omits the special votive Mass and the marriage blessing when the bride has received this blessing at her previous marriage. The Byzantine liturgy, far more severe, implores the pity of the Lord "for the iniquities of your servants . . . not having the strength to bear the heat and weight of the day and the ardors of the flesh." Canon law refuses access to holy orders to the widower of a second marriage (Can. 984, 5). For some persons, certainly, widowhood constitutes a call of the Lord to the life of perfection. As St. Paul says after stating the legitimacy of second marriages: "However, she will be happier if she remains as she is" (1 Cor. 7:40).

SUMMARY: THE CHRISTIAN VOCATION

As we have seen in the course of our study, Christian marriage can be understood only in the light of the reality it signifies in the plan of salvation: the self-sacrificing love of Christ for His Church and of the Church

---

[21] Obviously, where there are children still to be brought up, for example, a second marriage may be indicated by Christian prudence. Moreover, entering on such a marriage is not a bar to sanctity, or even to canonization; witness the case of St. Thomas More.

for Christ, the final union of the Church with Christ, of redeemed mankind with God. But, equally, we come to know the reality through the
sign studied in the light of revelation. A true appreciation of virginity
and of celibacy undertaken for the sake of the kingdom of heaven must be
based on an appreciation of Christian marriage. Virginity renounces the
sign in order the more directly and speedily to attain the reality signified.
Only by understanding the value of the sign, though, can virginity be
rightly oriented toward this reality.

Both marriage and consecrated virginity, then, lead us toward a fuller
understanding of the Christian vocation as such. For every Christian is
incorporated at baptism into the one Bride of Christ, the Church. Every
Christian is called to share in her unique intimacy with Him in her
sacramental life and in her prayer.[22] Every Christian is called to share in
one way or another in her work, which is His work. Every Christian is
called to obey Christ's command to love as He has loved us, even to the
sacrifice of life itself, and to share in His sufferings so as to share in His
glory. This is the picture of the Christian vocation presented throughout
the New Testament. And, as we saw, particularly in our study of the sacrament of orders and of baptism, the Christian receives and carries out this
vocation as a member of the one Body of Christ. He is shepherded, led
and guided by those who share Christ's priestly office by the sacrament of
orders.

Christian tradition has always seen the martyr as the supreme model of
the Christian vocation, the perfect witness to Christ, the word "martyr"
meaning precisely "witness." Martyrdom is perfect following of Christ,
total self-giving to Christ, in the joyful and infallible hope of immediately
"attaining Him," of "being found in Him."[23]

Again, the "poor" in Israel had already seen the renouncement of
earthly blessings as the best preparation for the coming Kingdom. Christ
Himself not only called men to follow Him in His pastoral ministry, but
also to follow Him simply by renunciation: "If you will be perfect, go,
sell all that you have and give it to the poor, and come, follow Me" (Matthew 19:21). In Christianity the primary emphasis within this total self-
deprivation came to be placed on the renouncement of marriage. As we
have seen, Christ exalted complete continence for the sake of the kingdom
of heaven at the time when He restored marriage to its primal state and
beauty. And St. Paul, who sets out the full Christian meaning of marriage, also shows the greater possibilities of self-giving to Christ by renouncing marriage so as to be free for the Lord's service.

During the first Christian centuries there grew up in local churches
groups of virgins consecrated to the Lord by an act of definitive self-

---

[22] See H. U. von Balthasar, *Prayer*, pp. 68-80.

[23] See St. Ignatius of Antioch, *Epistle to the Romans*.

oblation. Each remained with her own family, but had a recognized status and was the object of special care on the part of the hierarchy. From the third century on, Christian writers began to set out more and more explicitly the ideal of Christian virginity. For example, St. Cyprian writes:

> Virginity is the flower of the seed of the Church, the beauty and orna-
> ment of spiritual grace, nature opening up in joy, the sound and
> perfect work of praise and honor, the image of God responding to the
> holiness of the Lord, the most illustrious part of the flock of Christ
> (*On the Habit of the Virgin*, PL 443).

During the same centuries, as it became clear in the great persecutions that not every Christian was prepared to lay down his life in martyrdom, the life of the Christian ascetic, the "athlete" of Christ, came to be seen as a special way of preparing for martyrdom. Willingly to renounce earthly blessings, including marriage, and to undertake a life of hardship, prayer and prolonged meditation on the Scriptures in order to grow in the knowledge and love of Christ was seen as the training needed to be ready for the call to martyrdom, should it come. Then when the persecutions finally ceased, the ascetic life was seen to be itself a form of martyrdom, and the first great flowering of monasticism began.[24] From monasticism on the one hand and the requirements of the apostolic ministry on the other, the various forms of the "religious life," both for men and women, gradually developed through the centuries.[25]

Throughout this development, masters of the spiritual life, from the Desert Fathers on, never failed to point out that a Christian who was neither priest, monk, nor religious might in fact excel in charity and Christian perfection those in the priestly ministry or those vowed to the "state of perfection to be acquired." Again, through the centuries, guides have never been lacking to show the ordinary Christian how to attain holiness. The title "confessor" (meaning one who publicly witnesses to Christ—a synonym for "martyr") first given to Christians imprisoned for the faith and awaiting martyrdom has always been given to heroically holy men, whatever their state of life, who did not actually die for the faith. In the missal and breviary, the "Common for Holy Women" contains many elements from the Masses and Offices for both virgins and women martyrs. Yet it cannot be denied that somewhat lost to view was the idea that every Christian is, by the very fact of his baptism, called to holiness.

In our own times this ideal is once again being emphasized. Recent popes have pointed out how the Christian life itself, if led fully and con-

---

[24] See E. Malone, *The Monk and the Martyr.*

[25] See L. Bouyer, *Introduction to Spirituality*, pp. 185-241.

sistently in accordance with the demands of any state of life, can be a real martyrdom, a laying-down of life for love of Christ and neighbor.[26]

In this light the special graces, demands and opportunities of each state of Christian life are being studied and brought out. Christian marriage is being viewed afresh in the light of St. Paul's Epistle to the Ephesians.

> The relations of husband and wife, based on their bodily union, are to be seen, not as an alternative to the life of sacrifice in imitation of Christ, but as a new way of realizing it and carrying it into effect. . . . Viewed in this light, the life of each of the partners is no longer to be one of self-seeking, in however licit a manner. It becomes, on the contrary, wholly centered on self-giving, on supernatural charity, with all that this involves.[27]

The possibilities of the Christian single life "in the world" as a special service of Christ are similarly being explored. All this does not imply the derogation of the priestly, the monastic, or the religious life, but rather the bringing out of their special and higher glories and demands, all in relation to the growth of the whole Mystical Body through the varied functions and contributions of its members.

It is no accident that this whole development has accompanied a renewed emphasis on active participation in the sacramental and prayer-life of the Church, centered in the celebration of the Eucharist as the "primary and indispensable source of the true Christian spirit" (St. Pius X, *Motu Proprio, Tra le sollecitudini*), and that the popes of recent times have more and more urgently invited the laity to take their rightful part both in the Church's worship and in her work.

For, as we have seen through our study of the sacraments, the Christian life flows from baptism and confirmation, is renewed by penance and the anointing of the sick, activated and nourished by the Eucharist, while the reality contained in the Eucharistic mystery is signified by marriage. And the whole sacramental life of the Church and her organic structure flows from the sacrament of orders.

Our study of the sacraments, then, leads us by its very nature to a deeper understanding of the Christian life in all its forms. It should lead us also to a deeper and more fruitful living of our own way of Christian life, and to a more ardent desire to communicate the riches of Christ to others by our prayer and our witness, our words and our work. "I have come to cast fire on the earth, and what will I but that it be kindled?" (Luke 12:49).

---

[26] See Gabriel de Ste. Marie-Madeleine, "Present Norms of Holiness," *Conflict and Light,* (Bruno de Jesu-Marie, ed.) pp. 154-169.

[27] L. Bouyer, *The Seat of Wisdom,* p. 80.

BIBLIOGRAPHY*

GENERAL

Balthasar, Hans Urs von, *Science, Religion and Christianity* (Westminster, Md.: The Newman Press, 1959).

Bouyer, Louis, *Introduction to Spirituality* (New York: Desclee Co., 1961).

_____, *History of Christian Spirituality*, Vol. I (New York: Desclee Co., 1962).

Clement of Rome and Ignatius of Antioch, Sts., *Epistles, Ancient Christian Writers,* I (Westminster, Md.: The Newman Press, 1946).

Daniélou, Jean, *The Bible and the Liturgy* (Notre Dame, Ind.: University of Notre Dame Press, 1958) .

Davis, Charles, *Liturgy and Doctrine* (New York: Sheed and Ward, Inc., 1960)

Diekmann, Godfrey, *Come Let Us Worship* (Baltimore: Helicon Press, 1961).

Duchesne, Louis, *Christian Worship*: *Its Origin and Evolution* (New York: The Macmillan Co., 1903).

Durrwell, Francis X., *The Resurrection: A Biblical Study* (New York: Sheed and Ward, Inc., 1960).

Ellard, Gerald, *Christian Life and Worship*, rev. ed. (Milwaukee: Bruce Publishing Co., 1946).

Gelin, Albert, *Key Ideas of the Old Testament* (New York, Sheed and Ward, Inc., 1955).

Guillet, Jacques, *Themes of the Bible* (Notre Dame, Ind.: Fides Publishers, 1960).

Hippolytus of Rome, *The Apostolic Tradition,* Vol. I (New York: The Macmillan Co., 1957).

Hofinger, Johannes, ed., *Liturgy and the Missions* (Collegeville, Minn.: The Liturgical Press, 1962).

Jungmann, Josef A., *The Early Liturgy* (Notre Dame, Ind.: University of Notre Dame Press, 1959).

Liturgy and the Word of God, The, The Strasbourg Papers (Collegeville, Minn.: The Liturgical Press, 1959).

Martimort, Aimé-G., *In Remembrance of Me* (Collegeville, Minn.: The Liturgical Press, 1959).

Proceedings of the North American Liturgical Weeks (Washington, D. C.: The Liturgical Conference, 1940-1962).

Vagaggini, Cyprian, *Theological Dimensions of the Liturgy* (Collegeville, Minn.: The Liturgical Press, 1959).

*Works of the Fathers in translation other than those listed above may be found in one or more of the standard collections:

Fathers of the Church (Washington, D. C.; The Catholic University of America Press)

Ancient Christian Writers (Westminster, Md.: The Newman Press)

Society for the Preservation of Christian Knowledge—SPCK (New York: The Macmillan Co.)

The Ante-Nicene Fathers (New York: Charles Scribner Sons)

CHAPTER 1: A COMPREHENSIVE VIEW OF THE SACRAMENTS

(To avoid repetition, works are listed here which deal not only with the sacramental system as a whole, but also treat each sacrament separately.)

Ambrose, St., *On the Mysteries*, SPCK series (New York: The Macmillan Co., 1950).

————, *On the Sacraments*, SPCK series (New York: The Macmillan Co., 1950).

Augustine, St., *Sermons for Christmas and Epiphany*, in *Ancient Christian Writers*, 15 (Westminster, Md.: The Newman Press, 1952).

Brown, Raymond, *The Gospel of St. John and the Johannine Epistles*, in *New Testament Reading Guide*, 13 (Collegeville, Minn.: The Liturgical Press, 1961).

Davis, Charles, "Dom Odo Casel and the Theology of Mysteries," *Worship* 34:8 (1959).

d'Eypernon, Taymans, *The Blessed Trinity and the Sacraments* (Westminster, Md.: The Newman Press, 1961).

Fransen, P. F., *Faith and the Sacraments*, Aquinas Paper 31 (London: Blackfriars, 1958).

Hastings, Cecily, *The Sacraments* (New York: Sheed and Ward, Inc., 1961).

Henry, A.M., ed., *Christ in His Sacraments*, in *Theology Library*, 6 (Chicago: Fides Publishers, 1958).

Howell, Clifford, *Of Sacraments and Sacrifice* (Collegeville, Minn.: The Liturgical Press, 1952).

Leeming, Bernard, *Principles of Sacramental Theology* (Westminster, Md.: The Newman Press, 1960).

Lovel, F., and Putz, L., *Signs of Life* (Chicago: Fides Publishers, 1953).

O'Connell, Matthew,"The Sacraments in Theology Today," *Thought* 36 (1961).

Oesterreicher, John M., ed., *The Bridge*, I (New York: Pantheon Books, 1955).

Philipon, M., *The Sacraments in the Christian Life* (Westminster, Md.: The Newman Press, 1954).

Roguet, A. M., *Christ Acts Through Sacraments* (Collegeville, Minn.: The Liturgical Press, 1954).

Rush, Alfred, *Death and Burial in Christian Antiquity* (Washington, D. C.: The Catholic University of America Press, 1941).

Tardif, Henri, *The Sacraments Are Ours* (London: Challoner, 1956).

Schillebeeckx, Edward, "The Sacraments: An Encounter with God," *Theology Digest* 8 (1960).

Stanley, David M., articles on St. John's Gospel in *Worship* 32–34 (1957-1960).

Van der Meer, F., and Mohrmann, C., *Atlas of the Early Christian World* (New York: Thomas Nelson and Sons, 1958).

Vawter, Bruce, "The Johannine Sacramentary," *Theological Studies* 17 (1956).

CHAPTER 2: THE SACRAMENT OF ORDERS

Bligh, J., *Ordination to the Priesthood* (New York: Sheed and Ward, Inc., 1955).

Chrysostom, St. John, *On the Priesthood*, SPCK series (New York: The Macmillan Co., 1955).

Clement, St., *Letter to the Corinthians* in *The Epistles of St. Clement of Rome and St. Ignatius of Antioch*, tr. James M. Kleist, *Ancient Christian Writers*, I (Westminster, Md.: The Newman Press, 1946).

Congar, Yves, *Laity, Church and World* (Baltimore: Helicon Press, 1960).

Lécuyer, J., *What Is a Priest?* in *Twentieth Century Encyclopedia of Catholicism* (New York: Hawthorn, 1959).

Manning, Cardinal H., *The Eternal Priesthood* (Westminster, Md.: The Newman Press, 1944).

Marmion, Columba, *Christ, the Ideal of the Priest* (St. Louis: B. Herder Book Co., 1952).

Masure, E., *Parish Priest* (Chicago: Fides Publishers, 1955).

"Priesthood of Christ, The, "in *Proceedings of the North American Liturgical Week* (1951 and 1957).

Sellmair, J., *The Priest in the World* (Westminster, Md.: The Newman Press, 1954).

Spicq, C., *The Mystery of Godliness* (Chicago: Fides Publishers, 1954).

Stockums, W., *The Priesthood* (St. Louis: B. Herder Book Co., 1942).

Suhard, Cardinal E., "Priests Among Men," *The Church Today* (Chicago: Fides Publishers, 1953).

Theas, Most Rev. P., *Only Through These Hands: A Treatise on the Office of the Bishop in the Catholic Church* (St. Louis: Pio Decimo Press, 1957).

Veuillot, P., *The Catholic Priesthood according to the Teaching of the Church: Papal Documents from St. Pius X to Pius XII* (Westminster, Md.: The Newman Press, 1943).

CHAPTER 3: CHRISTIAN INITIATION

Biser, E., "He Descended into Hell," *Theology Digest* 8 (1960).

Bouman, Cornelius, "He Descended into Hell," *Worship* 33:4 (1959).

Bouyer, Louis, *Christian Initiation* (New York: The Macmillan Co., 1960).

————, *The Paschal Mystery* (Chicago: Henry Regnery Co., 1950).

Camelot, P. T., "Towards a Theology of Confirmation," *Theology Digest* 7 (1959).

Charles, Sister M., *Preparing Your Child for First Holy Communion* (Techny, Ill.: Divine Word Publications, 1961).

Crehan, J., *Early Christian Baptism and the Creed* (Westminster, Md.: The Newman Press, 1950).

Chrism Mass of Holy Thursday, The (Collegeville, Minn.: The Liturgical Press, 1956).

Gaillard, Jean, *Holy Week and Easter* (Collegeville, Minn.: The Liturgical Press, 1957).

Gumpel, P., "Unbaptized Infants—May They Be Saved?," *Downside Review* 72 1954).

Howell, Clifford, *Preparing for Easter* (Collegeville, Minn.: The Liturgical Press, 1955).

Journet, Charles, *The Meaning of Grace* (New York: P. J. Kenedy and Sons, 1960).

Kenny, J. P., "The Age for Confirmation," *Worship* 35:1 (1960).

Marsch, T., "Confirmation in Its Relation to Baptism," *Irish Theological Quarterly* (1960), pp. 259-293.

"New Man in Christ, The," *Proceedings of the North American Liturgical Week* (1945).

Parsch, Pius, *The Church's Year of Grace,* Vols. II and III (Collegeville, Minn.: The Liturgical Press, 1953 and 1954).

Smith, G., "Confirmed to Bear Witness," *Worship* 26:1 (1952).

Stanley, David M., "The New Testament Doctrine of Baptism: An Essay in Biblical Theology," *Theological Studies* (1957), pp. 169-215.

Waszink, J. H., "Pompa Diaboli," *Vigiliae Christianae,* I (1947).

Wilkin, Vincent, *From Limbo to Heaven* (New York: Sheed and Ward, Inc., 1961).

Winzen, Damasus, *The Great Sabbath Rest* (Washington, D. C.: The Liturgical Conference, 1957).

CHAPTER 4: THE HOLY EUCHARIST

Assisi Papers, The (Collegeville, Minn.: The Liturgical Press, 1957).

Bouman, C., and Ryan, M., *Key to the Missal* (Notre Dame, Ind.: Fides Publishers, 1960).

Byzantine Liturgy, The (New York: Fordham University Press, 1953).

Cabislas, Nicholas, *A Commentary on the Divine Liturgy* (London: Society for the Preservation of Christian Knowledge, 1960).

Didache, The, in *Ancient Christian Writers,* 6 (Westminster, Md.: The Newman Press, 1948).

Divine Liturgy of St. John Chrysostom, The (Collegeville, Minn.: The Liturgical Press, 1961).

Ellard, Gerald, *The Mass in Transition* (Milwaukee: Bruce Publishing Co., 1956).

Instruction on Sacred Music and the Sacred Liturgy, September 1958 Decree (Collegeville, Minn.: The Liturgical Press, 1958).

Jungmann, Josef A., *The Eucharistic Prayer* (Chicago: Fides Publishers, 1956).

———, *The Mass of the Roman Rite,* 2 vols. (New York: Benziger Bros., 1950-1955; one vol. without notes, 1960).

"Liturgy and Social Order, The," *Proceedings of the North American Liturgical Week* (1955).

"Liturgy and Unity in Christ, The," *Proceedings of the North American Liturgical Week* (1960).

Masure, Eugene, *The Christian Sacrifice* (New York: P. J. Kenedy and Sons, 1943).

Parsch, Pius, *The Liturgy of the Mass* (St. Louis: B. Herder Book Co., rev. ed. 1957).

"Participation in the Mass," *Proceedings of the North American Liturgical Week* (1959).

Reinhold, H. A., *Bringing the Mass to the People* (Baltimore: Helicon Press, 1960).

Robeyns, Anselme, "Rights of the Baptized," *Theology Digest* 10 (1962), pp. 106-112.

Roguet, A. M., *Holy Mass: Approaches to the Mystery* (Collegeville, Minn.: The Liturgical Press, 1953).

Vonier, Anscar, *A Key to the Doctrine of the Eucharist* (Westminster, Md.: The Newman Press, 1946).

CHAPTER 5: THE SACRAMENT OF PENANCE

Ahern, Barnabas M., *Mary, Queen of the Poor* (St. Louis: Pio Decimo Press, 1961).

Anciaux, Paul, *The Sacrament of Penance* (New York: Sheed and Ward, 1962).

Barton, John, *Penance and Absolution* in *Twentieth Century Encyclopedia of Catholicism*, 51 (New York : Hawthorn, 1961).

Confession: The Meaning and Practice of the Sacrament of Penance, Community of St. Severin (Westminster, Md.: The Newman Press, 1959).

Daniélou, Jean, "Blessed Are the Poor," *Cross Currents* 9 (1959).

Fraine, Jean de, "Adam and Christ as Corporate Personalities," *Theology Digest* 10 (1962).

Galtier, P., *Sin and Penance* (St. Louis: B. Herder Book Co., 1932).

Giblet, J., *The God of Israel, the God of Christians. The Great Themes of Scripture* (New York: Desclee Co., 1961).

Hardwick, Edgar, "Penance and the Church," *The Life of the Spirit* 14 (1959).

LeBeau, Walter, "The Sacrament of Penance in Parish Life," *Proceedings of the North American Liturgical Week* (1941).

Lebret, L., and Sauvet, T., "An Examination of Conscience for Modern Catholics," *Cross Currents* 7 (1957).

Lyonnet, Stanislaus, "The Saving Justice of God," *Theology Digest* 8 (1960).

MacRae, George, "With Me in Paradise," *Worship* 35:4 (1961).

McCauley, George, "The Ecclesial Nature of the Sacrament of Penance," *Worship* 36:4 (1962).

Prat, Ferdinand, *The Theology of St. Paul* (London: Burns, Oates & Washbourne, Ltd., 1926-27).

St. Benedict's Rule for Monasteries, tr. Leonard Doyle (Collegeville, Minn.: The Liturgical Press, 1948).

Sause, Bernard, *I Have Sinned* (St. Meinrad, Ind.: Grail Publications, 1952).

Sheerin, John, *The Sacrament of Freedom* (Milwaukee: Bruce Publishing Co., 1961).

Tertullian, *On Penance and on Purity* in *Ancient Christian Writers*, 28 (Westminster, Md.: The Newman Press, 1959).

Tillard, J., "Mary's Faith and Israel," *Sponsa Regis* 32:9 (1961).

Wilson, Alfred, *Pardon and Peace* (New York: Sheed and Ward, Inc., 1949).

CHAPTER 6: THE ANOINTING OF THE SICK

Alszeghy, Zoltan, "The Bodily Effects of Extreme Unction," *Theology Digest* 9 (1961).

Davis, Charles, "The Sacrament of the Sick," *Clergy Review* 43 (1958).

Didier, Jean-Charles, *Death and the Christian* in *Twentieth Century Encyclopedia of Catholicism*, 55 (New York: Hawthorn, 1961).

Furrow, The, 11 (1960). Papers read at the Seventh Irish Liturgical Congress on "the sick."

Palmer, Paul, "The Purpose of Anointing the Sick: A Re-appraisal," *Theological Studies* 19 (1958).

CHAPTER 7: MARRIAGE, CONSECRATED VIRGINITY, THE CHRISTIAN LIFE

A. Marriage.

Barbeau, Clayton, Head of the Family (Chicago: Henry Regnery, 1961).

Caffarel, Henri, *Love and Grace in Marriage* (Notre Dame, Ind.: Fides Publishers, 1960).

_____, ed., *Marriage Is Holy* (Chicago: Fides Publishers, 1957).

de Fabrégues, Jean, *Christian Marriage*, in *Twentieth Century Encyclopedia of Catholicism* (New York: Hawthorn, 1959).

Faherty, William B., *The Destiny of Modern Woman in the Light of Papal Teaching* (Westminster, Md.: The Newman Press, 1950).

"Family in Christ, The," *Proceedings of the North American Liturgical Week* (1946).

Ford, John, *The Validity of Virginal Marriage* (Washington, D. C.: The Catholic University of America Press).

Guitton, Jean, *Essay on Human Love* (London: Sheed and Ward, Ltd., 1953).

LeClercq, Jacques, *Marriage, A Great Sacrament* (New York: The Macmillan Co., 1951).

Mihanovich, Clement, and Werth, Alvin, *Papal Pronouncement on Marriage and the Family* (Milwaukee: Bruce Publishing Co., 1951).

Perrin, Joseph, *Christian Perfection and Married Life* (Westminster, Md.: The Newman Press, 1958).

Quay, Paul M., "Contraception and Conjugal Love," *Theological Studies* 22 (1961).

Sheed, Frank, *Nullity of Marriage* (New York: Sheed and Ward, Inc., rev. ed. 1959).

Tertullian, *Treatises on Marriage and Remarriage: To His Wife,* in *Ancient Christian Writers,* 13 (Westminster, Md.: The Newman Press, 1951).

Thibon, Gustave, *What God Hath Joined Together: An Essay on Love* (Chicago: Henry Regnery Co., 1952).

Wayne, T., *Morals and Marriage* (New York: Longmans Green and Co., 1936).

Zimmerman, Anthony, *The Catholic Viewpoint on Overpopulation* (Garden City, N. Y.: Hanover House, 1961).

B. Virginity, Christian celibacy, monasticism, the consecrated life.

Bouyer, Louis, *The Liturgy and the Religious Life* (St. Louis: Pio Decimo Press, 1961).

_____, *The Meaning of the Monastic Life* (New York: P. J. Kenedy and Sons, 1955).

_____, *The Seat of Wisdom* (New York: Pantheon Books, 1961).

Carpentier, René, *Life in the City of God* (New York: Benziger Bros., 1959).

Carré, Ambroise, ed., *The Vocation of the Single Woman* (New York: Benziger Bros., 1960).

Leclercq, Jean, *The Life of Perfection* (Collegeville, Minn.: The Liturgical Press, 1961).

Muenster, Ludwig, *Christ in His Consecrated Virgins* (Collegeville, Minn.: The Liturgical Press, 1957).

Perinelle, J., *God's Highways: The Religious Life and Secular Institutes.* (Westminster, Md.: The Newman Press, 1961).

Perrin, Joseph, *Virginity* (Westminster, Md.: The Newman Press, 1955).

_____, *Secular Institutes: Consecration to God and Life in the World* (New York: P. J. Kenedy and Sons, 1961).

Plé, Albert, *Chastity* (London: Blackfriars, 1955).

C. The Christian vocation.

Balthasar, Hans Urs von, *Prayer* (New York: Sheed and Ward, Inc., 1961).
Bouyer, Louis, *Introduction to Spirituality* (New York: Desclee Co., 1961).
Bruno de Jésus-Marie, ed., *Conflict and Light* (New York: Sheed and Ward, Inc., 1952).
Chautard, J. C., *The Soul of the Apostolate* (New York: P. J. Kenedy and Sons, reprint, 1937).
Marmion, Columba, *Christ, the Life of the Soul* (St. Louis: B. Herder Book Co., 1925).
Pinsk, Johannes, *Toward the Center of Christian Living* (New York: Herder and Herder, 1961).
Thils, Gustave, *Christian Holiness* (Tielt, Belgium: Lannoo Publishers, 1961).
Trese, Leo, *Many Are One* (Chicago: Fides Publishers, 1952).
Tyciak, Julius, *Life in Christ* (New York: Sheed and Ward, Inc., 1938).

INDEX OF SCRIPTURE REFERENCES

GENERAL INDEX

Abel 184f
Abraham 185
absolution 240f
acknowledging sin 230
acolyte 104
Adam Eve, in NT 288f
altar, imagery 162f
Ambrose 19, 45, 117, 174, 175, 178, 179, 180, 292
anamnesis 167f
anaphora 161
anointed 129f; symbolism 272
Aphraates 126
apostles as baptizers 77; as shepherds 77
apostolic blessing 262; succession 78f; necessity of 43, 79f
Apostolic Constitutions 145; *Apostolic Traditions* 97, 98, 102, 135 141, 148, 168, 242, 270
asceticism 306
Asperges 139
atonement 226
Augustine, 130, 235, 237; Sermons 115, 135, 229; on baptism 46; Conf. 212; *de bono conjugali* 299; *de genesi* 299; on the Epiphany 22; Homily on John vi, 23, 38, 45, 76, 213; letter to Parthos 215, 217; on punishment of sin 135

Baptism anniversary 139; anointing 119; candle 120, 129; character 130; of child 135; command of Christ 110; commitment to Christian living 131, 137; conditions for validity 134; baptism and confirmation 140; chrism 116; creed 115f; in danger 136n; defined 110; "door of sacraments" 64; effects 133; enlightenment 128f; eschatology 124f; baptism and Eucharist 149; exorcisms 114, 125; healing effect 121; of blood 137; of John 110, contrasted with Christ's 111; Lenten preparation 114; minister 136; necessity 137; not repeated 133; in NT 109ff, in St. Paul 111, in St. Peter, 111f, in St. John 112; Paschal time 108;

baptismal pool 123; baptism and perfect life 138; priestly mission 131; profession of faith 119; promises 133f; renouncing Satan 117; return to Paradise 124; reviviscence 133; rites 112f, change of location 113; ritual, introduction 114; Scriptural readings 114f; scrutinies 114; share in Christ's priesthood 129f, victory 132; baptismal washing 119, water 118; white garments 120
Bede 216
bishop, fulness of priesthood 99; indelible character 93n; consecration of 86f, 85; sacramental power 44; mission shared 83ff; appointment of 80, by state 81; exercising power outside Church 100
blood as life 232n; in pacts 192n
bread and wine as signs 176f, 191
breaking the bread 171f

Caesarius of Arles 273
canon 107 70; 108 67; 329 79; 218 79; 750 136; 889,890 252; 948 67; 1013 299; 1118 302; 1350 81
Canticle, meaning 289
care of souls 82
Casti Connubii 299, 300, 301.
catechumens 113
celibacy 73, 82; advantages 285f, in resurrection 286
central role liturgy 182f, Mass 153, priest's power to consecrate 97
chants, role 157
character, sacramental 52, 54
Christ as deacon 103; figures of 184ff; fragrance of (chrism) 145; grace, source of 35; mediator 74; Melchisedech 75f; Moses 76; minister of sacraments 38; passion source of sacramental grace 37; sacramental presence 180; sacrificial death 188, 189, 203f; priest 39, 95, 99; prophet New Law 74; presence at sacrifice 198f; reveals God's mercies 227; shepherd 75; words at Last Supper 176, words sign of passion 191; words, efficacy 178

316

Sacram Communionem 211
Sacramentum ordinis 33, 40, 91
sacramentals of the sick 277ff
sacrifice 195; OT and NT 95f; spiritual sacrifice of Christians 206
satisfaction 255f; medicinal 255f; punishment for sin 255
seal 53
self-abandon 223
"sending" 97
Severinus Gabalus 86
sickness and sin 264f; new meaning to sickness 268
sin, discovery of 220f; interiorization 222f; as death 222; sins that cause death 235; mortal 247; venial 258f; after Baptism 234
single life in the world 307
Stephen I 46
stream flowing from Christ's side 37
subdiaconate 88
Summa 18, 21, 37, 50, 51, 59, 70, 76, 82, 85n, 91n, 93, 97, 99, 127, 128, 133, 135, 140, 145, 147, 148, 152, 174, 191, 194, 195, 196, 214, 215, 216, 230, 236, 237, 243, 245, 246, 247, 248, 249, 250, 259, 265, 272, 273, 274, 289, 295, 296, 299, 300
Syriac marriage chant 88; anamnesis 198

Teaching authority 81
terminology, development 80

Tertullian 22, 49, 80, 101, 123, 181, 254, 299
Theodore of Mopsuestia 149, 164, 199
tonsure 69
transubstantiation 179f

Unfruitful reception 58
unworthiness in minister 45

Validity 42
viaticum 213, 216, 276
Vigil Mass, Paschal 118, 128
vine, symbol of God's people 177
virgin Israel 289
virgins, consecration preface 290
virginity in OT 284; in NT 284ff; community life, historical development 305ff
vocation, Christian 304ff; priestly 94
vows, exchange 293; ancient ritual 293f

Water, source of life 122; flood water 124; Spirit of God 122
wedding garment 132
widowhood 304
wife, Christian model, in liturgy 282f; in Scripture 282f
woman's dignity 301
words of institution 191f
Wycliff 45

p. 37 top
p. 39 Sac as Praise
p 58 show fourth resemblance to text
p 126 good for "Significance of Resurrection" (ad calc.)
p. 127 footnote 17 for further info on; "Descended into Hell"